# TO KIDNAP A POPE

## NAPOLEON AND PIUS VII

AMBROGIO
A. CAIANI

YALE UNIVERSITY PRESS
NEW HAVEN AND LONDON

Published with assistance from the Annie Burr Lewis Fund.

For information about this and other Yale University Press publications, please contact:
U.S. Office:    sales.press@yale.edu    yalebooks.com
Europe Office:    sales@yaleup.co.uk    yalebooks.co.uk

Set in Adobe Garamond Pro by IDSUK (DataConnection) Ltd
Printed in Great Britain by TJ Books, Padstow, Cornwall

Library of Congress Control Number: 2020950316

ISBN 978-0-300-25133-3

A catalogue record for this book is available from the British Library.

10 9 8 7 6 5 4 3 2 1

*A Mike,*
*Un grande amico ed un grande maestro*

# CONTENTS

# PLATES

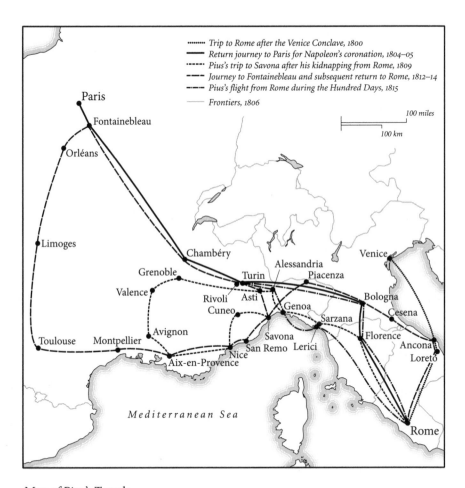

Map of Pius's Travels

# INTRODUCTION
## A SLEEPLESS NIGHT IN THE ETERNAL CITY, 1809

On the night of 5–6 July 1809, most of Rome's inhabitants were asleep, their windows and shutters open so that what breeze there was might chase away the intense summer heat. Those still awake could hear the regular patrols of French and Neapolitan soldiers marching through the streets. Their presence was deeply resented. When Napoleon's soldiers had first entered the city a year earlier, the sixty-six-year-old Pope Pius VII had moved to the Quirinal Palace, his preferred lodgings and an escape from the tribulations of his high office. Constructed during the sixteenth century, mushrooming in size ever since, the Quirinal is a labyrinth. Its structure is, more or less, L-shaped; its interiors comprise seemingly endless enfilades of antechambers and state rooms, while at the base of the L its large courtyard, or *cortile d'onore*, is arranged around a large clock tower. Perched atop a hill, the palace commands magnificent vistas over the city and looks directly onto the dome of Saint Peter's Basilica. A favourite residence of the popes, especially in the summer months, the cool ornamental gardens, English coffee house and ice boxes made it a haven from the sun, and, being on high ground, it was considered more salubrious than the Vatican, whose proximity to the Tiber was thought to be unhealthy.[1]

As 6 July dawned the sentries in the clock tower retired for the night feeling that their duty had been done. They were unaware that their movements were being closely watched. As soon as the lights in the tower had been extinguished, a flurry of activity began. The tight streets and square in front of the palace gradually filled with Neapolitan soldiers and French gendarmes. The leader of these 700 and more troops was the Frenchman Étienne Radet, resplendent in the blue uniform of a brigadier general of the Imperial Gendarmerie. He was an attractive man: tall, broad-shouldered, his cheeks sporting impressive auburn sideburns. This proud soldier, like the gendarmes he led, was a veteran of many campaigns of the revolutionary and Napoleonic wars. As he gained seniority, he had switched from traditional soldiering to specialise in counter-insurgency. He was by now one of the best bandit-catchers in Europe. A few years previously he had been instrumental in converting the Neapolitan brigand Sciabolone ('Big Sword') into a police agent.[2] In the early morning of 6 July he was about to face his biggest challenge.

In late June, the military governor of Rome, General Sextius Alexandre François de Miollis, had instructed Radet to take Pius VII into custody. The verbal orders stressed the delicacy of the operation: the pontiff must be extracted from the Quirinal without allowing time for the alarm to be raised. Radet spent weeks dutifully planning the pope's kidnapping. He discreetly reconnoitred Piazza di Monte Cavallo at the summit of the Quirinal. His task was made easier by the recruitment of a group of disgruntled papal servants and Roman aristocrats.[3] These renegades provided useful intelligence as to how to enter the palace unobserved. They also described the habits of the pope and, more importantly, his guards. It was thanks to their intelligence that Radet knew that the palace sentries retired at two o'clock in the morning.

The plan the general devised was bold, and bore many of the hallmarks of Napoleonic strategy. During the Empire, the French had divided their army into smaller units that would march swiftly on separate roads and then converge on the enemy's position to destroy him. This was known as the *corps d'armée* system. Radet hoped to achieve a similar outcome on a smaller scale. As in a battle, he would divide his forces into three detachments, which would take the papal palace in a pincer movement. Radet would personally lead thirty veterans onto the roof of the palace and then stealthily enter the main courtyard. His deputy, Colonel Siry, would head a similar contingent that would access the gardens and, through an open window, gain entry into the servants' quarters. Both groups would then rendezvous inside the palace and open the main gates leading to Piazza di Monte Cavallo, where the remaining forces would join them for the final assault. The critical phase would be to disarm and neutralise the Swiss Guard before they could raise the alarm. If Radet's careful plan proved successful, the pope and his court would be taken by surprise and spirited away in carriages in the dead of night before anybody realised what had occurred.[4]

All seemed to start according to plan. At 2.30 a.m. over 700 troops assembled outside Pius VII's summer residence. Colonel Siry scaled the walls of the gardens, but he and his men got lost in the vast papal gardens and wasted valuable time.

The darkness and obstacles – in the shape of the fine collection of exotic plants – made stealthy movement nearly impossible, and Siry's men could not identify the lighted window which a spy inside the Quirinal had promised to leave open. Meanwhile, Radet, a man of deeds, not words, had told his men that he would be the first to climb up to the palace roof, just under 30 feet high. Long scaling ladders had been requisitioned for this purpose. Radet ascended the ladder with grim determination, followed by his loyal gendarmes, but he immediately suffered an almost fatal setback: his men had forgotten to check the sturdiness of the scaling ladders and whether they could carry the weight of thirty brawny gendarmes. Radet had almost reached the roof when the ladder snapped in half and he fell indecorously to the ground.[5] The sound of the ladder breaking and men shouting awoke the inhabitants of the palace. Very soon cries of 'Treason, to arms, treason!' were heard.[6] Candlelight started to flicker in the windows of the Quirinal. To make matters worse, the sentries began tolling the palace bell and all the churches of Rome responded in kind. The element of surprise had been squandered.

Not a man to be discouraged, the now rather dishevelled Radet, his hat perched crookedly on his head, made his way to the main palace gate with an axe, and proceeded to deal violent blows to the wooden doors. In the previous months, however, the prefect of the papal household had taken the wise precaution of having both the locks and wooden gates reinforced in preparation for a likely incursion. Radet, despite his great physical strength, did not get very far, and only succeeded in making himself sweaty and breathless. One historian has described him as at this moment looking more like a poacher than an officer.[7] Nearing collapse from exhaustion, the general ceased his assault. He could hear sounds from the interior of the Quirinal: Colonel Siry, despite an unpromising start, had eventually found his way inside the palace. He now unbolted the gates and the imperial forces flooded into the state rooms. They were soon met by the Swiss Guard in full battle order, their armour and halberds glistening in the candlelight.

This was a stand-off the French had wanted to avoid. Any violence or shedding of blood in the attempt to kidnap Pius VII would have destroyed the Empire's already fragile reputation with Catholic Europe. The imperial officers demanded that the Swiss Guard surrender. To the Franco-Neapolitan soldiers' relief, the sound of the heavy halberds crashing down to the ground was a clear sign that there was not going to be a fight. Since the invasion of his states, the pope had ordered his troops to offer no resistance when faced with overwhelming force. As the soldiers penetrated deeper into the palace it was apparent that the papal court had had time to dress and prepare for their unwelcome visitors. Radet crossed the empty throne room, his footsteps echoing in the stillness of the night. He knocked on the door leading to the private apartments of Pius VII.[8] The sound of the lock turning greeted him. Tiberius, nephew of Cardinal Pacca, the papal secretary of state (foreign minister), admitted Radet. They walked down a dark corridor and eventually saw light emerging from the papal study.

Pius VII was sitting at his desk flanked by Cardinal Despuig and Cardinal Pacca. Radet, still sweating and panting, removed his hat as a mark of deference. A lengthy awkward silence ensued. Pius was no fool; he knew why the imperial general was there. After a decade of seeking conciliation with the French Empire, the moment of truth in the troubled relationship between emperor and pontiff had arrived.

Nervously, though respectfully, Radet addressed the following words to the pontiff: 'It is distressing for my heart to fulfil, before your sacred person, a severe and painful mission, which my oaths and duties bind me to fulfil.' The pope replied with irritation: 'Why do you come at this late hour to trouble my rest in my home?' The general declared: 'Holy Father, I come in the name of the government, to reiterate to Your Holiness the demand you renounce all temporal sovereignty.'[9] Pius VII raised his eyes and replied:

If you thought yourself obliged to follow these orders from the emperor due to your oath of allegiance, imagine how we must on our part maintain the rights of the Holy See to which we are bound by so many oaths! We can neither cede nor abandon that which does not belong to us. This state belongs to the church and we are but its caretaker. The emperor can tear us to pieces, but he will never obtain such a renunciation from us. After all we have done for him, we did not expect such treatment.[10]

According to the Chevalier Artaud, secretary to the French Embassy in Rome, the pope concluded with the words '*Non debemus, non possumus, non volumus*': we must not, we cannot, we will not.[11]

A brief discussion followed, during which the general pointed to the menacing crowds of ordinary Romans, who, having been awoken by the sounds of alarm, were gathering outside the palace. Surely the pope would not want to spread disorder, to see the blood of his subjects flow through the streets? Pius emphasised that this was far from his intention, but that he would not renounce his Italian kingdom willingly. Radet regretted this refusal and told the pope that he had orders to escort him out of Rome.[12] Pius accepted this and bowed before superior force. The memoirs of Cardinal Pacca differ from Radet's own account on this point. According to the pope's foreign minister, Pius had been told he was to be taken to the palace of General Miollis, the military governor of Rome, for further discussions.[13] Apparently, the pontiff was very upset when he realised he had been duped. Whatever the truth may be, the pope was now a prisoner of the French emperor. Pius VII must, at this stage, have regretted all the compromises and negotiations he had undertaken with Napoleon over the past decade. His reward was to be arrested and spirited out of his own capital and diocese like a prisoner.

Time was of the essence, especially given the anger of the Roman crowds at the violation of the Quirinal. When asked if there was anything he needed, the pope replied curtly that he cared little about material things. He briefly went to his bedroom to prepare for the journey. Radet was then surrounded by prelates and courtiers who begged to follow their master into exile. According to one account, Pius emerged from his private apartments carrying only his breviary. He was escorted down the ceremonial staircase into the main courtyard of the palace, where a carriage was waiting. Cardinal Pacca was the first to enter, followed by the pope, who seemed unsteady and visibly moved. Reportedly, he turned to bless his city for one last time and shed a tear.[14] In a clear sign that the travellers were in fact prisoners, the carriage door was locked from the outside. As the convoy of gendarmes, commanded by Radet, started on its journey, the Franco-Neapolitan troops presented arms in deference. The general sat next to the coachman as the carriage pulled out of the Quirinal. The people of Rome who lined the streets were ashen-faced, standing in ominous silence as the pope was removed from his city. Shortly after, an opportunistic group of anti-papal agitators looted the palace of much of its precious contents and fine Orvieto wine.[15] With a mounted escort of gendarmes, Napoleon's captives headed towards Porta Pia and thence on to Porta del Popolo where they changed post horses. As the exiles left Rome, the pope reassured his companions that Christ had suffered a far worse ordeal.

The convoy headed at great speed into Tuscany. Given the extreme heat, and the discomfort he had to endure, the pope was soon feverish. For some time Pius had suffered from a bladder complaint that was exacerbated by stress. After seventeen hours of uninterrupted travel the escort stopped at an inn in the Tuscan town of Radicofani, 65 miles south of Florence. Here Pius was allowed a few hours' rest before continuing the journey. He refused to move until those members of his household that he had requested accompany him joined him. Luckily, a few hours later two carriages arrived carrying a skeleton papal household. These included Pacca's nephew Tiberius, the pope's chaplain, his master of the wardrobe, valet, surgeon, cook and lackey.[16] The next stop was the Charterhouse of Florence. On his journey the pope was heartened by the large crowds that gathered to watch him pass and seek his blessing. The people of Italy were curious to see the man they revered as their spiritual leader. Crowds of women brought the pope fresh water and linen to help him fight the oppressive heat. They were less than friendly to the French gendarmes, whom they called *cani*, 'dogs'.

On the way to Florence, along a particularly steeply sloping road, the axle broke and the carriage toppled. The ailing pope was flung to one side and Cardinal Pacca fell on top of him. Bystanders extracted the pope and tried to provide comfort. Pius smiled and reassured all that he was unhurt. The angry crowd blamed the gendarmes for this accident and became threatening. An improvised change of carriage was organised, and the long journey continued in all haste. The party arrived at the Charterhouse at one o'clock in the morning on 7 July, the pope by now completely exhausted.[17] He received visits from the local commander of the Gendarmerie and the head of police. Elisa, Napoleon's eldest sister, was grand duchess of Tuscany, and she sent a chamberlain to welcome the pontiff into her domains.[18] All were much concerned by the pallor and feverishness of Pius VII. Untactfully, the monks of the Charterhouse informed the pope that he would sleep in the same bed in which his predecessor Pope Pius VI had reposed on his final journey to Valence, where he died as a French prisoner in 1799.[19] Grim parallels between his own situation and that of his predecessor must have troubled Pius's mind. What would happen to the church if he died in exile? Could the College of Cardinals, most of whom were Napoleon's prisoners, be counted upon to elect an independent and strong successor?

Throughout his captivity the pope would fight an intense inner battle to survive, to not yield. The French tried every psychological trick and form of emotional blackmail to weaken his resolve. Though he often came close to breaking, through prayer and mental discipline, and by drawing on his reserves of inner strength and spiritual resolve, he persisted in his gentle defiance. His captors found his determination both frustrating and incomprehensible.

The government took the decision that, on departure from Florence, Cardinal Pacca and his nephew would travel separately from the papal party along the Bologna road.[20] Radet, having completed his mission, was recalled to Rome, where he would try his best to impose law and order on the pope's former subjects. Security was now entrusted to the local commanders of the Imperial Gendarmerie. For her part, Elisa, as grand duchess of Tuscany, did not want to have the pope in her domains longer than was strictly necessary.[21] She washed her hands of Pius and passed responsibility for him on to others. Gravely ill, the pontiff was forced to continue his journey. The papal convoy first travelled towards Genoa and then veered west to enter Piedmont. They finally stopped in the large market town of Alessandria on 14 July. A hellish week of travel in stifling heat had finally come to an end. The convoy's journey had hardly been smooth, and highlighted that the imperial government was far from certain what the pope's final destination would be. Indeed, his odyssey was just beginning.

Prince Camillo Borghese, the military governor of Turin, and Napoleon's brother-in-law, was like Elisa reluctant to take responsibility for the pope's safety. Orders were given for the papal party to continue their journey across the Alps into France. The carriages flew through northern Piedmont and crossed the mountain pass of Mont-Cenis into Savoy.[22] On 21 July Pius took some long-awaited rest in Grenoble, where he received visits from the city's municipal authorities. Worryingly for the Empire's police, the pontiff received something of a hero's welcome from the French population. Their reaction mirrored that of the Italian peasants of Lazio, Tuscany and Piedmont, who had come to cheer the supreme head of the church. It became apparent that there was a significant danger that the pope's captivity could backfire and lead to public disorder. It was here, in Dauphiné, that Cardinal Pacca was briefly reunited with Pius. They would spend ten restorative days in Grenoble, where they were loaned books from local libraries so that they could continue their prayers and contemplation.[23] The imperial police kept the papal entourage under strict surveillance. Servants and chaplains had their conversations listened to and recorded by discreet police spies. All correspondence with the pope was opened and monitored lest there be any subversive messages. Some relief was now granted to Pius. He was given permission to communicate with his banker, the fabulously wealthy Giovanni Raimondo Torlonia of Rome.[24] He remained loyal to the pope and, thanks to his trans-European network of banks, the pope was rapidly sent bills of exchange for 10,000 francs to meet his immediate needs.

It was only when the pope reached Grenoble that Napoleon's attention turned to the fate of his prisoner. He had been engaged in the War of the Fifth Coalition, which had been one of his most problematic military campaigns to date.[25] Between 5 and 6 July he finally managed to defeat the Habsburg forces at the Battle of Wagram, a victory that ensured that Napoleon remained the military master of Europe. It was in the days following this triumph that he received a barrage of letters from his brother-in-law and king of Naples Joachim Murat, his sister Elisa and General Miollis. They all informed him of events in Rome and the pope's difficult journey through Italy. All were desperate to receive further instructions and resolve the situation. From the Habsburg palace of Schönbrunn, which he occupied in Vienna, Napoleon wrote to Joseph Fouché, his minister of police, with the following instructions:

> I am upset that the pope has been arrested, it is madness! They should have just detained Cardinal Pacca and left the pope in peace in Rome. But ultimately one cannot do anything about it; what's done is done. I have no idea what Prince Borghese has been up to, but it is my intention that the pope does not enter France. If he is still on the Genoese Riviera the best place for him is Savona. [The town] has a large house where he can be accommodated decently until it is decided what to do with him. I have no objection, if he desists from his insanities, to his being sent back to Rome. If he has entered France, make him head back towards Savona and San Remo. Make sure you intercept all his correspondence. As far as Cardinal Pacca is concerned, have him imprisoned in the fortress of Fenestrelle and let him know that if a single Frenchman is murdered due to his influence, he will pay for it with his head.[26]

The emperor's surprise at this turn of events was disingenuous in the extreme. Only weeks previously he had written to Murat in the following terms:

> If the pope, against the well-being of his office and the gospels, preaches revolt and hides behind his immunity in order to publish circulars and sow dissent, he must be arrested; the time for games has passed. Philip the Fair had Boniface [VIII] arrested, and Charles V kept Clement VII in prison for a long time; and he had done far less [than Pius VII]. A priest who preaches disorder and war instead of peace to the powers of the earth abuses his office.[27]

As Murat was in command of Miollis and the troops in Rome, there is little wonder that Napoleon's letter was interpreted as a direct order that needed to be executed urgently. Indeed, Radet's memoirs and own correspondence make it clear that he was told that his orders came directly from the emperor. A concerned Radet had insisted that his order to arrest the pope and take him out of Rome be confirmed in writing.[28]

Behind the pope's kidnapping there was one clear and unequivocal source: Napoleon. The emperor felt betrayed by this troublesome priest, and he wanted him to submit to his authority. After a decade of attempting to find a compromise with the Catholic Church, Napoleon ordered the kidnapping of Pius VII. It was probably one of the greatest miscalculations of his career. This book tells the story of that kidnapping – one of the great turning points in history. Today, in the West, the church is no longer the 'First Estate'. Rather, it is one among many institutions in modern civil society, and subordinated to the state. It was Napoleon's challenge to Pius VII which catalysed and accelerated this process. This book also tells the tale of the dysfunctional relationship between two men – one world-renowned, celebrated not only for his epic military victories but also for his administrative and legal reforms, which continue to cast a long shadow into the present day; the other a meek Italian Benedictine monk who became pope, whose life is largely unknown in today's English-speaking world. Both men were powerful players in European politics, but neither was a free agent. They were constrained by the legacy of the French Revolution, and had inherited heavy burdens from the final decade of the eighteenth century. This book explores the roots that led to the pivotal split between pope and emperor, which mirrored the period's larger battle between church and state.

# ONE

# GOD AND REVOLUTION
## FRANCE IN TURMOIL, 1789–99

Napoleon Bonaparte and Barnaba Chiaramonti, the future Pope Pius VII, were born into a world where the belfries of churches dominated the landscape. Before 1789, religious participation and worship were not mere notions, but were at the very marrow of European identity. The future emperor and pope were both born Italian Catholics. Both, too, had aristocratic roots. Physically they resembled each other. Their dark hair, eyes and tanned skin were decidedly Italian. Both were of average height, and of slim build. The biggest contrast was their gaze: where Napoleon's was fiery and intense, Pius's was beneficent, kindly. They shared little when it came to values and outlook. The deeply spiritual, phlegmatic and gentle pope was in decided contrast to the materialistic, cynical and energetic revolutionary emperor.

It was a mere accident of history that Bonaparte was not born Genoese, like all his ancestors. France had conquered Corsica on 9 May 1769 at the Battle of Ponte Novu.[1] Letizia Ramolino, wife of the lawyer Carlo Buonaparte, gave birth to a boy, christened Napoleone, soon afterwards on 15 August. He was born on an island that had become French only seventy days before. After the military conquest, the Corsican clergy were subsumed into the church of France, but their practices and culture still had a distinctly Italian flavour. Devotion to the Virgin Mary, the cults of the saints and processions remained a staple of eighteenth-century Corsican communities.

The Buonaparte family tree was populated with priests and, to a lesser extent, nuns. The same was true of the Ramolino and Baciocchi clans, who were first cousins to the future emperor.[2] Napoleon's great uncle Don Luciano was the well-to-do archdeacon of the cathedral of Ajaccio.[3] He lived in several rooms of the large Buonaparte house, and took meals with the family daily. By all accounts he was the family historian. His nine nephews and nieces were often amused with stories about their ancestors, which were no doubt embellished in the telling. The younger children were taken on pilgrimages to the chapel of Nostra Signora del Rosario in the cathedral, where many of their forebears were buried in the Buonaparte sepulchre.[4]

When Napoleon's father Carlo died prematurely in 1785, it was Father Luciano who became the head of the family and estate manager. The archdeacon was a conscientious administrator, who ensured that Carlo's many debts did not bankrupt his widow and orphans. This did not stop his grand-nephew from accusing him of being miserly when he recalled the archdeacon during his exile on Saint Helena. Clearly there was some resentment over just how tightly Luciano held the family's purse strings. One can only wonder if this might have instilled Napoleon's life-long distrust of clergymen interfering in secular matters. For him, priests and money were a bad mix.

By all accounts, Carlo Buonaparte was a lukewarm, even sceptical, Catholic, a man of legal education who distrusted superstition and flamboyant ritual. After Corsica's conquest by France he wanted his sons to become French gentlemen and make their careers in the army, bureaucracy or the courts. He had spent large sums of money, cultivated his friendship with the island's governor, and used his contacts to ensure that the family was registered as noble by the French courts.[5] This was a decidedly dubious operation, and these aristocratic affectations have remained the source of some debate to this day. The Buonapartes were certainly well-to-do patricians by Corsican standards, but they were hardly Italian grandees, as Napoleon would later claim on Saint Helena. Carlo was turning away from tradition by not seeking out ecclesiastical benefices for his many sons. For some time, Joseph, the eldest son of the family, was destined for an ecclesiastical career, and studied at the college of Autun in Burgundy.[6] His charms, eloquence and love of beautiful women, not to mention his over-achieving brother, ensured that he would follow a very different career path. The church in Corsica remained a prosperous institution, but in a changing world its status was hardly stable.

Napoleon's culture and instincts were in many ways Catholic, but he also grew up in a world where the church's supremacy was waning under direct challenge from an educated public. Admittedly, both the military academy in Brienne (run by the rather lax Franciscan Minims) and then the *école militaire* in Paris, where he trained, had a routine of prayers, Sunday Mass and religious education for its *cadets-gentilshommes*.[7] Yet few seemed to take this too seriously, and theology, especially for an aspirant artillery officer, came second to the best that French science and enlightenment could provide. Father Patrault, Brienne's mathematics professor, seems to have lacked any true vocation, living a dissolute life, but he knew his subject and managed to inculcate a passion for it in the young Bonaparte, his best student. Another teacher at this military academy, Father Berton, does not seem to have taken his vow of celibacy very seriously, as he seduced the wife of an officer and then married her during the Revolution.[8] Napoleon was aware of the church's power but, thanks to his progressive education, knew only too well the calls for it to be reformed and made more utilitarian. During his adolescence he lost the faith of childhood but retained Catholic instincts. Throughout his life, he remained devoted to the priests who had been charged with his primary and secondary education. As the 'local lad made good' he would shower these clerics with pensions and positions once he became the leader of France. Unlike so many boys sent to Catholic boarding schools, Napoleon fondly remembered the priests who taught him. They established a template, in his mind, as to what a 'good priest' should be like. Clergymen who taught and provided public benefit were to be encouraged. Lazy, parasitic, corrupt and dissolute monks were to be eradicated.

On 14 August 1742, twenty-seven years before the birth of Napoleon, Barnaba Chiaramonti was born, hundreds of miles away from Corsica, in Cesena on the Italian mainland. This market town was located on the borders of the ancient exarchate of Ravenna in the depths of Romagna. Cesena had also been the birthplace of Giovanni Angelo Braschi, later Pius VI, and who also happened to be a distant cousin of the Chiaramonti family.[9] The Catholic world, for better or worse, would be continuously ruled from 1775 to 1823 by popes born in Cesena. This was not entirely surprising, given its position as a prosperous agricultural town, and an important ecclesiastical centre on the northern fringes of the Papal States. The counts of Chiaramonti, unlike the Buonapartes, had a very distinguished pedigree. Originally from Catalonia – they could trace their roots back to the twelfth century[10] – the family had more recently produced important intellectuals and men of science. Of note was Scipione Chiaramonti, a famous astronomer of the seventeenth century, praised by the philosopher Blaise Pascal for his celestial discoveries.[11]

Like Napoleon, the future Pius VII was born into a large family of eight brothers and sisters. The death of Count Chiaramonti in 1750 left the young Barnaba an orphan, like his Corsican counterpart, at a formative age. His mother, the Countess Giovanna, was a woman of iron Christian principles who successfully transmitted her fervent Catholicism to her children. His brothers Giacinto and Gregorio and sister Olimpia all had religious vocations. They would eventually enter religious orders, though Gregorio ultimately abandoned the Jesuits after a severe bout of depression.[12] Barnaba, following his siblings' example and formidable mother's fervour, entered the Benedictine abbey of Sant Maria del Monte in Cesena. The future pope does not seem to have been a natural monk in his early years, and his superiors noted he had decidedly high spirits. It is rumoured that when a novice the young Barnaba had smuggled a donkey into his dormitory; the reaction of his fellows, and more particularly his superiors, was not recorded. Whatever the reason for this asinine prank, Barnarba seems to have exorcised his restlessness early in his ecclesiastical career. From his adolescence onwards he took to theology and monastic discipline like a duck to water. Later he would study at the prestigious University of Padua and at the Collegio Sant'Anselmo in Rome.[13]

From the painstaking research of the historian Jean Leflon, it is safe to assume that, during his studies, the young Chiaramonti came into contact with many of the great Catholic Enlightenment thinkers of his age, along with Jansenist theology. This was a theological movement which sought to improve Catholicism principally through spiritual renewal: frequent confession, moral severity and proper communion were vital ingredients in a diet that would ensure salvation. Jansenism, despite its theological essence, had political implications, and urged reform within Catholic governance. Many of its adherents believed the church was far too hierarchical and concerned with worldly power.[14] For Jansenist reformers, the church's worldliness and interference in politics damaged its pastoral mission to aid the poor and guide sinners to repentance. Chiaramonti may have spent the better part of his life in monasteries and universities, but he was no close-minded monk nor ivory-tower scholar. Both he and Napoleon knew that the church was being pressured into overdue reform. They were both sympathetic to this impulse and debated with their contemporaries how it could best be achieved.

Little could have prepared them for what the close of the eighteenth century had in store for Europe. As we shall see, in less than a decade, the church in France (known as the Gallican Church) lost its position of pre-eminence and became a persecuted clandestine organisation. The revolutionary armies of the 1790s that crossed the Rhine and Alps became anticlerical missionaries who attacked Catholicism throughout Europe. However, this process was hardly inevitable and stemmed from a dire mismanagement of eighteenth-century controversies about the role of the church in society. After decades of enlightened debate, the church had certainly been under pressure to let go of political power and provide public utility. It is a commonplace to think that the eighteenth century witnessed the birth of our modern secular world, and there is a general tendency amongst scholars to paint the intellectual ferment and the associated scientific discoveries of the eighteenth century in atheistic and anti-religious colours. The truth is rather more nuanced.

Few Enlightenment thinkers and *philosophes*, especially outside France, were militant atheists or radical secularists. On the contrary, many intellectuals of the Enlightenment believed that religion, science and knowledge were not mutually exclusive spheres of human endeavour, but rather might reinforce each other. They hoped that modern science and criticism would lead to stronger understandings of scripture and the workings of God's creation. A significant proportion of progressive writers at this time were clergymen or, at the very least, had started their careers in the church.[15] The religious – or in southern Europe, Catholic – Enlightenment strove to improve and strengthen the appeal of the church.[16] In many ways, the Enlightenment did not wish to destroy religion, but to improve it in the same way as it sought to free man from the shackles of arbitrary tradition and superstition. A better-educated clergy, and a more democratically accountable church, would not fear freedom but rather safeguard it. There was a general sense that the church's teachings on morality and conscience were vital for the preservation of both the social and political order.[17]

This was a vision that Napoleon would share. He saw religious morality as the bulwark that preserved public order.[18] He reportedly stated: 'It is by making myself Catholic that I brought peace to Brittany and the Vendée. It is by making myself a Muslim that I established myself in Egypt. If I governed a nation of Jews, I should re-establish the Temple of Solomon.'[19] This was diametrically opposed to the future Pius VII's sincere belief in both Catholic worship and the church's pastoral mission. Chiaramonti, as a university professor in Parma and later bishop of Imola, was a participant in these lively controversies about the purpose of the church in a modern society. He believed in the advantages of a more pastoral and charitable institution. Yet his allegiance to the church's hierarchy and authority was unshakeable. Chiaramonti wanted the church to lead social renewal, and not to be a mere spectator. In practice the millennial history of the church and the realities of its political role had made reform intractable.

This was certainly the case across the Alps in the Kingdom of France and Navarre. Here the system of governance, which we now call the *ancien régime*, or old order, was a complex living organism, which had not been created overnight but had developed, almost imperceptibly, over many centuries.[20] The Bourbon monarchy was the only national institution that presided over a vast array of interlocking jurisdictions, vested interests, corporate privileges and regional identities that characterised France before the Revolution and made reform highly controversial. Catholicism, paradoxically, legitimated the French crown whilst simultaneously resisting its attempts to centralise political power and curb social privilege.

The situation in Corsica was somewhat different: as the Bourbons' last conquest it was given a remarkably modern and centralised form of government. It was an administrative experiment that left an ambivalent legacy on the young Napoleon. On the one hand it made him resentful of foreign interference in his native island. Indeed, in his teenage years right up to his early twenties, he was a fervent Corsican patriot, dreaming of freeing his homeland from foreign domination. Despite resenting France's heavy-handed approach in Corsica, he was awed by the power and efficiency of the modern state and its ability to mould daily lives. This awe never left him. It is a decided paradox that he would visit on Europe the thing he most resented in his youth: imperial domination. As a Corsican, he realised that the church had an important function in ensuring social cohesion and public order. However, he viewed with decided hostility a clergy that interfered with public power and opposed the state. Catholicism's political pre-eminence during the *ancien régime* was something that many of Napoleon's generation wanted to put behind them completely.

The Gallican Church was one of the most important, wealthy and powerful institutions of the eighteenth century, something between an established church and a self-governing spiritual corporation.[21] In recognition that, after the fall of Rome, France had been one of the first barbarian polities to convert to Christianity, its king held the honorific title *rex Christianissimus*, or 'most Christian king'. This accolade symbolised the special relationship between the French monarchy and the Papacy. More spectacularly still, at his coronation, each king of France was anointed with the holy oil of Saint Remigius, which was supposed to bestow on him the miraculous power to heal scrofula (a glandular disease affecting the neck in particular).[22]

Despite this close relationship between the monarchy and Rome there was significant tension too. Bonaparte and Chiaramonti were both lovers of history.

They knew, from their reading, that the relationship between Paris and Rome had been fraught for centuries. The pope was nominally head of all French bishops but, since the Middle Ages, the clergy of France had claimed important rights, exemptions and privileges. The Pragmatic Sanction of Bourges of 1438 had made the Gallican Church virtually independent of the Papacy for the better part of a century.[23] One of its most distinguishing features was the power wielded by the kings of France over appointments for vacant dioceses. Since the Concordat of Bologna in 1516, monarchs nominated candidates for sees, and the pope, if the nominees were theologically qualified, would bestow canonical investiture.[24] The king, during the appointments process, claimed the right to collect all revenues of unfilled dioceses in his domains until a new incumbent was invested by the pope. This royal prerogative was controversial, and was often contested by Rome.

This dispute over episcopal appointments pitted Louis XIV against Pope Innocent XI for the better part of a decade during the late seventeenth century. This conflict culminated in the publication of the celebrated Gallican Articles of 1682 (see Appendix), drafted by Bishop Bossuet of Meaux (a staunch defender of royal absolutism).[25] These articles declared, with stinging finality, that the pope could not interfere in political and temporal matters in France. They went so far as to declare that the pope did not have the power to excommunicate the French monarch for political reasons. The Gallican Articles were vital in France's understanding of its relationship with the Papacy; as will be seen in Chapter 7 (pp. 193–4), they would be invoked later by Napoleon to claim supremacy over all ecclesiastical establishments within his empire. The Gallican legacy of autonomy from the Papacy was a powerful one, and will resurface constantly in the pages of this book.

Gallicanism's most significant repercussion was to rekindle the medieval notion of conciliarism.[26] This complicated theory claimed that church councils shared equal authority with the pope when it came to matters of faith and the internal governance of the church. In some ways, this alternative vision of church governance, or ecclesiology, called the pope's monarchical authority into question by making him subject to conciliar scrutiny. Simply put, the Gallican Church, assembled into a national council, could question and even veto papal authority. During the early modern period, not just the pope's supremacy was debated, but the powers of bishops were under challenge too. Edmond Richer, a theologian of the Sorbonne, had argued early in the seventeenth century for a more democratic ecclesiastical establishment.[27] He wished to see a church where priests would have a greater voice, and would not always be kept away from the levers of power by the episcopacy. These were arguments that Chiaramonti had studied carefully in his days in Padua. Though he was sympathetic to a more pastorally engaged church, he was horrified by the threat that conciliarism could bring to the authority of the Catholic hierarchy. Christ's resurrection had after all not created a democracy. The apostles and the disciples were princes of a church that was a spiritual monarchy governed by God, the ultimate king of the universe.

This ecclesiological controversy grew more acrimonious when it became associated with Jansenism. As we have seen above (p. 13), these sombre Catholics argued for a more austere and quasi-Calvinist understanding of salvation.[28] The principles and theological assumptions of this movement were condemned as heretical by the Papacy during both the seventeenth and eighteenth centuries, and the royal and papal persecution of Jansenist priests and believers created a significant backlash. Journalists and pamphleteers joined in a public campaign that defended Christian freedom of worship and conscience against external encroachments. Such debates re-emerged cyclically throughout the eighteenth century. It has been suggested that such theological and ecclesiological controversies exerted an important influence on the very outbreak of the French Revolution.[29] These disagreements over the governance of the Catholic Church mirrored debates over politics and good government in the lay sphere. Chiaramonti, and Napoleon to a much lesser extent, were aware and keenly attuned to such debates. They inherited the legacy of this eighteenth-century religious controversy on church governance which, despite their best endeavours, they failed ultimately to settle. The spectre of Gallicanism and Jansenism would cast a long shadow into the Napoleonic period.

The situation was made even more complex by the fact that the Gallican Church not only commanded vast wealth, but was also deeply enmeshed in the very fabric of *ancien régime* France. No fewer than three cardinals held the office of chief ('prime') minister during the eighteenth century.[30] The most significant advantage enjoyed by the clergy was exemption from both direct and indirect taxation. Clergymen held significant positions of authority in their communities, and each diocese had its own court or *officialité*. It was here that dispensations from consanguinity in marriage, annulments, sacramental discipline and issues of clerical behaviour were tried.[31] This institution would prove vital when Napoleon sought to have his marriage to Joséphine annulled in 1809 (see Chapter 6, pp. 170–5). During the eighteenth century, the secular laws of the realm also upheld the moral teachings of Catholicism: blasphemy, sacrilege or a refusal to attend Sunday Mass, for example, fell under the remit of ordinary justice. The grisly execution of the Chevalier de la Barre, who had his tongue ripped out for blasphemy before his execution, or the breaking on the wheel of the Protestant Jean Calas, falsely accused of murdering his own son, an alleged convert to Catholicism, were condemned as scandals in an age of Enlightenment.[32] The refusal of the sacraments to people suspected of heresy, the refusal to bury actors and showfolk in consecrated ground, shocked the sensibilities of a refined public. A gulf was emerging between religious morality and the call for a more humanitarian system of criminal justice.[33]

During the *ancien régime* the church had an overt presence in peoples' lives. To be a subject of the king of France implied being in communion with the church of Rome. Religious minorities such as Protestants and Jews faced severe restrictions, and were ineligible for public office.[34] The state's firm adherence to the church was not replicated with quite the same fervour by the French population as a whole. Many Catholics had a complicated and far from enthusiastic response to the Catholic magisterium (teachings). Regardless of how lukewarm the faith of some believers may have been, in practice, interaction with the clergy was unavoidable. A vast network of cathedrals, churches and convents held the French population in its tentacular embrace. There were roughly 140 dioceses in the kingdom, with about 40,000 parishes falling under their authority.[35] The church and its registers of births, marriages and deaths were the only form of bureaucracy that most peasants ever experienced. The pulpit and village bells were the social media of the age. They provided information from beyond the village confines and enabled royal edicts to be proclaimed. When Napoleon became first consul in November 1799 he was all too aware that religion was a vital instrument of governance. It was both a practical tool and a means of legitimating his regime. Yet his relationship with it was to be very different from that of his Bourbon predecessors, who had worked in partnership with their clergymen. Napoleon, as a man of the Enlightenment, tolerated all religions equally. In return he expected them to preach obedience and subordination to the state as the ultimate source of authority.

This had not been the case in the past; the French church had been independent of the state on many levels. The revenues and landed wealth of Gallican clergymen exceeded the private income of the French crown: it has been calculated that the church collected 120 million livres in tithes per year from farmers during the second half of the eighteenth century.[36] This excludes the revenue from rural land and urban properties under direct ecclesiastical control. Somewhere between 6 and 10 per cent of all arable land in France was church-owned.[37] In theory, the clergy were tax exempt, but every five years the General Assembly of the Gallican Church had to negotiate a *don gratuit*, or free gift, to the crown. This represented their contribution towards the running of the state and its administration. The *don gratuit* by the 1780s amounted to about 15 million livres per year, or 12.5 per cent of total tithes collected.[38]

The kingdom's nobility and the episcopacy of the Gallican Church had a symbiotic relationship. The second sons of aristocrats, or eldest sons in fragile health, were destined for an ecclesiastical career from early childhood. Bishops were powerful lords and, by 1789, all those who wore the mitre could boast noble pedigrees.[39] The archbishop of Paris commanded revenues totalling half a million livres, and his brother bishops in Strasbourg and Metz were not far behind. There were vast disparities in terms of episcopal wealth: the literally poor bishop of Vence collected a mere 12,000 livres per year.[40] These inequalities reverberated down the social pyramid. Rich parishes, urban prebendaries or abbeys *in commendam* could make French abbés immensely wealthy and independent. This was deeply unfair, considering that the bulk of pastorally committed parish priests had to make do with meagre tithes or, worse, the *portion congrue*. This payment, or salary, amounted to 700 livres and was paid to the meanest parishes that were barely economically viable. Such *congruistes* lived in a state of penury that mirrored that of their peasant flocks.[41] This economic gulf explains why the aristocratic episcopacy was portrayed as deeply out of touch with its priests, who worked hard on the peripheries of the realm.

Sixty thousand parish priests, or secular clergy, formed the very backbone of the Gallican Church. Many of them fought a harsh daily struggle to minister and assist their communities. They viewed with growing envy and resentment their brethren who followed a monastic rule or were part of religious orders. By 1789 there were 26,000 monks and 56,000 nuns, or regular clergy, in the Gallican Church.[42] As was the case during the Reformation in England, monasteries were viewed with suspicion because of their wealth and their perceived lack of social utility. Contemplative institutions, dedicated to study and spiritual discipline, did grate against the spirit of the age. Despite their bad press, these 3,000 monasteries and 5,000 nunneries did provide education, healthcare and poor relief, but this was far from their main function.[43] Withdrawal from the world and a life of contemplative prayer was their main *raison d'être*.

Predictably, most abbés and many canons were of aristocratic descent.[44] As was the case for the episcopacy, the nomination of abbés and abbesses (with some exceptions), was a royal prerogative, subject to little outside control or verification. The practice of granting abbeys *in commendam* was particularly criticised and seen as unethical. This process allowed a candidate of twenty-three years of age (who would vow to take priestly orders within a year) to enjoy over half the revenues of a monastic institution without having to reside in or minister to his community.[45] The career of Louis de Bourbon-Condé, comte de Clermont, who gathered a large collection of abbeys *in commendam* collecting a massive annual revenue of over 600,000 livres, was a scandal. He never wore clerical dress, was lax in his vow of celibacy and served as a military officer in the king's armies.[46] As the ecclesiastical historian John McManners has noted, the mausoleum he built for his pet monkey was the closest he ever came to exercising his spiritual ministry.[47]

Mercifully the Comte de Clermont was the exception rather than the rule when it came to abbés. Monasteries, convents and religious orders were under increasing pressure and public scrutiny as the eighteenth century drew to a close. They were among the key targets of enlightened anticlericalism. Napoleon was influenced by critiques of convents and he would become the scourge of monasticism in Europe. Wherever the Grande Armée conquered land, monasteries were confiscated and their properties nationalised or sold at auction. For the future emperor, parish priests provided services; monks, however, were parasites.

On the question of monasteries, the views of Napoleon and Chiaramonti could not have been more different. Pius VII, as a former Benedictine monk, saw convents as fulfilling a vital role in terms of prayer and study. He was a staunch defender of such institutions and shrines to piety. He would use his pontificate to promote such monastic associations and tried gradually to reform their worst abuses. The pope and the emperor's experiences of revolution led them both to reassess the role of Christianity in politics and society. They both appreciated the need for change, but their solutions were radically different.

As the eighteenth century reached its twilight, these religious tensions would erupt to the surface of politics with a vengeance. The 1780s were a decade of crisis for the French monarchy. Having helped – at great cost – the American colonists to win their independence, the royal government's indebtedness and budget deficit grew in peace time, leaving Louis XVI desperate to reform his finances, cut spending and find new revenues to control the kingdom's public debt.[48] Reform, counter-reform and U-turns exasperated the public and did little to reassure investors and taxpayers. A sign that the royal government was ready to countenance greater religious reform came in 1787, when Louis XVI granted an edict of toleration to the Protestant minority of the south of France; permission was even given for the construction of some synagogues in Lorraine. Under the edict's terms, Protestants were given limited recognition through the creation of non-Catholic registers in which they could record their own births, marriages and deaths.[49] The church's absolute monopoly on public worship was starting to slip.

The inability of the crown to control its spiralling deficit ultimately led to the summoning to Versailles of the Estates General of 1789. This advisory institution had not met since 1614,[50] and was composed of representatives emanating from the three orders of the realm. These were based on the old medieval division of society into those who prayed, those who fought and, basically, those who did everything else. The First Estate was made up of the clergy, and held the position of honour, followed by the Second Estate (the nobility) and the Third Estate (that is, everybody else in theory). It was hoped that the three orders' endorsement of new taxes and reforms would make the nation financially solvent and increase the crown's political control. As it happened, the summoning of the Estates General would backfire spectacularly.

Between January and March 1789, each of the three orders was invited to draw up *cahiers de doléances*, or lists of grievances, that would make the crown aware of the problems within the realm.[51] These lists highlighted that the people of France were sympathetic to ordinary poor parish priests, who were perceived to have suffered much at the hands of a power-hungry episcopacy and a corrupt regular clergy, whose monasteries and convents deprived them of vital income. Those lists of grievances, redacted by the clergy, demonstrated the order's willingness to reform ecclesiastical tax exemptions and the tithe. However, the most radical parish priests, given their poor relationship with their monastic colleagues, demanded that monastic wealth be confiscated and redistributed amongst poor parishes. These documents underline a church divided and seeking significant internal reform.[52]

This was particularly evident in the elections of the clergy's deputies at the Estates General. Only forty-six bishops were chosen as deputies, with a further fifty-six senior clerics selected to travel to Versailles.[53] The most impressive contingent was made up of 231 parish priests – against a mere ten monks – who were selected to represent the Gallican Church. The last time the Estates had met in 1614, only 10 per cent of clerical deputies could have been considered parish priests.[54] This hierarchical division between prelates and priests would become all too apparent after the Estates assembled and started their deliberations. Given the protestations of loyalty to Catholicism present throughout the *cahiers*, there are few grounds to suspect that the deputies had an anticlerical agenda. When the Estates opened in May 1789 Louis XVI did not anticipate that this assembly would act as the backdrop for an imminent revolution. He had even less reason to suspect that the unfolding political drama would unleash significant religious repercussions. In November 1788 the king and his reforming minister Chrétien-Guillaume de Lamoignon de Malesherbes discussed the parallels that the escalating crisis in France bore to the English Civil War. Despite agreeing with the king that the situation was alarming, the minister provided reassurance; at least, he stated, 'religious quarrels are not involved'.[55] These words proved decidedly ironic.

The opening ceremonies of the Estates General stressed the Gallican Church's pre-eminence in the realm. On 5 May 1789, a solemn procession traversed Versailles and culminated in a High Mass. The prelates and clergy of the ecclesiastical establishment were given places of honour. The cardinals, archbishops and bishops, dressed in their crimson and violet pontifical robes, emphasised that they were the 'First Estate' of the realm.[56] In the first six weeks of the Estates General the clergy behaved in a relatively pliant manner. This was not the case when it came to the Third Estate, whose deputies were uncertain of what to do and refused to deliberate on the reform programme put forward by the monarchy.[57] The deputies did not accept that they, as the Third Estate, were subordinate to the privileged orders of the clergy and nobility. It was at this moment that a radical clergyman came to the fore and made one of the most notable contributions in triggering the French Revolution.

The Abbé Emmanuel-Joseph Sieyès was born in Fréjus in the south of France and had from an early age been earmarked for a clerical career. He was educated at the seminary of Saint-Sulpice in Paris, the intellectual powerhouse of the Gallican Church. He made powerful friends and became the vicar-general to the diocese of Chartres. His later career brought him into close contact with Bonaparte, and he would play a crucial role in the events that ultimately resulted in the Coup of 18 Brumaire of 1799. His religious vocation was thin at best, and he was far more interested in philosophy and political economy than theology.[58] Despite being in holy orders, he had been elected a deputy of the Third Estate for the Paris region. Early in the year he had published a celebrated pamphlet entitled *What is the Third Estate?* Its opening lines – 'What is the Third Estate? Everything. What has it been hitherto in the political order? Nothing. What does it demand? To be something' – guaranteed that it would be a publishing sensation.[59]

According to the abbé, the Third Estate represented 96 per cent of the non-privileged population. It was the embodiment of the nation and had the right to legislate on its behalf. Sieyès urged his colleagues to declare themselves a National Assembly. This move would place sovereignty, or political power, in the hands of the Third Estate as representatives of the entire nation; this implied that the monarchy could be stripped of its ancient prerogatives and powers. Once the deputies had created a National Assembly, Sieyès urged them to give France a written constitution and reform the state thoroughly.[60] On 17 June 1789, in a true moment of history-making, the Third Estate heeded Sieyès's advice and declared itself to be the National Assembly. Breaking with Sieyès's pamphlet, the deputies of the Third Estate invited their colleagues from the other two orders to join them in common deliberation. The nobility of the Second Estate greeted the request with contempt. By contrast, many parish priests within the First Estate, who came from modest backgrounds, broke ranks with their prelates when, on 19 June, 149 clergymen (including some progressive bishops) voted to join the Third Estate in joint session.[61] Events soon accelerated, and the clergy played a secondary role in the growing struggle between Third Estate and crown. A tense stand-off followed over June and July, which culminated in a Parisian insurrection in support of the radical deputies that led to the violent taking of the Bastille.[62] Over the summer months, the French countryside erupted into violence in a phenomenon known as the 'Great Fear'.[63] Most accounts focus on attacks on royal bureaucrats and noble châteaux, but monasteries were also targeted, evidencing the long-held resentment against the regular orders.

In truth the French Revolution represented not so much the triumph of a pre-existing revolutionary movement or conspiracy, but rather the monarchy's implosion. France in 1789 was to all intents and purposes a failed state. The National Assembly tried desperately to fill this vacuum of authority with panicky and rushed legislation.[64] It would take the Constituent Assembly, as the deputies now described themselves, over two years to write a new constitution. These men, through the experience of revolution, gained an overarching sense that the traditions of the past centuries were obsolete and that former institutions were suspect, if not corrupt. Very soon, destructive legislation would be unleashed against the entire edifice that had upheld the *ancien régime*. Although the church had not been an initial priority it would soon occupy the Assembly's attention and become one of the most controversial areas of its reforms. Although at this time Napoleon was still trying to fulfil his ambitions as a Corsican patriot, and was eventually to seek election in the National Guard on his native island, the reforms of the Assembly made a deep impact on his thinking. He agreed with the deputies and believed that the church should be subordinate to the state.

It is unclear what Chiaramonti made of events in France in 1789. Although he had been made a cardinal and bishop of Imola in 1786, his priorities at this stage of his career were pastoral. Despite being related to Pius VI, the future pope was not a highflyer of the Roman Curia (the Papacy's central administration) and papal court. He was a liberal and open-minded prelate who possessed one of the best private libraries of Romagna. It was said even to hold some of the most recent works of the Enlightenment.

Across the Alps, the National Assembly passed some of its most celebrated legislation in August 1789. The Declaration of the Rights of Man and of the Citizen enshrined freedom of conscience as a fundamental human right in its tenth article.[65] This declaration severed the umbilical cord that had bound church and state for centuries. It disestablished the Gallican Church and bestowed citizenship implicitly on Protestants and Jews (it would take the Assembly several months to do this formally). This move was to have disastrous repercussions in the south, where sectarian violence erupted with a vengeance. Less than a year later, in June 1790, over 300 people lost their lives in street battles between Protestants and Catholics during the *bagarre de Nîmes*.[66] Article 10 of the Rights of Man broke the centuries-old axiom that to be French was to be Catholic. The politicians of the Revolution had the unshakeable certainty that loyalty to the state was the first duty of every citizen. All other allegiances were viewed at best with suspicion and at worst deemed to be a public danger. For the deputies of the Assembly, religious conscience was to be relegated to the private sphere. Public displays of loyalty to the Papacy came to be seen as traitorous. During the famous night of 4 August, the privileges of the nobility and feudal dues were voluntarily renounced with little consideration of the practicalities involved. It is often forgotten that the tithe was also renounced on this evening.[67] Unlike feudal dues, which were to be indemnified, compensation for the clergy's loss of income was not even entertained. This was a harbinger of things to come.

The church was to find itself at the epicentre of several political earthquakes. On 2 November 1789, in a move inspired by Charles Maurice de Talleyrand-

Périgord, bishop of Autun, church property was placed at the disposal of the nation.[68] Ecclesiastical lands and buildings could now be sold and used to service France's public debt. Eventually a new paper currency, the *assignat*, secured on the value of these properties, was floated on 19 April 1790 on the promised sale of over 400 million livres' worth of ecclesiastical real estate. The faithful sought to defend church land, arguing that it originated in private bequests rather than through public funding. However, such appeals against the seizure of ecclesiastical property fell on deaf ears. The nationalisation of church lands was only the beginning.

On 13 February 1790, four months after Talleyrand's speech on the confiscation of church land, the National Assembly withdrew all recognition of monastic vows.[69] In this it claimed to be liberating monks and nuns from their incarceration in abbeys; only those monastic houses dedicated to education were spared in this measure. Many regular clergy bowed to the inevitable and left their monasteries. Yet many nuns proved unhappy with being evicted from their homes, with the question of where they would go and how they would live remaining unanswered. In reaction, the clergy, under the inspiration of the Carthusian monk and deputy Dom Antoine Christophe Gerle, tried, on 12 April 1790, to launch a counterstrike. Gerle had proposed that Catholicism should be the sole religion afforded the right of public worship, but the motion was soundly defeated.[70] It was at this time that many priests and abbés shifted their ground. They moved from sitting on the left or in the centre to taking positions on the right-hand side of the Assembly's debating chamber. None was more outspoken than Jean-Sifrein Maury, then prior of Lihons, a rather worldly political priest, who defended the traditional orders of society with great bravery and eloquence. He was eventually forced to flee to Rome, where he was rewarded for his defence of the church and elevated into the College of Cardinals in 1794. He would remain an influential figure throughout the period, eventually becoming a key collaborator of Napoleon.[71] The first few months of the Revolution had weakened the church significantly. It was very hard to imagine how it could survive now that tithes had been abolished and its properties confiscated.

As John McManners put it, the revolution 'started to go off course when the Constituent Assembly imposed the oath of the Civil Constitution of the Clergy on 27 November 1790'.[72] The question of how to finance the church had been left unanswered since the end of 1789. With the passing of the Civil Constitution on 12 July 1790 the Gallican Church became again a government-funded church. All priests and bishops would become salaried officials of the state. The number of dioceses would be reduced from 139 to 83. This would mirror the new administrative reorganisation implemented by the Assembly. Administrative departments, which would deal with civil, military and judicial matters, would be congruent with dioceses. This was supposed to avoid the overlapping and complicated jurisdictional mess that had characterised the *ancien régime*. If rationalisation had been the sole object of the reformers of the Assembly, then papal approval might have been possible. After all, Pius VI had agreed in 1782 to the suppression of the monasteries in the Habsburg lands during the reign of Joseph II, Holy Roman Emperor. However, the Civil Constitution was much more radical in its intent and scope.

The most drastic proposal was that priests and bishops be subject to election, like any other functionary in the regenerated French state. This was bound to elicit hostility, especially as Jews and Protestants now formed part of the electorate. The church saw itself as the sole vehicle that could guarantee the apostolic succession; only the king and pope could make decisions relating to the hierarchy.[73] The Civil Constitution was a decidedly odd religious settlement. Its articles essentially created an established church without a monopoly on public worship (a toothless form of Anglicanism). Under the terms of this reform, the annual salaries of parish priests would range from 600 to 1,200 livres, representing a marked improvement on the old *portion congrue*. In comparison to the halcyon days of the *ancien régime*, bishops would fare significantly worse, and receive a yearly stipend of a mere 12,000 livres. The archbishop of Paris would continue to be the richest clergyman, receiving 50,000 livres a year, but this amounted to only a tenth of his pre-1789 income. The Civil Constitution sought to rationalise church governance, but the National Assembly failed to realise that tampering with faith was a delicate business. The deputies showed themselves deeply unsympathetic to the concerns of Catholic believers and their spiritual head in Rome.

Preventing divided loyalties or conflicts of conscience amongst the French citizenry was the National Assembly's prime concern. Its most radical action was to require newly appointed bishops and priests to swear an oath to uphold the French Constitution.[74] This decision transformed a political revolution into a religious schism. Essentially, Catholics were asked to choose between their faith and their politics. There is a tendency, at times, to see the French Revolution as a successor to the Reformation. In some ways there are obvious parallels between these two movements. They both challenged the traditional order and sought to limit the power of the Roman Church. Yet the religious reformers of the sixteenth century were deeply concerned with theology and salvation. For them, politics was a means by which the faithful were guided onto the right path which led to God and, ultimately, heaven.[75] For French radicals it was all about the politics of religion, rather than about theology.

The Civil Constitution created massive divisions that reverberated across the Kingdom of France. All but seven bishops refused to swear the oath to uphold the Constitution.[76] Amongst the lower clergy the situation was less clear-cut, with just over half of parish priests swearing. There were huge regional variations, with 80 per cent of priests in the west of the country refusing to swear, while in the Loire Valley and Provence the overwhelming majority accepted the Constituent Assembly's requirements.[77] The non-juring ('non-swearing') clergy and their loyal flock of religious dissidents became decided proponents of counter-revolution. The Assembly's treatment of the Papacy horrified and enraged large swathes of the population. In June 1790, the municipal government of Avignon, then a papal enclave within France, rebelled against the pope, with the help of the French National Guard, and declared its wish to be annexed to France.[78] On 20 November 1790 French troops were sent to occupy the entire Comtat Venaissin, an enclave of the Papal States in the south of France. This unilateral annexation was a direct violation of papal sovereignty, and did little to dispose the Papacy favourably towards the Civil Constitution of the Clergy.

After several months of discussion, Pope Pius VI, on the advice of the College of Cardinals, solemnly condemned the Civil Constitution on 30 March 1791 in his brief *quod aliquantam*.[79] This document stopped short of excommunicating those deputies who had voted in favour of the measure, but Pius did exhort Louis XVI not to sanction this act. Above all else the pope felt aggrieved at being presented with a *fait accompli* and a refusal to negotiate terms. A decade later both Pius VII and Napoleon would try to hammer out the compromise that so eluded the National Assembly. Unlike his predecessors, the first consul sought clerical consent for his ecclesiastical reform programme. During his rule, memories of the disastrous fallout and civil war stoked by the Civil Constitution were never far from his mind. A reoccurrence of this schism was something that both the future leader of France and pope desperately wanted to avoid.

The Constitutional Church created by the French Revolution inherited Gallicanism's distrust of Rome and the pope. The real paradox of such religious turmoil was to convert *ancien régime* bishops and king of France towards a more ultramontane (belief in the supremacy of the pope over the church) outlook. This new allegiance to Rome went against the grain of three centuries of French ecclesiastical tradition. Confrontations between the Constitutional Church and its refractory opponents, tacitly supported by the crown, were not in short supply. On 18 April 1791 the king, on the advice of the bishop of Clermont, sought to leave for the palace of Saint-Cloud, on the outskirts of Paris. Here, at a safe distance from his capital, he might take communion discreetly from a non-juring priest. Louis XVI, however, was prevented from leaving the Tuileries Palace by a mob, who manhandled his courtiers.[80] The fallout from the Civil Constitution and the intimidation of the church loyal to Rome formed part of a constellation of factors that prompted the king's ill-fated flight to Varennes in June 1791.[81] The revolutionaries felt deeply betrayed by the king, who had fled his capital and disowned the Revolution. His attempted escape led to a radicalisation of French politics and the birth of a republican movement.

In the subsequent two years, a steady stream of bishops and priests left France for exiles that would last the better part of a decade. Perhaps as many as 8,000 ecclesiastical refugees may have made their way to the Papal States.[82] It is likely that Chiaramonti, like so many prelates in central Italy, had to assist and find accommodation for these French ecclesiastical exiles. This mass migration of priests and nuns may well have given him his first inkling of the growing revolutionary crisis; perhaps it galvanised his determination to avoid a similar fate. Predictably, France's declaration of war on Austria on 20 April 1792 heightened passions and fears and amplified the need to annihilate internal foes.[83] The press increasingly painted ultramontane priests as dangerous fifth columnists hidden amidst virtuous citizens, while Louis XVI's decision to veto a law that would have allowed priests to be deported if denounced by twenty or more citizens caused outrage.[84] The war and the king's veto damaged the monarchy's already tenuous grip on executive power. The press disparaged Louis as he appeared to defend disloyal priests, rather than vigorously to oppose the enemies of the Revolution. On 10 August 1792, crowds stormed the Tuileries and deposed the king.[85]

As the allied armies came within 125 miles of the French capital, panic gripped the population. The September Massacres that followed were one of the most anarchic and horrifying spectacles of the 1790s. Mobs set up kangaroo courts, which tried suspects and inmates of Parisian gaols with little in terms of judicial process, and with no consideration for presumption of innocence. The majority of those unlucky enough to fall into their clutches were despatched with unmitigated cruelty. Of the estimated 1,400 victims of the Massacres were 220 priests and 3 bishops.[86] Napoleon had been in Paris on leave, awaiting reassignment, during the fall of the French monarchy. The spectacle of violence against soldiers, priests and counter-revolutionaries gave him a horror of mob violence that remained with him all his life. Witnessing such riotous behaviour and lawlessness ensured that in future he would do whatever was necessary to establish the rule of law, even if this meant he had to resort to authoritarian measures. Arrest, intimidation and military tribunals would in the future be important instruments in his attempts to ensure stability and security after a decade of revolutionary lawlessness.

The ongoing persecution of the non-revolutionary church caused massive dissatisfaction and scandal in the west of France and parts of eastern Languedoc. The fires of religious turmoil stoked those of the civil war. On 21 September 1792, after national elections, a new parliamentary body met; the first order of business for this new National Convention was to declare a new republic and proclaim monarchy abolished forever. The greatest pillar of ecclesiastical support was thus erased in one fell swoop. Louis XVI was tried and convicted of treason in December.[87] Before his execution on 21 January 1793 he received the last rites and confession from a French-educated Irish priest, the Abbé Edgeworth de Firmont, who had refused the constitutional oath. As he mounted the scaffold to meet his end, he heard his confessor exhort him with the words, 'Son of Saint Louis, ascend to heaven!'

The beheading of the king marked the death of *ancien régime* Gallicanism. Never again would the alliance of throne and altar re-emerge on an equal footing. Almost every monarchy in Europe declared war on the new French Republic, which now fought a desperate struggle for its very survival. The rebellion in the Vendée in the west of France seemed to confirm the revolutionaries' worst fears that the refractory church was fanning the flames of counter-revolution. The rebellious Catholic and Royal Army of the Vendée used the sacred heart of Jesus as the emblem for its banners, symbolising its devotion to the true church. It marched as far as the outskirts of Angers in the Loire Valley in July 1793. For the Convention it proved just how religion could electrify its enemies. Naturally the motivations of the Vendeans were more complex: conscription had been deeply unpopular in the west, and they had profited little economically from the Assembly's reforms. Eventually the armies of the Republic did crush the Catholic and Royal Army at the Battle of Savenay on 23 December 1793.[88] Yet the civil war was not over, and pacification proved intractable. Republican troops were subject to ambush, sneak attacks and gruesome torture. In response, General Louis-Marie Turreau developed an effective tool of counter-insurgency with his infamous infernal columns. Unlike large regular units, which found movement in difficult terrain cumbersome, these columns made up of small numbers were able to penetrate deep into the *bocage* (or hedge lands) to seek out and destroy rebels. They burnt villages and terrified non-combatants with brutal reprisals.[89] This campaign of repression did little to endear the Republic to the population of the west. The Vendeans and Bretons would remain hostile to Paris and its government for most of the nineteenth century.

Civil war and insurrection led many in the Republic to believe that the Constituent Assembly had not gone far enough in its ecclesiastical reforms. For France to be fully regenerated into a virtuous republic, an active campaign of anticlericalism and de-Christianisation was needed. The Catholic religion came to be perceived as irredeemably compromised by its association with the *ancien régime*. The year 1793 had been characterised by civil war and the constant threat of foreign invasion. By the autumn, the military situation had stabilised. Radicals outside of the Convention decided to unleash a deeper cultural revolution. They felt that the democratic regeneration of the population was essential if the Republic was to survive. The attempt to extirpate the church of Rome, and to create an alternative secular culture, was one of the most radical experiments of this time.[90] It was by no means centrally organised by the Committee of Public Safety, the Republic's government in all but name. It was the product of independent and unco-ordinated initiatives, taken by individuals and groups of fanatics.

This anti-Christian campaign had a remarkable effect on the acoustic landscape of France when, in July 1793, churches were limited to a single small bell and, a year later, bell ropes were confiscated.[91] Any bells in excess of the one allotted per parish were seized to be recast as cannons for the Republic's armies. This deeply symbolic requisition met with stiff resistance in some parishes. Yet by 1794 an eerie silence descended over France, as thousands of belfries were rendered unserviceable. Scattered across half a million square miles lay 40,000 parishes, whose sense of connection to a wider religious-political community had been experienced through the distant echoes of ringing bells. The bells announced moments of prayer, grief and joy; most importantly they marked the changing agricultural seasons. Their sound was one of the few ways in which communities had been held together. The ominous silence of the Revolution marked a new conception of time: one in which the Christian God was to have no part.

In September 1793 the radical deputy Gilbert Romme proclaimed that the present Gregorian calendar:

> began amongst an ignorant and credulous people and in the midst of troubles that foreshadowed the impending fall of the Roman Empire. For eighteen centuries, it served to date the progress of fanaticism, the degradation of nations, the scandalous triumph of pride, vice and stupidity, the persecutions and debasements endured by virtue, talent and philosophy at the hand of cruel despots.[92]

He proposed that the new year start on 22 September 1792, the anniversary of the proclamation of the Republic, and that France was now in Year II of a post-Christian calendar.[93] The year remained divided into twelve months, but each month had three ten-day weeks known as *décadi*. The months would be named after the weather or other seasonal characteristics rather than any political or subjective criteria. The final product that emerged was very romantic. Each new month received a very evocative name, such as *Brumaire, Frimaire, Floréal* and *Messidor* (roughly translated, 'the Misty One', 'the Frosty One', 'the Blossomy One' and 'the time of Harvest').[94] The calendar unexpectedly proved an effective tool for uncovering the Republic's enemies. Those who refused to use it by continuing to observe Sunday, or who bought fish on Fridays, as the church prescribed, revealed themselves to be suspects and were often denounced as public enemies.[95]

During the winter of 1793, groups of activists took the war against God further than anyone had anticipated, and escalated the campaign against religion. It was a decided irony that the Constitutional Church, created by the Constituent Assembly in 1790, was to be one of its main targets. By this time, the refractory church was an illegal underground organisation, and non-juring priests had either emigrated or were in hiding. It was a shocking betrayal when those priests who had taken an oath to the Revolution now found themselves persecuted like their former refractory colleagues. The Revolutionary Army sent from Paris to requisition grain and other essentials from the provinces took unquestionable pleasure in terrorising the clergy. They also enjoyed using clerical vestments and holy vessels for sham rituals aimed at undermining Catholicism before the eyes of the faithful. In waves of iconoclasm statues were knocked down from cathedral façades and interior church décor damaged beyond repair. One need only visit French cathedrals today to see evidence of this barbarism that sought to destroy the work of some of the most brilliant artists of the medieval and early modern age.

Simultaneously, some deputies, sent on a mission to the departments to ensure that the Convention's legislation was followed, took it upon themselves to irritate, if not persecute, Catholics. Joseph Fouché, Napoleon's future minister of police, and a former Oratorian lay brother, while on mission to the Nièvre department, put iron signs over cemeteries which stated 'Death is but an eternal sleep'. Some, like the former Capuchin monk François Chabot, bullied priests into renouncing their vocations. The Protestant Philippe-Jacques Rühl, armed with a hammer, visited the monastery of Saint-Rémi near Reims, and smashed the holy ampoule containing the sacred oil used to crown the kings of France.[96] In October 1793 crowds of vandals penetrated the royal necropolis of Saint-Denis on the outskirts of Paris. Here all precious objects and relics were requisitioned by agents of the Convention. Then the crowds exhumed the remains of dozens of kings and queens of France and threw these into a common grave. The magnificent statues and monuments would have been damaged beyond repair but for the intervention of the archaeologist Alexandre Lenoir. He persuaded the Convention to save the remains of these masterpieces of the late medieval, Renaissance and Baroque periods and placed them on public display in a museum of French monuments.[97]

The historian Michel Vovelle has calculated that about 18,000 constitutional priests were 'persuaded' to abandon their vocation during this period. The most high-profile figure caught up in this dismal process was Jean-Baptiste Gobel, the constitutional archbishop of Paris, who, under pressure from the Sans-Culottes, renounced his archdiocese on 6 November 1793. The next day, wearing the revolutionary red bonnet, he laid down his mitre, ring and crozier before the National Convention. His lack of resolve failed to impress the deputies; Gobel was eventually guillotined on 13 April 1794, a victim of the Terror.[98] During this time, over 3,000 priests married. Motivations for doing so must have differed enormously. Some undoubtedly were coerced with the threat of violence, while others probably liked the idea of domestic companionship and family life during a time of mayhem. How to deal with those priests who had forsaken their sacred vows of celibacy was to pose a decided headache for the Papacy after 1800.[99]

People sought to refashion themselves, their identity and their behaviour according to the new canons of republican culture. Some, like the prosecutor of the Paris municipality, Pierre-Gaspard Chaumette, renounced his Christian name and replaced it with that of the philosopher Anaxagoras, who had denied the divinity of the Sun. Others took on the names of republican heroes of ancient Rome, such as Brutus or Gracchus. Because it was not official state policy but rather the work of extremists, acting without government sanction, this movement has been described as 'anarchic de-Christianisation'. Chiaramonti and Napoleon both viewed such fanatical atheism with concern, not to say horror. For the future pope, spiritual renewal was the church's greatest priority. It alone could return peace to France. In Napoleon's case, he was certain that a well-regulated religion was one of the pillars on which political stability rested.

They were not alone in their views. The spiralling violence and the disorder it created caused concern amongst many in the Convention. By early 1794 Maximilien Robespierre, one of the most prominent members of the Committee of Public Safety, was appalled by what he observed unfolding in the provinces.[100] Robespierre was no friend of Catholicism, or the clerical establishment, but he believed that atheism's inherent immorality would damage any hope of instilling virtue into the Republic's citizenry. Deeply inspired by the philosopher Rousseau, he believed in the goodness of nature and its beneficent effects on man. He took the belief further, arguing that there was a Supreme Being who was the source of goodness and morality in the world, and that the soul was immortal. He suspected that the de-Christianisers of the winter of 1793 were not sincere patriots; atheism, he believed, kept people in ignorance and impeded their moral education. He decided that a counterstrike was necessary.[101] For Robespierre, republican virtue, that is an individual's selfless devotion to public good and society, lay at the heart of government and revolutionary culture. A new cult or religion was needed to instil 'virtue' on the French population at large and celebrate the Republic.

Largely inspired by Robespierre, a proposal was ratified by the Convention for the establishment of a new state religion. On 7 May 1794, it proclaimed that a special festival recognising the existence of the Supreme Being and the immortality of the soul would be celebrated in six weeks' time. This 'Cult of the Supreme Being' would replace Catholic morality with thirty-five festivals – celebrating virtues as diverse as 'hatred of tyrants', 'modesty', 'youth', 'agriculture' and 'misfortune' – which would be celebrated throughout the year.[102] It followed Enlightenment deism by recognising that some being or intelligent design lay at the origin of the universe. At its heart it promoted individual virtue and good works as the core of republican morality and identity. It was hoped that this regenerated religion would provide a necessary cultural and social adhesive to bind together the young Republic.

It is difficult to know what to make of this new religion. A minority genuinely engaged with the Supreme Being, while others ridiculed it and many more hoped that it signalled the end of the Terror against suspected enemies of the French Republic. Nothing could have been further from the truth: a few days after the festival, the Convention passed the Prairial Law (10 June 1794), which deprived those accused of political crimes of defence counsel. June and July saw an intensification of the Terror, which deeply disturbed politicians and their constituents alike.[103] The fate of the Cult of the Supreme Being was very much tied to that of the man who had inspired it. Robespierre had, throughout his time on the Committee of Public Safety, made many enemies, antagonising influential groups. He had contributed to a culture of paranoia and fear that eventually turned on him at the end of July 1794. Robespierre was now denounced as tyrant, and subsequently guillotined.[104] The religion he had tried to create followed him into oblivion. With the benefit of hindsight, one could argue that it was impossible to create religious feeling and belief overnight. The demolition of the Gallican Church had not just created a spiritual void, but a cultural one. There were times when former republicans tempted Napoleon to establish a new religion or a new church. The future emperor was deeply unimpressed with the Revolution's track record with seeking to build new religions from the ground up. He well understood that spiritual belief could neither be willed nor legislated into existence. This was an important political lesson learned from the chaos of the 1790s.

The period that followed the death of Robespierre saw the Terror gradually dismantled.[105] Almost as if by accident, in September 1794, the Convention abolished state salaries for constitutional priests, and in February the ringing of bells as well as the wearing of ecclesiastical dress were prohibited. For the first time in French history there was an effective separation of church and state.[106] The Constitutional Church had survived the Terror, but it was in dismal condition. Of the eighty-three bishops appointed during the Constituent Assembly a mere twenty-five were still in post. As many as five out of six constitutional priests may have renounced their vows during the late 1790s.[107] Between 1795 and 1799 a more moderate republican government, known as the Directory, took over the administration of France. For a time, Catholics, privately, started to attend discreet church services and, in some cases, sent their children to former priests for catechism and religious education. The years following the end of the Terror witnessed a hesitant rebirth in church attendance and worship.

Although the Directory initially decreased the persecution of the church, it remained deeply anticlerical and unsympathetic to religion. In its first two years it tried half-heartedly to heal the wounds created by the Revolution, but after royalists made troubling gains in the elections of 1797, the Directory was obliged to use military force to annul the result. The regime suspected that the growth of royalism was due to refractory missionaries spreading anti-republican propaganda, and even suspected the Constitutional Church of being lukewarm in its loyalty. A new oath of 'hatred of royalty' was imposed on priests practising their ministry. This new oath was quickly condemned by the Papacy. The Curia's disappointment was palpable, as Rome had secretly sought to establish a dialogue with Paris, but to no avail. Roughly 10,000 priests who refused to swear their hatred of royalty were arrested and sentenced to deportation to the South American colony of French Guiana, known as the 'dry guillotine', given the insalubrious climate and disease-ridden conditions. About 230 priests were actually shipped to this colony and a further 700 detained awaiting deportation.[108]

The most remarkable figure at this time in resisting directorial persecution was Henri Grégoire, constitutional bishop of Blois, who would later become a major opponent of the French Empire.[109] He had been a deputy since 1789 and was deeply committed to creating a less hierarchical and more primitive church. With remarkable vigour, he reached out to the surviving two dozen bishops of the Constitutional Church. In 1797 a synod with priests and bishops was held in Paris, where the basis for the reconstruction of the Constitutional Church was laid out. Under his zealous and determined pastoral care the church witnessed a remarkable – but ultimately wasted – rebirth. The number of bishops rose to fifty-eight, and new priests started to be appointed in parishes across France (excluding the west, where murders of constitutional clergy were endemic).[110] It must be admitted that the ultra-Gallican Church, born out of the Constituent Assembly's breach with Rome, was deeply vulnerable, especially given that the umbilical cord which had once linked it to the state had been severed. In terms of ritual, belief and spirituality it was remarkably similar to the refractory church that had remained loyal to Rome.[111] This made many wonder if the schism of 1791 was beyond repair. During the Directory, Napoleon had witnessed the ultimate failure of the experiment with the Constitutional Church. This made him wary of splitting the French church from the Papacy. The 1790s had taught him that disorder and civil war were the consequences of schism.

The Revolution's final years were characterised by increasing military success. During the early 1790s Cadet Buonaparte had come to reject his Corsican heritage after his family was expelled from the island due a feud with the patriot leader Pasquale Paoli. Following this trauma Napoleon concentrated on his military career, achieving outstanding successes first at the siege of Toulon in 1793 and then by quelling the Vendémiaire uprising in Paris in 1795 with a 'whiff of grapeshot'. At only twenty-six years of age, Bonaparte (he now spelled his surname in a more French fashion) was promoted to general and would win a string of unexpected military victories in northern Italy. This brought the frontiers of the French Republic into direct contact with the Papacy, which had, for the better part of a decade, been beyond its reach. Threatened with invasion and retribution, Pius VI signed the treaty of Tolentino on 19 February 1797.[112] Its terms forced Rome to pay an eye-watering indemnity of 30 million livres, while around 100 priceless artworks were shipped to France. It also ceded to France the Papal Legations of Romagna, the most prosperous region of the Papal States. In reality, the treaty was little more than a truce. The territories that fell under French occupation included the diocese of Imola, whose bishop was Cardinal Barnaba Chiaramonti. For the future pope, it was his first experience of revolution. During this time, he witnessed local radicals attack the power of the aristocracy and church; the French army showed little respect for traditional and ecclesiastical Italian elites. He sought to walk a fine line between the French occupier's anticlericalism and the expectations of his congregation.

On Christmas Day 1797 he preached a sermon in which he reminded all present that there was nothing in sacred scripture that precluded democracy, and that liberty could be enjoyed responsibly by Christians.[113] His sermon impressed not only the French government but Bonaparte in particular, as commander in chief. Those who read it came to believe that the bishop of Imola was a pragmatic peacemaker and enlightened reformer. Chiaramonti wanted to restore tranquillity and pre-empt violence, but to underestimate his commitment to the Catholic Church was unwise. He was a loyal servant of Pius VI, Vicar of Christ: obedience was hardly open to question. His belief in a spiritually renewed church did not imply that he accepted the supremacy of the state. He did not trust his new republican masters and in this he would be proved right. French territorial ambitions knew few limitations; for republicans, inspired by Roman antiquity, the eternal city was too appetising a prize to be ignored. Using the assassination of a French diplomatic agent, General Mathurin-Léonard Duphot, as a pretext, France declared war, and invaded the Papal States on 10 February 1798. A short-lived Roman Republic was founded. The biggest repercussion was the arrest of Pope Pius VI, who was first taken to Florence and thence across the Alps. His death in French captivity in Valence on 29 August 1799 marked the nadir in the fortunes of the modern Catholic Church. The republican authorities did their best to de-sacralise the dead bishop of Rome. Indeed, the head of the Catholic world and 'universal' church was described laconically on his death certificate as 'citizen Jean-Ange Braschi exercising the profession of pontiff'.[114] With the pope dead and the College of Cardinals scattered across southern Europe, many wondered whether Catholicism could weather this latest storm in its millennial history.

The French Revolution's tempestuous relationship with Catholicism raised issues that would trouble European history throughout the nineteenth century. The revolutionaries became pathologically distrustful of the Catholic Church after their ecclesiastical reforms met with dogged clerical resistance. They persecuted the church to an extent unseen since Roman antiquity or the Reformation. By 1799 France was a country riven by divisions, the most notable of which was between pious Catholics and fervent republicans. Catholics were disunited, and the Civil Constitution of the Clergy had succeeded in sowing much dissent amongst the faithful. The refractories were hungry for revenge, wanting to humiliate a constitutional clergy that they saw as renegades and traitors. Violence, lawlessness and horror was the daily experience for those opposed to the Revolution in France.[115]

Having said this, few peasants regretted the abolition of the tithe and other ecclesiastical dues. The state's refusal to impose Catholic morals and prohibitions liberalised private society in a hitherto unknown manner. Sexual freedom and religious satire exploded in this period. Unexpectedly, the new penal code of 1791 failed to criminalise homosexuality and the state withdrew from the bedroom in an unprecedented fashion. The Directory witnessed a vibrant cultural rebirth of elegant society, which enjoyed fully these new sexual freedoms. Many availed themselves of divorce by mutual consent, thus calling into question the very sacramentality of marriage. Anywhere between 38,000 and 50,000 divorces took place in the period between 1792 and 1803.[116] For many women this presented the opportunity to free themselves from abusive spouses and to start new lives. However, the Revolution was hardly a moment of female enfranchisement. The abolition of dowries and the subjugation of female property to male tutelage was certainly not an improvement. Women were actively discouraged from participation in politics, which was viewed as one of the vices that had brought down the *ancien régime*.

As the Revolution reached its first decade France remained a deeply unstable country. Political rivalries were bad enough, but the schism with the church had dramatically affected law and order. The creation of stability and public order would continue to prove elusive, so long as Catholics were forced into the counter-revolutionary camp. When Napoleon Bonaparte returned from his ill-fated Egyptian campaign on 8 October 1799, he was something of an unknown quantity.[117] In the Orient he had portrayed himself as an admirer of Muhammad and the monotheistic faith he had created during the seventh century. Islamic clerics had been vital to France's ephemeral rule in the Nile Delta. Such practices highlight that, wherever Napoleon went, the creation of religious stability was a priority.[118] In this approach he was in marked contrast with the radical revolutionaries who had tried to extirpate Catholicism and replace it with new cults. Here was a man who would surprise his contemporaries in trying to steer a middle course between the Revolution and the *ancien régime*.

# — TWO —
# ELECTING THE POPE IN VENICE, 1799–1800

At the turn of the nineteenth century, the lives of Chiaramonti and Bonaparte changed dramatically. Up to this point, they had been important players in the unfolding drama of revolution, but their positions had been subordinated to the higher authority of the Directory and the Papacy. As the new century dawned, the political and military situation was inauspicious for both. During the winter of 1799 the Catholic Church wavered on the brink of collapse. Shortly before the War of the Second Coalition (1798–1802), the French had invaded the Papal States, exiled the College of Cardinals from Rome, and Pope Pius VI had been taken prisoner. The Directory was soon to find itself in an equally precarious position. In April 1799 Austro-Russian forces, under the command of General Alexander Suvorov, had swept across northern Italy, chasing most of the French and their erstwhile Italian collaborators from the peninsula.[1] All of Napoleon's previous victories and conquests had been nullified by this bold allied offensive. Bonaparte, for his part, was fighting in Egypt, in a campaign which would end in disaster.[2]

As mentioned in the previous chapter, Pius VI, after a twenty-four-year pontificate, had died a prisoner in Valence on 29 August 1799. Giuseppe Maria Spina, the butler of the Sacred Apostolic Palaces, removed the fisherman's ring and other effects from the dead pontiff's body. The French authorities offered the late 'Citizen Braschi' a secular funeral, which his entourage indignantly refused.[3] Spina was to play a pivotal role in the conflict that would define Franco-papal relations for the following decade. He was a highly skilled canon lawyer and bureaucrat who, prior to the French occupation of Rome, had been entrusted with the delicate mission of preparing contingency plans for the pope's arrest and exile. During Pius VI's captivity, he had received the honorific title of archbishop of Corinth as a reward for his loyalty. Following the pope's death, he, along with the surviving members of the papal court, were interned by the French as a precaution. On 29 August 1799, he received permission to write to the College of Cardinals to inform them of the pope's death and that he was negotiating, with little success, the return of Pius VI's mortal remains to Rome.[4] Given the complex military situation in Europe it would take over a month for Archbishop Spina's letter to reach its destination. Everything would depend on the outcome of the conflict between the Revolution and the *ancien régime* monarchies.

The War of the Second Coalition proved a mortal blow for the Directory.[5] French armies were in retreat on all fronts, and recent elections had increased instability by bringing Jacobin extremists back into active politics. Lawlessness, rebellion and civil war were endemic throughout France.[6] As the situation reached crisis point, Napoleon decided to return from Egypt, landing in Fréjus in Provence on 8 October 1799. On his return he was fêted in the press as a new Alexander the Great, the conqueror of the Orient; in reality, he was a defeated general who had virtually abandoned his troops. News of the catastrophic situation of the French forces in the East had been kept from the population. If this information were released, Napoleon knew that the public's goodwill towards him would evaporate. For the weeks following his homecoming, he kept a low profile, dressing in civilian attire and attending meetings with audiences hungry to learn about his adventures and discoveries in the Orient.[7]

The military, political and economic crisis in France was becoming desperate. A confederacy of disgruntled politicians and public servants within the republican establishment saw the Directory as hindering the war effort and fomenting disorder. This group came to favour a coup d'état, which would replace the directorial government with a more powerful executive. They coalesced around the figure of Emmanuel-Joseph Sieyès, who, as described in the previous chapter (see pp. 22–3), had played such a decisive role in transforming the Estates General of 1789 into a revolutionary assembly. These men knew that their plot had no hope of succeeding without military support. They had initially approached General Barthélemy-Catherine Joubert for assistance, but he was killed in battle at Novi in Italy before coup preparations could begin in earnest. Napoleon was co-opted by the conspirators at a late stage in their plans. He was a decided second- if not third-choice candidate for the military leadership of the coup.[8] For its organisers he was something of an unknown quantity. Sieyès anticipated (unwisely as it turned out) that he could be easily manipulated once the dust had settled.

On 18 Brumaire (9 November 1799), after many hours of uncertainty, the conspirators seized power. The Consulate they created to govern France inherited, from the Directory, a republic defeated in battle, economically bankrupt and riven by civil discord. Napoleon soon showed himself to be no puppet, snatching the initiative away from his fellow conspirators. As first consul he was the head of state and government.[9] He drafted a short constitution with the help of his allies from the coup. This charter was then ratified in a plebiscite, or referendum, which gave his government the semblance of a popular mandate. In reality, voter turn-out, especially amongst the army, had been so low that the numbers had to be 'corrected', massaged to give the appearance of a landslide in favour of the Consulate.[10] As the year 1800 approached, it was clear that the first consul's position was very far from secure. He needed to achieve military victory against the Second Coalition, establish economic stability and restore law and order to ensure the new regime's survival. As Napoleon's future foreign minister, the apostate bishop Charles Maurice de Talleyrand-Périgord, put it: 'If he survives the year, he'll go far!'[11]

The situation for the Catholic Church was similarly perilous. Cardinal Giovanni Francesco Albani, the dean of the College of Cardinals (effectively its president), had sought refuge in the nearby Kingdom of Naples.[12] He had been a strong supporter of the rights of the Papacy throughout his career; so much so that he had advised the late Pius VI to resist the French invasion of the Papal States with military force. In 1799 he was seventy-nine years of age, hopelessly infirm and no longer possessed the energy to lead the church through the crisis it faced. Unlike him, most of his brethren had fled to the safety of Venice, which was under the control of the Holy Roman Emperor Francis II.

Not all of these prelates had taken the revolutionary challenge lying down. Cardinal Fabrizio Ruffo had put himself at the head of a peasant uprising against the French in southern Italy. Wearing his crimson robes and a steel breastplate, he crossed Calabria on horseback raising recruits for his army of the *Santa Fede* ('Holy Faith').[13] He led his followers, an unseemly crew of bandits, peasants and devout Catholics, in a brutal guerrilla and irregular war that contributed to expelling the French from Calabria. Ruffo's 'Sanfedists', with British and Russian assistance, restored Ferdinand IV of Naples to his throne in June 1799.

The actions of Cardinal Ruffo highlighted how a prince of the church could command a widespread popular uprising. He channelled, successfully, peasant religious fervour into a steely resolve to resist invasion. His followers gained a reputation for bloodlust, as they exacted brutal revenge on French soldiers and their Italian supporters. This violence shocked Ruffo, who tried his best to restrain it and to show mercy to the vanquished. Localist 'piety' became a catalyst that mobilised many Italians throughout the peninsula to butcher the godless invaders who had imprisoned the pope and threatened the heartlands of Catholicism. The counter-revolutionary spark lit in Calabria spread like wildfire across Italy. Certainly, the massacres and violence that followed in the wake of this Sanfedist insurrection did much to confirm the worst fears of the occupiers.[14] French republicans, and their Italian clients, identified the church as a dangerous anti-progressive power. The mutual distrust that characterised both sides made dialogue impossible. Compromise, courage and fresh leadership were needed to bridge the chasm that divided the church from the revolutionary state.

At this time there were forty-six cardinals scattered across Europe. Exactly where a conclave should assemble to elect a new pope had been an open question ever since the elderly and moribund Pius VI had been captured by the Directory in 1798. As winter drew near, the majority of the College of Cardinals gathered in Venice at the invitation of Francis II. By early December 1799 thirty-five cardinals were present on the Laguna.[15] The once proud and independent Republic of Saint Mark was a shadow of its former self. Looted by Napoleon's troops in 1797, the city had lost not only its greatest art treasures but also its independence. During the negotiations for the Peace of Campo Formio (17 October 1797), the Most Serene Republic of Venice was ceded by the French to the Habsburgs, without any regard for the wishes of the Venetians.[16] Local elites viewed the forthcoming Conclave with curiosity, but there is little evidence that the population as a whole was enthused.[17]

The word 'conclave' has its origins in the Latin expression *cum clave*, meaning 'under key'. During the early Middle Ages and early modern period, papal elections had been long affairs that had been disrupted by outside interference so, in the thirteenth century, the College of Cardinals began to be isolated during these decisions by being placed literally under lock and key during voting.[18] This was seen as a good way to speed up deliberations and produce an apparently independent result. The municipal authorities decided that the large Benedictine monastery of San Giorgio Maggiore was the best venue for the papal election.[19] Built on an island separate from the main city, it was felt that this location would guarantee the seclusion and security of the College of Cardinals during their deliberations – and, conveniently, it was only a short gondola punt from Saint Mark's Square. San Giorgio was undeniably one of the great monastic houses of

Europe. The monastery's refectory and basilica were originally designed (but not finished) by Andrea Palladio, and its chapels, oratories, cells, cloisters and refectory housed some of the great works of the Italian Renaissance and Baroque. (It had been home to Veronese's celebrated *Wedding Feast at Cana* until the French had plundered it in 1797 to hang, as it still does today, in the Louvre.) As a venue for an election it was certainly spacious and imposing, but could hardly be described as comfortable; the spartan monks' cells, coupled with the dampness, vile smells and cold rising up from the Laguna, were in decided contrast to the mild winters of Rome.[20] The winter choir was selected as the chamber where the cardinals would vote for Saint Peter's successor. Overlooking the proceedings was Vittore Carpaccio's gruesome painting of Saint George spearing a dragon.[21]

Of the thirty-five papal electors assembled in San Giorgio, only four were non-Italian. The circumstances of this gathering were almost unique. The last time a pope had been chosen outside Rome had been at the Council of Constance (1414–18), where Oddone Colonna had been elected Pope Martin V, to replace two schismatic popes, thus ending the Great Western Schism of the Middle Ages.[22] As early as 1796, Pius VI had been aware of the danger posed by the French Revolutionary Army stationed in Lombardy. He had authorised the dean and cardinals to elect his successor outside Rome by seeking refuge in the domains of a Catholic prince. He had relaxed rules on seclusion, communication and quorums to take account of the extraordinary nature of an election away from the eternal city.[23] He had also hoped, a little optimistically as it turned out, that a more streamlined procedure would lead to the swift election of his successor.

In 1799–1800, the cardinals faced a difficult choice when it came to select a suitable candidate to succeed Pius VI. The judgement of posterity has been that the Venice Conclave sought to find a personality that would respond to the challenge of the French Revolution in determined fashion. To an extent this is true: the upheavals across the Alps had done untold damage to the Roman Church, and a pope who would accelerate the process of reconstruction was highly desirable. Yet to portray the cardinal-electors who entered the San Giorgio Maggiore monastery as seeking a pious spiritual leader, who would guide the church through stormy waters, is unhistorical. In the early modern period, conclaves were highly political and secular events. Indeed, papal elections, up to 1903, were subject to the *jus exclusivae* ('right of exclusion'), which enabled the Habsburg emperor, the king of France and the king of Spain to appoint an ambassador, usually a cardinal, to attend the conclave: these delegates then had the right to intervene and veto the candidates least acceptable to their royal masters.[24] By the eighteenth century, most papal elections lasted several months, due to behind-the-scenes politicking and delicate negotiations with the chancelleries of Catholic Europe. Bitter divisions and slow correspondence with Vienna, Paris and Madrid meant that it took literally hundreds of ballots to reach consensus.

The representatives of these European powers rarely revealed their hand. Vetoing a candidate could only be done once, so the royal prelate-envoys preferred to keep the cardinals guessing for as long as possible as to who might be vetoed. Thus, the great Catholic sovereigns of Europe could influence the election decisively. Those cardinals acting as prelate-envoys were allowed to correspond with their masters, and seek instructions as the election developed. The correspondence between these cardinals and their sovereigns provides a veritable treasure trove of information relating to the day-to-day politicking within papal elections. Indeed, Charles IV of Spain, Louis XVIII in exile and Francis II were given a regular running commentary by their agents as to what was happening behind the scenes. As in the past, throughout the Venice Conclave the kings of Europe supported those candidates whom they felt would promote their territorial ambitions and recognise their regalian rights over the church. Pliant cardinals, who would ratify the decisions of secular governments, were ideal candidates.

There is an old Italian saying: 'He who enters the Conclave a pope, leaves it a cardinal.' That of 1800 was no exception. Cardinal Chiaramonti, bishop of Imola, seemed a very unlikely contender for the top job. His supposed liberalism and his pro-democracy Christmas homily had hardly endeared him to his more conservative colleagues.[25] Furthermore, he was born in Cesena and a distant cousin to Pius VI. His association with the powerful Braschi clan smacked of the old vice of nepotism. Pro-Habsburg electors and Roman nobles, neglected by the dead pope, were unlikely to elect one of his relatives. To his advantage, Chiaramonti was a man of genuine faith, who showed little interest in the intrigues and cabals of his more politically minded colleagues. Unlike the other, more opulent, princes of the church, he was a former Benedictine monk and felt perfectly at home in the monastery of San Giorgio Maggiore.

The four most important protagonists of the Conclave were the three representatives of Spain, France and the Holy Roman Empire – Latin Patriarch of Antioch Antonio Despuig y Dameto, Cardinal Jean-Sifrein Maury and Cardinal Franziskus von Paula Herzan von Harras – and the Conclave's secretary, Monsignor

Ercole Consalvi. Consalvi was one of the brightest rising stars of the papal bureaucracy. He had been a favourite and protégé of both Henry, cardinal duke of York (the last Stuart pretender to the British throne), and Pius VI. Despite serving the church all his life, he only took minor orders and was never fully ordained a priest.[26] Highly trained in law and diplomacy, as secretary to the Conclave he facilitated its proceedings and was to be highly influential during the election. His tact, diplomacy, administrative brilliance and energy would make him one of the key players in papal politics during the first two decades of the nineteenth century.

Antonio Despuig y Dameto was the representative of the king of Spain and had been given a generous fund of 40,000 scudi with which to 'persuade' cardinals to make the 'right' choice.[27] Essentially, he was to oppose the election of a pro-Habsburg client. As noted in the previous chapter (p. 25), Cardinal Maury had been one of the most eloquent counter-revolutionary orators of the age. As a deputy of the French National Assembly he had attacked the ecclesiastical reforms of the French Revolution with bravery and vigour. He had fled France after receiving death threats, and had been rewarded with the *galero*, the cardinal's traditional red broad-brimmed hat, and the bishopric of Montefiascone, near Viterbo, by Pius VI. He was Louis XVIII's official delegate, but, as the representative of an exiled pretender, his right to exercise the *jus exclusivae* was unclear; Cardinal Albani, as dean of the Sacred College, had written a letter to Louis XVIII to inform him of the forthcoming Conclave. In this epistle the French pretender was hailed as *Galliarum Regi*, 'king of the Gauls'.[28] Pius VI had not confirmed Louis's claim to the French throne: the cardinals, through their dean, now explicitly recognised the Bourbon pretender as the legitimate ruler of France. Maury was not given any specific instructions by Louis XVIII on which candidates to support or to veto. He was free to act as he saw fit.[29] The most important man of all was Cardinal Herzan, representing the Holy Roman Emperor Francis II, in whose lands the Conclave was taking place. The Prague-born cardinal had enjoyed a long diplomatic career as Austrian ambassador in Rome, and had been instrumental in organising Pius VI's journey to Vienna in 1782. Given his experience of Roman and ecclesiastical politics he was thought to be the ideal candidate to represent imperial interests in Venice.[30] His veto and influence would be of paramount importance during the election.[31]

This papal election, despite its revolutionary context, was still imbued to its core with *ancien régime* politics. Primarily, the search for a successor to Pius VI was a diplomatic struggle between the dynasties of Europe, a contest in which the Bourbons aimed to contain Habsburg influence in Italy. Charles IV of Spain and Louis XVIII were joined in this objective by the kings of Sardinia and Naples. To complicate matters further, any papal election had a Roman dimension that had to be taken into consideration. The pope was both a spiritual leader and an Italian prince. The Papacy commanded not just supreme spiritual authority, but was a worldly institution in its outlook, and a source of immense political and economic patronage in Italy. Thus, understandably, the great princely clans of Rome wanted a candidate who would shower their kin with gifts, positions and pensions.[32] Throughout the early modern period, pontiffs had appointed their nephews as cardinals to act as their deputies and most trusted advisers, a corrupt practice that gave rise to the term 'nepotism'. (This was an Italian custom which the Bonapartes embraced with remarkable gusto when Napoleon became emperor after 1804.)

Pius VI had showered his family with gifts of titles and pensions. He had commissioned the neoclassical architect Cosimo Morelli to build his family a sumptuous city palace near the beautiful Campo de' Fiori district of Rome.[33] The formal institution of the cardinal-nephew may have been abolished by 1700 in theory, but in practice it remained a powerful force.[34] Cardinal Romoaldo Braschi-Onesti, the nephew of the late pope, was to be an important powerbroker in the Venice election, and the Braschi clan and their clients would exert a powerful influence over this Conclave. Several cardinals appointed by his uncle looked to Braschi-Onesti for leadership. Dynastic competition, Roman princely politics, the challenge of the French Revolution and religious considerations all played their part in a descending order of importance.

The Conclave, as was tradition, was opened by a nine-day period, or *novendiale*, of mourning for the late pope.[35] After these ceremonies had been completed, the electoral process began. The official opening was delayed by a week to 12 December 1799: Cardinal Herzan, the imperial envoy, had not yet arrived from Vienna.[36] The Austrian foreign minister, Baron Thugut, was keen to use the Conclave to increase Habsburg influence in northern and central Italy.[37] He provided Herzan with both official and secret instructions on his mission. The Habsburgs paid lip service to the need to provide the church with an energetic younger man who would lead the Papacy in a time of crisis; in reality, the key ambition of the Emperor Francis was territorial expansion into Italy.

There is an argument to be made that the successful Austro-Russian offensive through northern Italy had made the Habsburgs overly confident. They expected that the Bourbons would soon be restored to their French throne and that counter-revolution would make the disasters of the Revolution a distant memory.[38] As already mentioned in the previous chapter (p. 36), Pius VI had ceded the three Papal Legations of Romagna to the French in 1797 with the treaty of Tolentino.[39] Due to recent victories on the battlefield, these former papal territories had fallen under Austrian occupation. It was Thugut's expectation that a defeated France would surrender these provinces to Francis II. It was thus essential to find a papal candidate who would accept these hypothetical Austrian territorial gains in Italy. The loss of the Legations in 1797 had made the economic viability of the Papal States precarious. The ability to disguise the Holy Roman Emperor's true objectives would be vital in this conclave; however, though Cardinal Herzan had many fine qualities, subtlety, tact and discretion were not among them.

He would place pressure on the cardinals, reminding them that they were the guests of the most powerful Catholic prince in Europe. For the Habsburg delegate, the restoration of the pope's Italian possessions rested on the benevolence of Francis II. Given the emperor's military and financial investment in defeating republican France, he, and Thugut, felt they had the right to direct the election on the island of San Giorgio Maggiore. Accepting the permanent loss of Bologna, Ferrara and Ravenna was a small price to pay for the continued existence and protection of the church. The Italian cardinals soon showed that they did not quite share their German colleague's point of view. On 14 December 1799 Maury wrote to Louis XVIII: 'Arriving at the Conclave Cardinal Herzan said that the emperor was master of Italy and that he desired a pope that would suit him, and that it was not necessary to elect a man of talent, as one can acquire these skills in Rome, and that we needed to select a good man agreeable to the court of Vienna.'[40]

Maury may have exaggerated the uncouthness of Herzan's behaviour and conversation. The Austrian cardinal's despatches to Thugut convey a more diplomatic timbre:

I had a long interview with Despuig, formerly archbishop of Seville, today patriarch of Antioch. His confidences have confirmed my [good] opinion of him which I had the honour of relating to Your Excellency [Baron Thugut] in the past . . . He told me confidentially that his court cared deeply about this future election and that there were three parties in play at this conclave: those following the dean want Cardinal Gerdil, those loyal to the cardinal-nephew want Chiaramonti, to whom he is related by blood, and finally there are some who want Bellisomi.[41]

Reflecting on Despuig's confidences, Herzan, in his despatches to Thugut, argued, not unreasonably, that the election of Cardinal Giacinto Sigismondo Gerdil as pope would be unfortunate. During his early life, this Savoyard prelate had been one of the standard bearers of the Catholic Enlightenment and his erudition was celebrated throughout Europe.[42] However, as he was now eighty-four years of age his pontificate would be brief and would not promote stability in the Catholic Church. During informal discussions with his fellow electors Herzan revealed his intentions too soon. He praised Cardinal Alessandro Mattei as the best candidate because he was the scion of one of Rome's oldest families, and would please the population of the city.[43] Nobody was fooled by this limp reasoning, and the agenda behind Herzan's favoured candidate was apparent. Mattei had been the chief negotiator of the treaty of Tolentino: Vienna was convinced that this cardinal, who had proved so pliant towards the French, would prove equally so before Francis II's claims to the Legations.

One suspects that Despuig had lured Herzan into a false sense of security by claiming that Charles IV of Spain was on the Holy Roman Emperor's side.[44] On the contrary, the Spanish ambassador's remit was to impede the election of an imperial papal candidate. Spain's ally France, and its new head of state Bonaparte, wanted to thwart Habsburg ambitions in Italy. The French foreign ministry was kept informed, albeit slowly, of events in Venice through its embassy in Madrid.[45] None of the European powers wanted to return the Legations of Romagna to the Papacy. The forthcoming French counter-offensive into northern Italy in 1800 would decide who would control Italy and hold these rich agricultural provinces.

During the first week, a clear candidate failed to materialise. Exploratory ballots highlighted what all had suspected: namely that the Sacred College was divided more or less in two. Throughout this time the pious and well-meaning Cardinal Carlo Bellisomi, bishop of Cesena, a diplomat who had served as papal nuncio in Lisbon and Cologne, commanded a healthy fifteen votes (almost half the electorate).[46] After another week of ballots, on 21 December Bellisomi came very close to the three-quarters majority which would have seen him crowned as

Saint Peter's successor.[47] At this point Cardinal Albani, as dean, inquired if Herzan would veto Bellisomi's election as pope. The Habsburg cardinal admitted that his court had not instructed him to do so. Given his lack of a formal mandate, Herzan requested he be given time to write to Vienna for clarification. Consalvi, in his memoirs, saw Albani's permission for Herzan to seek instructions from his court as the greatest mistake of the entire Conclave.[48] Thugut took his time sending fresh instructions. The Austrian chancellery hoped a delay would dampen the cardinals' enthusiasm for Bellisomi's candidature. During this hiatus Herzan did his best to canvass for extra votes for Mattei. According to Consalvi, the extended delay for the Habsburg emperor's instructions to arrive broke the momentum behind Bellisomi's candidature. Great uncertainty about who should become pope developed, and the Venice Conclave was thus prolonged, confounding growing hopes for a speedy election.

By January the situation had stalled at nineteen votes for Bellisomi and fifteen for Mattei. The cardinals' mutual resentment began to grow, and icy conditions in Venice made it decidedly unpleasant for elderly prelates used to Rome's warmer climate. At one point, Despuig's gondola was almost sunk by ice floes on the Laguna.[49] The city government proved mean when it came to fuel supplies, and it took all of Consalvi's resourcefulness to keep the winter cloister heated during these debates.[50] When fresh secret instructions from Vienna arrived, they did not prove very helpful in breaking the impasse. Thugut reaffirmed that the emperor was unshakeable in his determination that Mattei be elected pope. Only very grudgingly was a reserve candidate, Cardinal Valenti, put forward by Vienna as an alternative.[51]

Luigi Valenti Gonzaga was seventy-four years of age, in poor health and almost blind. His candidacy appears to have been a delaying tactic rather than a genuine attempt at compromise. The deadlock between the two factions ossified during January and February 1800. Loyal to his court's instructions, Herzan campaigned overtly for Mattei and tried to woo more cardinals into the Habsburg camp.[52] The stalemate became acrimonious, as both sides accused the other of acting in bad faith. On 22 February the monotony and tedium of this papal election away from Rome determined the cardinals to seek a compromise. To act as chief negotiators in the search for an alternative candidate who would satisfy all, the Bellisomi group chose Cardinal Albani, the dean, while Mattei's party chose Cardinal Leonardo Antonelli, a conservative and ultramontane defender of the Papacy and the Curia's supremacy over the church.[53]

TO KIDNAP A POPE

Antonelli put forward the names of five cardinals from his party and the dean responded with a list of five alternative candidates from his own faction. [54] Armed with these lists, the negotiators returned to their respective allies and started exploring how many votes these ten compromise candidates might receive. In order to do this, they devised a very complex system of exploratory tallies, where each candidate would be eligible to receive either outright or conditional votes. These efforts to identify a pope acceptable to both parties were interrupted almost as soon as they began; it was suddenly announced that four cardinals in Bellisomi's camp had shifted their votes abruptly in favour of Cardinal Valenti, who was Francis II's reserve choice. Herzan was excited: a pro-Habsburg victory seemed near, and he sought to persuade the dean to accept this solution.[55] The Valenti candidature, however, proved an imbroglio. It seems unlikely that the Conclave considered this decrepit and exhausted cardinal a real prospect for the Papacy. The parties were probably buying time, as they sought to redirect votes to more sturdy candidates.

Maury described the deplorable state of Valenti's health in a despatch sent to Louis XVIII on 1 March:

This poor man is pretty much paralysed, deaf as a doorpost, and almost blind. For the past ten years he has benefited from a 'blindness indult' which dispenses him from having to recite the office and permits him to deliver [from memory] daily the votive Mass of the Holy Virgin. Your Majesty should know that yesterday we were immersed in thick fog all day. One could not see ten steps ahead. The cardinal dean every day draws lots to appoint the officers who monitor each vote. He decided to profit [from circumstances] and nominate Valenti as scrutineer, this gave the College of Cardinals some reason to laugh. The incumbent was very embarrassed, but dared not decline this commission, for fear of the conclusions that would be drawn from his refusal. He sat before the desk and could not read the names on the [voting] slips, indeed he read them upside down and was obliged to turn to his neighbour for help in reading the name of the candidate. This jest was repeated seventy times in a row prolonging the session by an hour. The atmosphere became increasingly jocular as we drew deeper into the night . . . [Valenti's] partisans despaired in seeing his infirmities revealed in such a cruel manner, while those who did not have the honour of voting for him laughed under their breath at this [comedy].[56]

In fairness, Valenti did have great diplomatic experience and Spanish support, but his infirmities meant it would be impossible for him to shoulder the burden of the Papacy.[57] During the first two weeks of March 1800 the Conclave failed to find a route out of the impasse. Valenti continued to receive votes, but few saw him as a serious contender.[58] As one compromise candidate after another proved unable to garner sufficient support, significant momentum began to build up behind Cardinal Guido Calcagnini.[59] Maury described him in less than flattering terms: 'It is said that he lacks application and is an enemy of all work; which all things considered is a mortal sin, for a pope, at all times, but especially in the present circumstances', and that he was viewed generally as a 'virtuous savage'.[60] Bellisomi's faction was not convinced that Calcagnini was their man. Herzan's interview with him was disastrous: he found him cold about the Habsburg emperor and evasive about his intentions if he were elected to the Papacy.

The Conclave had by now lasted for more than three months, and the cardinals' patience was all but exhausted. Rumours started to circulate that Despuig had received an official mandate from Charles IV of Spain to exercise the *jus exclusivae* against Cardinal Mattei. These whispers turned out to be untrue, but they did nevertheless create an atmosphere of urgency.[61] According to Consalvi's memoirs, it was at this point that a mysterious cardinal came to the rescue.[62] This was to be the most questionable turning point of the Conclave:

> One of the cardinals of Mattei's party, endowed by nature with a rare perspicacity and an excellent heart, found himself in his party less by conviction than by an overwhelming necessity to which he felt he had to yield. Convinced of the impossibility of success for either competitor, he began to reflect that it would be very difficult, if not impossible, given the circumstances in which both parties found themselves, that one side would consent to the election of the other's candidate, and that the Conclave was thus at a standstill. He was further convinced that the pope needed to emerge from one of the two parties . . . He remarked that the only means of reconciling the interest of both camps was for the opposing party to select the new pope within the bosom of the rival [faction].[63]

Admittedly, these words are unreliable, as they were written long after these events, with the benefit of hindsight (Consalvi recorded his recollections when he was Napoleon's prisoner in Reims in 1810).[64] The name of the cardinal who proposed this way of resolving the deadlock has never been revealed.[65] He apparently managed to persuade Cardinal Antonelli that Chiaramonti was the best compromise.

The dean, Cardinal Albani, had become exasperated by the intrigue of the two factions, and found the overbearing Cardinal Herzan impossible. He felt his infirmities keenly during the cold and damp Venetian winter; indeed, he was bedridden and confined to his cell for most of the Conclave. From his bed he commanded Cardinal Antonelli to visit the Habsburg envoy.[66] By mid-March, Chiaramonti was emerging as the one candidate agreeable to both camps. Antonelli went to Herzan and persuaded him that the election of Chiaramonti was the solution to the deadlock.[67]

Realising that the Conclave could not last forever, the Habsburg representative rushed to meet Chiaramonti. He recorded the outcome in a despatch to Thugut in Vienna:

I took the resolution to tell him in confidence that many cardinals of my party would give their votes to him. On hearing this revelation, he went pale. I told him that my court had no objection to him personally but that his entourage did not command the same confidence. He needed to destroy this bad impression by taking on Cardinal Flangini, who has the emperor's confidence, as secretary of state. He replied that he had no wish to become pope, that he was perfectly happy where he was. Rather than allowing him to fulfil his sacred duties as a bishop, they [the cardinals] seemed determined to cast him into stormy seas. I replied that the seas could be calmed if he threw himself into the arms of the emperor. I humbly advised him . . . that the only hope for the Holy See was to seek the emperor's protection.[68]

Chiaramonti agreed that Austrian goodwill was necessary, and that he would try to be worthy of the emperor's esteem. He was concerned that Flangini had a chequered past, having been a freemason in his earlier life, and reminded Herzan politely that promising papal offices and patronage in return for votes was an offence worthy of excommunication. Ultimately, he refused to provide any undertaking to the Habsburg court about future papal appointments.

As Herzan put it, in a postscript note sent to Thugut, he was no longer in a position to prevent the election of the pope, and the Mattei candidature was dead in the water.[69] He thought it best for the chosen candidate to be given every support. The imperial party was forced to accept Chiaramonti's election with little enthusiasm. Chiaramonti's election was now a formality. It was decided that 12 and 13 March were to be kept free to give time to the future pope to prepare for the burden he was about to assume. On the night before his election he was visited by each cardinal in his cell. One by one, they kissed his hands and pledged to support him as pontiff.[70] During the night, the pope-elect drafted the standard letters to inform the crowned heads of Europe of his election. When it came to France, the letter was addressed to Louis XVIII in exile rather than to Napoleon as first consul.[71] Maury exulted: his hope that the new pope was a legitimist at heart, who would support the rightful king of France, seemed to be confirmed.

An unexpected technical problem now emerged: the two white cassocks prepared for the incumbent were of the wrong size. A tailor had to work all night cutting and sewing a robe to fit the slight new pontiff.[72] The next day, 14 March 1800, during the early afternoon vote, Chiaramonti was unanimously elected as the 251st successor to Saint Peter. When asked if he accepted his election, the new pope retired for some silent prayer. After this brief moment of meditation, he returned and accepted the cardinals' decision. He announced that in honour of his predecessor he would be known as Pius VII.[73] Then, from the loggia of the chapel of San Giorgio Maggiore, news of the election was announced to the population of Venice.

The appointment of the new pontiff was greeted by several ceremonial gun salutes. Seven months after the death of Pius VI, and following four months of bitter politicking, the Catholic Church had a new leader. Like Napoleon, Chiaramonti had not been the first choice for his exalted position. He would soon prove to be a man full of surprises. As one cardinal allegedly put it: 'he will be a modest pope in modest events, but if circumstances become great, he will be commensurate to them'.[74]

Vienna acknowledged the election of Pius VII with disappointment (their candidate had always remained Mattei). The imperial chancellery felt Herzan's mission had been a failure, and relations with the new pope were frosty at first. From Thugut's perspective, this election changed nothing in terms of territorial ambitions, and the retention of the Papal Legations of Romagna remained of utmost concern for the Austrians. The Habsburg Empire would exert pressure on the Papacy, by reminding Chiaramonti, indelicately, that the survival and restoration of the Papal States remained dependent on imperial goodwill. Indeed, the church's precarious position became all too apparent when one considers the manner in which the new pope was crowned. Everybody expected that the papal coronation would take place in Saint Mark's Basilica in Venice. As the mother church of the city, overlooking its largest square, this Byzantine architectural masterpiece was an obvious location for the ceremony. However, the imperial court sulked and gave no direct instructions to the city's authorities on whether to accept the papal court's request that Pius VII be crowned in Saint Mark's. The municipal government of Venice refused permission for the coronation on the grounds that the papal tiara was a symbol of the pope's temporal power: it would thus be inappropriate for it to be displayed inside a Habsburg cathedral.[75]

The basilica of San Giorgio Maggiore was considered the best alternative. It was the chapel of the monastery in which the Conclave had just taken place, and it was monumental in size. However, its austere neoclassical interiors were a decided contrast to the Baroque splendour of Saint Peter's in Rome. This papal inauguration, given that it was taking place in exile, was to be sober, less ostentatious than previous ones, reflecting the mood and the straitened financial circumstances of the new pope. Indeed, without access to the Vatican's collections and treasury, none of the traditional papal crown jewels nor symbols of power were available for the ceremony.

The papal tiara, the 'triregnum', a conical crown bearing three diadems, one above the other, was the supreme symbol of the pope's authority. What exactly it symbolised was a matter of some controversy. Many saw it as a symbol of papal monarchy, representing the pope's supremacy and sovereignty over all monarchs; others still, believed that it represented the three fundamental aspects of the pope's office: teacher, lawmaker and judge; for Protestants it was the sign of the anti-Christ as described in the Book of Revelation.[76]

Whatever it represented, no tiara was available in Venice. Lack of time meant that the gold- and silversmiths of Venice had to improvise and make do with whatever came to hand. Chiaramonti was eventually crowned with a tiara made of papier-mâché covered with a cloth woven with silver threads and decorated with some jewels gifted by pious aristocratic Venetian ladies.[77] (It is still visible today in the Vatican collection, as a reminder of one of the most unusual coronations in history.) Another Venetian aristocrat donated an ornate sedan chair, which was hastily refashioned into a *sedia gestatoria*, a papal throne which could be carried and raised high in a procession.[78] This allowed the pope to be visible above the crowd when he gave his blessing (a precursor to today's popemobile). By all accounts, the coronation was well attended, the Grand Canal flooded with gondolas carrying the great families of the city, while the curious people struggled to get a glimpse of the new pope. All received a special papal blessing and plenary indulgence in remission of their sins. At the solemn moment of the crowning, Pius VII was presented with a torch of burning flax. The Latin formula *Pater Sancte, sic transit gloria mundi* ('Holy Father, thus vanishes the glory of the world') was intoned – an important warning to the new pontiff against the dangers of vainglory and materialism. (Indeed, Pius VII, more than any of his predecessors, knew the precariousness of his position. Like Napoleon, his reign began unsteadily and was to be filled with unexpected successes, disasters and reversals of fortune.)

Despite their frosty initial response to the election, the Habsburgs soon tried to regain some favour with the Papacy. On 30 March, the pope received a visit from the emperor's sister, the Archduchess Maria Anna, abbess of the Teresian convent in Prague.[79] She was part of an attempt to persuade Pius that he had nothing to fear from Austria. Cardinal Herzan officially invited the pope to travel to Vienna to meet the emperor and discuss the future of the Papal States in his capital.[80] Chiaramonti was no fool: he knew such a journey would make the pope seem a mere imperial puppet. After all, there was a negative precedent. Pius VI had travelled to the Habsburg capital in 1782 to hold a summit with Joseph II to discuss the suppression of monasteries and other ecclesiastical reforms; once in Vienna Pius VI had been unable to resist imperial demands.[81] His successor feared that the same might happen if he negotiated directly with the emperor on the question of the Legations.

Indeed, the Austrians already behaved as if these territories had been annexed to their empire. As far as they were concerned, Bologna, Ferrara and Ravenna were imperial cities. For example, after the death of Cardinal Giovanetti, archbishop of Bologna, in early April 1800, Francis II arrogated the right to nominate his successor.[82] The archdiocese of Bologna was one of the most important sees in the Papal States, and it was impossible for the Papacy to accept any temporal interference in episcopal appointments in these cities. Ultimately the pope, through Consalvi, as interim secretary of state, thanked Herzan for the invitation to Vienna but argued that he needed to return to Rome before making any further travel arrangements.[83] Consalvi explained, politely, that only once the Papal States had been restored and stabilised could the pope consider undertaking such a journey. Herzan's failure was complete. He was appointed to the diocese of Szombathely in Hungary – which was an internal exile away from mainstream politics; Pius VII personally consecrated him bishop in Saint Mark's Basilica on 18 May.[84] He was replaced as Habsburg envoy to the pope by the Marquis Filippo Ghislieri. The following weeks were characterised by Ghislieri's polite, but firm, attempts to persuade the pope and Consalvi to accept territorial concessions to Austria.

At this time, central Italy seemed to be securely in Habsburg hands. The pope insisted on being allowed to return to Rome. A disappointed Baron Thugut agreed, on condition that Pius travel by sea and not cross the Legations by land: some in Vienna were concerned that the local population would cheer Pius VII and demand a return to his rule. On 6 June the pope, several cardinals and Ghislieri boarded the frigate *Bellona* (named after the Roman goddess of war). Its ultimate destination was either Ancona or Fano.[85] The vessel was utterly unprepared for the voyage. As it left Venice's harbour it began to sink. The ship was able, however, to return to port, where its cannons were unloaded. The crew was barely competent when it came to navigation, and what should have been a twenty-four-hour journey became an eleven-day ordeal, as storms and unfavourable winds forced the *Bellona* towards the Croatian coast. Only on 17 June did the ship finally make landfall at Pesaro, a port on the northern border of the papal Marche. Here Pius VII, finally, landed in his kingdom to a rapturous welcome. He presented the crew of the *Bellona* with a gift of 200 scudi, despite their having bungled his voyage.[86]

The journey from Pesaro to Rome was a triumphal progress as the subjects of the Papal States welcomed the return of the Papacy as a symbol of peace and an end to instability. The pope finally entered Rome on 3 July 1800. He proceeded directly to Saint Peter's Basilica for the adoration of the Blessed Sacrament and then, in a carriage pulled by eight horses, processed to the Piazza di Monte Cavallo, where he took up residence in the Quirinal Palace.[87] Throughout this time, the imperial envoy Ghislieri continued to press the pope to accept the loss of the Legations. It seemed like a small sacrifice, given that the Habsburg emperor had restored to Pius the lion's share of his domains. These negotiations were to be quickly superseded by events elsewhere.[88] If the population of central Italy had hoped that Pius VII's election would herald a period of peace and prosperity, they were to be disappointed. Austrian overconfidence was soon to be transformed into hubris.

On the other side of the Alps, Napoleon realised that his regime, born of a coup d'état, could not long survive while military defeat and uncertainty hung over him. The armies of the Second Coalition were approaching France's borders and needed to be repulsed. He decided to stake everything on battle, something that would become the leitmotif of his remarkable career. He formed a new Army of Italy which was to catch his enemies by surprise by hitting them in the rear. Instead of invading from Nice into south-western Piedmont, as he had done in 1796, the first consul decided, in a feat reminiscent of Hannibal, to use the great northern passes of the Alps. His army of 50,000 men crossed the Simplon, Great Saint Bernard and Gotthard passes in May 1800.[89] The French entered northern Piedmont, positioning themselves behind the main Austrian army and cutting off their supply lines from Lombardy. On 2 June Milan was occupied and the population welcomed Napoleon as a hero. The main Austrian force, under General Michael von Melas, operating in Piedmont, was taken entirely by surprise by Napoleon's daring invasion.[90] Napoleon was not one to rest on his laurels: he now decided to advance into Piedmont and meet Melas in battle near Alessandria.

On 14 June Melas launched a surprise attack on the French near the village of Marengo. Astonished by this Austrian assault, the French seemed all but defeated by the early afternoon. However, thanks to the miraculous arrival of General Louis Desaix and reinforcements, Napoleon's men were able to rally and counter-attack furiously, turning defeat into victory.[91] By evening the Austrians were in retreat and the next day requested an armistice. They agreed to withdraw into the Veneto, return to the French most of their territorial gains and suspend hostilities in Italy.[92] Marengo had been an uncertain victory, but it sealed Napoleon's fate. The Consulate would survive, and Napoleonic rule cement itself in France.

News of Marengo changed everything for Pius VII. Indeed, Ghislieri admitted that this reversal made his mission redundant.[93] The French had reoccupied the Legations, and, strengthened by the terms of the treaty of Tolentino, they would hardly return them to the Papacy. The papal court viewed this reversal of fortunes gloomily. In the aftermath of Marengo, both the Papacy and the Habsburgs appeared to be losers diplomatically. However, from this seeming disaster unexpected developments soon emerged. Bonaparte showed himself, at least superficially, very different from previous revolutionary leaders. On 5 June, three days after occupying Milan, Napoleon gave the following speech in Italian to the city's priests in the Duomo:

It is my formal intention that the Roman Catholic and Christian Religion be preserved in its entirety, that it be exercised publicly and that it enjoy this exercise with as full, complete and inviolable freedom as when I first arrived to these happy provinces ... Without religion one walks constantly in darkness; and the Catholic religion is the only one that gives man certainty and unfailing enlightenment about his nature and ultimate purpose. No society can exist without morality, there is no good morality without religion; thus, only religion can give the state firm and stable support. A society without religion is like a vessel without a compass; such a vessel has no hope of securing its route, nor can it hope to enter port . . . France through its woes has finally opened its eyes; she has recognised that the Catholic religion was like an anchor, which alone could keep it steady in distress and save it from the storm; as a consequence, it has taken it back to its bosom. I cannot deny that I have put much effort into this magnificent cause. I can certify that in France churches have reopened, that the Catholic religion has regained its ancient splendour, and that the population views, with respect, its sacred pastors, who have now returned to their abandoned flocks.[94]

The first consul here highlighted that he was different from the Jacobins and their anticlerical revolution: for his regime the re-establishment of Catholic worship and peace would be a top priority. On his return journey to France Napoleon stopped in the Piedmontese city of Vercelli, an important ecclesiastical centre with an impressive seminary.[95] Here he met with the cardinal-bishop of the city, Carlo Giuseppe Filippo della Martiniana, upon whom Napoleon made a very positive impression. The first consul reiterated his desire that Catholics resume free and public worship in France. Essentially, Napoleon was exploring the possibility of opening negotiations and future discussions with the Roman church. The conferences at Vercelli were a major turning point in European history.

This was the first time that the heirs of the French Revolution had sought to find an accommodation with their papal nemesis.[96] Napoleon's vision was ambitious in its scope and desire for conciliation. Allowing the Catholic Church to enjoy full freedom and independence within the state as a private institution was not satisfactory to either party. Instead, the first consul believed that a modernised but unequal alliance of throne and altar, similar to the one that had existed during the *ancien régime*, was the only way in which normality could be restored. For him, the supremacy of the secular state over all other institutions was axiomatic. Cardinal Martiniana was deeply impressed by the first consul's words, and wrote to the pope on 26 June to inform him of these overtures. Pius replied to the cardinal that:

> The assurances made to you, by First Consul Bonaparte, that it is his aim to regulate the ecclesiastical affairs of France in such a way as to allow the Catholic religion to flourish cannot but fill us with great joy as they would bring back millions of souls to Jesus Christ, whose place we occupy so unworthily on this earth. We certainly see it as a glorious and happy object for us, and useful to all the Catholic world to see this holy religion re-established in France, as it brought happiness [to this country] for so many centuries. Thus, we seize with eagerness this favourable moment which has emerged, which is why you may respond to the first consul that we would participate gladly in a negotiation having such a praiseworthy goal, so worthy of our apostolic ministry, and so in keeping with the wishes of our own heart.[97]

It was a great act of bravery to engage in talks which would be unpopular with the supporters of both sides. Bonaparte had many close friends and collaborators who had been committed revolutionaries and remained enemies of Catholicism. The army had little love for priests and was decidedly anticlerical in outlook. It had categorically refused to allow any chaplains within its ranks, and had sacked monastic houses with relish. Napoleon's decision to meet the pope halfway was thus to meet with some resistance.[98] Similarly, Pius had allies, many in the College of Cardinals, who viewed the French as untrustworthy. They were convinced that it would be impossible to negotiate any meaningful understanding with those who had so recently persecuted the church. Each side felt as if they were negotiating with terrorists, and that the very process was highly distasteful. Maury wrote a detailed report to Louis XVIII in which he stated that Bonaparte's approach to the church was a sign of his weakness.[99] For ultra-conservatives the Consulate's peace overtures were a cynical ploy to make the church an accessory to the crimes of the Revolution.

Both Pius and Napoleon knew that coming to an understanding would be an uphill struggle. As events accelerated it was decided that the ailing seventy-six-year-old Cardinal Martiniana was somewhat out of his depth in the world of high diplomacy. In the meantime, Consalvi had received the cardinal's *galero* on 11 August 1800.[100] As secretary of state (he was now the papal foreign minister) he would play a supremely important role in the climax of future negotiations. Yet the man who was first sent to Paris to prepare the groundwork was Spina, archbishop of Corinth. He would need all his resources as he entered the lion's den to discuss Catholicism's future within the heartland of the French Revolution.

The nineteenth century had opened as a time of uncertainty for both Pius and Napoleon. Against all the odds, they had succeeded in rising to become heads of state and government. More unexpectedly they had sought each other out in the hope that, after more than a decade of turmoil, they could put the past behind them. Historians have been less than kind to Napoleon about this ambitious plan to make peace with the Roman Church, dismissing it as cynical opportunism.[101] There is of course some truth to this, but one must guard against hindsight. It would be wrong to read the future Concordat, the treaty between Paris and Rome, from the vantage point of its ultimate failure. (Worse still would be to see it as a precursor to the concordats of Mussolini and Hitler in the first half of the twentieth century.[102] Such comparisons are deeply unfair, and underplay the importance of the contexts in which these agreements were forged.) In 1800 the prospect of religious peace was intoxicating. It had the potential to heal the greatest wound inflicted by the Revolution on the population of France. The difficulties were immense, but the rewards were commensurate to the perils. Napoleon and Pius knew that both their authority and their credibility were at stake.

# — THREE —
## DIVISIONS HEALED?
### THE CONCORDAT OF 1801

The peasant revolts of the 1790s in western France are among the most controversial episodes of the Revolution. Some have described the bloody repression visited on these rebels as an early form of genocide.[1] More moderate eyes view the events as representing a brutal war of attrition, in which tens of thousands on both sides perished. The government in Paris saw the insurgents as fanatics and barbarians, but ethnic cleansing was an unknown concept at the time.[2] The Vendeans were liquidated for their counter-revolutionary views, and not because they were a race apart. At their worst, these conflicts gave rise to bloody guerrilla warfare and military reprisals, a constant stream of ambushes, massacres and mutilations that foreshadowed some of the worst excesses of the twentieth century.[3] The peasants fought bravely for their God, and to a lesser extent their king, against *les Bleus* (the Revolutionary Army).

The Vendée, Brittany and Normandy became killing fields for those young republican conscripts unfortunate enough to be despatched to these rebellious provinces. This insurgency was the last thing the revolutionaries needed: they were already after all facing war against all the major European powers. The Republic was forced to send a permanent army into the west, and this drained troops away from other critical fronts. Their aim was to bleed the region into submission. As mentioned in Chapter 1 (p. 30), the 'infernal columns' were sent deep into the countryside to burn villages and to carry out reprisals against the local population. These brutal counter-insurgency techniques made the Republic despised by many of the very citizens it was supposed to protect. It was ironic that in 1789 most peasants had welcomed the Revolution, but that, by 1793, the attack on religion, new taxes and conscription pushed the west into open revolt.[4]

During January 1800, two strangers, dressed in civilian clothes, rode into the hamlet of Les Ponts-de-Cé (now a southern suburb of the town of Angers on the Loire).[5] The republican forces in control of this area viewed all newcomers with suspicion. After all, in October 1793, Vendean rebels had invaded the region, laying siege to the citadel of Angers, 190 miles from Paris. The assault represented the most easterly advance in the Vendean insurgents' offensive against the Jacobin Republic.[6] The failure to seize this fortified town on the Loire doomed the Catholic and Royal Army's rebellion. Surveillance remained high, and a state of permanent alert was imposed. The sentries immediately challenged the two strangers, demanding that they identify themselves. The first to speak was Lin-Loup-Lô-Luc Barré, who explained that he was a commissioner to the Revolutionary Army and was on a special mission. He produced a safe-conduct to enter the city of Angers signed by General Gabriel Hédouville.[7] The sergeant commanding the sentries was unimpressed. He informed Barré that General Guillaume Brune had replaced Hédouville as commander in the region, and that his safe-conduct had therefore expired.

It was at this point that the troops recognised the second stranger. This gave rise to enormous excitement. The notorious Étienne-Alexandre Bernier, parish priest of Saint-Laud in Angers, was in their hands. This fugitive was a big prize for any republican solider. For almost a decade, he had been effectively the prime minister, or civilian governor, of all areas controlled by the rebel warlords of the west. At this point Bernier must have felt betrayed, must have wondered if he had fallen into a trap. The sentries debated what to do next; some wanted to shoot the strangers as spies. In the end, the sergeant ordered his men to escort their indignant captives to Angers to verify their story.[8]

In so doing they saved the life of the man who was to be a protagonist in the story of France's rapprochement with the Papacy, the man who would reinforce Napoleon's conviction that only religious peace could bring stability to France. Bernier, the former guerrilla leader turned fervent Bonapartist, has been unjustly neglected by history. He was born in 1762 in the Loire Valley into a modest family of weavers.[9] He must have been a bright child, as his family paid for him to be educated and he went on to follow a career in the church. He was a brilliant student at the University of Angers, and, for a time, taught theology to younger students. After several years spent roaming local parishes as a curate, he was appointed to the prosperous parish of Saint-Laud in the heart of the city.[10] In the normal course of events Bernier might have expected to rise no further in the Gallican Church and to have ended his days in comfortable obscurity. His modest origins and lack of resources made any ambition to become a bishop virtually impossible.

As for so many, the Revolution of 1789 was to change his life dramatically. Initially Bernier was receptive to the new order, and participated in attempts to improve the administration of his parish. However, when, in 1791, he was compelled to swear an oath to the new French Constitution, he categorically refused to do so, as did most priests in the west.[11] He was deprived of his parish by the municipal authorities, who installed a more compliant candidate in his place. Bernier resented his removal, and remained in the area, stirring up trouble. There is little doubt that he encouraged his former parishioners to resist the intruder who had taken his place. The moment of truth arrived on All Souls' Day, when it was traditional for a procession of clergy and parishioners to visit the local graveyard. Here, Bernier's loyal followers greeted the intruder priest with a hail of stones.[12] At this stage, the revolutionary authorities decided to intervene and protect their candidate. Bernier was forced to flee the city and became an outlaw for almost a decade.

The abbé's life from 1792 to 1800 was to be one filled with adventure and would earn him the nickname 'Machiavelli in a cassock'.[13] After some initial hesitation he joined the rebels of the west in their famous military campaign of 1793.[14] His learning, charisma and organisational skills made him vital to their cause. He was at the same time a divisive and argumentative figure, who often stoked severe disagreements amongst the rebels, while his ambition and self-confidence, which verged on arrogance, made him some enemies. Indeed, one of Bernier's first actions was to pick a fight with Gabriel Guyot de Folleville, the self-styled bishop of Agra and president of the rebel civilian administration. Bernier wrote to Rome seeking information on this mysterious soldier-bishop, who seemed to have emerged from nowhere.[15] Soon the Curia responded that they knew of no bishop of Agra, thus exposing Folleville as a fraud who had no legitimate authority.[16] This unmasking of the fake bishop impressed Jean-Nicolas Stofflet, one of the principal leaders of the revolt, who delegated to Bernier much of the civilian administration of the areas under their military control. The abbé was also a lucky man, who survived one of the most dangerous periods of the Revolution. The Catholic and Royal Army in the First War of the Vendée suffered horrendous casualties, estimated to have been close to 90 per cent for the rebel side.[17] After the 1793 Battle of Savenay, which almost exterminated the Vendeans, the abbé managed to flee, evade capture and then rejoin the rebels when they eventually rallied in 1794.

After this time, Bernier was vital in rebuilding the insurgency against the Republic. He issued decrees conscripting youths into the rebel militia. He became a proto-minister of finance, requisitioning food, clothing and other essentials for the army; he also made a failed attempt to create a royalist paper currency to finance the insurrection in the west. There were initiatives to create rudimentary welfare for the orphans and widows of the war, and to improve the local cottage weaving industry to give the rebellion an economic base.[18] The abbé was an articulate and persuasive politician, blessed with charisma and sound organisational abilities. These qualities were counterbalanced by unbridled ambition and an unctuousness that often alienated his fellow royalists. At an assembly of Vendean delegates at Morozière in 1794 he tried to be elected by acclamation as commissioner-general of the Catholic and Royal Army, but his plan was scuppered by the objections raised by a deputy called Dupuis.[19] Bernier was incensed at this unexpected blow, and had his opponent arrested.

In 1795, with the fall of Robespierre and the creation of a more moderate republican regime known as the Directory (see above, pp. 34–5), the insurgency in the west seemed to grind to a halt. The abbé proved an able negotiator, achieving a temporary cessation of hostilities with General Lazare Hoche in December 1795, but this truce lasted barely two months before breaking down.[20] The leaders of the revolt had little faith in the French Republic. There was hardly any hope that the directors, in Paris, would honour Vendean demands to grant religious freedom and limit conscription.[21] The Directory resumed the persecution of priests, and conscription became an annual process with the introduction of the Jourdan Law in 1798. Thus the struggle against the Republic resumed, with little reduction in its brutality; Bernier resumed his role as virtual prime minister of the insurgents.

This time around he succeeded in being appointed to the new position of *agent général* for the rebels. In this capacity he was to travel to London on a special mission to meet with Louis XVIII's representatives and co-ordinate all future counter-revolutionary activity.[22] Bernier, realising that he was now among the most senior and influential leaders of the rebellion, decided against heading to England. He felt his absence would reduce his hard-won influence and erode his power base. The war in the west would be decided in France and not abroad. Despite his determined opposition to the French Revolution he was no dogmatic bigot. Ultimately his negotiations with Hoche in 1795 had demonstrated that he was willing to reach an accommodation with his enemies in the interests of peace.[23]

When Napoleon overthrew the Directory in November 1799 it was apparent that the pacification of the west was far from accomplished. Although the insurrection alone had little chance of toppling the Republic, it was a highly damaging drain on resources and manpower. Faced with a coalition of European powers advancing towards France, the last thing the new first consul needed were enemies to his rear. A mere two weeks after the Brumaire coup General Hédouville concluded a preliminary ceasefire with the rebels. On 28 December 1799 Bonaparte issued a proclamation to the inhabitants of the west, promising freedom of religion, a return to law and order, and amnesty to all who would lay down their arms.[24] Bernier saw immediately the opportunity that Bonaparte's rise to power represented, and sought to become a spokesman for the rebels. After some promising initial discussions with General Hédouville, the abbé set off on the four-day journey to Paris. There he was to negotiate with the highest officials of the new regime.

On 26 January 1800, Bernier, carrying 1,800 francs for expenses, and bearing false identity papers identifying him as a Citizen Deschamps (he was on the strictest instructions to maintain his incognito throughout his stay in Paris), arrived at the Petit Hôtel on the rue de la Loi.[25] Within two days, in the dark of night, he was summoned to a secret meeting with Napoleon at the Tuileries Palace. Napoleon saw in Bernier exactly the sort of collaborator and agent his regime needed. The consular government wanted to unite the winners and losers of the Revolution into a new composite elite that would bring social cohesion to France.[26] The first consul could offer this priest the respect, advancement and official status he had always craved. The obstacles to promotion that the low-born Bernier had faced during the *ancien régime* and subsequent rebellion melted away. For his part, the abbé assured Bonaparte that the west's loyalty to the Bourbon dynasty was superficial and that the real 'sticking-point' was the restoration of religion and public worship. His willingness to negotiate and re-establish order was a welcome sign of compromise to the consular regime. Throughout February, Bernier was hosted by some of the greatest dignitaries of the Republic, and was a guest at Napoleon's country retreat at the Malmaison. He was also invited to receptions by Talleyrand, who, as foreign minister, introduced him to the diplomatic corps.[27] The humble parish priest of Saint-Laud was making impressive inroads into the highest levels of the French establishment.

The dividends for the consular regime were palpable. On his return to the west, Bernier convinced his followers to lay down their arms and begin formal peace talks.[28] He even briefly persuaded Georges Cadoudal, the most indomitable of the Breton rebels, to come to the negotiating table.[29] The extent to which all these successes can be attributed to Bernier's intervention alone is debatable. It took other rebel leaders and a good deal of carrot and stick from Napoleon to ensure the temporary pacification of the west in 1800. The abbé had gambled on what he believed would be the winning side. He was convinced that the consulate would survive, and that Napoleon was a man with whom one could do business. He was rewarded in his wager with the victory at Marengo.[30] As described in the previous chapter (pp. 58–9), Napoleon, after the conferences at Vercelli with Cardinal Martiniana, needed a religious adviser who could help him make peace with the church. He knew that Talleyrand was unacceptable to the Catholic Church. This apostate and schismatic bishop and notorious libertine was detested in Rome as a renegade.[31] Bernier on the other hand had been steadfast to the church throughout the 1790s, and had spent most of his career fighting the Revolution. His credentials as a go-between, acceptable to both parties, were unimpeachable. He was to become one of the most redoubtable figures in the negotiation of the Concordat.

As Adolphe Thiers has stated, in his classic history of the Napoleonic Consulate and Empire, there were five options open to the first consul in 1800:

1. to completely separate church and state, that is to have complete neutrality in matters of religion;
2. to negotiate a peace with the Catholic Church, re-establishing the old alliance of throne and altar on a different footing;
3. to create an established Gallican Church with the first consul as its head, a solution resembling Henry VIII's reorganisation of the Anglican Church after the breach with Rome;
4. to make France Protestant, essentially abandoning Rome and supporting the Calvinist minority in France;
5. to create a new civic religion, along the lines of Robespierre's Cult of the Supreme Being.

The third, fourth and fifth options were radical and would require a massive campaign to change the culture, traditions and habits of the vast majority of the population.[32] Such drastic measures did not appeal to Bonaparte the realist. He had seen how the Constitutional Church and Cult of the Supreme Being had failed to garner substantial grassroots support during 1790s. The first option, a complete separation of church and state, had been pioneered in the Constitution of the United States and briefly by the Directory in France. It was, as yet, an unproven system and carried risks. Bonaparte feared that it would create a fifth column within France over which the state would have little or no control. Unsupervised Catholics and clergy, he worried, would stealthily continue to oppose the Consulate, preaching disobedience and subversion.

The second option had been tried and tested in the past. The Concordat of Bologna of 1516 had, for over two centuries, regulated the relations between the French monarchy and the Holy See. It had mostly done so very successfully (except for during the investiture crisis of the 1680s: see Appendix). Napoleon hoped to re-establish most of its content, but on much more favourable terms for the French Republic. On 25 June 1800, during his meeting with Martiniana in Vercelli, he had sketched out his vision. All *ancien régime* bishops and constitutional usurpers would be asked to resign their sees. All future bishops would be nominated by the first consul as the kings of France had done in the preceding centuries. The number of dioceses would be reduced, and the church would renounce all claims on those ecclesiastical properties confiscated during the Revolution. In return, the parish priests and new bishops would receive state salaries guaranteed by government bonds. There would also be an attempt to forgive and forget past misdemeanours, on both sides. In return, the French state would protect Catholicism and guarantee public worship, giving it official recognition as the dominant faith in France.[33]

The preliminary discussions in Vercelli elicited hope and disappointment in equal measure. Pius VII commissioned Michele di Pietro, a former professor of theology at the University of Sapienza and bishop of Isauropolis, to form a committee to examine Bonaparte's preliminary terms.[34] During the *ancien régime* the Gallican Church had possessed significant freedoms and autonomies, but such an independently wealthy church, enjoying immunity in the civilian courts, was unthinkable for the new order in France. The concessions demanded by the Republic were eye-wateringly painful for the church.[35] The trade-off was that the state would bankroll Catholicism in France and even support seminaries to train priests, but, in return, expected its bishops and priests to teach obedience and submission. The free exercise of Catholicism in post-revolutionary France came at the price of legitimating Napoleon's rule.

For Louis XVIII, who had been recognised as king of France by the new pope in March 1800, news that a peace agreement with the first consul was being seriously considered caused alarm. In exile, he had been informed of the talks in Vercelli by Cardinal Maury. He protested to Pius VII, begging him not to abandon his legitimate Gallican Church whose loyalty had been unwavering throughout the tides of revolution. After all, as Louis put it, the bishops' only crime was steadfastness to Rome and its dogmas.[36] The proposed betrayal of the old Gallican and legitimist bishops caused much consternation in the committee rooms of the Curia.

The Concordat was approached from two competing negotiating positions that seemed difficult to reconcile. Both parties, ultimately, never quite understood the other's point of view. Napoleon, inspired by the Emperor Constantine's rule in antiquity, wanted an ecclesiastical establishment subordinate to the state, whereas the Roman Curia and its cardinals saw this agreement as a first step in the rebirth of Catholicism as the state religion of France. The distance that separated the two sides was vast. It would take Bernier, the French negotiator, and the pope's emissary, Archbishop Spina, almost a year, and nine drafts of the Concordat, to find common ground. Most of Napoleon's secular collaborators, especially Talleyrand, were vehemently opposed to conciliation with Rome. Similarly, the College of Cardinals in Rome viewed the negotiations in Paris as a trap, and advised delay and caution. The distrust between a rational modernising state and Catholicism, whose traditions were millennial, was understandable. The Revolution's failure to settle the religious question had led to instability, lawlessness and civil war. The consular regime was all too aware that domestic tranquillity was as important as international harmony in establishing a political order that would endure.[37] In the context of 1800–02, the Concordat was as important as the peace negotiations with the Habsburgs and the British taking place at the same time.

Archbishop Spina was to travel to Cardinal Martiniana in Vercelli where it was expected that a French delegation would join him to begin preliminary negotiations. Cardinal Consalvi sent detailed instructions on 15 September.[38] The pope's secretary of state was uncertain of Bonaparte's 'true' intentions. If the first consul's objective was to restore religion on its pre-revolutionary footing, then concessions, even generous ones, could be made. Consalvi speculated that a legate could be sent to France after an agreement had been signed to oversee the restoration of the church. He compared this hypothetical situation to when

Cardinal Pole and Cardinal Campeggio had been sent to England to supervise the reintroduction of Catholicism to England during the reign of Mary Tudor.[39] Yet he feared such an outcome was optimistic. The Revolution of 1789 still had many followers who did not want a powerful independent church to re-emerge. Convincing them that any official recognition of Catholicism was necessary was an uphill struggle. Consalvi suspected that mere toleration of the church was the best they could hope for in the circumstances. If this was the official government offer, then the room for negotiation would be limited. According to Consalvi's instructions, the greatest points of contention would be the resignation of all Catholic bishops, the reduction of the number of the dioceses and the renunciation of all claims on church lands. Spina was not given plenipotentiary powers, and was not authorised to sign any binding conventions on behalf of the Holy See. He could merely inform the French authorities of the pope's intentions and feelings about the future of the Gallican Church.

As he approached Florence on 25 September 1800, Spina was informed that there would be no diplomatic conference in Vercelli. The request was made that he should proceed with all due haste to Paris. The consular government believed that negotiations would be more rapid at the heart of the Republic; it is equally true that the pope's agent would be more vulnerable to persuasion and compulsion so far away from home. Sensing that the nature of the mission was changing, Spina halted his journey. Three weeks of uncertainty followed. The archbishop wrote to Consalvi seeking new instructions and permission to head to the French capital, and the Curia and several cardinals hurriedly prepared revised directions for Spina. The ultramontane Cardinal Antonelli, who wanted the pope's emissary to be circumspect and avoid any reduction in the spiritual authority of the church, was then given the task of redacting this document taking into account the opinion of his colleagues. The new instructions took weeks to be written and only left Rome on 13 October 1800.[40]

This lengthy and convoluted document provided reflections on how to act in several hypothetical scenarios. The greatest fear was that Spina would be trapped into conceding too much ground: he was told to hold his own counsel and avoid socialising with French elites, especially members of the Constitutional Church. There was a fear that *philosophes* and Jacobins were still too influential in France: these enemies of the Roman Church were assumed to be working behind the scenes to undermine any treaty with the Papacy. Equally, legitimate clergy and agents of Louis XVIII were not to be trusted with the details of his confidential mission. Spina was permitted only to meet with the Spanish delegation and seek their support in the negotiations. Otherwise the papal emissary's sole contact was to be with French ministers and the official negotiating team led by Bernier. Talleyrand was described as *molesto* ('irritating'), but was to be treated with courtesy; as a minister of the Republic his presence was a necessary evil. Meanwhile, to alienate the apostate bishop of Autun would be an unwise move, given his influence and prestige over Bonaparte. Spina realised that his life in Paris would be lonely and isolated.

Perplexingly, Cardinal Antonelli's directions were much less well structured than the first instructions prepared by Consalvi. Spina's mission was primarily spiritual in character, although the Papacy did have temporal aims too. Like any prince, the pope wanted to enlarge his domains; it was thought that if the religious question could be solved to France's satisfaction the Republic would look more favourably on returning to the pope those lands lost during the 1790s. In the original instructions Consalvi had directed his agent to seek, informally, the return of the Comtat Venaissin and the Legations of Romagna to the Papacy (whereas Antonelli's guidelines were more circumspect when it came to temporal matters). As noted in the previous two chapters (p. 36 and p. 47), these territories had been ceded in the treaty of Tolentino in 1797 and were vital for the economy of the Papal States. Without the rich agricultural lands of Bologna, Ferrara and Ravenna the pope would be in constant danger of bankruptcy. The French had no intention of returning territories they had annexed by international treaty. Nevertheless, both Bonaparte and Talleyrand insincerely hinted that once spiritual peace had been restored in France such questions might be reopened to the benefit of the Holy See. Finally, Spina was provided with a learned counselor to assist him in his deliberations. Carlo Caselli, who was a former general of the Servite Order, was a renowned theologian who had served as *consultore* for the congregation of rites. He would be Spina's closest companion and adviser during the negotiations.[41]

As Spina left Florence and headed towards Piedmont, and then onwards to France, he must have known the most arduous mission of his life awaited him. The outcome would decide the future of Catholicism and the survival of the Papacy. For five weeks Spina travelled through the French countryside. For this Italian prelate the situation was shocking, the effects of the Revolution plain. Priests were nowhere to be seen. Clergy were required to dress in normal clothes, which made them indistinguishable from the rest of the population. Many churches remained shut, with nobody to minister to local congregations. Several Catholic chapels and shrines had been rededicated to the republican cults of youth, womanhood, prosperity and old age. The republican calendar had abolished Sundays and the ten-day week seemed to take France away from Catholic rhythms of life. The archbishop felt as if he had entered a heathen land.

Spina reached Paris on 5 November and took up residence at the aptly named Hôtel de Rome on the rue Saint-Dominique; he would remain incognito for some time by dressing in civilian clothes and keeping a low profile. Three days after his arrival, Spina received a note from Bernier explaining that he would represent the French government in all future negotiations. This initial message was optimistic in tone and detailed how the restoration of religion for the benefit of French society was the government's top priority.[42] The issue of the surviving *ancien régime* bishops was discussed immediately in this document. Their return to their former dioceses was impossible: they were after all seen as the enemies of the Republic, and opposed to the first consul's rule. Bernier deployed his immense learning to propose an ingenious historical solution to this problem.[43] He referred to the Donatist crisis in North Africa which had occurred during the fourth and fifth centuries AD. Here a schism had erupted between those who suffered, during the Roman persecution of Christianity, and those who had collaborated with the pagan authorities. The followers of Donatus Magnus, bishop of Carthage, were puritanical in their views and believed that collaborationist clergy were unworthy of their office. Donatists did not recognise candidates appointed by Rome: these quislings, in their eyes, had sullied their ordination by co-operating with the empire's pagans. The parallels between the Donatist and the legitimist clergy were striking. Ultimately, Bernier invoked the decision of Saint Augustine of Hippo and Saint Aurelius at the Council of Carthage of 411, which resulted in the forced resignation from their sees of over 300 bishops, ending the schism within the church.[44] In their stead a new generation of bishops was invested to heal the wounds of Donatism. Surely, Bernier stressed, a similar mass resignation on both sides could allow for a new composite French episcopate to emerge to heal the wounds of revolution?

Spina was not convinced by the parallel put forward, but he was delighted to have an interlocutor whose credentials were unimpeachable. Setting out from Rome, he had been concerned that he would be forced to negotiate with constitutional bishops, or worse, with the renegade Talleyrand. Bernier was a good priest, who had been loyal to the Papacy throughout the 1790s. Although his allegiance to Louis XVIII had been transferred to Bonaparte, from the Papacy's perspective he was an unexpectedly suitable intermediary. After all, he was a former enemy of the Revolution, who had refused the oath to the Civil Constitution of the Clergy. The next day, 9 November, after a brief meeting with Talleyrand, Spina was received by the first consul in the Tuileries Palace.[45] The initial interview was described as cordial and positive. Despite this, Napoleon could not resist noting that Chiaramonti had not written to him directly to announce his election as Pius VII in March 1800. Clear resentment lingered over the fact that Louis XVIII had been recognised as king of France immediately after the Venice Conclave.[46] The first consul reiterated that his position had not changed since Vercelli. Spina asserted that his presence in Paris demonstrated the pope's earnest desire to make peace with the French Republic, going on to explain that he would need to maintain his incognito to avoid eliciting resentment among those foreign powers still at war with France; the Papacy's decision to extend an olive branch to the Consulate was an implicit admission that it no longer supported the anti-French coalition. The true extent of the diplomatic powers entrusted to Pius VII's agent were not discussed, and Bonaparte assumed mistakenly that Spina was authorised to negotiate and sign a treaty. This cordial audience lasted thirty minutes, and highlighted that both sides wanted to begin discussions quickly.[47]

Early negotiations for the Concordat were overshadowed by the final stages of the War of the Second Coalition. In November 1800 France had resumed military operations against Austria and Britain. Although Marengo had been a blow to the Habsburgs, they still had powerful armies in Germany. There remained uncertainty about how the outcome of the fighting would change the map of Europe. Negotiations would be difficult so long as uncertainty reigned over the territorial outcomes of the war. Spina had replied to Bernier's note stating that the mass resignation of bishops would be difficult for the pope to accept. It was true that, during the Middle Ages, schisms had been resolved by depriving popes and bishops of their sees. This, however, had been achieved with the assistance of ecumenical councils whose membership comprised a quorum of all Catholic bishops. Since the Council of Trent (1545–63), popes had been jealous of such councils' prerogatives and felt uneasy about any conciliarist tendencies. The summoning of a church council was impossible, and the pope alone could only exhort bishops to resign their sees. What would happen if a majority of *ancien régime* bishops refused to accept this exhortation?[48] The damage to papal authority would be significant.

Napoleon's rationale behind these negotiations was complex and, at times, contradictory. On the one hand he saw the Gallican Church as subordinate to the state, and believed that its duty was to preach submission to his regime. The clergy of France had always claimed autonomy from Rome, so the consular government believed it had every right to regulate its hierarchy, administration and teachings. Nevertheless, Bonaparte recognised that the pope was the supreme spiritual head of this institution, and that only his goodwill could reconcile the schism of the 1790s. The tension between the autonomous tendencies of Gallicanism and centralising ultramontane thinking was one that he was never able to resolve to his satisfaction.[49] Indeed, the question of whether the Gallican Church was self-regulating or tied to Rome's authority was to remain a vexed one throughout much of the nineteenth century.[50] The historical self-sufficiency of the French church when it came to Rome's authority provided the first consul with a pretext to disregard the pope when convenient. Yet Napoleon was at heart a dictator who admired centralised hierarchies. The pope's claims to absolute spiritual supremacy over the church was useful at this juncture: the primacy of the Roman See could be used to force the legitimate and constitutional clergy to accept his new ecclesiastical structures. One of the major social policies of the Consulate was that of *amalgame*, that is the amalgamation of both supporters and opponents of the Revolution into a permanent working elite. Napoleon hoped to achieve in the church what he had managed to do in his secular civil service, where Jacobins and former nobles had been persuaded to work together for the good of the state. Could not refractory and constitutional clergy enter into a similar arrangement? Certainly, this pill of uniting rival churches was a bitter one for the Curia to swallow. For the cardinals in Rome, the constitutional clergy were traitors and abject sinners. They could only extinguish their disobedience through a public and humiliating retraction of their past errors.[51]

Spina and Bernier met almost daily throughout November and December 1800, making good progress on the issue of nationalised land. The church was willing to accept the loss of its former properties in return for state salaries and a possible re-establishment of the tithe.[52] Spina expressed the hope that confiscated churches and other ecclesiastical buildings that had not been sold might be returned to the church. The preliminary discussions at Vercelli had indicated that the state would accept to pay for future priestly training in seminaries. Initial discussions defined Catholicism as the 'dominant' religion in France, and as such it would enjoy special treatment, not to mention official patronage. The government seemed amenable to this definition, but it was built on a misunderstanding. For Rome, 'dominant' meant that Catholicism was to be the state religion of France and that future consuls would profess it. From the consular regime's perspective, 'dominant' signified simply that the Catholic faith was to be professed by the majority of the French population, and in consequence, would receive a generous financial endowment. This did not, in any sense, imply that the French state professed or preferred it to any other faith. For the Republic, all religions were equal. The state had the right to oversee and regulate them all in the interest of public order. Catholicism's prestige was due strictly to the number of its followers, and not to the content, let alone truth, of its beliefs and dogmas. The state's legislation was grounded in rationalism, not the revealed religion of Catholic dogma. The church's position on family, marriage and other matters of morality were irrelevant for the Consulate. Unlike under the *ancien régime*, state law and religious morality were separate entities after 1800.[53]

Nevertheless, Bernier intimated that the French government was willing to make some concessions to allay Rome's fears. He also made hopeful noises to the effect that the reduction of dioceses might be less drastic than envisaged. Some effort might also be made to preserve cathedral chapters and other ecclesiastical institutions with state subsidy. The problem, as ever, was the question of the episcopacy. Spina was unhappy with the Donatist solution proposed by Bernier. He saw this as a betrayal of those priests and prelates who had been loyal to the pope. He inquired if the government might reappoint several *ancien régime* bishops to the new dioceses and exclude constitutional clergy. Bernier feared that this would be extremely difficult. As an alternative, Spina advised that the pope could appoint apostolic administrators who could take charge of the government of the dioceses held by legitimate bishops. These clergymen would be selected with governmental approval, would exercise all episcopal powers without necessarily holding the title of bishop: they would in effect lay the groundwork for future church reform. The French government considered this a messy solution to the problem, and one that would delay the reorganisation of the church. The decision was made to suspend discussion on the problem of the legitimate bishops and continue with other issues.

On 22 November 1800 Bernier presented Spina with the first half of the draft Concordat. It sought to re-establish Catholicism in France along the lines that had already been defined by the Concordat of Bologna in 1516. Essentially, the executive would retain the right to appoint the church's hierarchy.[54] The first two titles concerned the reorganisation of the church and the removal of the *ancien régime* bishops. The first article of title II was cleverly worded to give the impression that a significant number of legitimate prelates would be reappointed to new dioceses once the Concordat was ratified.[55] Four days later the second half of this draft version was presented to Spina. The number of dioceses in France was reduced to sixty-two, fewer than half the number that had existed during the *ancien régime*. According to these terms, bishops were to take an oath to the French Constitution in the presence of the first consul before being enthroned in their dioceses. Article V of title III was very important: it granted the right to the first consul and his successors to nominate bishops to vacant sees. It also stipulated that future heads of state in France would be Catholic. Superficially, this was a return to the tradition by which the kings of France nominated candidates when dioceses fell empty. Bernier had also conceded that only Catholics, in future, would be eligible to become first consuls. Spina was delighted that present and future French heads of state would be Catholic, whereas Napoleon was furious that his negotiator had made an impossible concession in the name of his government: Bernier had taken this initiative without any direct instructions from his republican masters. This was a serious mistake on the part of Bernier, and one which Bonaparte refused to accept under any circumstance. An article prescribing the religion of the government would have transformed France into a confessional state, and made Catholicism its official religion, thus nullifying the changes brought by the Revolution of 1789. Furthermore, title IX, article I declared explicitly that Catholicism was the religion of the state. Again, Bernier made this concession without government approval and this move would have made Jacobin factions in the Council of State and French parliament deeply unhappy. Domestic opposition to the Concordat needed to be avoided where possible. Bonaparte wanted to present his parliaments with a *fait accompli*, and not allow any debate. Anything that adulterated the changes established by the French Revolution would have made this impossible.[56]

This first draft of the Concordat gave the French church extraordinary powers. It stipulated that bishops for the next two decades would receive from the pope the power to absolve married clergy and others guilty of grave sins committed during the Revolution. Furthermore, each diocese was to reduce the number of parishes and rationalise its internal administration. This preliminary version promised the return of all church property confiscated during the 1790s which had not been already sold at auction. In return, Rome accepted that the alienation of the properties lost in 1789 was permanent. There was a promise to repeal all existing anticlerical legislation, while the draft also stated that all provisions of the Concordat of 1516 that did not clash with current laws would once again come into force. It was a bold first draft and showed that both parties shared some common ground on the internal reform of the church. Yet the clauses pertaining to Catholicism's future position in France and the rebirth of a neo-Gallican episcopacy remained far from resolved. The initial draft contained nine titles and thirty-seven articles in total. It was an overly complex document, which would evolve significantly in 1801.

It took Spina nine days to digest this draft and its implications. His response was sent to Bernier as an official diplomatic note on 9 December. He suggested that the number and size of the new dioceses should not be part of the official terms of the Concordat: this could be decided at a later stage. This was important, as the ongoing war made the extent of French territory in Europe uncertain: which dioceses would fall under French authority in future remained an open question.[57] Equally, the articles on the appointment of future bishops were too detailed, Spina felt: he was of the opinion that such matters should be dealt with separately from the actual terms of the Concordat. The pope's emissary insisted that all future candidates for the episcopacy would need to possess theology degrees and that their doctrinal views be in line with church teaching. Furthermore, the draft made no mention at all of the constitutional clergy. Spina had several questions as to why this was the case. Was the first consul abandoning them? Would they be required to retract their constitutional oaths? Were these schismatics to make a public declaration admitting their past crimes and heresies? The Holy See was willing to be merciful, but these renegades must request forgiveness publicly and retract their oath to the Civil Constitution.[58] The pope could not allow schismatics to continue in ministry without penitence and absolution.

The French government had no intention of forcing priests who had favoured the Revolution to retract their past oaths. The government saw the Concordat as the implicit abrogation of the Civil Constitution and believed that no further discussion on the matter would be necessary. Rome would be surprised by this reasoning in later stages of the negotiations, and would bitterly oppose it.[59] After these remarks, Spina attached a revised version of the draft which streamlined the articles and sought to give the Holy See greater discretion over the episcopacy in France. Bonaparte's powers of appointment were to be temporary, and his successors would need to negotiate future arrangements with Rome. The first draft of the Concordat was promising, but reaching an agreement proved difficult.

Little did the negotiators know that, a week previously, on 3 December, a French army, under General Jean-Victor Moreau, had engaged Austrian forces commanded by the Archduke John in Bavaria. On the plains of Hohenlinden, east of Munich, the French had inflicted a crushing defeat on the Habsburgs.[60] Utterly overwhelmed, Austria was forced to enter peace negotiations at Lunéville.[61] It was clear that France had triumphed in the War of the Second Coalition, and that its territory would remain the same for the foreseeable future. Only England and Naples stood alone against the Republic and their resolve was starting to buckle. Within six months they too would take their seats at the negotiating table. General Moreau's victory made him the man of the hour. The opposition to Bonaparte saw him as a figurehead around which they could rally. He was a committed republican seen by many as a credible rival to Bonaparte. The French government became fearful of Jacobin conspiracies and sought to nip them in the bud.[62] Consequently, leniency towards the church became difficult to justify, given the new climate. Any further consideration of making Catholicism the state's official faith was impossible, as it would give rise to dangerous republican dissent.

In his report to Consalvi, on 10 December 1800, Spina announced the news of the French triumph at Hohenlinden. He expected that the French would continue to consider that the Italian peninsula fell within their sphere of influence.[63] The transfer of the Habsburg grand duke of Tuscany to a German principality meant that a French puppet would now be installed in Florence. The enlarged French Republic would now, indirectly, border the Papal States. Spina speculated that, in return for official recognition of the French Republic, the Holy See might expect to be invited to the negotiations at Lunéville. This hope proved illusory: as winter set in, little was left to do but await the arrival of the revised Concordat. Appropriately enough, Bernier transmitted a second draft to the Hôtel de Rome on Christmas Eve 1800.[64] Although it contained nine titles like the first text, this version had eliminated seventeen articles and was much shorter. Bernier had been forced to claw back many early concessions. Catholicism would now be the 'religion of majority' rather than the official state religion.

Equally, cathedral chapters and seminaries would not be entitled to receive state funding. The financial provisions would be significantly less generous than in the draft's first incarnation, and there was no mention of unsold properties being returned. The document's tone was ambiguous throughout, and made the church entirely subordinate to the state.

On the very night this text was presented to Spina, the first consul was due to attend a gala performance of Haydn's *Creation* at the Paris Opéra. His coachman César was apparently inebriated and in a hurry.[65] Napoleon's carriage sped in front of the cortège, and as it turned off the rue Saint-Nicaise into the rue de Chartres an enormous explosion sounded. The horses of the consular carriage bolted, hurtling forward out of control. It was only the quick thinking of General Lannes that managed to stop their flight, and they came to a halt in front of the opera house.[66] Initially the passengers thought that a cannon had been fired in their direction but soon the grim reality became apparent. A bomb had killed four people instantly; the death toll would later rise to over twenty and more than eighty wounded. It was only César's impatience that had saved the first consul from certain death.[67] Bonaparte attended the performance with sangfroid, but deep down he was shaken, and left early in a furious mood. Napoleon summoned his police minister Joseph Fouché, the former Oratorian lay brother and one-time Jacobin terrorist. Convinced that he had almost fallen victim to a republican conspiracy against his life, he berated his police minister for his inefficiency.[68] He ordered Fouché to round up all known radical Jacobins and place them in custody. Over the next few days, the Council of State and legislative assemblies authorised summary trials, followed by immediate deportation to the colonies. Ninety-three former associates of Fouché were sentenced to the dry guillotine. Fewer than a dozen would live to see France again.[69]

The minister of police was none too sure that his former Jacobin associates were responsible for the Christmas Eve assassination plot. For Napoleon this pre-emptive purge against disloyal republicans served to strengthen his grip on power. Fouché instructed Pierre-Marie Desmarest to take charge of the forensic investigation. This former canon of Chartres Cathedral had become a brilliant crime-scene investigator and a pioneering detective.[70] The bomb – which the newspapers christened the 'infernal machine' – was an early example of an improvised explosive device. Placed on a cart pulled by an unfortunate mare, the conspirators had lit a slow-burning fuse and had clearly survived the assassination attempt. Debris from the cart was used in a reconstruction, and a skilled veterinarian sewed the remains of the horse back together. Remarkably the nag's head was still intact, and this allowed a local blacksmith to recognise her. He remembered that she had belonged to a mysterious individual with a Breton accent called 'Little François'.[71] The investigation soon pointed to the truth that it was not the republicans but the royalists of the west who were behind the attempt on the first consul's life. The leaders of the Breton revolts were soon apprehended; Georges Cadoudal, the Breton guerrilla leader, whom Bernier had persuaded to take part in peace talks in early 1800, would later pay for his conspiracy with his head (see below, p. 115).

The assassination attempt in the rue Saint-Nicaise strengthened the Consulate by creating a pretext by which Bonaparte was able to liquidate his most extreme opponents of both the left and the right.[72] It rid him of some of the most dogged enemies to any conciliation attempt with the church. Yet the first consul was uncertain of how far the Curia was committed to his peace plan. Spina had responded with unconcealed disappointment to the second draft of the Concordat. From his perspective, it was a decided step backwards. The removal of the recognition of Catholicism as the established faith of the state implied that it was to be treated like any other religion. The archbishop was puzzled as to why Rome should grant the first consul the power to nominate bishops when he was giving the pope so little in return. At this time, Spina was also hindered by an inexplicable communications blackout with Consalvi.[73] He kept receiving requests for letters but no instructions as to how to negotiate. Mysteriously, Spina's correspondence was not reaching the Papal States. The diplomat felt isolated; things were soon to get worse. When the archbishop heard of the attempt on Bonaparte's life, he joined the corps diplomatique in writing to express relief at his survival.[74] He also penned a letter to Consalvi informing him of what had happened.[75] Rumours abounded that Fouché was trying to blame former nobles and priests for the bombing.

On 8 January 1801 Spina had a second meeting with Bonaparte. There were concerns about the ongoing delays.[76] The intention was that the Concordat would be published together with the general peace treaties signed with other European powers. However, several sticking-points remained insoluble: Catholicism's position as the predominant religion in France; how the new episcopate was to be appointed; and what would happen to confiscated church property. The first consul assured the archbishop that the Catholic faith would always reflect the executive's beliefs, and would always be that of the majority of the Republic's population. Although Catholicism could not be officially recognised as the state religion, it would be so in practice. For the Consulate an amalgamated episcopate, made up of both legitimate and constitutional clergy, was the sole means of putting the divisions created by the French Revolution to rest. Although Bonaparte understood that the pope's emissary's primary mission was to discuss spiritual matters, he insinuated that territorial questions in Italy were far from decided and might be reopened. This was Bonaparte at his most cynical, trying to extract spiritual concessions in return for vague promises about the return of the Legations of Romagna to the Papacy.[77] Spina left the meeting feeling that the French government was still on side, but that pressure was mounting to reach a final agreement.

Two further drafts of the Concordat emerged in January 1801. These documents represented, in Spina's view, improvements on the second version. Their articles recognised Catholicism as the religion of the majority and that of the consuls. They promised that a legate would be sent from Rome to supervise the re-establishment of the church in France. Furthermore, these drafts promised generous salaries to clergymen and enshrined the restoration of unsold properties. Stealthily, the French team had inserted a clause stating that the Vatican would forgive constitutional clergy and accept them back into the fold.[78] Talleyrand was probably behind this clause. He wanted forgiveness for all married clergy to be part of the deal, and it was not mere altruism – he wanted his own marriage to be acknowledged by the church.

Despite some cosmetic improvement, little real progress was made in January and February. Pressure and a sense of grim foreboding started to take hold of Spina. The future map of Europe remained uncertain: the Neapolitans had failed to join the peace negotiations in Lunéville and military operations continued in Italy. In February, General Murat, Napoleon's brother-in-law, sent an observation corps into the Papal States and occupied the port city of Ancona on the Adriatic.[79] Although the papal civilian administration was left unmolested, the fortress and citadel of the city were garrisoned by French troops. Local authorities were obliged to requisition the supplies and food necessary to maintain these foreign invaders. Alarm bells sounded loudly in Rome: many wondered if the first consul had made this move to exert pressure on the negotiations over the Concordat.[80]

As talks stalled, on 2 February 1801 Bonaparte decided to take matters into his own hands and produce his own Concordat. He felt that his version would represent the bottom line. Characteristically military and peremptory in tone, it was the shortest document produced throughout the entire negotiations, containing only fifteen articles.[81] It was vague when it came to the reduction of dioceses, while no figure was given for clerical salaries. Napoleon reprised the points he had made to Cardinal Martiniana at Vercelli eight months before. All bishops would have to resign their sees and the government would appoint all future incumbents. The most stunning innovation was forgiveness and laicisation for all priests who had married during the 1790s. Talleyrand's influence was again palpable in this last area. Spina swallowed hard when he received a document which felt very much like an ultimatum. It was difficult for Spina to further negotiations at this stage, and a recourse to Rome became vital.[82]

The treaty of Lunéville, enshrining peace with the Habsburgs, was signed on 9 February 1801.[83] Diplomatic success made the failure to reach spiritual peace with the church even more glaring. Throughout the negotiations, Bernier was at an advantage in comparison to Spina. A short carriage ride was all that was necessary for him to receive direct instructions from Talleyrand and Napoleon himself. The situation for Spina meanwhile became increasingly fraught when in February, during a stormy meeting with Talleyrand, he was accused of being a decoy sent by the pope to forestall the occupation of Rome.[84] The fact that he was not empowered to sign or ratify an agreement was now interpreted as a direct slight towards the French government. His hesitations were viewed by the foreign minister as delaying tactics. Spina appealed directly to the first consul, asking for time to seek fresh guidance from Rome.

On 22 February 1801 General Murat embarked on an important diplomatic mission. The commander of all French forces in Italy decided to visit the pope to bring reassurances that his troops were in the Papal States solely to prevent a Neapolitan offensive and to protect Italy's Adriatic coast from Britain's Royal Navy. He met with Pius VII: gifts were given, compliments exchanged.[85] The general also asked to visit the historical sites, collections and palaces of the eternal city. He wanted to demonstrate France's admiration for classical civilisation and its respect for papal sovereignty. This brief visit did much to allay some of Rome's fears that a French invasion was imminent.

On 10 March a papal courier, exhausted and breathing heavily, dismounted before the secretariat of state in Rome.[86] The heavy bags he carried contained not only documents but also the statue of the Madonna of Loreto which the French had pillaged during the 1790s. An object of fervent Catholic veneration for the population of the Papal States, its return symbolised French goodwill towards the church. The courier also brought the fifth version of the Concordat, the aggressive tone of which shocked Consalvi.[87] The document was initially presented to three cardinals and to di Pietro (who had been elevated in December to patriarch of Jerusalem). Within a week, this commission of prelates understood that haste and secrecy were of the utmost importance: the Roman Church could not accept the fifth draft, and it was recommended that two counter-proposals be drafted.[88] The first followed the templates established by the negotiations in Paris, but reworded them in a manner such that the church did not acknowledge the supremacy of the state. The second counter-proposal departed more from previous versions, and sought to make Catholicism the state religion of France. Instead of submitting these documents to the entire College of Cardinals, di Pietro advised that a smaller congregation of twelve be organised to deliberate on the Concordat with France. His recommendation was accepted, and these twelve cardinals would report back on Napoleon's draft. Despite being streamlined, this committee still operated within the mindset and ethos of the church's bureaucracy.

The Roman Curia, the papal administration, has been the subject of bad press ever since it was first established during the Middle Ages and developed into one of the great bureaucracies of the world. Its decision-making system was (and remains) complex: navigating the meanderings of canon law was a complicated business.[89] It centred around congregations of cardinals and theologians, which were given substantial time to consider the documentation relating to theological conundrums and judicial appeals. Each member was asked to give his *voto* (literally 'vote' or 'opinion') in writing. Most of these committees were composed of over twenty cardinals, and each brought their own theological counsel to advise them on their *voto*. This decision-making process highlighted the fact that the pope, although theoretically an absolute monarch, was not so in practice: he was required, like any wise prince, to seek counsel and benefit from the expertise of his fellow clergymen. The process of writing extensive *voti* and debating them meant that decisions could take many months or years to be finalised.

In striking contrast, Napoleon's bureaucracy was one of the most streamlined and efficient in the world.[90] French law derived, or at least claimed to derive, from reason and natural law, and was practical in nature.[91] The legal system was geared towards the quick resolution of disputes and deployed authoritarianism so that opposition, once a decision had been taken, became impossible. The

Council of State, the key institution where legislation was drafted, was a site of intense debate. Its sessions lasted hours, but once the first consul and a majority supported him, that was the bottom line.[92]

From Spina's despatches, and their intelligence on France, di Pietro accepted that Rome's response to the draft Concordat would need to be swift. A congregation of twelve was considered exceedingly small and would take a few months to report back. In this instance the Vatican was deliberating with unprecedented and precipitant haste: never in the annals of church history had priests and cardinals been asked to work so fast. Despite this, the congregation of cardinals was working on a glaring misunderstanding of Bonaparte's intentions. For the first consul, the next step was ratification, not further negotiation or amendment. The secretive and ponderous nature of curial deliberations was interpreted by Napoleon as malevolent, the deafening silence from the eternal city taken for a sign of duplicitous priestcraft.[93] As the weeks became months his limited patience exhausted itself.

It had been some years since France had sent a diplomatic agent to Rome. Bonaparte now felt that he needed an emissary there to reassure the pope of his continued good intentions. A man was needed who would fight the *zelanti* (conservative) faction in the College of Cardinals who were not in favour of a treaty with France. This task fell to François Cacault, a lover of Italian art and culture, and a wily diplomat with many years of experience.[94] He had started his career in Naples, just before the fall of the Bastille, and had risen eventually to become Bonaparte's negotiator for the treaty of Tolentino with the Papacy in 1797 (see above, p. 36).[95] A more able, discreet and well-known figure in elite circles in Rome was difficult to imagine. Although an ideal candidate for the position, Cacault initially refused the appointment. Now in his sixties, he was in ill health and from December 1799 had been elected to represent his local Breton constituency in Napoleon's parliament. After some persuasion, he agreed in February 1801 to travel to the eternal city. Ostensibly his mission was to help deliver the first consul's basic version of the Concordat to Rome and to ensure that the pope ratified this document. According to legend, Napoleon told Cacault: 'Treat the pope as if he had 200,000 troops.'[96] As it happened, Cacault would play a critical role in salvaging the negotiations at one of the most difficult moments.

An exhausted François Cacault arrived in Rome on 9 April 1801.[97] One of the few former royal diplomats to have bridged the transition from monarchy to Republic during the 1790s without great difficulty, he was a man of the

Enlightenment, and a polymath of voracious intellectual curiosity.[98] Despite this, and unlike so many of his contemporaries, he maintained an admiration for the role that religion played in society in fostering morals and a sense of community. As a Breton he knew just how important such religious belief was for his region. He had a deep appreciation of Rome and the church's cultural position on the Italian peninsula. It was his utmost priority to keep the Concordat alive: his tactfulness made him ideally suited to this task.

During his first day in the eternal city he had a long interview with Consalvi in the morning, and afterwards was admitted to an official audience at the Quirinal Palace. He spent over two hours with Pius VII, during which he presented his diplomatic credentials.[99] Pius expressed the hope that the future Concordat would mark a great chapter in the history of Christianity. This was, he recognised, a remarkable opportunity, and one which would change profoundly the nature of the institution over which he presided. Cacault was told that a congregation of twelve cardinals was deliberating, in strict secrecy, over the draft. In confidence the pope told the French agent that the written reports were ready, and that he hoped the final conclusion could be sent to Paris within the space of two weeks. Cacault recognised that the Concordat would be the cornerstone of the new consular regime, that its success would bring peace and stability after a decade of revolutionary turmoil. Failure, on the other hand, would mean a return to lawlessness and civil war.

One of the key stumbling blocks was that the cardinals believed they could rewrite much of the Concordat. During April they held congregations in which they debated two alternative versions drawn up by the patriarch of Jerusalem, di Pietro. At some of the most important meetings, Pius VII himself was present, chairing the debates. Cardinal Stefano Borgia (a distant descendant of the Renaissance dynasty established by the infamous Rodrigo Borgia, later Pope Alexander VI) was the most problematic member. Taking the lead, he opposed making overly generous concessions to France.[100] Borgia had accompanied the late Pius VI to Valence, and shared his imprisonment; as a witness to the death of a pope in captivity, he was far from well-disposed to the French Republic. He advised caution, standing firm and defending the church's prerogatives. The counter-proposal drafted by di Pietro was broadly acceptable to the cardinals and garnered their favourable opinions.

Under these proposals, the first article proclaimed that the consular government recognised the Catholic religion as that of the majority of the French population. The text also affirmed that the government of the Republic would protect the liberty and public worship of Catholicism, and that it would also defend the purity of church dogmas and abolish any laws that conflicted with the church's internal discipline. Essentially, the French government was to accept that its executive would be Catholic, thus turning the Republic into a confessional state.[101] The clause on the episcopate stated that the pope would exhort the *ancien régime* bishops to make any sacrifice necessary for the re-establishment of peace and religious harmony in France. The article in question contained no direct mention of resignation, and was vague to the point of being meaningless. The counter-proposal stated explicitly that the first consul would need to profess the Catholic faith if he wished to appoint bishops in future. Finally, Catholics were to be allowed to create endowments to fund clerical establishments: as trusts and property entails had been abolished by the French Revolution, it was unlikely that the government would allow this exception to normal property laws.

For the most part, the cardinals accepted that the French government would redraw the administrative map of the Gallican Church and that it would appoint future incumbents. The counter-proposal also accepted that church lands, lost during the French Revolution, could not be returned. However, it did not accept the French government's refusal to recognise Catholicism as the religion of the state. Theoretical equality with all other 'false religions' upset Rome greatly.[102] Consalvi was determined that the treaty would be dated using the Gregorian, and not the republican calendar invented by the Jacobins in 1793 (see above, p. 31).[103] Its anti-religious nature, and refusal to recognise Sundays, offended the sensibilities of the Roman Curia. For the princes of the church, religious dominance over France remained the price to be paid for a final agreement. The vague wording over the resignation of the legitimate bishops, which stated that sacrifices would be necessary in future, would never satisfy Paris. From the French point of view, *ancien régime* bishops must be removed from office, a painful action as the church considered them innocent of any wrongdoing. Ultimately, the church found it difficult to accept that it was being relegated to the private sphere. Any idea that Catholicism would be rewoven into the fabric of the French state and its official machinery was in reality unthinkable. The church was to be wholly subordinate to the state and legitimise its rule. This was a painful step which Rome never fully accepted.

Almost immediately after reading the Curia's drafts, Cacault advised Consalvi that this counter-proposal was unacceptable. He issued an official diplomatic protest against its terms.[104] Regardless, on 12 May 1801 the counter-proposal, di Pietro's notes and a covering letter from the pope were despatched to Paris with new instructions for Spina. On the very same day, the archbishop of Corinth had been summoned to the Malmaison. The first consul was in a dark mood and was looking to do battle.[105] After some initial pleasantries, Bonaparte viciously turned on the archbishop, saying that he was displeased with the court of Rome.[106] He was angry to learn that his fifth draft had not been accepted and, as Cacault had informed him, that a counter-proposal was on its way. He believed that the Curia was temporising in the hope that political disorder would strengthen its negotiating hand. The pope was praised as an individual, but deep mistrust towards the College of Cardinals was expressed. Bonaparte shouted that he knew from Cacault that in the Curia's version of the Concordat the *ancien régime* bishops were not explicitly asked to resign. He could not help but feel that the cardinals were behaving with extreme bad faith.

The restoration of Catholicism and unity with the pontiff in Rome were Napoleon's most ardent desire. However, if this could not be achieved, he would resurrect the Pragmatic Sanction of 1438. As stated in Chapter 1 (p. 16), this medieval charter, issued during the reign of Charles VII, had made the Gallican Church virtually independent of Rome.[107] This document had proclaimed the supremacy of councils over the pope, and established the king's power to appoint bishops without hindrance within the realm. Bonaparte threatened the Papacy with an independent French church, which would not be in communion with Rome. Spina tried to placate him with reassurances of the pope's genuine desire for France to return to the true faith. At this point, the first consul complained that the Holy See was in league with Protestant and Orthodox powers against the Catholic nations of Europe. The king of Sardinia had trusted Russia more than France, and had lost his provinces on the mainland. Surely the pope would not wish to risk the same fate![108] With these threats he urged Spina to write at once to Consalvi asking for greater alacrity. The poor archbishop rushed to the Hôtel de Rome and wrote to the secretary of state, begging for a positive reply. A day later Bernier too decided to write directly to Consalvi. This was a highly unusual course of action. The parish priest of Saint-Laud, in so doing, proved himself a committed adherent to the consular regime. He went so far as to suggest that, if negotiations collapsed, Napoleon would hold the cardinal secretary of state personally responsible. Bernier's exhortation was emotive:

Monseigneur, consider my reflections deeply and, without delay, or any further adjournment, act. France demands its old religion, Italy wants to preserve it, and Germany to protect it. The Papal States demand an end to their burdens, the sovereign pontiff an enlargement of his territory, and the apostolic chamber a decision on church lands. French priests, languishing in exile, want to return to the bosom of their fatherland. And so! Monseigneur, none of this can happen until the decision of the Holy See arrives! How many lost opportunities! How many souls saved, how many evils avoided, how much good done, how many obstacles surmounted, if only you work with greater haste![109]

For an ordinary priest to chastise a cardinal shows just how much Bernier's experience of civil war and collaboration with Napoleon had transformed him. He had become a leader unafraid to challenge the institution he had loyally served all his life. To end the schism of the 1790s major sacrifices would be necessary for a regenerated church in France to emerge.

The official courier failed to appear at the gates of the French capital despite Spina's fervent prayers and solicitations. On 19 May an ultimatum was delivered by Bernier to the pope's emissary stating that if within five days the papal bull approving the Concordat did not arrive, then Cacault would be recalled and ordered to head to General Murat's headquarters in Florence.[110] This threat to break off diplomatic relations with Rome seemed to hasten the point of no return. The Concordat seemed doomed, and a renewed split with the Papacy inevitable. Spina despaired of the future and remained uncertain of how to react. The next moves would take place on the other side of the Alps.

The ultimatum took nine days to reach Rome and caused the deepest consternation. Consalvi was ill with fever and received Cacault on his sickbed to discuss the situation.[111] He begged the French minister not to leave Rome: the pope would die of anguish if the negotiations collapsed.[112] Cacault could not disobey his orders; two days later he presented Bonaparte's ultimatum in an official diplomatic note, announcing that if within five days the Concordat was not ratified then diplomatic relations would cease.[113] The wily Cacault knew that it was time to take matters in hand. He decided to follow the spirit of his diplomatic mission, not just to obey the letter of his orders. His departure was delayed, and he advised the pope secretly on how to try to avoid a rupture with Paris. The situation was embarrassing: Consalvi had been identified personally by Bonaparte in correspondence as a direct hindrance to all future agreements with the Catholic Church. In response, the secretary of state offered the pope his resignation so that a candidate more agreeable to the first consul could be found. Pius VII felt that such a course of action would compromise his sovereignty, and refused the resignation of his first minister.[114]

It was decided that Consalvi would follow Cacault to Tuscany. From Florence he would demonstrate his goodwill by offering to come to Paris to conclude negotiations directly.[115] This offer to send the pope's chief minister in person to negotiate with a foreign power was without precedent. Technically, Cacault had been in breach of his orders by delaying his departure, but he was a veteran pragmatist. In persuading both Consalvi and Pius that this extraordinary journey was vital, he saved the Concordat. If one person deserves the credit for rescuing this agreement, then that man was certainly Cacault. He broke the deadlock that had emerged since February 1801 with his disobedience and original solution. On 6 June, in his own carriage, seated next to Cacault, Consalvi left Rome. His baggage was heavy, given his long journey, but heavier still was the burden on his shoulders. In his hand he held a letter of credence, written in arcane Latin and signed and sealed by the pope, bestowing on him plenipotentiary powers.[116] In comparison to Spina his powers of negotiation were vast. The cardinal secretary of state was empowered to sign and approve the Concordat on behalf of the pope. The final phase of the negotiations was now beginning.

As we have seen, Consalvi, while imprisoned by Napoleon almost a decade later, wrote his memoirs. They are grippingly narrated and filled with theatrical detail. They are, to an extent, corroborated by correspondence written at the time of the negotiations, but there is a decided tendency towards exaggeration.[117] These memoirs present the cardinal secretary of state as a reluctant negotiator who concluded a deal that was far from wholly satisfactory. There is some truth to this, but it is compromised by the benefit of hindsight. Consalvi earnestly wanted to conclude an agreement with Napoleon and, when he had done so, enthusiastically believed that he had brought religious peace to Europe.

After midnight on 20 June the cardinal's carriage and entourage arrived at the Hôtel de Rome. Although exhausted by the long journey, he was immediately briefed by Spina on the present situation. After a few hours of sleep, he was roused by Bernier, who informed him that the first consul would receive him in a formal audience at two in the afternoon.[118] He was instructed 'to come dressed as a cardinal as much as he could'. Napoleon wanted to show Europe, not to mention his own domestic public, that he had forced the pope's chief minister to come all the way to Paris.

Consalvi objected that full red robes were the standard court dress in Rome and in some European courts. Until the Concordat was ratified, and normal diplomatic relations established, he could not appear in full crimson. Instead, he wore black choir dress but with a red collar and biretta hat which was standard dress outside of ceremonial functions.[119] The Tuileries Palace was arrayed in full pomp for this diplomatic reception, with troops in gala uniform and musicians in attendance. All three chambers of Napoleon's parliament were present: the Senate, Tribunate and Corps Législatif ('Legislative Body'). Talleyrand guided the cardinal into the audience hall, where he was greeted by the first consul wearing the magnificent red and gold uniform of the head of state. According to Consalvi's memoirs, Bonaparte said to him: 'I am familiar with the reasons for your journey to France. I wish that discussions be opened immediately. I give you five days, and if on the fifth day your negotiations are not concluded you will have to return to Rome.'[120] Consalvi responded that his presence was testament to the Holy See's goodwill and genuine desire to approve a Concordat with the French Republic. A discussion ensued about the situation of religion in France and the key sticking-points in the drafts. The issue Bonaparte most resented was the close relations that the Papacy enjoyed with Russia and England. He warned that no good would come of such duplicity. They were Protestant and Orthodox heretics, who could not have Rome's best interests at heart. Consalvi was difficult to intimidate: he showed that he was open to discussion but would not capitulate without argument.

Although Napoleon had given the cardinal five days, the real deadline was set for the 14 July, the anniversary of the taking of the Bastille. The first consul had planned to publicly announce both the peace with Austria and the conclusion of a Concordat with Rome at a large diplomatic reception. This would be testament that his regime had succeeded where so many previous revolutionaries had failed. He had brought peace, religious harmony, and law and order back to France. The daily conferences between Consalvi and Bernier were to be frenetic, and all worked at breakneck speed to meet the deadline. It is unnecessary to go through the exact details of the negotiations. No fewer than four further drafts of the Concordat were produced during this time. The key sticking-points remained the status of Catholicism in France, the resignation of bishops, the oath of allegiance and the wording surrounding the pope's acceptance of the renunciation of claims over confiscated church land that had been auctioned during the 1790s.

Talleyrand had been awkward about reaching an accommodation with the Papacy throughout these months. As an apostate bishop who had consecrated the first constitutional prelates in 1791, he was an interested party in the outcome of the negotiations. The question of clerical marriage was decidedly on his agenda, as has been seen: he had recently married the wealthy English divorcee Catherine Grant. His presence in Paris had not helped the negotiation of the Concordat: he had often thrown a spanner in the works. Somewhat inexplicably, in June 1801, he left the capital and took the waters at Bourbon-l'Archambault for his poor health.[121] It is difficult to know whether this was a political illness or whether it was a genuine leave of absence. Talleyrand was rarely an individual to let an opportunity slip through his fingers. One suspects he felt that, as a renegade cleric, he would be unable to guide the discussions to his benefit. Ultimately, the Holy See was willing to forgive all priests who, because of the maelstrom of revolution, had married due to difficult circumstances. Yet, the Curia reported categorically that never in the history of the church had an ordained bishop been allowed such a dispensation. Some unordained archbishops and cardinals, most famously Cesare Borgia, had been laicised and then allowed to wed. However, Talleyrand, as the consecrated and anointed former bishop of Autun, could not be given similar permission. Most priests who had married in the extraordinary situation of revolution would be forgiven for their 'sin', but Napoleon's foreign minister remained beyond the pale. From his perspective the Concordat would prove a personal defeat.

The negotiations focused on Consalvi and Bernier's effort to reword the contentious articles of the Concordat in such a way as to make them acceptable to both parties. Like Spina before him the pope's chief minister's sense of isolation was almost unbearable. Unlike Bernier, he was not received by the first consul every evening to discuss progress. Consalvi's repeated requests to seek clarification, or further instructions from Rome, were denied. As a plenipotentiary he was deemed to be empowered to come to a final decision on the agreement. As it was the easiest one to resolve, the negotiators started with article XIII, on church property. The church could not condone or officially sanction the seizure of its lands and property. Bernier worded the text so that it stated that His Holiness and his successors would not trouble those who had purchased and acquired former church lands for the good of Catholicism in France. Consequently, it was accepted that these lands would remain in perpetuity with their new owners.

Eventually, the wording of article III, on *ancien régime* bishops, was rephrased with extreme delicacy. No direct reference was made to resignations nor to the removal of legitimate bishops from their dioceses. The article now stated that the pope would exhort the holders of French bishoprics to make every sacrifice for the good of peace and unity, including the sacrifice of their own dioceses. In case of refusal, which the Holy See did not expect, new bishops would be appointed to the government of the new dioceses created by the Concordat. While the end result was the same, the careful wording preserved the illusion that the loyal legitimate bishops would not be punished and deprived of their offices. This article was revolutionary in terms of papal monarchy, and had the unintended consequence of strengthening the pope's supremacy over the church. It affirmed, tacitly, the pope's authority to remove bishops who had committed no crime but whose removal benefited the unity and good of the church. Such powers would have been impossible during the *ancien régime* and this was certainly an important milestone towards creating an absolute, almost infallible, pope, with complete authority over the episcopacy of the entire globe. It is a decided irony that Napoleon would live to regret this step, when seven years later the pope refused to accept his appointments to French dioceses (see Chapters 6 and 7, pp. 168–9 and pp. 197–205).[122]

The question of the oath of allegiance to the Republic was likewise solved by careful wording. The church objected to any reference to the laws of the state, as these contained anti-Catholic principles, such as divorce. It was decided to resurrect the old oath that bishops had taken to the kings of France. New bishops would swear obedience to the government established by the French Constitution.[123] They also promised never to conspire against the state, nor to enter into secret negotiations with foreign powers to the detriment of the Republic. The oath was silent on the subject of those civil laws of the French state that were contrary to church teaching. The church had no intention of accepting anything contrary to its doctrines.

The real difficulty pertained to the preamble and first article. Essentially, the government wanted to avoid any direct reference to its confessional identity. The First Consul could not commit his successors to being Catholic. In contrast, the church wanted a position of privilege above other religions. There was an expectation that it would be free from government interference in terms of religious practices, dogma and teaching. Resolving this issue was going to be extremely delicate: the church could not sanction the Consulate's idea that all religions were valid and that its people were citizens first and Catholics second. Meaningful agreement on this issue proved impossible; a way out of this impasse was found through word games. The preamble of the Concordat affirmed that the pope recognised the consuls' profession of Catholicism. This wording provided an ingenious solution, as the French government was not compelled to give a written undertaking to prescribe the religion of its head of state. What Catholicism's position as the religion of the vast 'majority of the population' meant in practice was never defined.[124] Equally, the assumption that the executive power would profess the teachings of the Roman Church was something that had no basis in French law. But the preamble's ambiguity allowed for the Papacy to enter into an agreement with the French Republic.

Given these compromises, the expectation was that the Concordat's signing ceremony would take place on 13 July, in good time for the celebration the next day. The Abbé Bernier sent a cryptic note to Consalvi:

> I wish to give you notice that tonight's conference will take place at 8 p.m. at the home of Joseph Bonaparte. I will come to you at 7 p.m.. This [the attached text] is what will be presented to you initially: read it well, examine everything and above all else do not despair of anything. I have just had a long meeting with Joseph [Bonaparte] and [the jurist Emmanuel] Crétet. You are dealing with honest and reasonable men. All will go well tonight.[125]

To Consalvi's immense surprise the text presented to him was not the one to which he had agreed beforehand during negotiations. One did not need to read far to see the problem. Article I now stated that: 'The Roman, Catholic and Apostolic religion will be exercised freely in France. Its worship shall be public, and it will conform to all police regulations that the government will deem necessary.'[126]

This article was to create a new crisis that once more threatened the viability of the Concordat. The preamble had also been altered to remove any mention of the government's Catholic faith, and the pope was required in this version to confirm all new bishops immediately. Napoleon's brother Joseph, who had been delegated to sign the Concordat on his brother's behalf, was endowed with charm and natural diplomatic talent. He suggested that the team gather to work through the night to amend the text in order to make it admissible to all parties. They redacted a revised text, agreeable to all present, just in time by noon on 14 July. It was sent to Napoleon, who furiously rejected it. The first consul – according to one account shouting obscenities – ripped the revised Concordat to shreds; another telling has him throwing it into the fireplace.[127]

Despite this diplomatic failure all had to attend the gala dinner meant to celebrate both peace with Austria and with the church. As Consalvi put it, rarely did food taste so bitter. Napoleon's humour was dark with fury. As soon as he saw the cardinal secretary of state, he shouted:

> So, Monsieur Cardinal, you want a breach! I have no need of Rome. I will act alone. I have no need of the pope. If Henry VIII who had barely an eighth of my power could change the religion of his country and succeed in this endeavour, well I know how, and will be able to do the same. In changing the religion of France, I will change it in almost all of Europe, wherever the influence of my power extends. Rome will realise its loss, it will shed tears, but there will be no remedy. So, you wanted a breach: so be it, since you want it [you have it]. When are you leaving?[128]

Napoleon's ability to cause a scene was legendary and his fiery Mediterranean temper was fearsome. Towards the end of the banquet Consalvi drew all his courage and stated calmly that the first consul's attack was unfair. If he had wished for a deliberate breach would he have agreed to all articles except one? Surely this was a sign of good faith; a sign, too, that all was far from lost. Unphased, Bonaparte replied that it was all or nothing, and that the church would shed tears of blood in regret over its poor decision. According to Consalvi, the Habsburg ambassador Count Philipp von Cobenzl intervened at this point. Napoleon, seeing Cobenzl speaking with Consalvi, interrupted: 'Do not reason with a minister of the pope.' The ambassador replied that it seemed to him that the cardinal secretary of state was very much open to the possibility of dialogue. Only one article needed modification: could not a final effort be made between the commissioners to find an agreement on this final question? Napoleon allowed them to have a further meeting the next day. But as he turned his back he shouted 'But on that article I will brook no changes!'[129]

The next day the delegates met in Joseph Bonaparte's Parisian town house. For eleven hours they debated article I. These interminable controversies may now seem trivial and overcomplicated; yet at the heart of the Concordat's first article was the struggle between the modern non-confessional state and Catholic teaching and tradition. The state saw itself as supreme, and demanded the right to supervise the public worship and teachings of Catholicism in the interest of public harmony and order.[130] The Catholic Church, on the contrary, believed itself instituted of Jesus Christ and that its origins in divine revelation entitled it to preach its faith freely without external hindrance from the laity.

Near exhaustion, both parties managed to find a compromise for article I. It was now to read: 'The Roman, Catholic and Apostolic religion will be freely exercised in France. Its worship shall be public, and it will conform to those police regulations that the government will deem necessary to promote public tranquillity.'[131] The delegates understood this article to mean that after the turmoil of the Revolution the government retained the right to legislate over those areas of public worship that took place outside church buildings: that is to say, public authorities might if they saw fit restrict processions, pilgrimages, public prayers and any other exterior signs of the faith. In order to avoid anti-religious riots or disorder, the government might intervene in the interests of all citizens to pre-empt turmoil.[132]

With this modification, the document was now ready to be signed. The French Republic was represented by Joseph Bonaparte, the Abbé Bernier and the jurist Emmanuel Crétet, the Holy See by Consalvi, Spina and the theologian Carlo Caselli, who all signed this historic document. An exhausted – but pleased – Joseph Bonaparte now rushed to the Tuileries to present his brother with the finished document. Napoleon grumbled that too much had been conceded in article I, but that it would have to do. Thirteen months had passed since his meeting with Cardinal Martiniana in Vercelli.

The ratification process was going to be long-drawn-out, but this was not the church's responsibility. Consalvi had a distressing departure meeting with Napoleon at which he was informed that some of the schismatic constitutional clergy would need to be appointed to positions within the newly reorganised French church. Consalvi protested that this was not part of the agreement, but the first consul insisted that it was the only means of healing the divisions of the 1790s.[133] An amalgamated clerical elite, made up of those who had followed and those who had defied the French Revolution, was the sole means of forgetting the past and moving forward. The cardinal secretary of state said that the Papacy would require some declaration of retraction, penitence or unity with Rome before accepting constitutionals back into communion.[134] The government also intimated that police regulations would be issued concerning public worship. There was a discussion about whether the papal brief ratifying the Concordat could be agreed and drafted in Paris in advance. This request was for Consalvi impossible. No pope could accept interference in the drafting of official briefs, bulls and encyclicals. The meeting was tense but cordial; both parties said farewell in the hope that they had achieved a historic milestone. On 25 July Consalvi departed Paris. He had spent four very fraught weeks at the heart of the French Republic, but he felt he was bringing home a good deal to the church for final ratification.

In early August the carriage carrying the cardinal secretary of state wheeled back into the eternal city.[135] Rome's state courier had already brought the signed version of the Concordat to Pius VII who had charged a commission of cardinals and theologians to examine the treaty.[136] Most were urging the pope to ratify the document, but with conditions. Of the five theologians, three were in favour of ratification, while two opposed it. According to Cacault, Consalvi, seeing the danger that his work might be rejected, pushed the pope to work quickly and summon the College of Cardinals to vote on the treaty in a solemn congregation.[137] Pius agreed, and the cardinals present in Rome gathered in their crimson robes on 11 August 1801 to vote on each article of the Concordat with the French Republic.[138] Each tally was tense, especially as the pope and Consalvi knew that article I, on worship being subject to police regulations, would make ratification difficult. The secretary of state spoke at length and persuasively about the reasons that had pushed him to sign the treaty. He admitted it was imperfect, but that it was a good basis on which to start rebuilding the church in France. As each cardinal voted individually in the congregation everyone held their breath. The result for article I was fifteen in favour to ten against.[139] Di Pietro, the patriarch of Jerusalem and secretary to the congregation, wondered bitterly whether realpolitik or a true appreciation of the theological implications of the text had guided the cardinals' votes. On 15 August 1801 Pius VII ratified the Concordat. Many hoped that this would be the beginning of a new era of harmonious relations between church and state in France. Cacault commented that never in all the annals of history had a pope moved with greater haste on a diplomatic negotiation.[140]

The ball was now firmly in the first consul's court, but he was to move extremely slowly in getting his legislature to ratify his agreement with the church. The parliamentary session was due to start in November. Two chambers would be involved in the ratification process. The Tribunate would debate the Concordat, and present an opinion on whether it should be approved. The Corps Législatif would then vote simply to adopt or to reject the text.[141] Given that the chambers were populated with significant factions of former Jacobins, constitutional clergy and some radical intellectuals, it was feared that ratification might prove difficult. The first signs as the session opened were not promising. Charles-François Dupuis, a renegade former priest and an enemy of all religions, was elected president of the Corps Législatif.[142] The peace treaties with Austria and England passed, but to Napoleon's immense irritation the vote was not unanimous, with one or two dissenting voices. The early years of the Consulate were a frenetic age of reform, and the executive sent to its legislature mountains of bills to ratify. With potential opposition, the government felt unable to present the Concordat to the chambers.

The solution was to purge the assemblies of Napoleon's political opponents. The Constitution written after the Brumaire coup specified that during Year X (September 1801–September 1802 in the republican calendar) one-fifth of the chambers would be renewed. Most understood this to mean that newly elected deputies would take their seats at the end of the republican calendar year, that is after 22 September 1802. Bonaparte, keen to keep the momentum going and to rid himself of his bitterest opponents, persuaded the Council of State to interpret the Constitution so that new deputies could be appointed at any time in Year X. Cleverly, Napoleon did not list those to be removed, but rather specified those deputies who could remain until the next session. He then chose candidates for election who were known supporters of the government. With the number of republican anti-religious candidates reduced significantly, a new parliamentary session was scheduled to take place between 5 April and 21 May 1802.[143]

The government chose the jurist Jean-Étienne-Marie Portalis to present the government's case in support of the Concordat.[144] On 5 April Portalis spoke for two hours before both chambers. He praised the beneficent effects of religion on societies, and spoke of how wise governments nurtured private morality. The impression was given that the Catholic Church, like all other religions, had accepted subordination to the state. From the rostrum the old conflict of the Civil Constitution was declared dead. The pope, by recognising the Republic and accepting the terms of the Concordat, was now a friend. He and the clergy would no longer exert a dangerous subversive influence on French politics. This Concordat made religion an instrument of social stability, and legitimated the state further in the eyes of the population. This shrewd jurist advised acceptance in the strongest terms.[145] A committee from the Tribunate discussed the treaty in private and recommended its acceptance. This chamber proposed ratification, with seventy-eight in favour to seven against. The Corps Législatif then approved the final ratification with 228 votes in favour to only 21 against.[146] After twenty-two months of negotiation, and convoluted ratification processes, the Concordat was now accepted by both church and state. It was an immense achievement. But there were dark clouds on the horizon.

Very soon the church would cry bad faith as events moved in unexpected directions. Indeed, the text ratified by the French parliament included seventy-seven organic articles which had not been part of the original negotiation. They had been appended to the final ratified text of the Concordat without any consultation of ecclesiastical officials.[147] The initial appointments to dioceses included constitutional clergy despite Rome's protests. More seriously still, little effort was made to discuss the territory of the Holy See. The return of the Papal Legations of Romagna and the question of the Comtat Venaissin was not on the table. In Rome the disappointment was palpable; the Concordat should not, however, be analysed with the benefit of hindsight. After a decade of intractable religious turmoil, any settlement with the Catholic Church seemed at the time a miracle. All involved in the negotiations would receive enormous rewards. Spina and Caselli were both made cardinals and were eventually given the prosperous archdioceses of Genoa and Parma to govern.[148] Bernier, the former warrior priest, was rewarded with the bishopric of Orléans, fulfilling his lifelong ambition to become a prelate. Throughout the rest of his existence he would remain one of Bonaparte's most committed ecclesiastical collaborators. He was raised to the status of cardinal *in pectore* by Pius VII. This was a secret elevation to the crimson often made by popes for controversial candidates or for when the College of Cardinals had no vacancies for voting members. (The practice continues to this day.) Sadly for Bernier, he died in 1806 before his elevation to a prince of the church was made public.[149]

The truest symbol of peace with the church had arrived in Rome some months before the ratification of the Concordat by the Corps Législatif in April 1802.[150] It took the form of a coffin, carried with great pomp by a guard of honour including representatives of the French Republic. Inside were the earthly remains of Pope Pius VI, who as we have seen had died a French prisoner in Valence in

1799.[151] On 17 February 1802 his coffin solemnly re-entered Rome through Porta del Popolo. A huge procession followed the remains through the streets of the eternal city. Cannon salvos saluted the dead pontiff's return to his final resting place. The funeral in Saint Peter's was solemn, a celebration not only of the return of the former pope's mortal remains but of peace in Europe. It seemed to promise that never again would a pope be kidnapped and die a captive. This assumption would prove only partially correct.[152]

# — FOUR —
# CROWNING CHARLEMAGNE
## NAPOLEON'S CORONATION, 1802–05

On 25 March 1802 the French Revolutionary Wars ended. After almost a decade of conflict, France signed a peace treaty with Great Britain in Amiens.[1] Armed struggle ceased on the European continent, and lasting tranquillity seemed to have been achieved. Bonaparte was at the zenith of his popularity. His propaganda machine portrayed him as a peacemaker, a restorer of public order. According to the regime, he had brought an end to the chaos of the Revolution. Not all of those who lived through the consular regime shared this positive assessment. A few weeks later, on 18 April 1802, General Moreau was pacing up and down the Tuileries' terrace smoking a cigar, visibly disgusted and cursing under his breath. As already discussed in the previous chapter (p. 77), the victor of Hohenlinden had been, at best, a lukewarm supporter of the first consul.[2] He distrusted Bonaparte, and wondered if he was a sincere republican, a point of view that was shared by a significant number of other officers and soldiers. Although these military men wore their resplendent uniforms, this day would prove difficult to stomach. Moreau had instructed his wife to cause as much mischief as possible.[3] It was Easter Day. Bonaparte had decided that the most important feast in the Christian calendar was the perfect moment to rejoice, not only in the peace with Britain, but also in the publication of the Concordat, and in the restoration of Catholicism to France.[4] A solemn paschal Mass, followed by a *Te Deum* at Notre-Dame, would celebrate these notable achievements. All members of the government, senior civil servants and deputies of the parliamentary chambers were to attend.

The prelate who presided over the ceremony was Cardinal Giovanni Battista Caprara Montecuccoli, an affable and intelligent Bolognese aristocrat, who had spent most of his career as a diplomat. Although Caprara was sixty-nine and in poor health, Bonaparte had requested that he be appointed papal legate *a latere* to France. The position was akin to that of special envoy. Not since Cardinal Reginald Pole's mission to restore Catholicism to England during the reign of

Mary Tudor had a clergyman wielded so much authority.[5] Pius VII had delegated many of his apostolic powers to this cardinal to facilitate the implementation of the Concordat: Caprara was given a list with no fewer than twenty-two prerogatives which the pope had entrusted to him as legate.[6] The papal legate, to all intents and purposes, was the pope in France. He could annul marriages, lift clergymen from their vows, forgive constitutional clergy for their schismatic pasts and absolve myriad sins. Though his powers were not unlimited, he had been temporarily authorised to invest and confirm newly appointed bishops, a prerogative usually jealously guarded by Saint Peter's successor. Pius's decision to authorise his legate to wield supreme authority demonstrated that returning France to the Catholic fold was, for Rome, the utmost priority.

Caprara was no stranger to controversial missions. During the 1770s he had been one of the first papal emissaries to Britain since the seventeenth century, and had been presented incognito to George III.[7] Here he had urged greater toleration of Catholics and sought to establish better relations. He had also served as papal nuncio to Lucerne, Cologne and Vienna, where he learned the intricacies of diplomacy at the court of the Holy Roman Emperor. Caprara was an innate ambassador for whom conciliation, concession and compromise were instinctual. He had met Napoleon during the first Italian campaign and was well-qualified for the delicate role of papal legate to France. However, unlike Consalvi or Spina, Caprara was intimidated by the first consul and found it difficult to resist French demands. The papal court would live to regret not sending a more headstrong candidate to Paris.

The solemn Easter Mass of 1802 preoccupied the consular regime, who feared it would give rise to opposition. Fouché, as police minister, sent disheartening reports of just how many important generals, who had fought alongside Bonaparte on so many campaigns, had criticised the peace with the church. On the day itself, General André Masséna pushed several priests out of his way as he moved down the nave of Notre-Dame.[8] More hopeful signs emerged from the monarchist right. The writer and royalist François-René de Chateaubriand celebrated this paschal Mass as the culmination of the rebirth of Catholicism in France. He had just published his great work, the *Génie du christianisme*, an ode to the church's positive social role for almost two millennia.[9] It was a sign of how times had changed. Now, the government encouraged rather than persecuted authors loyal to the church.

The ceremony, however, could not hide from sight the scars of revolution. The cathedral of Notre-Dame, the metropolitan church of Paris, had emerged from the 1790s badly damaged and in a state of deep neglect. A decade of revolutionary iconoclasm had deeply compromised the fabric of the building. The statues of the kings of Judah on its façade had been destroyed in the maelstrom that followed the fall of the French monarchy in 1792. Many of its precious relics and treasures had also been looted. By 1802, it was in need of urgent repair, along with the restoration of its nave. Teams of builders, masons and glaziers were to work furiously to make the building serviceable as a place of worship.[10] The great bells of its towers, which for centuries had called Parisians to prayer, had been silenced during the revolutionary wars, and these great drones had to be recast in time for the ceremony. After a decade of eerie Jacobin silence, the soundscape of Paris resounded anew to the chimes of the great bells of its cathedral.[11] Inside the building, tapestries and other decorations hid from sight the damage done to the side chapels along with the graffiti from the anti-Christian festivals of the 1790s.

According to press and police reports, large numbers of Parisians were pleased that the religious upheavals of the past appeared to have come to an end. They turned out in crowds to celebrate the dual peace with Great Britain and the church.[12] Many, however, especially members of the army, observed a different development with concern. The previous revolutionary governments had been noted for their informality and lack of pomp. Initially the consular regime had followed this republican template. However, as the government became more stable, a change in tone was perceived. The first consul's household and the Tuileries Palace became organised along more monarchical lines.[13] Lavish court uniforms were introduced, and intricate ceremonial routines guided the rhythm of life in Bonaparte's court. On Easter Day 1802 it was decided that Louis XVI's coronation coach would be restored in order to carry the first consul in triumph to Notre-Dame. Jean de Dieu-Raymond de Boisgelin de Cucé, the new archbishop of Tours, was invited to preach the Easter sermon in Notre-Dame. Boisgelin was a man of venerable age and distinguished aristocratic pedigree, who had given the homily for Louis XVI's coronation in Reims in 1774.[14] He was among the *ancien régime* bishops who had willingly resigned their old sees (Boisgelin's had been that of Aix-en-Provence) and rallied to the Consulate. From his exile in London in 1801 he had transferred his allegiance from Louis XVIII to the first consul.[15] The return of such an important cleric from the past monarchical regime was for Napoleon a propaganda coup.

The solemn paschal Mass in Notre-Dame in 1802 was not just a celebration of the peace: it also showcased Bonaparte's role as the restorer of order and religion in

France. He claimed to have achieved in less than two years what the Revolution had failed to do in a decade. There was one concession he categorically refused to give Rome, however: he would not confess his sins and would not receive communion from Cardinal Caprara. As the head of a modern secular state he would never recognise the church's jurisdiction over his conscience. Catholicism could legitimate his power, but would never share in it. There has been a tendency to see this as evidence of Bonaparte's atheism or indifference in matters of religious ritual.[16] It is difficult to tell what he really thought about his spiritual heritage. A non-religious person would have had little difficulty in receiving the Host: after all, for the atheist it is but a wafer. However, Napoleon did once say that his first communion had been the happiest day of his childhood.[17] There were probably residual Catholic sensibilities that made him hesitant of taking the Host, which could only be received by a penitent Christian in a state of grace and which symbolised complete acceptance of the church's teachings. Such a spiritual commitment would have conflicted with his duties as the head of a post-revolutionary state.

The day, though initially filled with tension due to the presence of dubious military officers, was quite the spectacle. Napoleon's wife Joséphine was surprised to find Madame Moreau occupying her seat. After a minor scene, Madame Bonaparte managed to have her rival ejected.[18] But such hitches did not detract from the *éclat* of the ceremony. For the first time in a decade Catholics and their prelates, wearing their full pontifical robes, were free to worship their God and celebrate their rituals unmolested by republican authorities. The culmination of the day was the solemn *Te Deum* sung at the end of Mass. This prayer, composed by Saint Ambrose of Milan during the fourth century, was Catholicism's quintessential hymn of praise.[19] The task of setting this Ambrosian hymn to contemporary music was given to the Neapolitan composer Giovanni Paisiello. Hundreds of choristers from the national conservatory were engaged to sing, and two orchestras to perform, the ancient Latin words of the *Te Deum*.[20] One group of musicians was conducted by the diehard republican Étienne Nicolas Méhul, who had composed the *Chant du départ* in 1794, the great revolutionary war anthem of the previous decade. Now, baton in hand, he presided over one of the most traditional of Christian hymns. On Easter Day, 18 April 1802, the consular government, through Catholic ritual, attempted symbolically to heal the divisions of the Revolution.

Not all were convinced by what they had witnessed, as Napoleon discovered that evening. He commented to General Antoine Guillaume Delmas that the ceremony had been beautiful. The crotchety veteran replied witheringly: 'You just need to replace our [sword] straps with rosary beads. As for France, how can she console herself over the loss of a million men, which she sacrificed uselessly to put an end to the farces which you have just resurrected.'[21] Furious at such insubordination, Napoleon relieved Delmas of his command and sent him into internal exile.[22] But the general's angry comment demonstrated the extent to which republicans who had supported Napoleon's Brumaire coup felt betrayed by the peace with the church. In many ways the Concordat with Rome, like the peace of Amiens with Britain, was hardly permanent, but a fragile truce.

For the church, the process of communicating the terms of the Concordat to the *ancien régime* bishops was agonising. On 15 August 1801, the feast of the assumption of the Virgin Mary (and also Napoleon's birthday), Pius VII issued the solemn brief *Tam multa*, a revolutionary document, the contents of which, although composed in the traditional courtly Latin of the Curia, was remarkable.[23] The supreme head of the church exhorted all *ancien régime* bishops to resign their dioceses for the good of the church. Although the document called for bishops to resign willingly, it did imply that the reorganisation of the French church was going to occur irrespective of their consent. Following Bernier's advice, the brief cited the example of the Donatist bishops of the fifth century, who had resigned their dioceses for the good of the church (see above, p. 71). The pope also reminded his bishops of a promise made in September 1791 by senior Gallican bishops to vacate their sees if the Holy See demanded it.

Although the brief was couched in the language of tradition and legalism, its content was revolutionary. For the first time since antiquity, a Roman pontiff was to purge an entire episcopacy in order resurrect a national church. Those clergymen of more Jansenist leanings had demanded a more democratic church, one in which councils took the most important decisions. Given these eighteenth-century tendencies towards conciliarism, *Tam multa* came as a surprise.[24] The Concordat headed in the opposite direction, reinforcing the pope's monarchical powers over the clergy. During the autumn of 1801 Michele di Pietro, patriarch of Jerusalem, as the head of the Curia's extraordinary congregation on the French church, wrote to all papal nuncios across Europe instructing them to compile lists of the addresses of all Gallican bishops in exile. Few *ancien régime* prelates would meekly accept the brief as a *fait accompli*. A group of ultra-Gallican prelates in London protested furiously against *Tam multa*: they denied the Papacy's right to compel them to resign, and vindicated the liberties of their national church against the encroachments of Rome.[25] Others, like the duke-bishop of Langres, worded their resignation letter so as to make them conditional.[26] He stated that he would resign willingly once a new incumbent was selected for his diocese. Langres had misunderstood the situation completely: his response was judged unacceptable by the Vatican. The bishops of the *ancien régime* were resigning from dioceses that no longer existed; in fact the Concordat had abolished all 139 dioceses of the old order.

Perhaps the most emotive resignation letter came from Aymar Claude de Nicolaï, bishop of Béziers. He refused to resign to the pope but instead wrote to Louis XVIII on 29 August 1802, offering his resignation to the head of the dynasty which had nominated him to his diocese.[27] Others used emotional blackmail as a tactic, knowing that it would upset the pope. Indeed, the bishops of Pamiers and La Rochelle reminded Pius VII of the many church martyrs who had died during the Revolution.[28] For them this impious treaty made peace with murderers and the worst enemies of religion. Not all resignation letters were hostile: those of Cardinal Rohan and the ecclesiastical electors of the Holy Roman Empire were complex for technical reasons. These princes resigned their French dioceses, but retained all benefices within Germany.[29] A principle emerged that French bishops should preside over French Catholics. This notion, that bishops should hold sway over congregations who shared their ethnicity, had always made the church uneasy. After all, was it not a universal institution, whose mission was to care for the spiritual well-being of all humanity rather than catering to specific national groupings?

By early 1802 Rome began to tally the numbers of resignations against the refusals to do so. According to the figures in the Vatican Archives, by April, of the ninety-four surviving Gallican bishops, only forty-nine had willingly relinquished their dioceses; the other forty-five had refused.[30] Even allowing for a margin of error in the arithmetic (and some resignations did not arrive until late in 1803) this was certainly far from ideal for the pope.[31] These episcopal irredentists allowed for the emergence of a 'Petite Église' ('Little Church') that recognised neither the consular church founded by Napoleon nor the authority of the Papacy.[32] These Gallican Catholics were a minority movement, but they did prosper in rural areas, especially in the Lyonnais and around Angoulême.[33] Their continuing existence showed just how difficult it was to heal the schism created by the French Revolution.

In the short term, the attempt to force the *ancien régime* episcopate to recognise the post-revolutionary world was a draw at best. Some divisions, rather than disappearing beneath the authority of the Concordat, hardened. The situation became fraught with the question of the appointment of candidates to the sixty new French dioceses created in 1801.[34] Essentially, the first consul's nominations privileged new men without previous episcopal experience. Exactly half of those appointed were clergymen who had survived the Revolution uncompromised by its politics, while eighteen were chosen from among the old Gallican bishops as a concession to the Papacy. The final twelve nominees were to prove controversial. These were men who had taken the oath required by the Civil Constitution of the Clergy.

As stated in the previous chapter (p. 73), this policy of amalgamating the winners and losers of the French Revolution into a composite elite mirrored what had occurred in secular government after the Brumaire coup. The regime created by Bonaparte wanted to transcend the divisions of the past and move beyond ideology. Indeed, Napoleon had warned Consalvi that this would be the case during the negotiations over the Concordat. Nevertheless, the church remained outraged, as theological rigour and clerical allegiance were not concepts it could easily discard. These wayward prelates could only be confirmed in their dioceses if they admitted and publicly retracted their past errors.[35] Ultimately, these bishops from the 1790s remained traitorous apostates in the eyes of Rome.

The constitutional clergy loyal to the Revolution issued a declaration, drafted by the ministry of religion in Paris, stating that they accepted the Concordat and that they had always recognised the spiritual supremacy of the pope. Cardinal Caprara deemed this document to be insufficient. He refused to invest such clergymen, and would not confirm their election to their dioceses. With mechanical predictability, the government threatened that this would cause a breach with Rome and an end to diplomatic relations with the Holy See. The ever-resourceful Bernier was summoned to resolve the impasse. Now bishop of Orléans, he had gained the status, prestige and power he had coveted for so long. Bernier advised that he and the bishop of Vannes, under the guidance of Portalis, now Bonaparte's minister of religions, should meet in private with the twelve constitutionals individually.

Each candidate would be asked to explain their past schism and then retract all errors. Caprara insisted that reports of these meetings and retractions should be published in the state newspaper, the *Moniteur*. Bernier, after consulting Portalis on these requests, reported back to the legate. In his presence most of the constitutionals had broken down in tears, admitted their errors and retracted their schismatic oaths. Caprara's doubts sufficiently assuaged by these reassurances, he confirmed the twelve constitutional bishops. The Curia in Rome was furious and felt that Caprara had proved invertebrate in the face of governmental pressure.[36] Soon these former constitutionals demonstrated through their behaviour that they were unrepentant, and indeed their pastoral letters vindicated their loyalty to the Revolution.[37] They claimed to have been always loyal to both France and the Papacy. Of all the things that were to infuriate the Curia in Rome, the presence of unrepentant schismatics among the French episcopacy was among the greatest embarrassments.[38] Vatican theologians deemed that the private interviews conducted by Bernier were deficient, and that a full public retraction was needed.

Despite these ongoing tensions, the period between 1802 and 1806 is generally seen as one of relative harmony in Franco-papal relations. There is some truth to this, but several crises did disturb this time of apparent tranquillity. After Easter 1802, Napoleon demanded that France be awarded an appropriate number of cardinals to sit in the Sacred College in Rome. In a letter sent on 14 June, Napoleon demanded no fewer than seven, which would equal the number that had been bestowed on the Habsburg emperor.[39] The officials in the Vatican replied that France already had four cardinals, the exiles Maury, Rohan, La Rochefoucauld and Montmorency. The government icily retorted that, by their emigration, they had rendered themselves stateless: the émigré bishops were no longer French. Pius VII reacted by complaining about the behaviour of the constitutionals and their failure to repent in a genuine way. Nevertheless, he did concede that the first consul's request for more cardinals was not unreasonable.[40] Currently there were only five vacancies which, in principle, had been filled already. The French government would have to be patient. But, the pope observed, with gallows humour, as twenty-three cardinals were in their eighties it would probably not be too long before vacancies emerged.

The pope expected in return that the first consul would reward the church and guarantee the integrity of the Papal States in the same way as Charlemagne had done. As already noted, Pius had elevated Bernier to the crimson privately, knowing that this would please Napoleon.[41] In early July it was decided that five cardinals would be allotted to the French Republic. By December the list was finalised: it included Napoleon's half-uncle Joseph Fesch, the second consul's brother Étienne Hubert de Cambacérès, Boisgelin, archbishop of Tours, and Jean-Baptiste de Belloy, archbishop of Paris. Bonaparte's decision to elevate a family member within the church was in keeping with his Italo-Corsican roots, roots that Chiaramonti, as an Italian, well understood. In their world family members were an asset and a repository of trust that should not be squandered. Fesch, the younger half-brother of Napoleon's mother Letizia, was a genuine priest, who, after a brief interlude in business during the Revolution, had kept his vocation. Although loyal to his family, he did possess a tendency towards pedantry, a trait that frustrated his nephew. Fesch also often found himself undecided as to where his ultimate loyalties lay: were they with God or with the Bonaparte family? It was a dilemma he never resolved, to the extreme irritation of Napoleon.

The final cardinal on the list was selected internally by the Curia. Their choice fell on the aristocratic Alphonse-Hubert de Latier de Bayanne, an auditor of the Holy Rota (that is to say a canon lawyer-magistrate on a Roman ecclesiastical tribunal).[42] As previously explained (p. 97), without any vacancies Bernier could only become a cardinal through a process of nomination known as *in pectore*.[43] It is unclear whether Bernier was aware of this deal. The crimson robes and membership of the Sacred College would have been the culmination of all his ambitions. The clever young seminarian from Angers had risen through sheer talent, not to mention savage ambition, to the very summits of the Roman hierarchy.

Resurrecting Catholicism in France was a difficult and unsteady process. The new church that emerged after 1801 bore scant resemblance to the *ancien régime* institutions it supplanted. First and foremost, there was an acute shortage of priests. This was not due to a lack of vocations, but to the destruction of seminaries which had taken place during the 1790s and which meant that opportunities to train for the priesthood were now limited. Barely 1,000 seminarians graduated yearly to the priesthood. Second, in many communities scattered across France, a decade of revolution had bred indifference towards spiritual matters. Furthermore, the monastic orders, except for a few teaching and hospital congregations, were not re-established. This all served to create a shortfall of between 80,000 and 100,000 clergy of both sexes. According the historian Jean Leflon, the secular clergy that ministered directly to parishes was less than half the size of that during the *ancien régime*, its numbers hovering around 35,000 priests.[44] More than 80 per cent of these clerics were over the age of fifty.

The finest minds and theologians of the Gallican Church had been scattered throughout Europe in exile. A notable exception was to be found in the courageous Abbé Jacques-André Emery of Saint-Sulpice, a brilliant teacher and theologian. Once the archbishop of Paris had fled into exile, Emery had exercised episcopal powers as vicar-general of this archdiocese throughout the 1790s, and had in many ways become the clandestine leader of the Gallican Church through its darkest hour.[45] It was a miracle he survived the ordeal. He bemoaned the collapse in the quality of ecclesiastical teaching across France: those priests who had survived the Revolution were far from the best, while the constitutional clergy ordained during the 1790s lacked legitimacy and had received a lamentable education. They were viewed with contempt by their non-juring colleagues, who viewed their continued priesthood as a scandal. The Concordat remoulded Catholicism socially as well as politically. As Roger Price has shown, the French church, throughout the nineteenth century, became more middle-class and less patrician.[46] Ministerial lists of vacant parishes were kept by Portalis and his civil servants, and, unsurprisingly, cosmopolitan and rich postings were filled easily, while tiny and isolated rural parishes remained without a pastor; the aristocracy and the wealthy still coveted bishoprics, but they seemed unwilling to pay the price of ministering to poor peasants in obscurity in order to rise to the top.

Forgetting the schism of 1790 was easier said than done. Its wounds resurfaced cyclically. Refractory and constitutional clergy continued to fight old battles with undiminished rancour. The issue of constitutional bishops had been resolved to the satisfaction of the government in Paris, but what to do with those ordinary priests loyal to the French Revolution, or – worse – married, was delegated to the discretion of local bishops and prefects.[47] Some, like cardinals Fesch and Cambacérès, showed themselves hostile to the old constitutionals and demanded humiliating retractions from those eligible for parish service.[48] Many clergy who had not sworn the oath to the Civil Constitution in 1791, but who had sworn the oath of hatred of monarchy in 1797, or the oath to the Brumaire Constitution in 1800, were unfairly included among the constitutionals.[49] They, with much justification, remonstrated that theirs was a case apart. Such pettiness led to a disunited clergy that found it difficult to recreate the corporate identity which had been a hallmark of the First Estate before 1789. French bishops and priests became dependent on leadership from Rome in ways which would have been unthinkable in the past.

The question of those clergymen and women who had married during the Terror was difficult to resolve. There were substantial regional differences, but many of these unions were born of convenience rather than being genuine love matches.[50] Leflon identifies a number of clergymen in their thirties who, during the 1790s, married their sixty-year-old housekeepers.[51] While there is no accounting for taste, one does suspect that such marriages were contrived by clergymen in order to keep revolutionary authorities off their backs. In other cases, priests did cause genuine scandal by bringing their wives to Mass and seating them in the pews.[52] Dealing with the issue of married clergy would keep Cardinal Caprara, along with the secretary of his legation, Monsignor Giuseppe Antonio Sala, busy for the better part of six years. Revolution had forced significant numbers of priests and nuns to make choices they normally would never have made. Allowing them some peace and forgiveness, after the turmoil they had experienced, was a priority for Rome. A return to normality was the illusory goal of the Concordat, but the more the Curia pursued this target the more distant it seemed to become.

Dispiritingly, the new French church saw past recriminations erupt easily. In some dioceses, especially those held by former constitutional bishops, accusations were rife that such prelates favoured their former revolutionary brethren.[53] Rome kept a close eye on them and transmitted litanies of complaints on their behaviour to Minister Portalis in Paris. In some cases, when it became known that a priest had sworn the oath of 1791, masses and confessionals remained empty. The constitutionals who had been loyal to the Revolution and had stayed in their parishes throughout the 1790s might well complain that they were more sinned against that sinning. But their ultramontane colleagues saw their betrayal of Rome as unforgivable. A conflict occurred in Rouen between 1802 and 1805 between Cardinal Cambacérès, the city's archbishop, and Jacques Claude Beugnot, prefect of the department of Seine-Inférieure. They were at daggers drawn over the cardinal's refusal to employ constitutional clergy for the parishes of his archdiocese.[54] The situation became so poisonous that Beugnot sought a transfer. What *amalgame* had achieved for the French government's civilian bureaucracy (see above, p. 73) failed in the ecclesiastical realm. The Consulate could not impose easy reconciliation.

The legacy of the 1790s cast a long shadow over the post-Concordat church and sowed much division. Despite Napoleon and Pius's best intentions, the settlement failed to create a completely harmonious clerical establishment. Nevertheless, the new ecclesiastical institution born in 1801 did usher in several irreversible changes. The priest of the *ancien régime* had been a privileged lord, above and separate from his community. He was the recognised representative of the First Estate and was legally distinct, in terms of the privileges he enjoyed, from the peasants and commoners to whom he ministered. He was implicated deeply in the worldly power structures of the Gallican Church. The priests that emerged after the Concordat of 1801 were generally less privileged and were subject to the criminal and civil laws of the state, like everybody else. Indeed, the failure to grant legal immunity to the clergy was a sore point for Rome. One could speculate that the poorer-quality education of rural priests probably made them more sympathetic to folk beliefs and superstitions than had been the intellectually brilliant seminarians who had graduated from Saint-Sulpice during the eighteenth century.[55] Certainly, this newfound attachment to communities, and their most fervently held beliefs, became a source of strength for the church. It would serve Catholics well in what was to be a decade of crisis.

This depiction of the French clergy after the Concordat inadequately reflects the great regional diversity and complex realities that characterised the over 40,000 parishes that stretched across France. Yet, for this new church born of the Concordat, now shorn of its wealth and power, it was back to basics on so many levels. The church, through the cataclysm of revolution, rediscovered its social vocation and resilience. The nobility and monarchy had collapsed with unnerving rapidity a decade earlier, whereas the church, through its underground capillaries and clandestine networks, survived. Religious opposition had given the politicians in Paris many headaches: atavistic beliefs could not simply be legislated away.[56] Throughout the 1790s the clergy could not communicate easily with its émigré bishops, who had sought shelter in the distant courts of Europe. In their stead, apostolic delegates from Rome co-ordinated their activities, and they thus learned to look across the Alps rather than to Paris, Lyon or Reims for leadership. The thirty new bishops appointed in 1802 had lived through this unsettling experience. They had little nostalgia for the Gallicanism of 1682.[57] Their loyalties were bound firmly to the pope in Rome. This point cannot be stressed enough: the paradox of the Concordat was that, despite Bonaparte's intentions, it did not create a loyal, well-policed and state-sponsored church. Instead, the ecclesiastical establishment, risen from the ashes of the *ancien régime*, was ultramontane to its core. By using the pope's authority to eliminate 130 Gallican bishoprics, Napoleon had manifestly shown that the French church was subject to the pope's authority. This surge in papalism, within France, would haunt Napoleon as the decade inexorably rolled onwards.

The key bone of contention pitting the modern French imperial state against the 'universal' Catholic Church concerned the nature of the Concordat. For Rome it was an emergency measure that reflected the extraordinary circumstances in which France had found itself. This treaty was a beginning – an incentive – in rebuilding one of the great regional churches in Europe from the ground up. The Papacy longed for the gradual re-creation of the equal partnership embodied in the alliance of throne and altar. This sentiment was opposed to that of the consular regime, which desired an unequal partnership between church and state. Napoleon may have had some residual attachments to the faith of his youth, but the modern state was his true religion. His view was that the Concordat defined clearly the primacy of the state over the church. What had worked so well for France was equally applicable to the rest of Europe. Indeed, this treaty served as a template for inter-faith relations throughout the period. Over the first decade of the nineteenth century, Concordat-like agreements were concluded with the Lutherans, Calvinists and Jews who lived under French hegemony.[58] The Concordat was a monument to French civilisation, intended very much for export.

Piedmont, in north-western Italy, was annexed formally to France in 1802. To the great surprise of the Curia, the provisions of the Concordat were extended unilaterally to this corner of Italy. The theologians and cardinals protested vociferously that, as the Piedmontese Church had not suffered any disruption during the Revolution, it should be exempt from the provisions of the Concordat.[59] The French ignored such remonstrances and redrew the diocesan boundaries, confiscated monasteries and reduced the number of parishes in the region. The Concordat, it became clear, was not a unique arrangement, but had become the blueprint for French imperial hegemony over religion. The Piedmontese case was not to be the last. In January 1802 those areas of Lombardy and Romagna under French influence were converted into a satellite state called the Italian Republic. Although nominally autonomous from France, the president of this state was Napoleon, while a French army of occupation was positioned within its borders. To the horror of Rome, organic laws, similar to those in force in France, were issued by the pro-French government in Milan.[60] Cunningly, Napoleon suggested that the best solution for the church to solve its disagreement with his satellite state was to negotiate a separate Concordat.

The newly elevated Cardinal di Pietro, on Pius VII's behalf, argued with conviction that the Lombard Church, the second richest in Christendom, had not suffered any disruption comparable to that of the church in France.[61] He and his theologians contended that the *ancien régime* structures of ecclesiastical life should be left to continue unmolested. He conceded without hesitation that the Habsburg emperor's former right to nominate bishops in Lombardy could be transferred to Napoleon as president of the Italian Republic. However, he hesitated in granting this right for Bologna, Ferrara and Ravenna: the Papacy still coveted these former Legations. To accept the Republic's right to nominate bishops in Romagna was akin to renouncing claims to these territories forever.[62] For Bonaparte an informal arrangement was unsatisfactory: he wanted negotiations to be opened. The Curia agreed, but did so reluctantly, sensing a trap. Cardinal Caprara was empowered by Rome to negotiate with Ferdinando Marescalchi, the foreign minister of the Italian Republic.[63] The compromises and discussions over the Italian Concordat were almost as long and as complicated as those of 1801. By mid-1802, despite growing disgruntlement in Rome, Pius remained remarkably optimistic. He still believed an entente had been established with Paris. He wrote to Napoleon, warmly suggesting that, if the first consul intended to visit Milan, he should include Rome in his itinerary.[64] Napoleon's actions were to shape profoundly the eternal city and the church. It was a decided irony that he never took up Pius's invitation.

The organic laws of the Italian Republic reduced the number of parishes, cathedral chapters, monasteries and diocesan properties, while priests were placed under government tutelage and subject to police powers.[65] If the church wanted these regulations removed, then it would have to agree to a separate Concordat for the north Italian territory. Bernier was asked to send to the pope a detailed justification of why an Italian Concordat was essential. He argued that if the church negotiated with the Republic, many of its properties in Italy would not be confiscated and sold at auction, as had happened in France.[66] In these negotiations Napoleon tried to make it seem as if he was sympathetic in comparison to his vice-president, Francesco Melzi d'Eril, who was portrayed as deeply anticlerical.[67] In reality Melzi and Napoleon shared the same vision: both wanted religion to serve the state, and not vice versa. From September 1802 to October 1803 a host of draft treaties and counter-proposals made their way across the Alps.[68] A state courier, as always, braved the elements to bring these vital documents back and forth between Paris and Rome.

The second article of the final counter-proposal from Rome stated that the Italian Republic would abrogate the organic laws of January 1802.[69] All seemed set for both parties to sign this document. At the last minute Napoleon intervened, stating that any such article could not be agreed to. The church could not compel the state to withdraw legislation. This caused panic in the papal legation in Paris during September 1803. Caprara was obliged to think quickly. He now decided to drop article II and, in its place, stated in article XXI that the Italian Concordat superseded all previous laws.[70] It was an elegant solution and seemed to give the church what it wanted without embarrassing the government.

The greatest concession made by Paris was article I, which declared that Catholicism was the state religion of the Italian Republic.[71] This was something of a meaningless statement, as all other religions were tolerated, and no special privileges were bestowed on the Catholic clergy. Only two dioceses in the Italian Republic were to be abolished; a gesture that was offset by the confiscation of several monasteries and chapters, which were sold or used as military barracks.[72] Despite its misgivings, Rome ratified this new treaty in October and Napoleon, as the president of Italy, followed suit in December. Imitating the French revisory example of 1801, Melzi, as vice-president, issued new police regulations, which were pasted onto the Italian Concordat, without consultation, when it was published in January 1804.[73] These articles imposed new organic laws in northern Italy, making the church subordinate to the state.[74]

The Italian Concordat of 1803 made Rome conscious that concessions to the French Imperium did not have the desired effect. Each surrender seemed to embolden Paris in its demands. Concordats had become instruments of an empire that wanted to bend Catholicism to its will. Wherever French influence cast its shadow, it was assumed that the provisions of the Concordat could be automatically extended. This challenged the church's freedom to organise itself according to its traditions and teachings.

Legacies from the past made it difficult for both Napoleon and Pius to move forward as they would have liked. Throughout the 1790s, the Papal States, following the example of other Italian principalities, had been generous in their hospitality towards refugees and émigrés from France.[75] The Papacy had promoted counter-revolution within its domains with conviction; indeed, Maury had been rewarded with a cardinal's hat for his role in resisting the Revolution. Those who were enemies of the Jacobin Republic became friends of the church. In 1797, during the first Italian campaign, the comte d'Antraigues, a spy and émigré, was arrested and interrogated by Bonaparte. He revealed just how bound up several politicians and generals in France were by anti-revolutionary spy networks.[76] Suspicion that émigrés were stirring up trouble and plotting assassination were rife. Rome was aware of these fears and did its best to dispel them.

In order to facilitate negotiations over the Concordat, and to prove his goodwill, Pius VII had asked Maury to leave Rome, resume his diocese of Montefiascone, and not interfere in politics.[77] The Curia tried to distance itself from the agents of Louis XVIII who had once been welcome in the eternal city.

Despite this conciliatory policy, the news reached Paris that Joseph Hilarion de Gautier du Poët, chevalier de Vernègues, the former cavalry officer who had tried to provoke a counter-revolutionary insurrection in Provence in 1790, was in Rome. As an agent of Louis XVIII, and a close associate of his nephew the duc de Berry, he was suspected of being linked to a royalist plot against the first consul's life. Cardinal Fesch, now French ambassador in Rome, wanting to impress his nephew with his zeal, demanded that he be arrested and questioned.[78] The Papacy, as a sign of goodwill, consented to this request.

A large bundle of papers was confiscated (they now lie in the Vatican Archives). Papal policemen on reading these impenetrable letters, which were probably written in code, found little incriminating evidence to compromise the chevalier.[79] At this point Count Vittorio Cassini-Capizucchi, the Russian chargé d'affaires to the Holy See, intervened. He wrote to Consalvi: Vernègues had been naturalised a Russian subject and was thus not a French citizen. His emigration in 1790 had rendered him stateless until the Russians had provided him with a passport.[80] The request for his liberation came directly from Tsar Alexander I. Cardinal Fesch protested, demanding that Vernègues should be placed in the fortress of Castel Sant'Angelo and extradited to France.[81] Cassini complained that such an act would compromise the sovereign rights of the Tsar to protect his subjects abroad. By December 1803 a triangular diplomatic crisis was brewing between France, Russia and the Papal States. Consalvi was forced to consult international lawyers and hear arguments from both sides. (Vernègues became, briefly, the Julian Assange of his day.)

The Russians were prepared to accept some form of international arbitration, but France steadfastly refused this option.[82] For Pius VII the choice was now a difficult one. The Tsars had undertaken to protect and assist Catholics within their domains. Any diplomatic difficulty could imperil the relationship with this friendly Orthodox power. Equally, giving offence to France could compromise the Concordat. According to some accounts, Napoleon the pragmatist was not keen to take Vernègues into custody, hinting that during the extradition process he could discreetly disappear and make his escape. Caprara from Paris, for some reason, failed to impress this solution on Consalvi.[83] On 4 May 1804 the Gendarmerie of the Italian Republic were surprised to be informed that Vernègues would be surrendered to them at the border, near Pesaro.[84] The chevalier became a French prisoner and would languish in the fortress of Vincennes for several months. Alexander I was furious and recalled Count Cassini, thus breaking diplomatic relations with the Holy See. It would take the better part of a year for these to be resumed.[85] The Vernègues affair was a comedy of errors: although the Papacy had shown itself loyal to France, it left a bitter aftertaste. Pius hoped that an opportunity to clear the air might emerge.

In the aftermath of the peace of Amiens with the British in 1802, Bonaparte was triumphant: he had reached the zenith of his popularity. On 2 August he had been rewarded with the title of first consul for life, a role that was then ratified by a referendum. Soon after his coup d'état, Napoleon's brother Lucien and the intellectual Louis de Fontanes had urged him to assume monarchical powers: he had demurred.[86] He feared that his position was not secure, and did not wish to appear as if he was seizing power directly. The first consul was all too aware that from a constitutional point of view the Brumaire coup had not been a good start. That is why the rule of law and political legitimacy remained an important aspiration for his regime. Napoleon always stressed that he was not a military dictator, but that his was a civilian regime, based on popular consent; his acceptance of the consulship for life consolidated his rule and the popular referendum confirming it legitimated his power constitutionally. As Sieyès's adage had put it: authority from above, consent from below.

During the Consulate, republican and monarchical plots seeking to topple Bonaparte's hold on power continued unabated. The year 1804 was to be one of reckoning, one which would exorcise many of the ghosts of 1789. The elusive Breton guerrilla leader Georges Cadoudal, after years in hiding, had gathered a coalition of generals and politicians to assassinate the first consul and unseat his government, in order to spark a Bourbon restoration.[87] General Moreau, very unwisely, became embroiled in this plot through the shady politicking of a former colleague, Jean-Charles Pichegru. Eventually the consular police discovered the conspiracy and started rounding up those involved. Although the evidence was thin, Moreau was tried and allowed to escape to the United States.[88] After his arrest, Pichegru was found hanged, conveniently, in his cell; Cadoudal was later captured and guillotined. The government, under pressure from assassination attempts, both real and imagined, decided to launch a pre-emptive strike against the émigrés. It was suspected that a cousin to Louis XVIII, Louis-Antoine de Bourbon-Condé, duc d'Enghien, was behind the plots against Bonaparte. Troops were sent into his place of exile in Baden where, with little respect for international law, he was kidnapped. He was then taken to the

Château de Vincennes on the outskirts of Paris where he was court-martialled and executed by firing squad on 21 March 1804.[89]

It is difficult to know the extent to which Bonaparte's position was genuinely under threat at this time. A group of politicians close to him certainly felt this conspiracy could be used as a pretext to tighten the first consul for life's grip on power. The argument was made that if he were to die, France would be plunged into renewed chaos, as there was no clear system of succession to replace him. The moderate core of those who had supported the Brumaire coup, like Talleyrand and Cambacérès, sought to stabilise the situation. They argued that only a return to hereditary rule could stabilise France's system of governance.[90] What is remarkable is how little Napoleon himself seems to have been directly involved in these plans. Indeed, his correspondence and other writings give little sense that he orchestrated what happened next. Joseph Fouché, after a period in disgrace, was back in favour and was a leading member of the senatorial commission, charged with investigating the Cadoudal conspiracy.[91] It emerged that British money was still financing attempts against the first consul's life. The commission's report recommended that not only should the guilty be punished by severe justice, but also that the man who had brought stability to France should consider any means necessary to maintain order and prosperity in the future.[92] A carefully orchestrated campaign of public addresses from members of the army and civil society urged Napoleon to heed this advice.

Louis XVI had been offered the title emperor of the French by the Jacobin Club in 1790.[93] At the time this proposal was seen as eccentric, but by 1804 it had two distinct advantages: it was not a title used by the Bourbon dynasty, and was thus uncontaminated by the *ancien régime*; and it recalled the glory days of ancient Rome. In an age of neoclassicism in both art and architecture, this would prove compelling as propaganda. The title also brought to the surface vague memories of Charlemagne and a Europe-wide imperial state.[94] Eventually, the motion to declare Napoleon hereditary emperor of the French was considered by the Council of State. Most were in favour, and the proposal was brought forward for debate before the Tribunate. Here, Jean-François Curée, a former revolutionary and associate of Fouché, was chosen to present a motion before the house. After almost fifteen years of revolution, it was proposed that the first consul be made hereditary emperor of the Republic (a solution that bore striking similarities to when Octavian became the supreme ruler and imperator of ancient Rome).

Curée argued that this would end the French Revolution for good. It would put the state back on course, by returning to the constitutional monarchy first envisioned by the Constituent Assembly in 1791. France, he argued, had veered off track by declaring a republic which brought in its wake global warfare and political terror.[95] A constitutional, parliamentary and hereditary monarchy was the only means of ensuring stability. Lazare Carnot, a former member of the Committee of Public Safety, was alone in boldly speaking against Curée's motion. His intervention was a rhetorical masterpiece. He did not deny Bonaparte's many virtues, but reminded his colleagues that biological whim rarely produced stability. Marcus Aurelius, the great philosopher-emperor of Rome, had spawned the vile monster Commodus. This was but one example given of many other good monarchs who were succeeded by vile offspring. Carnot made an impassioned plea for his fellow tribunes to reconsider.[96] However, given the growing momentum behind an imperial solution, he remained a lonely voice (apart from the Abbé Gregoire, the former leader of the Constitutional Church).

Curée's motion was overwhelmingly carried through the parliamentary chambers. On 18 May 1804 the senators of the French Republic declared Napoleon emperor of the French and vested this office in the Bonaparte family.[97] In theory, this was no absolute monarchy, but a constitutional one, restrained by the rule of law. In many ways Napoleon accepted the constitutional monarchy that Louis XVI had failed to implement after 1791. The parallels are striking: Napoleon's civil list of 25 million francs was the same as that of the previous Bourbon king.[98] In June, the French people ratified this change in a referendum. Over 3.5 million voters accepted Napoleon as their emperor, with a mere 2,579 against.[99] Two months later Cardinal Maury, one of the bitterest enemies of the Revolution, wrote to Napoleon to offer his felicitations.[100] After a decade and a half of exile he could take no more of being cut off from Paris. In a difficult letter, he pledged his allegiance to the new emperor, thus implicitly abandoning the counter-revolutionary royalism he had defended for over fifteen years, and even came to terms with the Concordat. This marked the beginning of Maury's rallying to the French imperial regime. His letter was published in the *Moniteur*, the state newspaper, to the immense fury of Louis XVIII who viewed it as a complete betrayal of the Bourbon cause. The birth of the Empire sent the royalist and counter-revolutionary movement into dormancy.[101]

The plebiscite may have settled the issue of constitutional legitimacy, but more was needed to make Napoleon a monarch. The Senate had created the legislation necessary to make him emperor, and French voters had ratified it. But in comparison with the other dynasties of Europe his dynasty reeked of novelty. How to inaugurate the new regime and symbolically celebrate Napoleon's accession became the object of a heated debate in the Council of State.[102] Some wanted a purely civil ceremony shorn of the traditional incense, religious ceremonial and platitudes. The barbarian Franks had proclaimed their kings on the Champ de Mars in Paris, lifting them up on their shields in triumph. A similar ceremony was proposed, with the emperor swearing an oath before the army and public authorities. This solution would have been reminiscent of the revolutionary festivals of the 1790s which had taken place on this parade ground.[103] The spectacle presented according to this format would, however, appear too republican, and would do little to convince Europe that Napoleon was as much of an emperor as his Habsburg and Romanov counterparts.

Indeed, the response of the European courts to the birth of the French Empire was lukewarm at best. The breakdown of the peace of Amiens with Britain meant that a new European war loomed on the horizon.[104] Russia meanwhile, as a deliberate snub to France, had gone into official court mourning after the execution of the duc d'Enghien; it had recalled its diplomats from France and now failed to recognise Napoleon's new imperial title. Pius VII, however, did seem genuinely pleased that France was again a monarchy. He was among the first sovereigns to write to congratulate the new emperor of the French.[105] From the church's perspective, a Catholic emperor might be easier to deal with than a republican and non-denominational first consul. The French Empire created in 1804 needed both the lustre of popularity and tradition to gain legitimacy, both at home and abroad.

The decision to invite the pope to Paris to crown the emperor of the French was born from an oversimplification of history. The intellectual and writer Louis de Fontanes claimed that all new imperial dynasties needed the papal seal of approval. After all, Pepin the Short had been crowned directly by Pope Stephen II in Saint-Denis near Paris in 754 (his second coronation, as it happened).[106] Theologians in the Curia later observed that Pope Stephen had not travelled to France simply to crown Pepin king of the Franks, but also to seek his assistance in expelling the Lombards from the Papal States. For the French Council of State, a coronation ceremony that combined religious and constitutional legitimacy was the ideal solution. The most important thing was to avoid any sense that Napoleon recognised the spiritual supremacy of the pope. Under no circumstances must it appear as if it was the church that bestowed sovereignty on him. The people of France had already done this.

In preparation for the ceremony, Napoleon travelled to Aachen to visit the tomb of Charlemagne, where he stood in quiet reflection over the Frankish emperor's relics. Some jewels and trinkets purported to be the regalia of the long dead Holy Roman Emperor had conveniently been recently discovered.[107] These proved important when it came to manufacturing a complex heritage, combining a strange mixture of Roman and Carolingian icons. The ultimate aim was to bestow on the Bonaparte dynasty a veneer of historic legitimacy. All sites of memory linked to the Bourbon dynasty had to be avoided. So, Reims Cathedral, where the kings of France had been crowned for almost a thousand years, was out of the question. Bonaparte was tempted by Aachen because of the Charlemagne connection.[108] In the end, it was decided that Notre-Dame was the most practical location, as the chief church of the capital of the Republic. There was a precedent, of course, though not an auspicious one: Henry VI of England had been crowned king of France there in 1431 during the Hundred Years' War.[109]

Cardinal Fesch, as ambassador in Rome, was given the delicate mission of approaching the Curia and inquiring whether Pius VII might accept an invitation to Paris. As was to be expected, the pope expressed delight, but delegated the negotiations relating to his journey to the French capital to an extraordinary congregation of cardinals. There was a feeling that, while France's resumption of the path of monarchy was a step in the right direction, there were a number of unknowns and other perils to consider.[110] First, the extraordinary council contested Fontanes's vision of history. No pope had ever undertaken a journey outside the Papal States merely to crown an emperor. A better pretext would need to be found if this voyage was to take place. It was suggested that Napoleon might reopen negotiations in some areas: an agenda for direct discussions with the pope might include the return of the Papal Legations of Romagna, the abrogation of the organic laws, formal retractions from the constitutional bishops, and the revocation of all civil laws allowing divorce. Only if the French government promised further discussions and new concessions in religious matters might the Holy Father be persuaded to travel so far. Equally, it would be impossible for the pope to reach Paris by October: the heat of the Italian summer was too torrid for him to undertake such a trip. Thus the ceremony would need to be delayed until December if Pius was to arrive in time.

The problems mounted as the details of the ceremony filtered through to the cardinals. Napoleon's coronation oath struck at the heart of Catholic teaching: the new emperor was to promise to respect all religions equally and to protect those who had purchased church lands. This part of the ceremony could not be performed in the Holy Father's presence. Particularly upsetting were the provisions within the Imperial Constitution recognising freedom of conscience and which put all religions under the protection of the state; from the perspective of the theologians of the Curia such a juxtaposition of truth and heresy was scandalous. Under no circumstances could the pope sanction Catholicism's equality with other faiths.[111] The greatest dilemma was the French Embassy's notification that Napoleon was to crown himself, by his own hand. Grudgingly the cardinals conceded that the self-crowning could take place: they insisted however that the pope anoint the new emperor with chrism (holy oil).[112] With this gesture the coronation would be endowed with an aura of sacramentality. The placing of chrism on the emperor's head, hands and chest was a sign of divine approbation and would give the ceremony an important Christian veneer. The congregation of cardinals probably enjoyed refusing Napoleon permission to use the liturgy contained in the *pro coronando imperator* ceremonial: this text was reserved exclusively for the Holy Roman Emperor. Instead, the generic liturgy used for the crowning of kings in the episcopal handbook, the *Pontificale romanum*, was suggested for the ritual in Notre-Dame. It was a simple solution: the only necessary modification was that the word *rex* be substituted for *imperator*. This was a cold shower for the organisers in Paris, but they realised that the Curia at this stage would not budge.

Popes in the early modern period had travelled infrequently in comparison to their medieval precursors. As mentioned in previous chapters (p. 26, p. 45 and p. 55), Chiaramonti's predecessor, Pius VI, had in 1782 made an important journey when he visited Emperor Joseph II in Vienna in the hope of putting a brake on his anti-monastic reforms.[113] The mission had ended in failure, making the church wary about undertaking journeys beyond the Papal States. Pius VII hoped – somewhat optimistically – that he could improve on this negative precedent. A face-to-face meeting with the man who had restored Catholicism to France was filled with potential benefits. The journey to Paris was to be an impressive logistical feat: as the negotiations had taken so long, the French wanted him to reach Paris quickly, whereas the pope still sought to maintain his dignity by travelling in style. The trip was not quite the dismal progress depicted in some histories: Chiaramonti brought with him six important cardinals, not to mention several members of the papal household and of the great Roman aristocratic families.[114]

Napoleon's aide-de-camp, General Marie-François de Caffarelli du Falga, travelled to the Quirinal Palace bearing the official invitation to the coronation. The wording and content of this letter had been negotiated in advance, and its delivery to Pius was supposed to be purely ceremonial. To everybody's chagrin the letter presented to the pope on 7 October 1804 departed significantly from what had been agreed.[115] It made no mention of the visit concerning negotiations on a wide variety of matters relating to the Christian faith, but only that the pope was to anoint the emperor. Initially the pope refused the invitation, with some resentment; only through Cardinal Fesch's good offices was it made clear to the pope that the mistake had been occasioned by Napoleon's absence from Paris, rather than being a deliberate slight. There would be ample opportunity to discuss matters of common interest once Pius met with Napoleon in person. Somewhat reassured, the pope took some rest in his summer residence of Castel Gandolfo, outside Rome, to prepare for the journey.

Four convoys were organised to transport the papal court to France, setting off on 2 November 1804. The first carried mostly luggage, along with – inexplicably – Cardinal Borgia, who travelled alone; the second brought the cream of the Roman nobility; in the third travelled the pope and his closest advisers, amongst whom was his friend, the almoner and theologian Francesco Bertazzoli, archbishop of Edessa (a man who would play an important role when the pope became a French prisoner in Savona); the final convoy carried papal servants and secretaries. In total 146 horses were needed to draw all these carriages and carts.[116] This number did not include the military escort, which added 100 cavalrymen to protect the papal entourage from the many bandits lurking in the Italian countryside. Fresh horses were needed at each postal relay: the directors of the French, Italian and papal postal services had spent weeks making arrangements for the journey.[117]

The decision was taken to avoid travelling through the Legations, as the pope did not want to recognise their annexation to the Italian Republic. This meant that the journey would go through Tuscany, passing through a *cordon sanitaire* established around Livorno due to an outbreak of yellow fever. After breaking the quarantine, the convoys headed into Piedmont, then directly through France. Rome's government had been left in the hands of Consalvi. All too often this cardinal's memoirs are quoted in relation to the trip to Paris. There he describes the imperial coronation as a complete disaster, and paints it in negative colours.[118] These pages portray Pius as receiving insults at every turn, being slighted by the

French as an almost unwelcome visitor. There is some truth in this: the trip did not improve Franco-papal relations, and was a disappointment. However, Consalvi was not present, so his words do need to be treated with care.

Although the journey has been described as a race to Paris, the pope did make several stops en route. Spending some nights in monasteries where he had once been a simple Benedictine monk, he must have looked back on his early life with some nostalgia. In Turin he visited the Holy Shroud in the chapel of the royal palace.[119] He spent time in quiet contemplation before this sacred object, which many Catholics, to this day, believe displays an impression of the face of Jesus Christ made by Saint Veronica during his passion. Here, Pius was joined by Cardinal Cambacérès, who headed the delegation sent to welcome the pope into French territory. Throughout the journey enormous throngs of people lined the route to greet the pope's progress and receive his blessing. There were fears that the welcome on the other side of the Alps might not be so warm after a decade of de-Christianisation.

Cardinal Antonelli's librarian, the abate Francesco Cancellieri, followed the papal suite. He described how, after the carriages had travelled over the Mont-Cenis Pass into France, swarms of people suddenly appeared on the mountain and hilltops in the distance.[120] Faithful Catholics had scaled these heights to glimpse the pope and receive his benediction from afar. Once arrived in Lyon, Cardinal Fesch's archdiocese, Pius VII was welcomed by a rapturous sea of people on Place Bellecour at the heart of the city's *presqu'île*, its historic centre at the confluence of the Rhône and Saône rivers.[121] Apparently, amidst the cheering crowds, Chiaramonti's eyes filled with tears as he entered the cathedral of Saint-Jean to give thanks for his safe journey. During his transit through France the pope liberally distributed rosaries, crosses, medals and images of saints to all who came to kiss his feet. On 23 November 1804, in Lyon, Cardinal Borgia's age caught up with him, and he passed away. He was to be the only casualty of the pope's first journey to Paris.

As the pope left Lyon, and the convoys sped through Burgundy, the moment of truth was looming. The omnipresent Bernier was sent ahead to negotiate and finalise the liturgy for the coronation. Pius conceded that the wording would not give the appearance that the emperor received his crown from the church, but rather from the people of France. Finally, on 25 November 1804, the papal carriages passed through the crossroads of the Croix de Saint-Herem near the palace of Fontainebleau, south-east of Paris.[122] As the pope's carriage approached the crossroads he heard the sound of hunting horns, horses galloping and hounds giving chase. Suddenly, the man with whom Pius had corresponded for almost four years appeared before him on horseback, in the green hunting livery of the Imperial Vénerie.[123]

This meeting had been contrived to appear as a chance encounter. Consalvi declared that it was a deliberate insult to the pope, whereas it appears that Napoleon wanted to avoid the rigidity of a formal ceremonial meeting.[124] This would have involved lengthy negotiations about who should dismount first, and whether Napoleon should genuflect before the pope. Any undue deference towards the head of the church would have been interpreted as a humiliation by the generals and politicians of Paris. Informality would avoid any embarrassment and, hopefully, allow the two men a chance to converse without inhibition. General Anne Jean Marie René Savary, in command of the emperor's personal bodyguard, was present at this encounter. He noted how the pope initially hesitated to descend from the carriage: the crossroads were a quagmire, and he was wearing delicate white silk slippers.[125] After some awkwardness the emperor of the French and the pope moved towards each other and warmly embraced. A specially prepared carriage arrived, in which Napoleon and Pius could continue the journey to Fontainebleau together. Here the pope would spend two days resting in preparation for his entry into Paris. The coronation was just a week away, and there was much to be discussed. After some refreshment in his apartments, the pope visited the emperor in formal procession, with state officials and officers in gala uniforms lining the rooms. Once this was over, the Empress Joséphine was visited by Pius and his entourage. To repay the compliment, Napoleon and his court officials later processed in the opposite direction to call on the pope in his apartments to pay their respects.

We do not know the exact content of the private conversations in Italian that took place between pope and emperor. Napoleon's recollections of these meetings, written on Saint Helena, are extremely unreliable. One issue the pope did insist upon immediately was a formal retraction and expression of regret by all twelve constitutional bishops. Napoleon promised that this would be settled soon, but the pope replied that he refused to leave Fontainebleau until written retractions were provided. Napoleon's face became bright red with fury, but he realised that, to avoid a diplomatic catastrophe, he could not refuse. Within hours, ten of the twelve constitutional bishops had signed the declaration required by the pope.

Only Claude Le Coz, archbishop of Besançon, and Jean-Baptiste Saurine, bishop of Strasbourg, initially held back.[126] Their refusal caused some embarrassment, as they could not attend the coronation. Only in January 1805 did they finally meet Pius and resolve the issue.[127]

Napoleon wanted to avoid a triumphal entry for the pope into Paris, so he decided to travel with him in the same carriage. On 28 November 1804 hundreds of thousands of Parisians greeted the pope with uncontained enthusiasm. Pius was given apartments in the Pavillon de Flore of the Tuileries Palace.[128] Here he found replicas of the furnishings that adorned his quarters in the Quirinal Palace; a small consolation, given that he was housed in the very wing that, ten years previously, had hosted the meeting rooms of the Jacobin Committee of Public Safety responsible for the death warrants for many priests. The crowds thronged into the palace gardens, demanding that the pope appear on the balcony to bestow an apostolic blessing. Napoleon, never one to be sidelined, also joined, unsolicited, the pope on the balcony. The next day was taken up with the formal presentation of the Senate, Tribunate and Corps Législatif to the pope. He was complimented in formal speeches by the president of each chamber. There was a sense in Louis de Fontanes's speech that the combined rebirth of Catholicism and monarchy were a perfect formula for prosperity. The pope had a noble and elegant bearing that exuded piety. Indeed, the revolutionary painter Jacques-Louis David, who would immortalise the coronation on canvas, apparently exclaimed on seeing the pontiff: 'My goodness, this is a real priest.'[129] Pius's voice was soft, and he seldom spoke, giving him something of a mystical aura. Indeed, when he did speak his words were bound to make an impression. His gentleness, dignity and piety certainly won over the Parisian public. Even the most revolutionary and republican soldiers found little to criticise. The only person the pope refused categorically to meet was the wife of Talleyrand.[130] It was painful for Pius to have to meet this apostate bishop who had presided over the schism of 1791. Diplomatic courtesies meant that this was unavoidable, but meeting the wife of man whom the church still considered an anointed bishop was something protocol could not permit.

Napoleon had succeeded, through Bernier's diplomatic efforts, to have the ceremonial prescriptions of the *Pontificale romanum* modified. There would be no coronation vigil, the emperor would not need to confess nor to receive communion. Most importantly, he would not be required to prostrate himself before the altar and the pope. The self-crowning was confirmed, and the papal blessing for the crown was also reworded.[131] Everything now seemed set for the ceremony to proceed without further delay. Yet a family drama of a different order was about to explode. The Empress Joséphine was hated by Napoleon's siblings: the emperor's brothers had urged him to divorce her as she had borne him no children.[132] On 1 December the empress beseeched the pope for an audience. Pius met with her, and to his immense surprise she broke into tears. She revealed that her marriage to the emperor in 1796 had been solely a civil wedding at a registry. Consequently, her union had not been blessed by a priest and was not sacramental. Deeply shocked, the pope promised to speak immediately with Napoleon. The emperor's irritation was immense, as he argued that a civil wedding was entirely legitimate in the eyes of the French state. The pope stated that he could not anoint a man who in the eyes of the church was unmarried and living with a concubine.

Pius, the good priest, would not budge: marriage was a sacrament, not a civil contract. Cardinal Fesch was told by his nephew to ask the pope for the necessary dispensation required so that the emperor could marry Joséphine in a private ceremony. The priest of Saint-Germain l'Auxerrois, the parish church of the Tuileries, was summoned amid some confusion. This simple priest had to give his permission for Cardinal Fesch to perform the religious wedding within his jurisdiction and then record the marriage in the parochial registers. In the Tuileries that afternoon, Fesch secretly blessed Napoleon and Joséphine. The official marriage act recorded Talleyrand and Marshal Berthier (the army's chief of staff) as witnesses to the marriage, but it is unclear if they were actually present.[133] After eight years of civil marriage, Napoleon and Joséphine were now also husband and wife in the eyes of God. The new empress was delighted: her membership of the imperial family was now more secure than it had ever been. Her sisters-in-law were commanded by Napoleon to carry Joséphine's train on the morning of the ceremony. They would do so with tears of fury in their eyes for a woman they despised.[134]

The days before the coronation had sealed some compromises in favour of Pius, but the gulf that separated state from church remained in evidence. For Napoleon, religion could legitimate his dynasty, but it was subordinate to the state, whereas Pius, the monk, saw the sacraments and God as paramount. Although they would share the stage in Paris, neither protagonist really spoke the same language. Despite the bitter cold of 2 December 1804, crowds turned out in droves to watch the unique spectacle of a modern coronation. The representatives of the provinces and the deputies of the three chambers were required to be seated and ready by 8 a.m. An impressive papal cortège left the Tuileries an hour later. There was a panic when it was realised that the mule, supposed to represent the donkey that carried Jesus into Jerusalem on Palm Sunday, and required to carry the papal cross ahead of the procession, was missing. After much searching a grey donkey was rented for the extortionate price of 67 francs.[135] The papal procession wound its way through the streets of Paris and arrived at Notre-Dame, where the pope was greeted by Cardinal Belloy, archbishop of Paris. One of Napoleon's personal chaplains, the Abbé Dominique Dufour de Pradt, had been nominated ecclesiastical master of ceremonies. He now arranged the papal entourage into a hierarchy that processed down the nave. As the pope entered the cathedral, the choir intoned the hymn *Tu es Petrus*, singing Christ's words from Saint Matthew's Gospel: 'that thou art Peter, and upon this rock I will build my church; and the gates of hell shall not prevail against it'. The pope took his place on a throne next to the altar and waited.

Cannon salvos at 10 a.m. announced that the emperor and empress had departed the Tuileries. They arrived at Notre-Dame with a grand military entourage. Unlike previous coronations, two sets of regalia had been commissioned. The imperial insignia were new, while the 'honours of Charlemagne' were claimed to be the crown jewels of the long dead Holy Roman Emperor.[136] Each of the most important officers of the court carried an item from the regalia in procession, which were then laid on the altar, in preparation for the ceremony. Many books have been written about the coronation: a debate has arisen amongst historians as to whether it represented a religious ritual or rather a secular one with religious symbolism.[137] This debate seems pedantic, given that the ceremony took place in Notre-Dame and was choreographed around the liturgy of the Catholic Mass. The opening part of the ceremony saw the pope invoke God to bless Napoleon in order for him to reign wisely and prudently. The emperor then knelt and was sealed by the pope on his head and on both hands, like the kings of old (his chest was avoided for modesty's sake). The empress then received the same anointing. This was a quintessentially religious moment, in which the emperor was sealed before God with holy oil. After the anointing, a solemn grand pontifical Mass commenced.

After the *Graduale* and *Alleluia* had been sung, each individual item of the regalia was blessed by the pope. Napoleon then descended from his throne and approached the altar, where he was invested by the great officers of state with the imperial insignia. The most notable breach with tradition came in the form of the Hand of Justice, an ornament representing the legislative power of kings. In the past, three fingers of the ivory hand were extended in the gesture of a trinitarian blessing, symbolising that all laws were of divine inspiration. The Imperial Hand of Justice (now lost) instead had all five fingers outstretched.[138] Was this a mistake or an ultimate symbol of the Enlightenment? Was it a symbol of mankind, reaching out with its own hand outstretched, seizing its own destiny, unaided by any supernatural power? Whether the Hand of Justice was a symbol of hubris denying divine providence was unclear, but it was ultimately striking that no monarch – before or since – dared to use such a secular version of this symbol. Once the emperor had been invested, he returned his sceptre and Hand of Justice to his grand officers. He approached the altar, lifted the crown and placed it on his own head. He then crowned Joséphine, who knelt at his feet. This was the scene that the artist David immortalised years later in his coronation tableau.[139] He rewrote history by placing Napoleon's mother Letizia in the foreground; she had not attended, but had stayed in Rome for the birth of a grandson. Given her hatred of Joséphine she probably had few regrets in not seeing her daughter-in-law crowned. Touchingly, Napoleon's wet nurse Camilla Illari, who had written him a letter begging to be present at the ceremony, was given a special place to view the child she had nursed at the tenderest age become emperor of the French.[140]

After his self-crowning, Napoleon returned to his throne. The pope approached the emperor and kissed him on both cheeks. He asked God to confirm his blessing on the newly crowned monarch. He then turned to the congregation and proclaimed: *Vivat Imperator in aeternum!* ('May the emperor live forever!'). To which all thunderously replied, 'Long live the emperor!', while a specially commissioned fanfare, by the Abbé Roze, proclaimed to the world that the emperor of the French had been crowned.[141] The Mass continued as normal, with the offertory performed by the great ladies and officers of the imperial court. At the elevation of the Host, the most sacred moment of the Mass, Napoleon removed his crown and knelt in respect before what the church believed was the living body of Christ. When the Mass ended, the pope and his entourage quickly headed to the sacristy at a less than dignified speed. They surely did not wish to be present for what would occur next.

It would be a decided exaggeration to define this ceremony as secular. While it was true that the Senate and a popular referendum had made Napoleon emperor, the church, with its ceremonies and liturgies, had added legitimacy to this claim. The Hand of Justice and the self-crowning were isolated secular elements in what was otherwise a Catholic High Mass. Once the pope was safely in the sacristy, Napoleon ascended the grand throne at the rear of the nave. Here he raised his hand and swore on the Gospels his coronation oath. The promises he now made, to treat all religions equally and to defend those who had purchased church lands, meant that the pope could not be present.[142] The kings of France, in the past, had sworn to extirpate heresy and protect the church's rights with all their might. None of this was present in the new version of the imperial oath. Like a true constitutional monarch, Napoleon swore to respect the civil and political rights of all citizens and to never levy taxes without the consent of the nation. This was a coronation oath worthy of an age that had witnessed the American Declaration of Independence and the Declaration of the Rights of Man and of the Citizen in France. This final part of the ceremony was supremely secular and non-religious. It was a constitutional pact between ruler and ruled. It signalled that the gains of the Revolution were irreversible.

The coronation was certainly magnificent and filled with pomp. Yet the attempt to blend tradition and modernity, religion and secular government led to an extremely complicated ritual. Spectators and journalists betrayed this confusion in the conflicting reports they gave of what they had observed. Napoleon had desperately tried to make monarchy into a rational modern institution. It is far from clear that he succeeded in his goal.[143] Certainly the coronation banquet did not ease relations with the Papacy. According to Consalvi, the pope was placed on the third rank in the seating arrangement, while other dignitaries and foreign ambassadors were placed ahead of him. The subsequent ceremonies in the Champ de Mars and Hôtel de Ville showed little consideration for religion, and made the pope wonder what his mission had actually achieved.

The Holy Father would stay in Paris for a further three months. He held consistories in which he bestowed the cardinal's *galero* on Belloy and Cambacérès, and also presented the imperial authorities with a list of eleven articles on reforms that would benefit the church.[144] These included reforms of spiritual matters, like the organic laws and divorce, but also the possible return of the Papal Legations of Romagna. Most of these papers were forwarded to the minister of religions, Portalis, who politely received the demands of the pope and wrote a very detailed, but somewhat lawyerly, response. On divorce, he regretted that the laws of a civil society were above confession, and that the state could not accept the church's view that marriage was indissoluble. The minister did concede that priests could refuse to bless in church the remarriage of divorcees. The request that priests should be judged by their bishops alone was rejected without hesitation; clergymen were citizens and subject to criminal proceedings, like anybody else. In terms of canon law, bishops could apply the appropriate sanctions if spiritual infractions were committed by priests, but for other matters they would appear before the civil courts.

Promises were made to increase priests' salaries and that civil servants would not work on Sundays, but the rest of the population would not be bound to keep the Sabbath holy. The church of Saint-Geneviève, which had been transformed into the Pantheon during the Revolution, and where the heroes of the 1790s were buried, was once more to be used for Catholic worship. While Napoleon did not allow the rebirth of religious orders in the Concordat, he did accept that the Sisters of Charity had an important role in assisting in hospitals as nurses, and placed them under the protection of his own mother.[145] He also promised personally to fund the Congregation of the Mission, more commonly known as Lazarists, to perform missions to China and elsewhere.[146] Finally, the imperial government agreed to fund the basilica of Saint John Lateran in Rome in return for the same privileges the kings of France had received in the past in this establishment. Although the responses on divorce and clerical immunity were unhelpful, there was some leeway on the other minor requests raised by the pope.

At this time the request was made for Vernègues to be pardoned and released. The imperial government consented, and he was given safe-conduct to Vienna; there the chevalier disappeared from history as abruptly as he had entered it.[147] In several conversations with the pope, the emperor claimed that he was the successor of Charlemagne. Pius stated that, if that was the case, he should return all former papal territories on the banks of the Po river. Had not Charlemagne seized these lands from the Lombards in the ninth century and given them to the pope? As the pope's stay drew to an end, Napoleon wrote a long letter in which he responded to his requests for negotiations over the return of lost papal territories. He affirmed that providence had allowed him to be the instrument through which the disorders of the Revolution had come to an end: he had restored religion and brought peace. However, the emperor stressed that he could not, under any circumstance, return those territories conquered in northern Italy at the expense of so much French blood. The penultimate paragraph concluded that if the future allowed for the opportunity to expand the pope's domains elsewhere in Italy, he would be happy to do so. He concluded with a reassurance that he was one of the firmest supporters of Catholicism in Europe, and that he would do his utmost to further the interests of Christianity.[148] Essentially, nothing but vague promises were given.

Ominously, the Italian Republic sent a delegation to Napoleon in early 1805 offering him the crown of Italy.[149] He accepted it and, to everybody's consternation, the keys of Saint Peter appeared in the arms of the new kingdom. By adding the emblems of provinces he did not rule, Napoleon gave the impression that he considered himself imperial suzerain over all of Italy. Pius was greatly disheartened. When the French government asked to open negotiations for a German Concordat to settle issues on the right bank of the Rhine, the pope replied that he could only enter into such negotiations with the consent of the Holy Roman Emperor Francis II who was, after all, the overlord of all these territories.[150] On 25 March 1805, shortly before his departure from Paris, the pope consented to baptise the youngest son of Louis Bonaparte and Hortense de Beauharnais, Napoléon-Louis, in the chapel of the palace of Saint-Cloud on the outskirts of Paris.[151] Pius thus again gave the dynasty a mark of legitimacy.

After the christening, the pope started out on the slow return across France back to Rome. Wherever Pius travelled, crowds of French citizens came to cheer his progress. What was the actual outcome of the coronation trip? The question of the constitutional bishops had been grudgingly settled by Napoleon, but none of the other issues had been resolved. The emperor had promised the pope lavish gifts, and members of the papal entourage had received generous cash gifts from the imperial government. Pius VII had been presented with a coronation tiara which, on close inspection, was encrusted with jewels that Rome had paid to France as war indemnities in 1797.[152] In some ways, he was being given back treasures which had originally belonged to the church. In the meantime, the pope's nephew Scipione Chiaramonti was appointed a chamberlain of the Italian kingdom and invited to Napoleon's Italian coronation in Milan. To the pope's horror his nephew spent lavishly in his new position and sent his uncle the bills. Pius was a patient man, but with his nephew he lost his cool and accused him of being financially foolish. His letters represent a rather uncharacteristic dressing-down.[153]

The pope entered Piedmont, where he was invited to spend time with Napoleon at the hunting lodge-cum-palace of Stupinigi on 25 April 1805. This was to be the last meeting between emperor and pope for several years. We do not know what took place there, but it seems that there was little intention on either side that the pope would crown Napoleon king of Italy. The pliant Cardinal Caprara, who was now archbishop of Milan, did so in May 1805 in an even more lavish ceremony involving no fewer than three crowns, including the ancient iron crown of the Lombards.[154] The royal motto Napoleon chose for his Italian kingdom was: 'God has granted it [the crown] to me, woe betide anyone who should dare touch it.' France seemed to claim the entirety of the Italian peninsula. While the pope had been away, the Tiber had burst its banks and badly flooded the countryside around Rome. Some saw this as an omen that when the pope was away disaster inevitably followed. On his return to the eternal city Pius was given a rapturous welcome.

# FIVE

# A NEW BABYLONIAN CAPTIVITY
## THE FRENCH ANNEXATION OF ROME, 1805–09

The coronation of 1804 failed to bring lasting benefits. Soon after, relations between the new emperor and the pope worsened sharply. Once Pius was back in Rome, he was sucked into another Bonaparte family drama which exploded in 1805. Jérôme, the emperor's youngest sibling, had been selected to undertake a naval career. While in port on the eastern seaboard of the United States, he met the charming and extremely beautiful Betsy Patterson, the daughter of a prosperous merchant family in Baltimore. On 24 December 1803, he decided to marry the girl without consulting his imperial brother, upsetting Napoleon's plan to wed Jérôme to one of the great ruling houses of Europe.[1] It was decided to seek a papal annulment to solve the situation. The truth was bent significantly to make it seem as if Letizia, the matriarch of the Bonaparte clan, was deeply upset that Jérôme had married an American Protestant without her consent. Knowing full well he was on thin ice, the emperor suggested to Pius VII that a marriage between a Catholic and a heretic could be easily annulled.[2]

Canon law, unlike the French Civil Code of 1804, did not require parental consent before the age of twenty-five for a marriage to be valid.[3] Pius, well versed in these matters, admitted that inter-faith marriages were unfortunate, but that they alone did not provide valid grounds for matrimonial nullity. Jérôme's case would need to be considered by the tribunal of the Holy Rota in Rome before he could come to a decision. Napoleon alleged that an unscrupulous Spanish priest had presided over the affair. This was a blatant lie: no less a personage than John Carroll, bishop of Baltimore, had officiated at the wedding.[4] To make matters worse, the shrewdly mercantile Patterson family had drawn up a marriage contract to protect their daughter. It stipulated that in case of separation a third of Jérôme's property would be devolved to Betsy.[5] Non-consummation was, usually, sufficient grounds for nullity, but this path was hardly open to the emperor: on 5 July 1805 Betsy delivered a son, who was christened Jérôme-

Napoléon in honour of his furious uncle. (Thanks to this child an American branch of the Bonaparte dynasty was born; it would eventually enter US politics after the Civil War of the 1860s. Indeed, Charles Joseph Bonaparte, a grandson of Jérôme, would serve between 1906 and 1909 as secretary to the US navy and then as attorney general, and in 1908 founded the Bureau of Investigation, later to become the FBI.)[6]

Although the Pattersons were by all accounts urbane and decent folk, the emperor was determined that his would-be sister-in-law would not set foot in France, and was resolute that her union to his youngest brother be dissolved. Rome was utterly unsympathetic to this domestic drama. Pius had obtained so few concessions during his recent trip to France that he had no wish to dissolve a marriage that in the eyes of Catholicism was perfectly valid.[7] A year later Napoleon was forced to re-establish the old Gallican diocesan courts of France, known as *officialités*. In October 1806 the *officialité* of Paris annulled Jérôme's marriage to Betsy, leaving him free to marry Princess Catherine of Württemberg.[8] This set an important precedent that Napoleon would use again in 1810.[9] The pope's refusal to annul Jérôme's marriage to Betsy Patterson in 1805 heralded the downward spiral in Franco-papal relations.

Through the 1801 Concordat Napoleon had put pressure on the Papacy to force the resignation of the *ancien régime* episcopate. In this treaty the pope's supremacy over the church and its hierarchy was implicit: this was an aspect of the Concordat that the emperor would live to regret. As his disagreements with the pope escalated, he came to see himself as the head of a Gallican Church that was autonomous from Rome.[10] Over the following three years, the emperor's personality evolved as events accelerated and made his wildest ambitions reality. The Battle of Austerlitz on 2 December 1805, coincidentally the anniversary of his coronation, made him master of Europe.[11] As first consul, he had heeded advice and sought to come to collective decisions about France's future. Now, the victorious emperor saw himself as a modernising genius, and would brook no opposition. From 1805 to 1807, through to a string of unbroken military victories, it seemed as if Europe was on the verge of a new Carolingian age. At Tilsit, on 7 July 1807, on a raft on the Neman river, Napoleon and Alexander I of Russia would sign treaties of alliance that transformed western Europe into a vast French federation of satellites, vassal states and vanquished foes.[12] Opposition to this grand design was viewed as traitorous.

For Pius VII his role as a secular prince in central Italy was vital. This, for nineteenth-century popes, was the *sine qua non* of their spiritual independence.[13] The pope, as king, was a precept of political theology, and his rule over central Italy, from the church's perspective, was the manifest outcome of divine providence. Only by being free from any obligations to secular princes could the pope freely exercise his position as supreme head of the church to the benefit of humanity. As the successor of Christ, the Prince of Peace, it was incumbent on the pope to remain neutral in the struggles that pitted Christian rulers against each other: a principle that the Papacy, admittedly, had not always adhered to in its medieval and Renaissance past.[14] For supporters of the modern French state, clerical interference in government had led to barbarism and inefficiency. During the Middle Ages the Papal States were the epitome of backwardness, underachievement and superstition. The pope's right to rule was not something the ministers, bureaucrats and diplomats of the French Empire viewed as self-evident.[15] Indeed, Napoleon believed that the Concordat had made him the successor, not just of Charlemagne, but also of Constantine I, the first Christian emperor of Rome.[16] He was the church's defender, but not its stooge. The pope could not be a free agent when it came to geopolitics: he might on the surface have seemed to be an independent prince, but, in terms of realpolitik, he was the head of a vassal state. In the same way it was expected that Pius's spiritual mission would conform to the modernising agenda and administrative reforms of the French Imperium.

The War of the Third Coalition in 1805 rapidly brought these tensions to the surface. Napoleon formally inquired, through Cardinal Fesch, his ambassador in Rome, whether the Papal States could defend the ports of Ancona, on the Adriatic, and Civitavecchia, the eternal city's main access into the Mediterranean. The Papacy's answer, that there were a thousand troops to defend both ports, did little to reassure the French government: would this be sufficient to repel Russo-Anglo-Neapolitan forces, should they attempt to seize these vital strategic points on the Italian coast?[17] The French had a transit arrangement with the Papacy allowing its military forces to pass through central Italy. Using this arrangement, French troops seized Ancona on 18 October 1805 and illegally started to requisition supplies in the region.[18] The French commanders also established hospitals and a supply base. Consalvi protested with great vehemence that such actions were a clear violation of Roman neutrality and demanded that the city be returned to papal control.[19] General Reynier, commander of the fortress of

Ancona, responded that he had respected papal neutrality by allowing enemy merchant ships into port to trade. Papal requests for the return of this Adriatic port were met with assurances from General de Gouvion de St Cyr that he was merely manoeuvring to check a likely Neapolitan advance, and hoped that the occupation would be brief.

On 17 November 1805, Pius, for the first time, reached the end of his patience. The occupation of Ancona compromised his sovereignty. He wrote to the emperor of the French accusing him of bad faith over the Italian Concordat and demanding the evacuation of Ancona. For the first time Pius threatened that, if the French failed to respond, he would break off diplomatic relations.[20] Many in Rome hoped that Habsburg forces in northern Italy might liberate the peninsula from French influence.[21] But the Curia did not realise that Napoleon had encircled and defeated the main Austrian army at Ulm. He soon occupied Vienna (something the Ottomans had twice failed to do).[22] Cardinal Fesch did his best to maintain good relations, but like so many members of the Bonaparte clan he was somewhat out of his depth in the world of high politics. It was one Napoleon's great regrets that his family did not share his energy, political acumen and administrative abilities. Only his adopted son Eugène de Beauharnais (Joséphine's son from her first marriage) shared these traits, proving an able viceroy in northern Italy. Fesch was pedantic, found it difficult to interpret his nephew's intentions and had a worrying tendency to undertake his own unauthorised initiatives, much to the chagrin of the imperial authorities. Like so many Bonapartes he owed everything to the head of the family; indeed it was unlikely that through his own merits Fesch would have become a bishop, let alone a cardinal and virtual head of the French church. As with his brothers, Napoleon interpreted his uncle's temporising, independent thinking and sluggishness as craven ingratitude. As the years progressed, the conflict with Pius VII brought the relationship between uncle and nephew to breaking point on a number of occasions. To make matters worse, Fesch experienced a crisis of conscience: he was torn between his loyalty to his emperor but, at the same time, admired the pope, whom he felt was being ill-advised by enemies of France. The relationship between the French ambassador and Consalvi, the papal secretary of state, deteriorated to the point of no return amidst bitter recriminations.

In Fesch's defence, he found his position doubly difficult, as he had no idea what the French army's ultimate intentions were, nor what the emperor's peace plan would encompass. When news arrived of victory at Austerlitz and the peace signed at Pressburg with the Habsburg monarchy, Fesch threw a lavish reception at his palace in Rome.[23] The entire diplomatic corps, excluding the Austrian and Prussian ministers, and many cardinals attended. Fesch had also been instructed by the French foreign ministry to seize the city's Habsburg-owned Palazzo Farnese and Palazzo Venezia as part of the spoils of war.[24] Unwisely Fesch, thinking that he would now play a key role in the Empire's policies in Italy, started writing to French generals in the Papal States advising them on what they should do. Most seriously of all he welcomed peace overtures from the Neapolitan warrior-cardinal Fabrizio Ruffo (see above, pp. 41–2). He had no authority from the French foreign ministry in Paris to undertake such initiatives.[25] News had not reached Rome that, in the palace of Schönbrunn in Vienna, Napoleon had declared that the Bourbons of Naples had ceased to reign. On 7 January 1806, Napoleon wrote to Fesch, incandescent with rage:

> The pope, his people believing me dead, wrote a letter, dated 13 November, that is extremely ridiculous and mad. I occupied the fortress of Ancona because, despite your representations, nothing had been done to defend it, and given the disorganisation [of papal forces] there they would not have been in a fit state to hold it against anyone. Let it be known that I will not suffer any more insults. I do not wish Sardinian or Russian representatives to be in Rome. It is my intention to recall you and replace you with a layman. As these imbeciles have no problem with a Protestant occupying the throne of France, I shall send them a Protestant ambassador.
>
> Tell Consalvi that if he loves his homeland he needs to leave [his] ministry; or that he must do what I demand. I am religious but I am not a bigot; [remind them] that Constantine separated the civil and the military [spheres], and that I can appoint a senator to rule in my name in Rome. These people may well talk of religion! They who have admitted the Russians [to their court] and rejected Malta, and who want to expel my minister! It is they who prostitute religion. Is there any [previous] example of an apostolic nuncio in Russia? Tell Consalvi, the pope too, that if they chase my minister from Rome, I can come back there to re-establish him.
>
> Can anything be done with these people apart from using the threat of force? They allow religion to die in Germany and refuse to negotiate for a Concordat there; they allow it to perish in Bavaria and Italy; they are the laughing stock of all the courts and peoples [in Europe]. I have given them

advice, but they never listen. Do they really think that the Russians, Neapolitans or English would have been more respectful of the pope's neutrality! For the pope I am Charlemagne, because like Charlemagne I unite the crown of France with that of the Lombards. My empire now stretches as far as the Orient. I wish him to understand this situation and behave accordingly. I will change nothing for appearance's sake as long as he behaves well; otherwise I shall reduce the pope to the mere bishop of Rome.

He complains that I have settled Italian affairs without him. Should I have let things slip as in Germany, where there are no solemnities, sacraments or religion? Tell them that if they don't stop, I'll show Europe that they are mere egoists and that I'll settle the affairs of Germany with the archchancellor [Dalberg] without them. In truth there is nothing in the world as unreasonable as the court of Rome.[26]

This lengthy rant highlighted that Napoleon would brook no disagreement. In February 1806 there was a crackdown on the Catholic press, many newspapers were abolished, and religious publications heavily censored.[27] A new government-sponsored periodical, the *Journal des Curés* ('Newspaper of Parish Priests') emerged. Its remit was to propagate a neo-Gallican and pro-imperial version of church affairs.[28] The government hoped this would pre-empt any ultramontane opposition to the regime. Simultaneously, a force of 40,000 troops crossed Italy towards Naples. In an abrupt about-face, the papal bureaucracy became more co-operative and more willingly provided the French troops with provisions during their transit. Joseph Bonaparte arrived in Rome as lieutenant of the army of Naples: his presence was a sign that Paris took the invasion of Naples very seriously.[29] He was granted an audience by the pope, who pledged that everything was being done to assure the quick passage of the troops. The emperor's brother, in turn, reassured the pope that his forces would not interfere with the magistrates and civil authorities of the Papal States.

On 15 February Joseph entered Naples at the head of the army. It would take the French months to capture the great fortress of Gaeta and suppress a peasant insurrection in Calabria.[30] This guerrilla conflict was a harbinger of things to come, as the population was stirred up by local priests and preachers to resist bitterly the French invaders. On 30 March Joseph was declared king of Naples by Napoleon, the second member of the Bonaparte dynasty to receive a crown.[31] The violent accession of Joseph to the throne of Naples created a complex diplomatic crisis, its origins going back to Charles of Anjou's defeat of Manfred of Sicily during his conquest of the Kingdom of Naples in 1266.[32] The Papacy had declared a crusade in favour of Charles's war. This support had been conditional on the proviso that the new king of Naples would recognise the pope as his overlord. The Anjous committed future monarchs to pay 8,000 ounces of gold and solemnly present the Chinea, or prize horse, in a ceremony in Rome every 28 June, the eve of the feast of the apostles Peter and Paul.[33]

The Papacy also held the enclaves of Benevento and Pontecorvo within the Kingdom of Naples.[34] Ever since the early eighteenth century, there had been a dispute between the Holy See and the Neapolitan monarchy over this so-called right of Chinea. The Bourbon kings of Naples and Sicily paid this feudal due grudgingly at best, and often suspended payments.[35] Indeed, Paris felt that the pope's suzerainty over Naples was a relic of the Middle Ages, with hardly any place in the modern world. Predictably, when Joseph acceded to his new throne, he refused to accept the pope as his overlord and pay the Chinea.[36] Pius's reaction was to refuse to recognise Joseph as the legitimate king of Naples. To escalate the already palpable tension, the French annexed the papal enclaves and turned them into sinecures. To the church's supreme annoyance Talleyrand was invested prince of Benevento and Marshal Jean-Baptiste Bernadotte became prince of Pontecorvo.[37] This was a clear breach of the Holy See's sovereign rights; papal protests against this violation were ignored. To make matters worse, Cardinal Luigi Ruffo-Scilla, archbishop of Naples (a distant cousin to the more famous Fabrizio), refused to allow prayers and devotions in favour of King Joseph to be celebrated in his archdiocese. He was arrested, imprisoned in Gaeta and then transferred to France, where he would remain a prisoner until 1814.[38]

Between March and April 1806 the Newmann–Sarconi affair erupted in the eternal city. Its catalyst was the arrival in Rome of Dorinda Roger (who used the pseudonym Mrs Newmann), the Irish mistress of Pignatelli Moliterno, Prince Marciconovo, a Neapolitan rebel who was in exile in Prussia (who used the name Sarconi). Roger's presence in the papal capital immediately gave rise to French suspicions that she was transmitting her lover's seditious correspondence to his confederates in Naples. As with Vernègues two years previously, Fesch demanded her arrest and extradition. The papal police took her into custody, placed her in a cell in Castel Sant'Angelo and interrogated her, but there were insufficient grounds for sending her to Paris unless more evidence of her guilt was found.[39] Napoleon furiously accused Consalvi of protecting bandit leaders and encouraging rebels to harass his lines of communication with Naples. Unlike with the Vernègues affair, on this occasion the Holy See refused to surrender a foreign national without due process.

After the peace of Pressburg with the Holy Roman Emperor Francis II was signed on 27 December 1805, the Habsburg Venetian provinces were ceded to the Napoleonic Kingdom of Italy. The French, without consulting the Holy See, extended the provisions of the Italian Concordat to these territories.[40] Pius VII protested against this unilateral act, but again was ignored. Wherever the French imperial standard was planted, the Concordat followed in its wake. During this time, Anglo-Russian naval squadrons started blockading the French-controlled Italian coast more intensely.[41] It was an omen of the economic war that Napoleon was about to unleash. The Continental System, as this foreign policy was known, and which sought to shut out Britain from trading with Europe, technically started with the Berlin Decree of 21 November 1806, issued by Napoleon after he had crushed Prussia at the twin battles of Jena and Auerstädt.[42] In many ways the occupations of both Ancona and Civitavecchia were pilots for the future blockade that Napoleon would visit on the continent. The further that relations with the Papacy deteriorated, the more British and other enemy merchants found themselves harassed in these ports by French troops and customs officials.

The end of the conflict with the Habsburgs witnessed the dissolution of the millennium-old Holy Roman Empire and its replacement by the Confederation of the Rhine under French hegemony.[43] This was the culmination of a process that had begun with the imperial recess of 1803, which had seen the elimination of a significant number of ecclesiastical electorates, prince-bishoprics and monastic lordships. In truth, those German princes who received rich monastic lands had little nostalgia for the ecclesiastical states that had been wiped from the map between 1803 and 1806.[44] The Catholic Church's situation in Germany became remarkably unclear. Karl Theodor von Dalberg, the last prince-elector and archbishop of Mainz, not to mention archchancellor of the Holy Roman Empire, rallied to the French emperor with enthusiasm. As a personal friend of Talleyrand, he became probably the French Empire's most important German client.[45] During Napoleon's coronation in Paris, Pius had been persuaded, reluctantly, to hold two consistories of cardinals in the French capital. During these solemn meetings important ecclesiastical appointments were announced or papal decisions made public. At these extraordinary Parisian consistories, Archbishop Dalberg was removed from Mainz, which was now part of metropolitan France, and given the new prince-archbishopric of Regensburg in compensation.[46] This made manifest Napoleon's ambitions: ecclesiastical patronage now extended into Germany. A year later Dalberg was further rewarded, becoming prince-primate of the Confederation of the Rhine.[47] Napoleon had hoped the pope's trip to Paris would witness the sealing of a German Concordat.

In early 1805, the ubiquitous Bernier campaigned to be invested as papal legate to Germany. He played both sides, hoping to become indispensable to both Papacy and Empire. On this occasion, the one-time parish priest of Saint-Laud miscalculated, and his campaign backfired.[48] The Curia laughed away his candidature and instead chose Annibale della Genga (the future Pope Leo XII), a diplomat with long experience of German affairs, to lead the negotiations. Napoleon, exasperated with the meddlesome Bernier, who was now in increasingly ill health, decided to retire him. He was ordered not to meddle in high politics again. Having returned to Orléans in semi-disgrace, he died in October 1806.[49] Although now largely forgotten, this talented priest embodied a remarkable attempt to bring church and state together. There were few like him, who had served Napoleon and his vision of the future so loyally. The negotiations for a German Concordat between Dalberg and della Genga now stalled. The church was unhappy with giving concessions to an empire that had violated its sovereignty repeatedly, and which was constantly meddling in spiritual matters.

To the surprise of the French bishops, and even more so of the Curia, the French ministry of religions on 4 April 1806 announced that a new Imperial Catechism was to be adopted throughout the Empire.[50] The catechism was a manual, which had been for almost three centuries the key instrument through which the Catholic faith was propagated throughout the world. It was structured in a simple question-and-answer format so that even the illiterate could listen to and memorise the dogmas and teachings of the church.[51] Indeed, until recently, Catholic youths were still examined through questions from the catechism in order to qualify for the sacrament of confirmation. Most of the world used the official catechism, crafted by Pope Paul V after the Council of Trent.[52] However, other versions had been created to take local circumstances into account. In Gallican France the catechism, drafted in 1698 by Bishop Bossuet for the diocese of Meaux, was particularly well-regarded.[53] There was nothing particularly strange in the French government's desire to create a national version of the church's teachings. Indeed, the theologians charged by the Curia to examine the text found little in it that was questionable.[54] The biggest problem, as ever, was that Napoleon and Portalis, his minister of religions, had taken this initiative without consulting the Catholic Church.

Michel'Angelo Toni de Miavi was among the expert theologians charged with examining this new Imperial Catechism. While its wording was generally uncontentious, omissions which were far from accidental. The notion that there was no salvation outside the church teaching had been glossed, while obedience to the ecclesiastical hierarchy, along with the pope's supremacy, was not emphasised; original sin, the economy of salvation and the condemnation of usury had been cut to a few sentences and downgraded in terms of importance.[55] But the most problematic area was a series of questions interpolated into the text, which presented Napoleon's rule as divinely mandated.[56] In most European countries, prayers for the well-being of the monarch were included in both the catechism and liturgy of the Mass. However, Napoleon was referenced personally, rather than as just emperor of the French. It was claimed that divine providence had brought him to the throne. The Imperial Catechism maintained that imperial subjects were commanded by God to pay the state taxes, provide service and conscription: such secular issues went well beyond the remit of what was usually prescribed by the church.[57] Saint Paul had taught that submission to the political regimes had been ordained by God, but this went too far. The theological commission led by Archbishop Bertazzoli did not believe the content of the Imperial Catechism could be condemned outright, but advised the pope to deplore the fact that it had been produced without consultation. In France itself the former constitutional Jean-Baptiste Saurine, bishop of Strasbourg and Louis-Mathias de Barral, the loyalist archbishop of Tours, both complained that it had been imposed on them without discussion. This being said, only Charles François d'Aviau du Bois de Sanzay, archbishop of Bordeaux, refused to publish it in his archdiocese.[58] The Curia's learned observations and objections to this text irritated the imperial government, who saw the new catechism as providing the regime with vital legitimation.

To add to the rising tensions, in 1806 it was decided that henceforth every 15 August, the emperor's birthday and a day traditionally celebrated by Catholics as the feast of the assumption of the Virgin Mary into heaven, or in Italy as the *Ferragosto*, would become a national holiday in honour of Saint Napoleon.[59] The imperial government thus hoped to fuse religious fervour, patriotism and dynastic loyalty into a single celebration. It must be said that the historical basis for Saint Napoleon was more than a little dubious. According to some acrobatic research, this saint was, apparently, an early Christian martyr in Egypt, whose name was sometimes spelt as Neopolis.[60] Attendance at the celebrations for Saint Napoleon would become a barometer for the regime's stability. As repression grew in the Empire, the day became a flashpoint between the authorities and those who protested against imperial rule. Priests who failed to mention the emperor in their sermons, or who did not recite the *domine salvum fac* prayers, could find themselves arrested. Rome did not condemn the feast outright, but its reaction was unenthusiastic. Pius seemed perennially caught in a vortex of political and religious crises not of his making.

On 18 April 1806 Napoleon made good on his threat to recall Fesch and downgrade his diplomatic agent in Rome. His half-uncle was given something of a promotion by being appointed as Dalberg's coadjutor in Regensburg. This made Fesch not only the most important cleric in France, he was also the successor to the senior German clergyman. The emperor was never clear what his ultimate intention was for Fesch, but one could speculate that he was being groomed to become the primate of a Neo-Carolingian Empire stretching across western Europe. He was replaced in Rome by Charles-Jean-Marie Alquier, a former moderate revolutionary deputy and experienced diplomat.[61] Fesch's departure audience with Pius VII was dramatic, and minuted by Consalvi. Apparently, the pope refused to rule out issuing canonical sanctions as a remedy against Napoleon's aggressions. These could involve anything from refusing to invest new bishops to excommunication. Fesch, in a furious fit of family loyalty, replied that, if any such action were undertaken, then the Gallican Church would convene a national council and invest their own bishops without recourse to Rome.[62] To add insult to injury, Alquier was appointed a minister plenipotentiary rather than ambassador. The downgrading of the diplomatic mission in Rome made manifest the French emperor's displeasure with Pius.

Consalvi suspected that, once back in Paris, Fesch would report that he was to blame for the Papacy's obstinacy and refusal to collaborate. The emperor had certainly become convinced that a more pliant secretary of state in Rome would be needed. The Empire wanted to negotiate a treaty of alliance with Rome, whereby the church acknowledged that the Papal States fell under imperial hegemony. The campaign to be rid of Consalvi was brutal, and certainly made him an implacable enemy of Napoleon.[63] Caprara, from Paris, sent panicked despatches stating that it was only through a miracle that the Papal States had not already been occupied. All of Europe, except Britain and Russia, had submitted to the French. Could the pope alone stand firm against the Napoleonic Empire?[64] On 17 June 1806, supported by the College of Cardinals, the pope transmitted a solemn diplomatic protest. Cardinal di Pietro had drafted a document which listed all the violations – both spiritual and temporal – inflicted on the pope's sovereignty. In the aftermath of this diatribe, Pius bowed to the inevitable: Cardinal Consalvi's resignation was accepted on 17 June 1806. Denounced as an enemy of France, his position had now become untenable. He was replaced by Cardinal Filippo Casoni, who had been nuncio to Madrid. Although more acceptable to France, this elderly prelate was as resolute as Consalvi in resisting aggression and maintaining neutrality. On 19 July 1806, Casoni informed the indecisive Caprara that, if France invaded Rome, he was to close the legation in Paris and withdraw immediately.[65] Throughout his tenure he would do his best to temporise and delay the French Empire's creep towards central Italy.

The years 1806 and 1807 were ones of grim foreboding in the Curia and the College of Cardinals. Historians have not drawn attention to a remarkable series of documents and drafts which demonstrate that Rome was preparing detailed contingency plans for its governance should the pope and College of Cardinals be arrested and unable to communicate freely with the universal church. These plans created a parallel hierarchy of secret agents and alternative decision-making structures to be put in place should the worst happen. When the French eventually annexed the Papal States, they were met with a campaign of passive resistance and civil disobedience propped up by a clandestine network that astounded them. After two years of planning, the cardinals, priests and civil officials knew what they were doing. They could not hope to confront the overwhelming force of French military might with armed resistance. Therefore, everything had to be done to remind the population that Pius VII was their legitimate ruler, and that the invaders were usurpers. It is difficult to reconstruct such plans minutely because much of the time instructions were given verbally and many documents were destroyed or lost during the French occupation. It would also seem that scores of agents, apostolic delegates and governors consigned such plans to memory in order to avoid being caught with compromising documents in their possession. From fresh research undertaken for this book, a new picture clearly emerges of Pius undoubtedly planning and preparing his clergy and subjects for an almost doomsday-like scenario. Even if the pope were absent, the government of state and the church would have to continue as best it could.

An undated document, probably from around July 1806 (judging from the bundle in which it is located in the Vatican Archives), sets out a series of questions for the College of Cardinals to consider.[66] These revolve around two potential scenarios: first, the occupation and annexation of Rome; second, the possibility that Napoleon might come in person to the eternal city to intimidate the church. The document, probably a brainstorming exercise, listed thirteen questions. Only one dealt directly with the frightful possibility of a French annexation of Rome into the Empire. Should the pope in this case first communicate his formal protest against the loss of his kingdom to the courts of Europe or to his subjects, appealing to them immediately to resist the invader? The remaining series of questions dealt with the hypothetical and very unwelcome arrival of Napoleon in Rome. Some were trivial, relating to his ceremonial reception at the border: should he be met with full honours or asked to visit incognito? More worrying was the issue of what was to be done if he tried to intimidate individual cardinals or used his troops to force his presence at papal congregations and/or consistories. What should the Curia do if Napoleon demanded that Joseph be crowned king of Naples in Rome, or, worse, if he insisted that he be crowned emperor of the West in Saint Peter's Basilica? Finally, the pope's advisers wondered whether Napoleon's offer to join a military federation should be accepted. These scenarios present a College of Cardinals preparing itself for the inevitable, and fearful that the emperor of the French was becoming a modern Nero. These hypotheticals were not as fanciful as they might seem on a first reading. The archbishop of Seleucia, Tommaso Arezzo, returning from a mission to Saint Petersburg, was asked to meet Napoleon in Berlin on 9 November 1806. He was told to inform the pope that he had until the end of February 1807 to join his federation.[67] A refusal would mean the occupation of Rome.

Even before Arezzo brought this ultimatum home, the Curia intensified its preparations. The Vatican Archives hold an unsigned agenda of items, dated 6 July 1806, requiring individual responses from every member of the Sacred College.[68] Its author believed that there were three possible outcomes if the French invaded:

1. that the entire Papal States would be annexed to France;
2. that all territory apart from Rome would be taken by the Empire;
3. that a temporary military occupation of the pope's domains would follow.

A series of seven questions dealt with these three scenarios. The key question was how the pope should condemn such an invasion, and how he should communicate it to the outside world. Only Cardinal di Pietro's answers appear to survive, but they provide a remarkable glimpse into papal planning for a French invasion.[69] The tone of resilience and determination contained in these pages was something the French were totally unprepared to confront. Some of the recommendations read like the plot of a Cold War spy novel. Sealed envelopes were to be given to the governors of the provinces and larger cities so that, even if Rome was conquered quickly and the pope imprisoned, they would still know what to do. The plan was that a papal bull, prohibiting any oath of loyalty and active collaboration with the occupying power, would be published and distributed throughout central Italy. Cardinals would need to be brave and keep all these preparations strictly secret should they be captured by the French.

The final questions dealt with contingency plans to come into force should the pope and the College of Cardinals be imprisoned by the French. Flight was deemed impossible, given that the Papal States were surrounded by enemy forces; di Pietro advised that the Holy Father might only leave Rome if threatened with violence. If he was taken prisoner, he would have to endure captivity with Christlike resignation; however, if a choice were offered, the pope should head for Catholic Germany.[70] Flight to Britain or Russia was not considered in these pages. One can only speculate that di Pietro felt that the pope could not seek asylum among the non-Catholic powers. For the Curia's chief theologian, it was axiomatic that the College of Cardinals should seek to remain close to the pontiff during this ordeal.

This panel of experts also considered the hypothetical question of what should be done were the pope to die as a captive (as had been the fate of Pius VI in 1799). It advised that a future conclave must not under any circumstances take place on French territory. In such circumstances the cardinal secretary of state and the dean of the College of Cardinals should head to a safe location, with Germany thought to be the best place to assemble cardinals for a conclave free from French interference. The protection of the Habsburgs would be sought to ensure the election of an independent pope who would not be a mere puppet of the French emperor. During this hypothetical time of crisis, the Curia advised that the regents and governors of the Papal States should go underground in order to continue secretly to exercise their authority, and ignore the illegitimate government that the French would establish in the pope's absence. These remarkable documents show that the church was very far from unprepared for the worst. Indeed, there was an entire programme of resistance in place for several contingencies. Papal government would continue beneath the surface, even if the pope and the College of Cardinals were impeded from communicating with the outside world.

While Rome contemplated the worst-case scenario, Napoleon wanted to exercise his right to nominate bishops to vacant sees in his Italian kingdom, claiming that this right extended over the recently annexed Venetian dioceses.[71] By the autumn, there were eleven positions that the emperor wanted to fill. Cardinal Casoni informed Napoleon that His Holiness was not inclined to bestow letters of investiture, given that the Italian Concordat had been breached, as had the sovereignty of the Papal States.[72] The refusal to nominate the candidates chosen by the emperor had echoes of the eleventh century, when a similar situation had pitted Pope Gregory VII against the Holy Roman Emperor Henry IV.[73] This crisis had reached its climax when Henry had been forced to appear, barefoot, clad in a hair shirt, in the freezing snow outside the castle of Canossa. Here Gregory VII made him wait as a penance for having defied him. Napoleon was no medieval emperor, and knew his history well enough to wish to avoid at all costs a reoccurrence of those events. The crisis over episcopal investiture in the French Empire was to prove intractable. For many years the Papacy refused to yield and confirm Napoleon's episcopal candidates.

By February 1807, Pius had refused to acquiesce to the ultimatum given to Monsignor Arezzo. The pope argued that he could not take sides in the conflict against Great Britain, and that he would not concede the automatic extension of the Concordat to all lands annexed by the French.[74] By the summer of 1807, Russia had been defeated at the Battle of Friedland. The emperor could now turn his attention to Rome. From Dresden, on 22 July 1807, he wrote a wrathful letter to his adopted son Eugène de Beauharnais, the viceroy of Italy, stating that if Rome published a denunciation of him as an enemy of religion he would regard Pius as the antipope:

> The current pope is too powerful, priests are not made to govern . . . Why then does the pope not wish to render unto Caesar what is due to Caesar, does he consider himself above Christ? Maybe the time is not far, if he continues to trouble my states, that I will only recognise the pope as bishop of Rome, as

equal and of the same rank as any other bishop in my states. I have no fear of summoning the Gallican, Italian, German and Polish churches in council to solve my affairs with the pope . . . I hold my crown from God and from my peoples, I am only accountable to God and my peoples. I will always be Charlemagne for the court of Rome and never Louis the Debonair.[75]

In a pre-arranged ruse, Eugène wrote to Pius VII attaching a copy of this letter. The viceroy of Italy, in a letter ghost-written by Napoleon, craftily tried to forewarn the pope of his stepfather's wrath, begging him to come to his senses and negotiate with the Empire for the good of the church and Italy.

The pope was clearly unsettled and deeply troubled by the ferocity of this menacing letter. He replied the following month that he was unmoved by threats and that his conscience was serene. He was willing, however, to send a cardinal to Paris to open discussions with the emperor. Initially, Alquier insisted that Caprara should be the man invested with the plenipotentiary powers to negotiate. Knowing that the easily intimidated and unreliable legate would collapse under French demands, the pope refused. The Curia initially proposed that Cardinal Lorenzo Litta, a Milanese prince of the church and thus a subject of the emperor, go to France to negotiate an alliance. However, this candidate proved unacceptable to Paris, and instead Cardinal Bayanne, an expert canon lawyer, was appointed as papal negotiator.[76]

Because of a disagreement with Napoleon, Talleyrand had quit the foreign ministry, where he was replaced by the career diplomat Jean-Baptiste Nompère de Champagny. On 21 September 1807, Champagny transmitted a list of demands to Bayanne.[77] This stated that the eastern provinces of the Papal States would be annexed to provide a vital corridor to link the Kingdom of Italy with the Kingdom of Naples. As far as the emperor was concerned there was nothing to negotiate when it came to France: it was his intention that there would be no monks in his domains, and that under no circumstances should the Society of Jesuits be resurrected.[78] Since the eighteenth century a trans-European myth had grown up around these stormtroopers of the Counter-Reformation, who were seen as far too worldly in their love of political power and far too lax in their moral teachings.[79] A joint Franco-Portuguese and Spanish campaign had led to the order's abolition in 1773. Since then, European rulers, with Napoleon no exception, had worried that former Jesuits were still operating, stealthily trying to recreate their defunct order. Given their ultimate loyalty to the Papacy and perceived love of political intrigue, the French government persecuted any priests suspected of having Jesuitical intentions. Indeed, the Congregation of the Fathers of Faith (made up of former Jesuits) was declared illegal and hounded all the way to Poland by imperial authorities.

Champagny stressed that the Italian Concordat should cover all territories on the peninsula, and that Italian bishops would not travel to Rome for their investiture. Finally, he demanded that a German Concordat be finalised in Paris. It was his expectation that Dalberg and della Genga would meet to finalise this treaty.[80] One can only imagine that Bayanne must have taken a very deep breath on reading over these ominous words. He was being asked to capitulate, to surrender the pope's sovereignty even before he reached Paris. Indeed, a few weeks later, in October, Eugène de Beauharnais's troops, from the Kingdom of Italy, occupied the Marche, the eastern coast of the Papal States, where the pope's governor Agostino Rivarola was arrested and deported. Half of the church's territory was now in Napoleon's hands.[81]

In November 1807 Bayanne was presented with a draft treaty in Fontainebleau. It prescribed that the Holy See would enter an 'offensive-defensive' alliance against the British and other infidels.[82] In return the emperor would offer his protection and defend papal shipping against the Barbary pirates. The pope would also observe the Continental System, refusing all British trade. The ports of Ancona, Civitavecchia and Ostia would be occupied permanently by French troops. It was expected that the Curia would pay for the upkeep of these occupying forces, while Napoleon would pay the costs for his soldiers transiting through the Papal States. It was also stipulated that the legitimacy of all of Napoleon's brothers and sisters who now reigned in Naples, Holland, Westphalia, Berg, Lucca and Piombino would be formally recognised by the Catholic Church. The treaty also demanded that Pius renounce his sovereignty over Pontecorvo and Benevento, and that the provisions of the Italian Concordat be extended to all territories under the Empire's control. There was in addition a stipulation that in future a third of the College of Cardinals would be assigned to the French Empire. Predictably, the treaty demanded that a Concordat on German affairs be negotiated as a priority.[83]

Bayanne was intimidated by Champagny and urged acceptance of these incredibly harsh terms. Candidly he advised that, if the Papacy refused, military occupation would automatically follow.[84] The emperor was determined to force Pius VII to yield. In December, he was on a state visit in northern Italy. Napoleon had much on his mind: he was about to become embroiled in the invasion of Spain, while in central Europe the Habsburgs were rearming.[85] The decision to beat Rome into submission was almost as bad a miscalculation as his strategic blunder of transforming Spain from an unreliable ally into an unstable satellite dominion riven by insurgency.[86] The Holy See attempted a final appeal: Cardinals Caselli and Oppizzoni were to meet with Napoleon during his Italian trip. The Holy See asked them to appeal to his moderation. It was well known that these two prelates were favourites of the emperor. As already mentioned (see p. 97), Caselli had been rewarded for his role in negotiating the French Concordat by being made a cardinal and by being granted the rich archdiocese of Parma.[87] Oppizzoni had been a long-standing supporter of the regime, and sanctioned the organic laws in Italy to the fury of the Curia. He was elevated to the crimson at the remarkably young age of thirty-five, and given the archdiocese of Bologna.[88] Here, despite his best intentions, he became mired in scandal. Unpopular with the Jacobin and Napoleonic administration of the city, he was accused of a sexual liaison with an underage prostitute. The charge was probably false and instigated by his enemies, chiefly Teodoro Somenzari, the city's prefect. In the end, Napoleon ordered a cover-up: it was also decided that both the young prostitute and her procuress would be detained until things simmered down.[89] The emperor was under the impression that he had done Oppizzoni a major favour; however, the cardinal, who strenuously protested his innocence, was upset that he had not been given the opportunity to clear his name in court.[90] Furthermore, none of his accusers had been punished. The Oppizzoni affair was a comedy of errors. Napoleon, despite his best efforts, had the uncanny ability of alienating his ecclesiastical collaborators.

At 11 a.m. on 20 December 1807, Oppizzoni and Caselli ascended the grand staircase into the throne room of the royal palace of Milan, adjacent to the city's magnificent Gothic Duomo. Thinking they were bearing a special message from Pius, the emperor showered them with a litany of abuse and uttered many 'disgusting things'. Napoleon said that he had always respected the pope's spiritual prerogatives, but that in secular matters he was a prince like any other and would be treated accordingly. Instead, the pope had continued to consort with the enemies of France. The cardinals, clearly terrified by this explosion of fury, reminded the emperor that Cardinal Bayanne was charged with negotiating a treaty of alliance. This was surely evidence of the Papacy's goodwill towards the Empire. Angrily, Bonaparte retorted that this individual had not been given sufficient powers and that he would be forced to annul Charlemagne's donation of lands to the Papal States. He admired the pope on a personal level, but no one appreciated how much he had done for Catholicism in France, Italy and Germany. He had even restored Catholic worship in Calvinist Holland! Surely Rome had no better friend than him? The pope had two months to make up his mind; after this, the emperor's patience would be exhausted completely. As was so often the case, these two prelates left the meeting feeling that their attempt to conciliate the French emperor had produced the opposite reaction.[91]

The secretary of state, Cardinal Casoni, was unable to temporise further: in letters dated 3 and 28 December he rejected the French treaty of alliance.[92] Cardinal Bayanne, in order to return to Rome, was forced to seek his passport back from Champagny.[93] The breach was now sealed. At the same time, in January 1808, the draft German Concordat, elaborated between Dalberg and Caprara, was roundly rejected by the theologians of the Curia.[94] Indeed, the author of the report condemning this draft (probably Cardinal di Pietro) did not recognise Napoleon's authority to contract such an agreement on behalf of the princes of the Confederation of the Rhine.[95] The collapse of the German Concordat sealed the formal breach with the French Empire. The imperial response was to be swift. Troops were already mustering on the borders of the Papal States in anticipation of the final collapse in negotiations.

It was decided to give the command of the forces entering the Papal States to General Sextius Alexandre François de Miollis, a veteran of the American War of Independence; he had been wounded at the siege of Yorktown in 1781, leaving him with a prominent facial scar.[96] He came from an old Provençal family of lawyers, and his older brother Bienvenu de Miollis was bishop of Digne (a clergyman of impeccable probity, who, apparently, served as the basis for the character of Monseigneur Myriel in Hugo's *Les Misérables*).[97] There is little evidence that General Miollis was particularly anticlerical and certainly later he did his best to treat the pope with respect. He was, however, a rigid military professional for whom orders were gospel. He had rallied to the Empire, had wide experience of campaigning in Italy and believed in the Napoleonic vision of a well-ordered modern state.

In late January French forces advanced towards Rome. It was exactly ten years after a similar force had captured Rome, established a Jacobin republic and arrested Pius VI.[98] For his successor, this moment must have represented complete failure. Despite his willingness to come to terms with modernity, not only by underwriting two concordats but also by crowning the emperor of the French in person, Pius's beloved Rome was now in peril. In a tavern near the Milvian Bridge the occupation of Rome began. According to legend, during the fourth century, the Emperor Constantine had experienced a vision. He looked up towards the sun and saw a cross with the words *In hoc signo vinces* ('With this symbol, you will be victorious'). Crosses were placed on the shields of his troops and at the Battle of the Milvian Bridge he defeated his rival Maxentius to become undisputed ruler of the Roman Empire.[99] This bridge, then, marked the point at which Catholicism had become a state religion. On 2 February 1808, at three in the afternoon, Count Filippo Resta, a colonel in the pontifical army, met with Miollis, who was taking some refreshment. He asked the general if he expected his troops to camp outside the city or to be billeted within the walls. Miollis replied that his 'forces would go through Rome like a thunderbolt!'[100] Resta was forced to mount a horse and follow a French column through Porta del Popolo, into one of the most beautiful squares in the world. From here, they marched to Porta Angelica, one of the main gates to the Vatican. Here the invaders halted, divided into small groups and started occupying the key strategic points of the city. General Miollis insisted that his occupation would be temporary and that he would not interfere with the civil authorities of the Papacy. This pretence was accepted, but one wonders how far the cardinals were truly fooled by such reassurances.

A significant detachment of infantry, cavalry, artillery and engineers appeared before the walls of Castel Sant'Angelo, the citadel of Rome. Angelo Colli, the commander of the fortress, was approached by Lieutenant-Colonel Briand of the 3rd Dragoons and ordered to surrender. Colli seems to have possessed little desire for heroism, let alone martyrdom. He stated that he did not have permission to surrender the fortress, but at the same time had been ordered not to resist if violence were used.[101] Briand intimated that force would be deployed to its fullest extent. Colli demanded that his garrison be allowed to evacuate the fortress with the honour of arms. This was agreed to, and Colli wrote a protest against the illegal seizure of his fortress, stating that he would not surrender the keys for the storehouses and munitions under his command. The papal garrison exited, flags unfurled, shouldering their arms, and headed to their barracks on Piazza Barberini. The French forces who occupied the fortress found the pope's political prisoners still in its cells. It would take them some time to decide what to do with these captives. After all, the enemies of the pope might potentially be transformed into loyal collaborators.[102] The next day Alquier requested an audience on behalf of Miollis with Pius VII. Although tension-filled, the occasion was cordial, with the general claiming that he was in transit towards Naples. He informed the authorities that he had occupied the Papal States as a police measure in order to apply the Continental System against Britain, and to hunt for brigands who were disrupting Napoleonic rule.[103]

The reaction of the people of Rome to the arrival of foreign soldiers was an ashen-faced stony silence. Some officers mistakenly believed that behind these inscrutable expressions the French were perceived as liberators from papal oppression.[104] It is true that a republican minority did feel this way, but they were hardly representative. For the people of the city and its nobility the invasion of the eternal city was a grim day. Initially Miollis did try to woo city elites to the pro-imperial camp. Balls and gala dinners were held for the cream of the Roman nobility. A curious Cardinal Consalvi even attended one such *soirée*.[105] Letters of disapproval and disappointment were immediately sent by the pope to those who joined these festivities. The papal government had been preparing for almost two years and discreetly reminded its subjects that to fraternise with the invaders was traitorous. Soon the French would be confronted by a campaign of passive resistance and civil disobedience. Certainly, the occupiers could be their own worst enemies. The decision to place artillery outside the gates of the Quirinal Palace caused a public scandal.[106] Miollis soon ordered these guns to be transferred to more discreet locations.

As the weeks passed a vacuum seemed to form wherever Miollis went. The Romans filled the churches of their king-pope to pray for deliverance from their godless invaders, and refused any interaction with the occupying forces. With his health now seriously impaired, Cardinal Casoni was forced to resign and was replaced in the interim by Cardinal Giuseppe Doria.[107] Unable to get the pope to yield to a military alliance, Alquier found himself recalled to Paris. The Holy See sent word to Caprara that his powers as legate were suspended, and he too was recalled.[108] Miollis decided not to leave any hostages to fortune. His troops began overseeing all the print shops of Rome and the papal postal service was taken over by French officials. There was a fear that Pius might use these printing presses to inform the outside world that he was now a prisoner. The imperial government started publishing a newspaper called *La Gazzetta Romana*, which printed official news for the occupied territories.[109] Meanwhile brick walls, reinforced doors and boarded-up windows started appearing in the Quirinal

Palace, a desperate attempt to prevent the French from gaining easy access to the pope's private apartments. At the end of February, six Neapolitan cardinals were forcibly removed from Rome and sent to Naples to swear allegiance to Joseph. By the end of March, a further fifteen princes of the church from the Kingdom of Italy, including Cardinal Doria, the secretary of state, were ordered to leave Rome and return to their dioceses.[110]

Throughout the pope's captivity, the French sought to isolate him from his closest advisers and prevent information from filtering through to the outside world. Such attempts proved a dismal failure. As already mentioned, the church had from 1806 established several clandestine information networks; these Napoleon's police managed to disrupt, but never completely to crack. On 16 March 1808 the pope published a formal allocution, condemning the occupation of Rome and other violations of papal sovereignty. It was one of the most ultramontane statements of papal authority to date:

> The government of the church is not based on any representative system but on the absolute power of the Vicar of Christ, [who] together in union with the Sacred College [of Cardinals], which is the supreme council of the head of the church, directs and administers the supreme authority given unto him by God for the edification and good of the church. It is absolutely contrary to the nature, institution and office of the supreme pontiff that any secular power should wish to influence or prescribe the numbers of members that compose [this body].[111]

The pope had no wish to join a military alliance, or bestow a third of cardinals to France. He reminded Napoleon that God was a far greater monarch than him, and that his wrath often struck the mighty in order to cast them down from their thrones.[112] Printed versions of this speech were in widespread circulation, while a formal diplomatic protest against the invasion of the Papal States reached all the courts of Europe. The pope would not have to wait long for the imperial response to arrive.

On 2 April 1808, an edict in Napoleon's name as king of Italy formally declared that, on 11 May, Urbino, Ancona, Macerata and Camerino would be annexed. Furthermore, these provinces were to be turned into three departments of the Kingdom of Italy and the French Civil Code would come into force there from 1 June. The decree also announced that all the institutions of the modern state would supplant ecclesiastical ones. All officials and bishops would be required to swear an oath of allegiance to the king of Italy.[113] Pius VII sent a secret brief to the loyal bishops of the Marche. Here he declared the annexation of these provinces sacrilegious. The Papacy's temporal rights over central Italy were ordained by God himself in order to guarantee the independence of the church from secular interference. The pope's principality was inalienable and divinely mandated. No subject should repudiate Pius's legitimacy by swearing allegiance to an occupying power. Equally, no clergy should collaborate with the French by singing *Te Deums* for military victories, let alone in celebrating Saint Napoleon's feast day. Pius VII was determined to avoid violence and disorder. Therefore, while active participation in the usurping government was prohibited, passive submission could be allowed under certain conditions. Papal functionaries and clergy were permitted to take the following modified oath: 'I promise and swear not to take part in any conspiracy, plot or sedition against the current government. I also promise to submit to and be obedient in all matters that do not contravene the laws of God and the church.'

No subjects of the pope were allowed, under any circumstances, to work for the French ministries of finance or religions. In these offices even the modified oath was unacceptable. The pope, with grim realism, advised that persecution would erupt in the wake of his instructions, and that all members of the church must follow the example of Christ. Rewards for such resistance awaited in the next life.[114] Reprisals occurred directly: Cardinal Gabrielli, who had succeeded Doria as secretary of state, was immediately arrested when the French learned of this modified oath. He was then ordered to leave Rome and to return to his diocese of Senigallia near Ancona.[115] Doria and Gabrielli held the office of secretary of state for barely two months each. Their tenures were among the briefest in the history of this office. Gabrielli's temporary successor Bartolomeo Pacca was determined to do better in these difficult circumstances.[116] He was a native of papal Benevento and a decided reactionary, with little sympathy for the upheavals of revolution. He had had a stellar diplomatic career, and in 1791 had been posted to Liège to negotiate with the anti-episcopal revolutionaries of that city. Pius VI had given him a letter of congratulations to deliver to Louis XVI in the expectation that his flight from Paris in June would end in success. The capture of the royal family at Varennes made this impossible: and he was never to be the pope's emissary to the French king at Montmedy. For the next ten years Pacca was papal nuncio to Lisbon, where he fought vigorously against the autonomy of the local episcopate from Rome, and tried to rid Portuguese seminaries of their Jansenist tendencies. He returned to the eternal city in 1802, was elevated to cardinal and became a closer collaborator of the *zelanti* faction. Although inflexible, Pacca was a man of spirit, as his memoirs make clear. His resolve to resist invasion and maintain papal supremacy over the church galvanised Pius as he entered the most difficult years of his life.

Napoleon, in the meantime, was embroiled in Spain, dealing with the consequences of one of the biggest mistakes of his career. The decision to depose the Spanish Bourbons and replace them with his brother Joseph was hugely unpopular, and led to a mass insurrection throughout the Iberian peninsula and the despatch of a British expedionary army to assist the insurgents.[117] The French pattern of confiscating church lands and requiring oaths from clergy was akin to pouring kerosene onto flames in many regions of Spain. The abolition of the Holy Inquisition may have been popular in the salons of Paris, but in Catholic Europe it was viewed, with decidedly mixed feelings, as another encroachment by an anti-religious imperial state.[118] The abolishing of monasteries, the harassment of priests, inflamed the passions of the Spanish peasantry against the invaders.[119] The archives of the Inquisition were transported to Paris, and Juan Antonio Llorente, a former inquisitor turned dissident, was charged with writing a negative history of this ecclesiastical tribunal.[120] This history was eventually completed in 1817; entitled *Histoire critique de l'Inquisition d'Espagne*, debate still rages on the so-called black legend of the Spanish Inquisition created by this multi-volume history.[121] In his study of the Inquisition Llorente had been given a clear agenda by Napoleon: to mud-rake and to exaggerate the brutality of this 'fanatical' court.[122]

While Napoleon was in Spain with the Grande Armée seeking to crush Anglo-Spanish forces, the Habsburgs accelerated their rearmament and, hoping that they might check the inexorable advance of the French Empire, launched a pre-emptive military strike.[123] A peasant revolt in the Tyrolean hills, led by Andreas Hofer, was deeply Catholic in nature; some interpreted it as a sign of an imminent general pan-German revolt against French oppression.[124] With some justification, Napoleon feared that his worst nightmare was becoming a reality. The Concordat of 1801 was supposed to defuse the bomb of religious opposition. It had been the intention of the consular regime to transform Catholics from enemies into allies, but imperial expansion and the mistreatment of the pope had produced the opposite effect. Napoleon, for the first time in his career, was uncertain of what to do with Rome. Faced with insurgencies in Spain and Tyrol, not to mention a Habsburg military offensive in his rear, he now had no fewer than four separate crises to resolve.[125]

General Miollis and his forces were meanwhile becoming increasingly frustrated in their attempts to win hearts and minds in Rome. The pontifical army was incorporated into the French armed forces. The supine Colonel Fries accepted this, but the vast majority of the officers of his regiment preferred arrest and imprisonment over the betrayal of their oaths to the pope.[126] It had been traditional for soldiers to wear the yellow-and-red cockade of the city of Rome to show their allegiance. Now, those troops who remained under the direct control of the Papacy, to emphasise their loyalty to Pius, started wearing a new cockade of yellow and white: these were the traditional colours of the city of Rome, but also replicated the silver and gold of Saint Peter's keys. These symbolised the pope's power, both spiritual and temporal. The Swiss Guard and the *Guardia Nobile* continued to wear these emblems to highlight their rejection of the French occupation.[127] Many priests and members of the population also did the same as a show of defiance. Near Piazza Navona there stands a fragment of a classical statue (some believe it to be part of a larger piece that portrayed Achilles grieving over the dead Patroclus).[128] In times of trouble Romans hung (and still hang) placards around the neck of this statue, known locally as Pasquino, bearing satirical verse written in the Roman dialect voicing the displeasure of the populace of the eternal city. During Napoleon's reign these placards, which had in the past been used to criticise the Borgia pope and many others, now turned their fire on the French emperor. Miollis himself received an anonymous wreath composed of musket balls with a note from Pasquino with the words 'Spanish olives', a clear reference to Napoleonic brutality in Spain. One placard hung around the statue's neck read:

Bears, not men, are made to dance with a stick
Let Napoleon know that
I, Pasquino, don't give a f—k about him.[129]

The attempt made by the French, in 1808, to create a civic guard or local militia loyal to them was to backfire dramatically. Ever since the French Revolution, militias of 'upstanding' citizens had been formed throughout the French

Imperium to ensure public order and to perform basic policing duties, constituting a home guard in case of invasion.[130] Miollis decided to import this institution into the Roman provinces. The Papacy had always outsourced its law and order on its peripheries to a very controversial group known as *sbirri*, or *birri*. They were essentially paid thugs, little better than the bandits they purportedly kept in check. They were a classic case of poachers turned gamekeepers: in return for money and a blind eye turned to their racketeering, they maintained a semblance of tranquillity outside the capital and major cities.[131] Where the modern state failed to penetrate, loose and inefficient arrangements, like the *sbirri*, flourished. As soon as Miollis started recruiting for his new civic guard, Pius issued an allocution warning his subjects that service on this force would lead to immediate excommunication and imperil their immortal souls.

To the French government's surprise, printed versions of this pronouncement appeared on the city's walls and across all of central Italy.[132] Perhaps predictably, many *sbirri* and other assorted members of the demi-monde joined the civic guard with what, for them, amounted to enthusiasm. In Piperno the civic guard became a means for the town's criminal underbelly to settle old scores. Brutal honour killings and punishments took place for several weeks.[133] To Cardinal Pacca's glee this gave him a pretext to protest formally about the bad behaviour of this militia.[134] For Miollis's military government, the *sbirrification* of the civic guard was immensely embarrassing. The Empire was supposed to showcase the benefits of modern government through efficient policing, probity and the maintenance of order. In the first years of the French occupation the opposite was the case. Renegades and political dissidents rallied enthusiastically to the French Tricolour. It was at this point that Napoleon intervened, ordering General Radet, the head of the Imperial Gendarmerie in Tuscany, to head to Rome. It was felt that the general and his 400 military policemen, made up of elite veterans, would do a better job than the *sbirro*-infested civic guard.

During this time the Quirinal Palace became the focus of French attention. In theory it had been safeguarded as the pope's place of residence. Those who entered and exited it were searched thoroughly. Despite this, papal communications still filtered through to the outside world. Miollis suspected that the campaign of passive resistance was being orchestrated from the very private apartments of the pope. On one occasion, French troops entered the offices of the secretary of state and removed documents which Miollis needed for the orderly administration of the Roman provinces.[135] On another, the papal armoury was breached, some

Swiss Guards maltreated and the *Guardia Nobile* disarmed.[136] The most serious violation occurred in September 1808, when an attempt was made to arrest Cardinal Pacca and spirit him away to an imperial fortress. Pius personally came to the apartments of his pro-secretary of state and interposed himself physically between the cardinal and his would-be captors.[137] This brave action stopped the arrest and deportation of his friend and adviser. After this incident, crowds of Romans flooded into Piazza di Monte Cavallo, shouting 'Bravo il Papa!'

Through the winter of 1808 and spring of 1809, the tense stand-off continued. The pope started to omit Napoleon's name in the bulls of investiture for French bishops (a clear insult against the emperor – it made it seem as if the pope appointed bishops without imperial direction): the investiture crisis, which had begun in Italy, now spread to metropolitan France.[138] The pope refused any further negotiations while his states were occupied. To Miollis it was clear that little could be done to administer Rome with Pius residing in his capital. With the pope in the Quirinal, the people of Rome rallied to him and regarded the French as usurpers. Fesch's familial loyalty showed the first signs of wavering during these tense months. He wrote to his nephew begging him, on behalf of the French clergy, not to create a new schism with the church.[139] The pope's predicament was wholly disconcerting to Catholic Europe, and was not helping the Empire's public image. Only Cardinal Maury was pleased with the turn of events: in a volte-face of epic proportions he merely expressed surprise that the pope had not yielded to the emperor.[140] The chanceries of Europe had received Pius's protest against the occupation and annexation of his states, but most monarchs and their ministers were too fearful of Napoleon's military might to support the papacy. Only the Habsburgs refused to recognise the occupation of Rome and the annexation of papal territory; when Austria declared war on Napoleon on 10 April 1809, it withdrew its diplomatic staff from Rome and all territories under occupation.

In December 1808 Pius VII had refused to receive Miollis and his staff for Christmas greetings. The pope also declined to send out the traditional season's compliments to the courts of Europe to highlight the fact that he was a prisoner. As carnival approached, the French administrators promised the traditional extravaganza of food, fireworks and entertainments. Immediately the Quirinal issued instructions that people should avoid these events at all costs.[141] Indeed, the carnival of 1809 was to be one of the dreariest and least well-attended in the history of Rome. The shops and windows of the *corso*, one of the most important commercial streets of the city, remained tightly sealed, and the absence of illuminations made the city seem as if it was in mourning.[142] Historically a festival that had always been the great favourite of the Roman population, the collective decision to desert their usual revelries was a sign of the extent of their displeasure with the French occupiers.

One group who did not long for a return to the past, though, were the Jews of the Ghetto of Rome, for whom the coming of the French Empire represented liberation.[143] Each carnival the Roman population would invade the ghetto and perform a pogrom of sorts. During the fifteenth and sixteenth centuries the *Palio dei judei* had been a particularly barbaric practice. This was no sporting occasion but rather a gratuitous humiliation; Jews were forced to eat a large (probably non-kosher) meal, before being run naked through the city as Romans flung mud and rotten vegetables at their Jewish neighbours. The custom was formally prohibited by the Papacy at the end of the seventeenth century and commuted into a tax.[144] Despite this interdict, the fishmongers' guild continued to dress up as Jews, while their leader was made up like a rabbi, leading his brethren in procession through the Ghetto.[145] Insults and incidents of violence remained common in the Jewish quarter during carnival time. But under Napoleonic rule this cruel custom did not occur. For all its authoritarianism, the modern state imposed religious equality on all. Napoleon's subjects were citizens first and people of faith second. He found superstitions and folk festivities disruptive to good order and was determined to stamp them out. The Jews were freed from the ghettos and permitted to own property, horses and vehicles like any other citizens, much to the annoyance of bigoted Catholics.

Finally, on 10 June 1809, the inevitable happened. The papal standard flying from Castel Sant'Angelo was lowered, and the French Tricolour raised in its place. A thunderous cannonade signalled to the population of the eternal city and the world that all remaining papal territory had been annexed to France. Rome had now become the second city of the Empire, and all its antiquities were placed under the protection of the French state.[146] According to legend, Pius observed the changing of the flag from a window of the Quirinal Palace and sighed '*Consummatum est!*', 'It has come to pass!' – the very words Christ uttered at the moment he died on the cross.[147] The end of the temporal power of the pope could not pass without response. During the night, a formal brief of excommunication, entitled *quum memoranda*, appeared on the doors of all the main churches of Rome.[148] Soon it would spread like wildfire throughout Europe. Its most damning paragraph stated that:

With the authority of almighty God, of Saints Peter & Paul, and our own, we declare that all who invaded our beloved city, usurped our jurisdiction, sacrilegiously violated the Patrimony of the Blessed Peter, Prince of the Apostles, as committed by French troops, which, on our command denounced, in aforementioned consistories was protested against and objected to, we lamented, within our good city and within the [greater] dominions of the church, the violation of ecclesiastical immunities and rights of the church, and this Holy See, which includes [our] temporal rights, [we again declare that] whosoever, even in part, facilitated these usurpations, so too those who mandated, committed, advised, adhered to or whosoever procured the execution of these aforementioned usurpations, have incurred 'major' excommunication, including those censures and ecclesiastical sanctions which emanate from the sacred canons, the apostolic constitutions and decrees of the general councils, especially the Council of Trent, we hereby excommunicate and anathemise [these persons] with the loss of all and sundry privileges, graces, indults given by us, or any previous Roman pontiff . . . these [persons] cannot be absolved of their crimes until they have publicly retracted all their violations, and repaired the damage caused and given due penance in order to satisfy proportionately the promises of satisfaction made to the church, us and this Holy See.

This excommunication encompassed those who, in future, would collaborate in the perpetration of similar sins and crimes. It was open-ended and flexible in terms of attributing blame for the annexation of the external city. Although Napoleon was not named personally in the bull, it was clearly directed against him. Indeed, documents in the Vatican Archives show that the pope had received advice from cardinals on whether it was possible to excommunicate the French monarch.[149] The king of France had, for centuries, claimed immunity from excommunication. This precept had been formally accepted by the bishops of France in the Four Gallican Articles of 1682 drafted by Bishop Bossuet (see Appendix).[150] However, the Curia reminded Pius that, according to the decrees of the Council of Trent, all secular rulers were subject to censure by the pope for violations of the Holy See's prerogatives.[151] The excommunication of the emperor and his administration was the point of no return for the Papacy. It was very difficult, after this, for Miollis and the Consulta (the provisional government of Rome), which was in the process of preparing Lazio for annexation, to continue operating as long as the pope was working actively against their reforms.[152]

The Introduction (pp. 1–5) has described the extraordinary events of the night of 5–6 July 1809. The decision to kidnap the pope was communicated to Murat and thence to the authorities in Rome. It was a remarkable coincidence that Radet's assault on the Quirinal Palace happened on the very same day that Napoleon defeated Habsburg forces at the Battle of Wagram, thus becoming, once again, undisputed overlord of Europe.[153] As Romans awoke to the news that their pope and king had been kidnapped, a pithy declaration from Pius spread throughout the city. It stated that the pope had only left Rome under threat of violence. His fate, like that of Saint Peter during the first century, was guided by an invisible hand; he placed himself at the mercy of divine providence. The faithful subjects of the Papal States were urged to behave like the Christians of the first century and accept persecution, but not to forget their loyalty to the Papacy.[154]

It would be almost five years before the pope would return to his capital. In the meantime, all the institutions of the Empire were rolled out in the former Papal States. Modern courts, elections and an efficient bureaucracy came to the eternal city. Freedom of conscience arrived too, much to the annoyance of anti-Semites. The empty Quirinal was soon confiscated and made part of the imperial domain; it was intended to become Napoleon's great summer palace, second only to the Tuileries. Frenetic work started to transform this monastic complex into a neoclassical jewel. The fabric and decorations of the building still bear the marks of the Napoleonic modification.[155] It was a supreme irony that the man who spent two years temporising on what to do with the pope's domain in central Italy would never visit the city whose history played such a vital part in his education and imperial imagination. Napoleon was now master of Rome. Yet the future remained uncertain, and the breach with the church was now irreversible.

# SIX

# ONE WEDDING AND THIRTEEN
# BLACK CARDINALS, 1809–10

After Pius VII had departed Grenoble, Napoleon instructed his police to arrest both Cardinal Pacca and his nephew Tiberius forthwith. They were to spend several years in the forbidding fortress of Fenestrelle above the Susa Valley, in the depths of the Piedmontese Alps, one the few forsaken places where Protestantism had made inroads into Italy and flourished unmolested.[1] The locals were decidedly unsympathetic to the cardinal. It was no coincidence that the imperial government had chosen this remote place of exile: Pacca would be completely unable to communicate with his master and the other princes of the church. In the meantime Pius was transported from Grenoble to Savona on a route that would take him in a semi-circular direction down the French Alps. Throughout his voyage he was forced by his captors to travel incognito to avoid any mass demonstrations of support. It was only in Nice that the townspeople recognised the pope and gave him a rousing reception. The final leg of the trip was through western Piedmont, via the scenic town of Mondovi and thence to the Ligurian coast. During these sweltering days, in France and across the Empire, the feast of Saint Napoleon on 15 August, the emperor's birthday, was due to be celebrated as a national holiday, with the accompanying prayers, hymns and festivities. In Rome and western Italy churches were deserted: people stayed at home in a sign of passive resistance to the man who had kidnapped Christ's vicar on earth.[2]

Pius's destination was the port city of Savona in the middle of Liguria, the snake-shaped region on the north-western coast of Italy, where the Alps and Apennines meet as both plunge into the sea. With its craggy hills, mountains and cliffs, its landscape is decidedly Mediterranean and rather desolate. Given the absence of flat land suitable for cultivation, it is difficult to farm; its inhabitants have consequently needed to trade to survive. Gradually, over many centuries, the port city of Genoa emerged as the region's great maritime republic.[3] During the

Middle Ages the Genoese had established colonies, not just on Corsica, but as far away as the Black Sea.[4] By the early modern period, Genoese bankers rivalled the Dutch in wealth and power. They had contributed enormously to financing the Spanish monarchy's expansion into South America.[5] For a region that possessed hardly any natural resources its seafaring inhabitants had done remarkably well. It is a decided irony that Napoleon, the scion of Ligurian colonists, who came originally from Sarzana in the region's east, destroyed the very republic which his family had served for generations in the *presidi* of Corsica.[6] He sent the pope here because it was by now a backwater, its glory days in the past. In the early nineteenth century there was not even a glimmer of that international tourism that would one day make the region renowned across Europe. Maritime trade was in decline to the extent that Genoa, once the commercial centre of the western Mediterranean, had been surpassed by Livorno.

Pius was out of the way, held where one did not naturally go, not without a good reason. Liguria would remain a place of exile in decades to come. During the twentieth century dethroned monarchs, including the last Ottoman sultan, came to these shores to die, forgotten by the world, longing for the kingdoms and empires they had lost.[7] It is a sleepy part of the world, where little happens. This was particularly the case for Savona. For a considerable part of its history, it had a natural deep-water harbour that had rivalled Genoa. One of its most important families, the della Rovere, gave the church no fewer than two popes: Sixtus IV and Julius II.[8] Indeed, the city has its own Sistine Chapel adjacent to the bishop's palace. (Despite the name it hardly rivals the splendours of the Vatican.) After its conquest by Genoa in 1528, however, Savona went into steep decline, its harbour filled with rocks by its conquerors.[9] From here on it picked up mere crumbs scattered by its more powerful trading neighbours. After its conquest in 1797, and gradual annexation to France, this decline accelerated.[10] The citadel, though, continued to have strategic importance for anyone wishing to control the Ligurian Sea. The Continental System and a blockade by the Royal Navy made matters worse. It was an unlikely location to host the head of the universal church for three years.

Napoleon had not been sure of what to do with Pius. Savona seemed sufficiently remote that the pope's capacity to communicate with the Catholic world would prove difficult. Pius's Ligurian exile was, ultimately, an attempt to place him in solitary confinement. As a former Benedictine monk, such isolation proved less onerous for the pope than the French authorities might have expected.

He had huge reserves of self-discipline, determination and moral resolve upon which to draw during his confinement. The local clergy was naturally sympathetic, but unable to provide concrete assistance. Indeed, the bishop of Savona, Vincenzo Maria Maggioli, could be relied upon by the imperial authorities not to cause trouble. He had a chequered past, now permanently put behind him. In 1796, when he was bishop of Luni-Sarzana, he had fled before Bonaparte's invading armies. He published letters condemning the godless invaders and urging his flock to resist. Three years later he returned with the Austro-Russian armies of Alexander Suvorov and praised the repression visited on republicans. The victory at Marengo in 1800 brought the French back, and Maggioli took flight once more. In his absence he was condemned to death by his enemies. He sought asylum in Rome and expected the church to vindicate his loyalty to the *ancien régime*, but after the Concordat he was abandoned, forced to make a grovelling public apology to the republican authorities in Liguria. He was then transferred from Sarzana to Savona (a decided demotion). Here he promised never again to cause trouble. Maggioli, technically, was the pope's host during these troubled years, but had no intention of playing the hero. He greeted the pope and sympathised over the plight of the church. After much sighing and cries of 'Lord save us all!' he left his palace to Pius and retired to a nearby convent. After the experience of being a fugitive and exile earlier in his career, the ageing bishop of Savona would now keep a low profile.[11]

After arriving in Savona on 17 August 1809 the pope spent his initial four days in the home of the town's mayor.[12] Pius's new residence was a palace in the town centre, a former Franciscan convent which had been transformed into an episcopal residence centuries earlier. It had a pleasant cloister, where he could hide from the heat, and a garden (no longer extant) where the pope read his breviary and strolled. The building had been neglected over the years: Savona was a poor diocese and it was apparent this complex would need a face-lift in order to provide the pope with a dignified confinement. The French would over time also feel the need to install spyholes and other means of surveillance in order to keep a closer eye on their 'guest'. The city garrison, meanwhile, was doubled, and Colonel Thouvenot of the 29th Legion of the Gendarmerie was given the task of guarding the prisoner.[13]

The key individual charged with supervising – and spying on – the pope was Gilbert Joseph Gaspard de Chabrol, the prefect of the department of Montenotte, of which Savona was the administrative centre. The son of a freshly ennobled family from Auvergne, Chabrol was a highly intelligent, erudite and well-qualified civil engineer. Early in his career, in 1798, he had joined Bonaparte on his expedition to Egypt, where he had been noted as an efficient scientist and proto-anthropologist.[14] His studies on the topography of the Nile Valley and the customs of the Egyptian peoples were later published to some acclaim.[15] (He eventually contributed to the massive *Description de l'Égypte*, published between 1809 and 1829, many years after the expedition.) On his return he had entered the civil service, married a rich heiress and experienced a meteoric rise.[16] He now unexpectedly found himself acting as gaoler to Pius VII.

It is difficult to judge whether Chabrol was hero or villain. At times he played both roles. His Catholic upbringing made him sympathetic to the church, but he was viciously ambitious. It could be suggested that he wanted to play the peacemaker who would reconcile emperor and pontiff. He was affable towards his 'guest' and tried to lift the pope's spirits during his daily visits. Although in his later career he became a loyal servant of the restored Bourbons, in 1809 he proved diligent in obeying Napoleon's orders and spying on Pius.[17] Initially he sent weekly bulletins, but these became daily as the crisis deepened. He found an ally in the pope's personal physician, Dr Carlo Porta. First noticed during the Conclave in Venice, where he had acted as physician to the College of Cardinals, Pius had subsequently selected him to be his private doctor.[18] Porta was a man of large family and limited means. Throughout this time as the pope's doctor, he received emoluments from the prefect in return for information on Pius's state of mind and his activities.[19] In private discussions, Porta pressed the pope to yield to imperial demands. The true difficulty in Savona was not the pope's isolation, but the constant psychological pressure he had to endure. His tormentors were Iago-like, and slyly weakened him, blackmailing him with embellished stories of the church suffering on account of his stubbornness. Pius at times fell into depression; he also suffered from stomach pains and a bladder complaint. His conscience troubled him, and he experienced panic attacks, during which he became extremely agitated, episodes that troubled both Chabrol and Porta.[20]

Technically, the person in overall control was Prince Camillo Borghese, the husband of Napoleon's sister Pauline, and governor of western Italy.[21] Although he came from one of the most celebrated princely families of Rome, Borghese avoided being drawn into the conflict between empire and church. He kept away from Savona, and obeyed the orders of his imperial brother-in-law with little regard for his former sovereign the pope, delegating most of the daily decisions and details to Chabrol. Large sums of money were made available for the refurbishment of the episcopal palace in Savona, while Napoleon had told the prince to send one of his masters of ceremonies to run the papal household, and authorised him to spend up to 100,000 francs per month on the upkeep of this important prisoner.[22] The pope's exile, at least at first, was to be comfortable, and the palace was lavishly redecorated. Indeed, the Napoleonic frescos and decorations still adorn the interiors of this residence.

During the initial phase of the pope's captivity, the imperial authorities kept their prisoner on a loose rein. He was permitted to impart blessings from the balcony of the episcopal palace, as if he were still in the Quirinal. He even presided over Mass and other festivities in the cathedral, a special gallery being built inside his apartments so that he could view the cathedral altar without having to leave the palace.[23] On set days, Pius received faithful Catholics and petitioners in private audience. The citizens of Savona flocked to be admitted into the pope's presence to kiss his feet ceremonially.[24] While the government of the church was impossible from his exile, the pope was allowed to receive correspondence from all over the Catholic world. Private petitions, requests for forgiveness of sins and special graces made their way to the pontiff in Savona. Indeed, Pius lamented that he had only one copyist and one secretary with which to govern the souls of millions of Catholics: two people could hardly replace the several thousand clerics who worked in the Curia. Predictably, the imperial police went through this correspondence meticulously. These officials sought out hidden messages and were instructed to crack any attempts to make the pope aware of what was happening in the outside world. The Vatican Archives possess no fewer than five boxes packed to bursting with private requests addressed to Chiaramonti.[25] Particularly moving is the letter of a Sardinian countess, determined to be granted a private chapel, as recurring bouts of illness made it impossible for her to travel to church to attend daily Mass.

The imperial authorities would live to regret granting these liberties. During the autumn, Pius visited the sanctuary of Nostra Signora della Misericordia in the nearby scenic valley of Saint Bernard.[26] According to local legend, the Virgin Mary had here appeared to the peasant Antonio Botta in 1536. She informed him that her son was angry with the world and that people needed to pray for forgiveness. Reassuringly though, on a second appearance, she informed Botta that she came to bestow 'mercy not justice'.[27] It was a site of fervent Marian veneration for the people of Liguria, and especially for seafarers, who had built an impressive Baroque shrine to the Virgin. There was a general belief that Mary answered the prayers of those who ventured on foot into the sanctuary of the Misericordia with a penitent heart.

Pius's pilgrimage to the shrine gained him notable popularity with the local people. He promised Mary that if he ever regained his freedom, he would return to thank the Virgin for his deliverance.[28] The Napoleonic persecution of Roman Catholicism brought the Papacy and ordinary people together in a way that would have been unthinkable in the past. During the early modern period popes had been remote figures, who remained firmly ensconced in the eternal city. They showed a distinct unease about popular devotions and local superstition. Pius VII, and his successors, came to appreciate that, rather than fearing the enthusiasm of ordinary peoples' dedication to local saints, relics and miracles, this was a force that could be harnessed to the benefit of the universal church.[29] During the nineteenth century, once Napoleon was vanquished, the worship of saints and pilgrimages were encouraged as part of a renewal of Catholic piety.[30] In the memory of the people of Savona, Pius continues to hold a special place. Even to this day, local history societies publish unverified stories of his stay in their city; a Savonan priest is currently promoting Pius's canonisation.[31] There are stories of miracles being performed during his captivity: one is depicted in an astonishing print, held by the British Museum, which shows Pius VII levitating during Mass on 15 August 1811.[32]

Throughout the autumn and winter months of 1809, hopes rose and sank in Savona as it became clear that the pope's stay was not transitory. Learning of the peace of Schönbrunn with the Habsburg monarchy, Pius hoped that the emperor might turn to his dispute with Rome and settle matters in a more conciliatory fashion.[33] Imperial memoranda, and a speech given to a delegation from the newly annexed Roman departments, showed that the opposite was the case. Napoleon furiously denounced the ways in which the Papacy had always sacrificed the spiritual well-being of Christianity to its temporal interests in central Italy.[34] The pope was to accept his subordination to the Empire in secular matters. In the end, the church was a mere auxiliary tool in the administration of the peoples of Europe. Pius lost his cool on hearing of these words. He went so far as to declare that the emperor was an agent for a revolutionary and Masonic plot to undermine both the church and the monarchies of Europe, which, he said, had been in existence for almost 150 years.[35] During October, several cardinals resident in Liguria were allowed to visit Pius in Savona to pay their respects. During these visits communication was strictly monitored.

Little did the residents of Savona know that the imperial vision for the church was becoming more ambitious and extreme. After the victory at Wagram and peace with the Habsburgs, Napoleon's determination to make the church an instrument of the modern state reached its apex. With the pope as his prisoner, it was now necessary to resolve the issue of church reform and episcopal investiture. For Napoleon it was vital to bypass papal authority and resolve these questions without any curial involvement. Portalis had died in August 1807 and had been replaced as minister of religions by Félix Bigot de Préameneu.[36] A Breton who enjoyed a distinguished career as jurist, little more is known about Bigot. His correspondence betrays an absolute loyalty to Napoleon: he continued to serve him through the Hundred Days (see Chapter 9), but with the fall of the Empire his career ended abruptly. Following Bigot's advice, an ecclesiastical committee was convened to discuss the crisis with the Papacy. This included five of the most loyal Gallican bishops in addition to Cardinal Fesch and Cardinal Maury. Francesco Fontana, then general of the Barnabite Order, one of the most eminent theologians in the world, and Jacques-André Emery, the superior of the great seminary of Saint-Sulpice in Paris, also took part, unwilling members of the *comité*,[37] which was to advise on the authority of the pope, episcopal investiture and other reforms in France, Italy and Germany. It would also give an opinion on the validity of the bull of excommunication issued on 10 June 1809. But the most important issue to be decided was whether a national council of all the bishops of the Empire could bypass papal authority and accept the emperor's reforms and ecclesiastical appointments.

The *comité* met privately for two months before producing a long report, which was presented to Napoleon on 10 January 1810. Its contents infuriated him and disappointed his hopes.[38] First, the *comité* believed that the church could not function as long as the pope was a prisoner. It was essential that he be liberated and allowed to communicate freely with his cardinals and bishops. The members of the *comité* also felt that a national council of French and imperial bishops was not empowered to settle matters that concerned the universal church and, to make matters worse, argued that a general (ecumenical) council, made up of all Catholic bishops from around the world, could only meet with the approval of the pope. The emperor alone could not legitimately convene such an assembly.

At the end of its deliberations, the *comité* declared that a national council of imperial bishops could discuss and propose non-binding solutions to the investiture crisis. This was far from an ideal outcome: it was not clear how such a council might decide on the matter of confirming new bishops without papal approval. Its members would be free to advise the emperor to reconcile with the pope, or even to deny the legitimacy of his candidates. The report's only good news was on the question of excommunication. For the *comité*, Napoleon was not named personally in the bull, and they accepted that the Four Gallican Articles of 1682 made the monarch of France immune from any church sanctions over temporal matters. Ultimately the *comité*, whose loyalty to Bonaparte was beyond reproach, advised that a Catholic Church shorn of papal authority was unthinkable.[39]

For the emperor, the pope could remain a spiritual figurehead, but could not be in the position to oppose the administrative and legal reforms of his Empire. The church should teach obedience and respect for civil authorities and state institutions. During these years of deep crisis, a vision of a church completely subordinate to the state crystallised. On 10 October 1809, Napoleon instructed Bigot to summon discreetly all members of the College of Cardinals to Paris.[40] A separate order was also transmitted to the tribunals of the Penitenzieria and Dataria, canon law courts, in Rome commanding them to transfer their sessions and archives to Reims. In the depths of eastern France these two supreme ecclesiastical tribunals would sit in judgement of spiritual matters such as the behaviour of clergy, the absolution of mortal sins and marital annulment, all under the watchful eye of the Empire's judges and bureaucrats.[41]

A major restructuring was soon under way on the palace of the archbishop of Paris, next to the cathedral of Notre-Dame, overlooking the Seine. The palace was to be expanded, improved and made worthy to host a prince.[42] In January 1810 it was decided that the archives of the Curia would be transferred to Paris and integrated into the imperial archives. The Napoleonic regime confiscated state papers across Europe, with the aim of creating one of the greatest historical research centres the world had ever seen.[43] The archivists in Paris were given the precise task of identifying Galileo's trial proceedings and publishing those of its contents that would be most embarrassing to the church.[44] This would highlight to the public the great ills committed by the church against scientific progress. Antoine Alexandre Barbier, a former priest who had married in 1793, and the imperial librarian charged with this task, took the papers to Napoleon's personal library, and some remained in his possession even after the fall of the Empire.

They were later sold at auction and bought by a library in Florence, where they remain to this day. Behind these individual acts lay the tantalising dream that Paris would become the Rome of the future. Politics and religion would be fused together in the capital of this vast Neo-Carolingian Empire.[45]

In the meantime, the emperor's gaze turned to his dynasty. It had been clear for some time that the Empress Joséphine was beyond childbearing age, and that she was highly unlikely to provide the desired heir.[46] Napoleon knew, from several extra-marital affairs, that he was well able to sire children. He realised that divorce and remarriage was the only way he could ensure a direct line of succession for his dynasty. Furthermore, the Bonapartes – as we have seen – had always hated the Beauharnais clan, and had been encouraging Napoleon to divorce Joséphine for over a decade.[47] Much has been written, of varying quality, about Napoleon's tempestuous first marriage. He had clearly been deeply infatuated with Joséphine during his youth, and her affairs had hurt him deeply. After his return from Egypt the pair had come to form an excellent working partnership. Joséphine was a charming hostess, and did much to protect the world from her husband's rougher edges.[48] She had also played a vital role in wooing her husband's co-conspirators just before the Brumaire coup. Her children from her first marriage, Eugène and Hortense, had become very dear to Napoleon, who had adopted them as his own. In some ways he favoured them above his own siblings, who often appeared ungrateful and unreliable in comparison. It was clear that this step would be painful: the emperor was being guided by realpolitik rather than mere whim.

On 5 December 1809 Napoleon asked his courtiers to leave him alone so that he could have much needed privacy. He called on the empress in her apartments to inform her of his intention to seek a divorce.[49] Joséphine immediately collapsed in a faint: a chamberlain had to be summoned to help revive her. Hortense, the empress's daughter and, through her marriage to Napoleon's brother Louis, queen of Holland, was also asked to be in attendance, which did not help matters: on hearing of the divorce she began to cry. Napoleon, furious, stated that such scenes would not change his mind: the good of the state was his utmost concern. Hortense replied that they well knew what they owed him, and that they would accept his decision with meekness and resignation. However, he could not command them not to be sad and distressed. Here the scene descended into one of despair: on hearing these words the emperor himself broke down in tears.

Joséphine was not just upset by the divorce: she would also now lose her rank and revenues. Although she would keep her title and dignity, she could not appear in court once a new empress-consort arrived to preside over the Tuileries. Nevertheless, after a few days, she accepted her fate, and Eugène was informed of this difficult news. He was a favourite of Napoleon and he would remain as his viceroy in Italy. However, it was decided that he would not succeed Napoleon as king of Italy, but rather would become grand duke of Frankfurt.[50] One of the most vexing aspects of the divorce for the Beauharnaises was to witness the delighted expressions worn by the Bonapartes at this time. They had finally rid themselves of the woman they despised.

The civil divorce should have been a simple matter. For most Frenchmen such a divorce was akin to resolving a simple contract. The grounds for ending a marriage tended to favour men; for women it was much harder to terminate unions with their spouses.[51] However, as the emperor had forbidden members of the imperial family from divorcing, ending his marriage to Joséphine would require legislation. It was decided that a formal ceremonial occasion at court was needed to seal the divorce. The highest officials in the land would witness both emperor and empress signing their names to the final legal act ending their marriage. On 15 December 1809 Joséphine was forced to progress through the entire state apartments of the Tuileries. Doing so in front of the smiling Bonaparte clan was humiliating. With determination, dignity and calm she, and other members of the imperial family, signed and witnessed this formal act. In return, Joséphine would retain the title of empress and receive a pension of 2 million francs per year, along with lands in Navarre, which she could leave to her family.[52] The next day the Senate met in a ceremonial session to approve the divorce with enabling legislation.[53] The good of the Empire and future of the dynasty required a natural male heir.

Napoleon was now technically a free man and could conclude a new dynastic marriage. He had asked the foreign ministry to draw up a list of eligible princesses. The priority was to seek a great lady from a reigning house who was healthy and likely to provide him with children. Initially, the hope was for a match with the Romanovs.[54] Napoleon discussed this possibility with Tsar Alexander I through diplomatic channels.[55] Either of the tsar's sisters, Anna and Catherine, would be ideal matches for the emperor of the French. Alexander replied that he had no objection, but that these princesses were wards of the dowager empress of all the Russias, and the decision was not his. Indeed, it immediately became apparent that the Dowager Empress Maria Feodorovna had no intention that either of her daughters would marry a Corsican usurper. Alexander deplored the situation, but nothing could be done to change his mother's mind and anti-French convictions. The attention of the French diplomatic corps now turned to the vanquished Habsburgs. The rulers of the Austrian monarchy needed to repair their relations with France: a match was likely to accelerate the process of reconciliation. However, a problem loomed large. As devout Catholics the Habsburgs would only consent to a religious wedding. Napoleon had no objection to this in principle, but soon realised that the demand threw up an unanticipated complication.

As described in Chapter 4 (p. 125), on the eve of his coronation Napoleon had been forced to marry Joséphine in a secret religious wedding performed by Cardinal Fesch.[56] It now dawned on him that, to the Catholic Church, his civil divorce was utterly valueless. No priest, let alone prelate, would marry a man while his first wife was alive. The only solution open to the imperial court was an annulment. Naturally, as a prisoner of the emperor, the pope was hardly well disposed to grant such a petition. Furthermore, in 1804 he had granted a special dispensation to allow Napoleon's hasty religious marriage to Joséphine. For Pius this marriage was valid, binding and impossible to annul. The imperial administrators turned to Cardinal di Pietro, as head of the Penitenzieria, for his opinion. Hostile to the imperial administration, he replied that, although he had been appointed apostolic delegate in the pope's absence, he had no authority to adjudicate on such extraordinary matters.[57] Essentially the church refused to even consider this request. Without an annulment the Habsburgs would not proceed with the marriage.

At this stage, Napoleon's memories of the eve of his coronation started to evolve. The parish priest of Saint-Germain l'Auxerrois, the parish church of the Tuileries Palace, had not actually consented to the marriage taking place. The witnesses to his nuptials with Joséphine had been fictitious, and nobody had been present to observe him wed Joséphine before the altar. Even more significantly, the emperor had not wished to get married, but had been coerced into it by both Joséphine and the pope.[58] Clearly, the emerging argument had it, the marriage had been irregular and could be easily annulled. Cardinal Fesch was summoned and stood in dumbfounded silence as his nephew shared his new recollection of events. Napoleon had an inexhaustible ability to believe his own lies. For all his pedantry, Fesch was a real priest and knew full well that the wedding of 1804, though unorthodox, was completely valid, having received the necessary papal dispensation. He quivered before his half-nephew's convenient recollection of events, which caused him massive discomfort and troubled his priestly conscience. The emperor, realising that Rome was not going to help, decided that only a Gallican solution would win the day. In 1806 the old church courts, or *officialités*, had been resurrected in France to adjudicate on matters relating to canon law. During October of that year, they had dissolved the union between Jérôme Bonaparte and Betsy Patterson (see above, pp. 132–3). Surely the same could be done for the emperor.[59] Soon, the priests and canon lawyers of the *officialité* of Paris were charged with examining the case. Their eyebrows rose when they saw that the grounds for the annulment were coercion. Ordinarily such cases involved teenage girls who had been beaten by their fathers to compel them to marry rich old men. Napoleon, who commanded a million soldiers and controlled most of western Europe, seemed unlikely to be easily intimidated by anybody.

These ecclesiastical judges were summoned by the archchancellor of the Empire, Jean-Jacques-Régis de Cambacérès, duc de Parme, to discuss the matter. Cambacérès, who had been Bonaparte's second consul, was a figure of titanic power. He had played a key role in choreographing the smooth transition from Consulate to Empire. As an immensely learned jurist his influence had been vital in the drafting of much of the Code Napoléon, and when the emperor was on campaign he served as his virtual regent. The archchancellor was an urbane and efficient statesman, whose bachelorhood, not to mention his friendships with younger men, gave rise to suspicions that he had a somewhat lukewarm interest in the fairer sex. Whenever a messy and controversial legal problem arose, it was standard procedure for Napoleon to delegate its resolution to Cambacérès. He would now exert massive pressure on this church court to grant an automatic and swift process.[60] The judges of the *officialité* returned that such important cases were usually referred to Rome for adjudication. They argued, with some alarm, that they were not competent to sit in judgement over such an important issue. Cambacérès brushed such concerns aside, replying that this issue of jurisdiction would be referred to the ecclesiastical committee set up by the ministry of religions in November 1809. This committee obediently gave its blessing and the judges of the *officialité* were commanded to proceed. The judges asked for the marriage act and baptismal certificate of the emperor. The archchancellor lied, saying that the marriage act did not exist, while assuring them that Napoleon was a baptised Catholic.[61] The judges concluded that they would need to interview the people involved. Cambacérès grumbled but agreed that Fesch and the three false witnesses (Berthier, Duroc and Talleyrand) could be interviewed by the judges of the *officialité*.

Over three days in January, these grandees of the great French Empire travelled to the archbishop's palace on the banks of the Seine. Here they gave depositions relating to the imperial marriage of 1804. Fesch, who had officiated over the wedding, could not pretend that he had not married his nephew on the eve of the coronation. However, he stressed that the emperor had been pressured against his will, by Joséphine and the pope, to undertake this ceremony. Napoleon had not allowed any witnesses to be present. Fesch had complained that this would nullify the marriage, but his nephew had angrily commanded him to proceed with the ritual. Therefore, the cardinal had had to seek out the pope and obtain special dispensation to marry the emperor in secret and without witnesses. In general, canon law held that clandestine marriages were invalid; it was a special favour that this wedding went ahead without third parties present.[62]

It was also stated that the local parish priest had not been consulted about the matter and that his jurisdiction had been violated; Fesch was acting as a mere imperial chaplain and had no powers outside his archdiocese. Technically, priests needed to obtain permission from their colleagues to perform sacraments outside their own parishes. This statement was generally truthful, if a little vague.[63] Fesch demurred from declaring his nephew's marriage invalid, but rather emphasised how unhappy the emperor had been when forced to formalise his union with Joséphine in the eyes of the church. The other three people interviewed were the fake witnesses to the marriage. It was clear that their statements had been pre-prepared and corroborated amongst themselves. They stated that the emperor had not wished to marry and that he had the nuptial blessing performed without witnesses or the parish priest to ensure that this ceremony would not be sacramentally valid. That they had not been physically present was stressed in their testimony. The judges found their statements odd, but felt it dangerous to press these important figures any further.[64] Like all good lies, the statements had some verisimilitude but significantly bent the truth to favour the emperor's version of events. The ecclesiastical lawyers realised that if they did not annul the wedding, they would face serious repercussions. The Gallican ecclesiastical committee set up to advise the emperor on church matters had ruled that they were competent to adjudicate on this issue without recourse to the pope. The issue of coercion was dismissed as ludicrous.[65] Aside from teenagers being compelled by their parents it was very difficult to prove.

The judges decided not to dwell on this aspect. They focused instead on the absence of witnesses and the failure of the local parish priest to give his permission to Fesch to perform the wedding within his parish. In ordinary circumstances, this would have been enough to invalidate the marriage. A problem remained in that the pope had bestowed special dispensations for the nuptial blessing to take place. Here the canon lawyers came up with a very neat solution, which would prove acceptable to the church, and save them from the prisons of the Empire. They considered that it was uncertain whether the pope's dispensation concerned the failure of the parish priest to authorise the wedding (and publish the necessary banns), or whether it encompassed the absence of witnesses. The judges felt that His Holiness's dispensation would have followed precedents already established in canon law. There were cases in which the jurisdictional rights of parish priests were ignored to expedite weddings. However, in their judgement it seemed unlikely that the pope would have dispensed the emperor from being married before witnesses. They believed there were sufficient grounds for the annulment of the emperor's church marriage. Their judgement stated that he and Joséphine must cease living as husband and wife.[66]

Cambacérès was happy with this outcome, but wanted to strengthen it in the eyes of the public. The ruling was thus referred to the metropolitan *officialité*, the highest ecclesiastical court in the Paris region.[67] Here a canon lawyer, acting as prosecutor against this referral, wrote that the validity of the marriage was beyond dispute. He stated that, though unorthodox, the wedding at the Tuileries had obtained papal dispensations, which could not simply be ignored. The judges of this appeal court, fearing the emperor's wrath would not spare them any more than their colleagues of the lower court, decided to uphold the first judgement. They added that, given that the Senate had dissolved the civil marriage between Napoleon and Joséphine, it would be impossible to reimpose a religious marriage on the couple.[68] It was exactly the sort of judgement that the imperial administration had craved. The primacy of civil law over canon law had been recognised. For Catholic opinion it was a betrayal: God's law was, after all, above man's law. (It is unclear whether the *officialité* of Lyon, the highest in all of France, reviewed any of these judgements. If this tribunal did offer an opinion on the matter, the papers relating to it seem to have been lost.)[69]

On 21 January 1810, bizarrely coinciding with the anniversary of the execution of Louis XVI, the Council of State met to consider the question of Napoleon's remarriage, now approved by the *officialité*.[70] Its members were divided. Some favoured a Russian match, while others felt that marrying into the royal house of Saxony would cement France's position in Germany and Poland. Some even suggested that Napoleon marry a French noblewoman for patriotic reasons. Gradually, however, favour turned towards the Habsburgs, who were one of the oldest and most prestigious reigning houses in Europe.[71] The Archduchess Marie-Louise was attractive, if not beautiful, intelligent and was known for her robust health. It seemed probable that she could deliver a healthy heir.

Essentially, Napoleon was to renew the Franco-Austrian alliance that had been sealed in 1770 by the marriage of Louis XVI to Marie-Antoinette.[72] He was to marry the grand-niece of the last queen of France. This union again seemed to augur military invincibility in western Europe. In this respect, Napoleon, his family and ministers showed themselves poor students of history. Marie-Antoinette had been universally loathed as a foreigner throughout her husband's reign.[73] Furthermore, during the second half of the eighteenth century both the French and Austrian chancelleries had failed to co-ordinate their foreign policies. They did not honour the terms of their alliance, but rather favoured political expediency.[74] The Emperor Francis certainly felt ambivalent, to say the very least, about his prospective son-in-law. On two occasions Napoleon had already occupied Vienna and forced humiliating peace treaties on the Austrian monarchy. This represented a shaky foundation on which to build a dynastic union and durable military alliance.

In Savona, the pope was furious that the Gallican ecclesiastical committee had accepted the *officialité*'s jurisdiction over the emperor's marriage. In the past, most of Catholic Europe had recognised the pope's supreme authority over the marriages of crowned monarchs. Indeed, during Henry VIII's reign, the failure to come to an accommodation over his marriage to Catherine of Aragon had led to disastrous consequences for Catholicism in England.[75] Similarly, the breach between Papacy and Empire threatened to usher another ecclesiastical rupture in Europe. The Gallican party, though loyal to the emperor, remained sympathetic to the Papacy. Despite their allegiance to the state, they wanted to avoid breaking France's historic communion with the Holy See.[76] The continued imprisonment of the pope was steering the Catholic Church into uncharted waters. The solution seemed ever more elusive, as Napoleon argued that the religious establishment within his domains was autonomous from Rome.

Klemens von Metternich, the Austrian chancellor, received the news of Joséphine's divorce with interest. The Habsburg ambassador in Paris, Karl Philipp, prince of Schwarzenberg, sent regular bulletins to Vienna. Although news of the annulment was greeted favourably by the Habsburgs, more information was requested. It was not clear how the *officialité* had come to its decision, and whether papal approval had been sought. The vagueness of French replies aroused Austrian anxiety. It was hardly ideal that Francis I was expected to marry his favourite daughter to the man who held the pope prisoner. Functionaries of the Habsburg Embassy in Rome advised that the *officialité*'s judgement, though unorthodox, was valid, and that the marriage could proceed.[77] The prospect of a Habsburg–Bonaparte prince in Paris, which would soften French hostility towards Vienna, outweighed all other considerations.

History has severely underestimated Marie-Louise of Habsburg, the woman who, for nearly five years, would be empress of the French. The nineteen-year-old archduchess, like many Habsburgs, was a notable polyglot, but her politics and technical education had been overlooked. She had artistic and musical interests, but, due to decades of war against France, she had been brought up to distrust and resent the heirs of the French Revolution who had guillotined her great-aunt.[78] It spoke highly of her sense of duty that she accepted this match, to a man she had once defined as the Antichrist in her correspondence, for the good of the Habsburg state.[79] Napoleon himself was deeply impressed with his spouse, so much so that a broad programme of education was prepared for her. She was later taught the rudiments of the mathematical sciences by the emperor himself, and given thorough grounding in French public law. When the fortunes of the Empire wavered in war, she was proclaimed regent and chaired the Council of State in person.[80]

On 28 February 1810, Marshal Berthier, prince of Neuchâtel, the emperor's highly competent chief of staff, arrived in Vienna to ask officially for the archduchess's hand in marriage.[81] The next day the emperor Francis accepted on his daughter's behalf. Following the precedent set by Anne of Austria in 1615, to make the wedding legally binding in both Austria and France there was to be a proxy marriage.[82] Some embarrassment occurred when Sigismund Anton von Hohenwart, archbishop of Vienna, set out a long list of questions about the nature of Napoleon's civil marriage to Joséphine and examined the basis on which the annulment was granted. He wanted to be reassured before he could preside over the proxy wedding. The French ambassador protested, saying that he had given his word of honour that the marriage had been annulled: a foreign

TO KIDNAP A POPE

prelate was not entitled to review judgements issued by French *officialités*. Metternich complained that, in this case, there was no possible harm in sending duplicates of these ecclesiastical judgements to Vienna for inspection. Instead of the documents requested, a solemn letter from Cardinal Fesch was delivered, assuring his colleague in Vienna that all was in order. Hohenwart, clearly a man of determination, insisted that he still wished to see the relevant documentation.[83]

With regret, the Emperor Francis had to lean on his own archbishop to accept Fesch's reassurances and proceed with the ceremony. On 11 March 1810 the marriage by proxy took place in the Augustinian church in Vienna. Marshal Berthier requested that the Archduke Charles, the emperor's brother, in a gesture symbolising Franco-Austrian reconciliation, have the honour of standing in for the French emperor during the ceremony.[84] After all, the archduke was a talented soldier, who had commanded the imperial armies against the French at the Battle of Wagram and in many previous campaigns. Not all present were overjoyed by this union. The bride's grandmother, Maria-Carolina of Naples, the sister of Marie-Antoinette, remained one of the bitterest opponents of the French Empire. Apparently, before her granddaughter departed for Paris, the queen exclaimed: 'This is the last thing missing in my misery, to become the devil's grandmother.'[85] When it came to international politics the Habsburgs put sentiment aside and were driven by a strong sense of duty. It must have been with a sense of grim foreboding that Marie-Louise headed towards a nation that had beheaded the last Habsburg queen-consort of France.

The journey of the new empress to her new homeland was a triumphal progress. Everywhere she stopped she was celebrated and cheered. The task of receiving Marie-Louise at the border was given to Caroline Murat, now queen of Naples, the emperor's sister.[86] Although they were initially cordial the sisters-in-law never warmed to each other. The Bonapartes were distrustful of outsiders; however, unlike Joséphine, Marie-Louise's pedigree far outshone that of her prospective in-laws. To cement the union, both civil and religious ceremonies would take place in Paris in full pomp.[87] For the emperor the spectacle of this dynastic alliance between the Habsburgs and Bonapartes would showcase the power and glory of his own Empire. The marriage ceremonies were to be lavish, and the pageantry was to cost millions of francs.

At this time twenty-nine members of the College of Cardinals were present in the French capital. Cardinal Pacca, blamed for the bull of excommunication, would remain in the fortress of Fenestrelle in Piedmont for the following three years, separated from his brethren.[88] Most cardinals had had their dioceses, properties and lands in Rome confiscated, and the government had decided to provide them with a state salary of 30,000 francs, drawn from the emperor's own private funds.[89] (Cardinal Consalvi and Cardinal di Pietro had declined the offer with indignation.)[90] It was the emperor's desire that the entire College of Cardinals would attend his wedding, thus dispelling any lingering doubts about the legitimacy of the annulment. Napoleon, at times, could be his own worst enemy. He wanted to charm the cardinals by integrating them into the life of the imperial court.

The ministry of religions severely underestimated these prelates. In co-ordination with the provisional government in Rome, Bigot produced intelligence files on each of these princes of the church, which were far from flattering.[91] For Cardinal di Pietro the following entry was recorded:

It is he who has thrown the pope over the abyss. He is an old and very mediocre professor of canon law at the University of La Sapienza, a doctor of law who neither knows the real world nor understands important affairs. He used to be very timid, but his fanaticism has become so bold that he is capable of ignoring the government's public advice. He is vengeful and indomitable. He should be treated with the coldest disdain. He is abhorred by all the Sacred College and by all the Romans who attribute to him, openly and with reason, all the decisions made [recently] by the pope. He is not a dangerous intriguer as he leads a very sheltered life. The government should, nevertheless, keep its eyes open and monitor his verbal and written communications. His rage against France is truly delirious.[92]

(For other cardinals the dismissal was even more brutal: 'Scotti: He is a useless man . . . [Chigi-]Zondadari: He also is absolutely useless.') These facile dismissals probably belie the extent to which the French government feared the resistance from these senior prelates. Upon their arrival in Paris, the imperial authorities did their best to integrate them into the elite life of the capital. Several cardinals attended Sunday Mass in the chapel of the Tuileries, others were invited to the *soirées* held by Napoleon's ministers and foreign ambassadors. Paris was to be their new home, and everything was done to rally them to the imperial regime.[93]

In an audience at the Tuileries in February, Napoleon met with several cardinals. Even at the best of times the emperor found small talk particularly painful.

When presented to some Neapolitan and Spanish cardinals he merely remarked on their nationality and said nothing else. He tried to be witty with Cardinal di Pietro, saying that he had put on weight since the coronation six years previously; it is unclear how this jest was received. When Consalvi's turn came, he commented that they had not seen each other since the signing of the Concordat ten years previously. The emperor joked that, unlike di Pietro, Consalvi had lost much weight. They both lamented that the benefits of the Concordat had all but vanished and that the situation was grave. Napoleon surprised all by repeating no fewer than three times that if Consalvi had remained secretary of state 'things would not have gone so far as they have now'. These remarks were patently insincere, as Consalvi's removal from office had been orchestrated by the emperor years previously. The cardinal, unmoved, replied dryly 'that he would have done his duty'. An indignant Napoleon turned his back on the cardinal, bellowing: 'You would have not sacrificed the spiritual to the temporal.'[94]

In the aftermath of this scene, Consalvi and di Pietro consulted their colleagues individually. Many felt uncomfortable that they were being charmed by their French hosts, hosts who had been formally excommunicated from the church. They took a straw poll about how they should react to the imperial government before writing a joint letter to the emperor to make him aware of the Sacred College's collective viewpoint. This stated that the cardinals were bound by all decisions and pronouncements made by the pope before his arrest on 6 July 1809. They could not, and had no wish to, reopen anything already decided by the Holy Father prior to this dark day: only in the presence of the pope could the cardinals deliberate on matters relevant to the government of the church. Loyal to Pius's instructions, his most senior advisers assumed a stance of passive resistance. On receiving this letter Napoleon ripped it to shreds and threw it into the fire.[95]

Formal invitations to the celebrations for the Habsburg marriage were sent to each cardinal. These caused much embarrassment. Consalvi suggested that his colleagues should hold a conference to decide their collective response to this unwelcome summons. They met in Consalvi's residence in the Hôtel d'Élisée, rue de Lille 7 in Paris.[96] Fesch, as the designated celebrant for the marriage, was not invited to these meetings: it was felt that he would not act impartially. They also feared that he would spy and inform his nephew on all that was said. Cardinal Caprara, meanwhile, was on his deathbed, and could not attend (he passed away on 21 June).[97] Many cardinals expressed the view that going to the civil ceremony was not improper, as this contractual arrangement had no sacramental value in the eyes of the church. In contrast, there was a feeling that attending the religious celebration would be impossible, given that Consalvi and di Pietro argued that the *officialité* had usurped the Papacy's exclusive jurisdiction over crowned heads of state. For the Sacred College, Napoleon and Joséphine remained married in an indissoluble bond.[98]

In the end, fourteen cardinals felt compelled to attend the wedding, regardless of the prescriptions of canon law. They argued that their presence did not imply approbation, but rather was simple compliance to an imperial command. These cardinals, essentially, wanted to avoid falling victim to the emperor's wrath. The remaining thirteen voted to refuse the invitation and not to attend the festivities. They informed Fesch that they wanted to preserve the prerogatives of the Holy See intact, and that the annulment had violated papal authority. Any collaboration with the French Empire would compromise their position. To avoid embarrassment, Consalvi suggested that the government could publish a face-saving story. A statement could be circulated explaining that, due to restrictions of space in the palace, only half of the College of Cardinals could attend these ceremonies.[99] Fesch brought this unwelcome news to his nephew who greeted this opposition with the words 'They would not dare!'[100] Fouché, as minister of police, was sent to intimidate some of these princes of the church, but failed to get very far.

In the meantime, Marie-Louise had entered French territory and rendezvoused with Caroline Murat. On 22 March 1810 she entered Strasbourg, where she was fêted at a magnificent reception. Here she was joined by Metternich and Schwarzenberg, who would represent Austria at the forthcoming nuptials. The first meeting between bride and groom was scheduled to take place in Soissons in specially constructed ceremonial tents. However, on 27 March, Napoleon lost his patience. He and Joachim-Napoléon Murat, king of Naples, left at a gallop. At the village of Courcelles they intercepted Marie-Louise.[101] In the pouring rain Napoleon met his future wife's carriage and entered it to make his formal introduction. They exchanged pleasantries before the emperor insisted that the couple head directly to the palace of Compiègne, north-east of Paris. At this great palace and hunting resort the empress was welcomed into the imperial court. She was introduced to members of her household and many of the great officers of the Empire. In this rural idyll she was given a week to prepare herself for the forthcoming wedding. The court seamstresses worked hard to get her wardrobe ready to suit French rather than Austrian fashions. Finally, on 31

March, the soon-to-be married couple headed for the palace of Saint-Cloud on the outskirts of Paris. It had been one of Marie-Antoinette's favourite retreats in the summer months.[102] It was here that the civil ceremony was to take place.

The great and the good of the Empire filed past the throne room to be presented to the new empress before her civil marriage was registered formally on 1 April. All the cardinals, with the exception of those who were too ill or elderly to attend, were conspicuous in their flowing crimson robes. The emperor and empress verbally consented to their union and then signed an official register before the assembled guests. This brief prosaic ceremony was all that was needed to make Napoleon and Marie-Louise husband and wife in the eyes of the state. According to Fouché's (far-from-reliable) memoirs, he pulled Consalvi to one side and asked if it was true that he and several other cardinals were thinking of not attending the religious wedding. Consalvi refused to give names but affirmed that it was difficult for them to be present at a marriage that was contrary to canon law. Fouché, as police minister, expressed his personal sympathy for the cardinal, whom he had first met in 1801. Yet he impressed on him in no uncertain terms that failure to attend would result in grave repercussions. Consalvi regretted that he was unable to give Fouché a positive answer.[103] In the end, the absence of thirteen cardinals from the civil ceremony did not draw much comment.

On 2 April 1810 the imperial couple made a triumphal entry into Paris. They were greeted by cannon salvos as they rode past the unfinished Arc de Triomphe. At three in the afternoon the 8,000 guests eagerly took their places in the great gallery of the Louvre, temporarily transformed into a chapel by the brilliant neoclassical architects Percier and Fontaine. The emperor processed down the *gallerie de Diane* in full ceremonial dress, and with great pomp.[104]

Napoleon was radiant as he arrived in the chapel. The coronation had marked his assumption of the crown: this wedding was to mark the recognition of his legitimacy by all of Europe. As he approached the altar, his eyes went to the special stalls set up for the College of Cardinals. Only twelve were present. Two had excused themselves with medical certificates, insisting that they would have attended if only their health had allowed. Napoleon's face went purple with anger.[105] Thirteen cardinals had defied him and made a mockery of his wedding by leaving their places empty. The emperor muttered, under his breath, to his chaplain, the Abbé de Pradt: 'Where are they? Ah the idiots! I see what they're up to: they are protesting against the legitimacy of my blood, they want to unsettle my dynasty. Idiots!'[106]

1. On 25 November 1804, Napoleon and Chiaramonti met for the first time at the Croix de Saint-Herem near Fontainebleau. The emperor can be seen wearing the green uniform of the imperial hunt. According to the memoirs of Savary, the pope had to descend from his carriage and walk through mud to meet his imperial host.

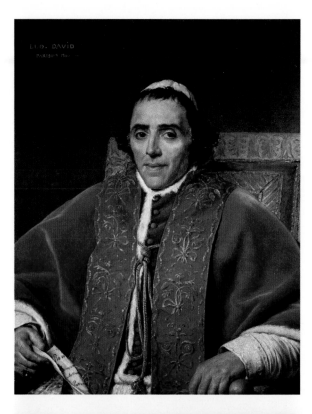

2. Despite being a former Jacobin and associate of Robespierre, the neoclassical artist Jacques-Louis David, like many others in Paris, was captivated by the pope's noble and elegant features. This portrait was a preparatory study for the more famous coronation portrait of 1807.

3. Cardinal Ercole Consalvi was one of the key architects of the Concordat and influenced the policy of papal neutrality. In 1806 he was dismissed due to Napoleon's ultimatum, but would return to office in 1814. He was to be one of the more moderate and reformist voices in the last years of Chiaramonti's pontificate.

4. David's iconic celebration of Napoleon's coronation in fact shows the moment the emperor crowned Joséphine empress, with Pius extending his fingers in a gesture of benediction behind them. Overlooking the entire scene is Letizia, Napoleon's mother, who was actually not present but in Rome to witness the birth of her first grandchild from Lucien Bonaparte.

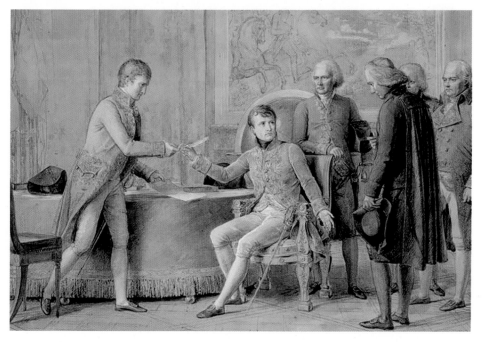

5. This unfinished painting by Gérard shows Napoleon countersigning the text of the Concordat which his delegates had concluded on 15 July 1801. In reality Bonaparte was unhappy with the concessions given to Rome and his rigidity almost wrecked the peace with the church.

6. This is a complicated allegory by François which celebrates the ratification of the Concordat. At its centre is a restored altar, with Pius VII and prelates on the left celebrating the divine mysteries; the people of France at their feet applaud the restoration of religion. On the right Bonaparte is represented naked with the flame of heroism burning on his forehead as he is crowned with victory. Further away Mars can be seen chasing away discord with a sword.

7. The Quirinal Palace, a favoured summer residence of eighteenth-century popes, is a large labyrinth of rooms and antechambers. The kidnapping of the pope proved a massive challenge for the Imperial Gendarmerie.

8. Cardinal Bartolomeo Pacca was the pope's faithful pro-secretary of state in July 1809. He advised Pius to excommunicate Napoleon after the annexation of Rome. He spent the next four years in the fortress of Fenestrelle above the Protestant Susa Valley in the Alps. On his return to Rome in 1814 he became a determined opponent of reform and liberalism.

9. This fresco from the Chiaramonti Museum section of the Vatican Museums shows Radet helping Pius VII enter the carriage that would take him into exile in Savona. He would not see Rome again for almost five years.

10. Elisa was Napoleon's eldest sister and deeply enjoyed the splendour of ruling Tuscany from Renaissance Florence. The transit of Pius VII through her lands proved very unwelcome. She sent her palace officials to greet the kidnapped pontiff to avoid an embarrassing personal audience.

11. This room, still in the green livery, was the pope's bedroom in Savona. It was routinely searched, and in early 1811 all writing materials and books were removed when the clandestine network that allowed the pope to communicate with the outside world was discovered. Colonel Lagorce's gendarmes became deeply paranoid, so much so that spyholes (bottom right) were drilled throughout the episcopal palace to keep a close eye on Pius.

12. Legends sprang up about the pope's piety and martyrdom in Savona. This post-Napoleonic print purports to show an ecstatic moment in which the pope levitated during a Mass for the feast of the assumption of the Virgin Mary on 15 August 1811 (incidentally also the birth of Napoleon). Even to this day there is a campaign to have Pius VII canonised a saint.

13. After 1814 the pope returned to Rome in triumph and restored his rule. This sumptuous image by Ingres shows a solemn service and consistory in the Sistine Chapel. It captures well the pomp and ritual of papal Rome.

14. In 1819 the great British portraitist Sir Thomas Lawrence travelled to Rome to paint Pius VII. The pope's physical decline after five years of exile is apparent. This dignified portrait can be found in the Waterloo Gallery at Windsor Castle, where the pope hangs among the generals and statesmen who defeated Napoleon.

15. Antonio Canova died in 1822, so the College of Cardinals commissioned his rival, the Danish neoclassical sculptor Bertel Thorvaldsen, to produce a funerary monument worthy of the pope who defied Napoleon. It was completed in 1832, almost a decade after Pius VII's death. As Thorvaldsen was Protestant, he was not allowed to sign his monument. It is apparently the only unsigned sculpture inside Saint Peter's Basilica.

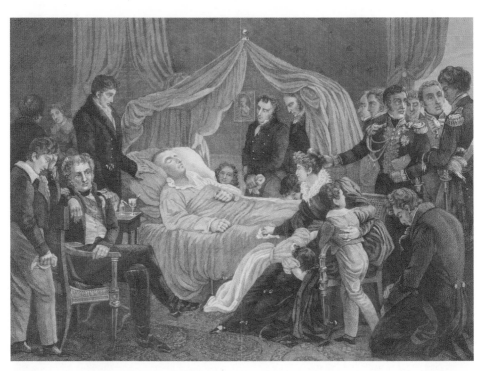

16. Charles de Steuben's painting shows Napoleon's death in a romantic composition. It portrays a dramatic moment where all of the exiles of Saint Helena gathered round to say goodbye to the 'spirit of the age'. To the extreme left the man with his back to the viewer is the Abbé Vignali. Nobody knows what he looked like and indeed whether he was able to reconcile the former emperor with the church at the last moment.

The festivities continued, but the emperor's fury knew no bounds. According to Consalvi, the emperor ordered that he, Oppizzoni and di Pietro should be put in front of a firing squad in the morning.[107] Although this story emphasises Napoleon's legendary rage, there is no actual evidence that he ever gave such an order, or at any rate seriously contemplated carrying it out. It is true that Napoleon felt particularly aggrieved towards Oppizzoni, whom he had favoured and elevated at such a young age to the crimson. He also felt that he had protected him from scandal in Bologna in 1806 when he had been accused of an affair with an underage prostitute.[108]

This challenge on the part of the thirteen cardinals needed to be met with a determined response. Very unwisely, they tried to attend a formal reception in the Tuileries the next day. An usher approached the thirteen cardinals individually and loudly informed them one by one that His Imperial Majesty would not receive them. The thirteen cardinals had to walk sheepishly through the antechambers of the state apartments in public humiliation. According to legend, Napoleon had ordered that their carriages be removed so that they had to walk all the way back to their homes. Bigot, the minister of religions, was asked to identify the offenders, stop their pensions and demand their resignations. Cardinal della Somaglia had been ill, so he would have been excused from any punishment. Bravely he declared that if he had been well, he would not have attended the ceremony.[109] The emperor ordered the absent cardinals to be summoned to the ministry of religions. Here they were informed that they had, for a decade, ill-advised the pope and conspired against the stability of the Empire. Essentially rebels against the crown, they had sown the seeds of civil war. The civil authorities reserved the right to try them for treason at an unspecified date.

At this point, Fouché arrived with even graver instructions to carry out. The cardinals were to be stripped of their crimson robes and all other symbols of their rank. From here on they would only be permitted to wear black cassocks, like ordinary priests. Immediately, in the public spheres, these prelates who had defied Napoleon became known as the 'black cardinals'.[110] They wore their demotion with dignity. Consalvi protested that the cardinals, far from being rebels or conspirators, had always acted in good faith. Indeed, they had warned the emperor in a letter that they could not accede to his wishes and suggested means of saving face. The cardinals produced a joint declaration stating that they were innocent of rebellion, but had not attended the marriage because the pope had not been consulted over the annulment.[111]

Despite the festivities for the marriage to Marie-Louise, the emperor's fury knew no bounds. He now insisted that those cardinals who were also bishops resign their dioceses. They wrote to Pius VII in Savona offering their resignations, but the pope refused to accept them.[112] After months of nervous waiting, the thirteen black cardinals were summoned again to the ministry of religions on 11 June 1810.[113] They were informed that they were to be sent into internal exile to eastern France. Napoleon chose fortress or garrison towns whose loyalty to his regime was proven. Here these princes of the church led a miserable and dull existence. They were given a meagre 250 francs per month on which to live. Consalvi was sent to Reims, the only one of these thirteen prelates exiled to a cathedral city. The rest would spend the subsequent years in obscurity, waiting for the fortunes of the Empire to collapse. After his wedding, the emperor had stripped almost a third of the College of Cardinals of their rank, and sent them into exile. The crisis with the Roman Church deepened; its resolution seemed ever more evanescent. Napoleon's second marriage was overshadowed by the scandal of the black cardinals, further reducing his position with the Catholic populations of Europe.

From Vienna, Francis I observed Pius VII's incarceration with increasing unease. He instructed Metternich to intercede as best he could in the pope's favour during the summer of 1810.[114] The imperial chancellor offered Austria's services as mediators in an attempt to settle the disagreement between Rome and Paris. The Habsburgs did not wish to appear indifferent to the Holy Father's plight. Yet Metternich the realist knew that any mediation was likely to be shipwrecked by Napoleon's determination to subjugate the church to his will. Equally, the pope was unlikely to yield to any requests until he could return to the Quirinal. But even if this mediation ended in failure, it would reflect well on Austria: the monarchy would appear simultaneously to be the champions of Catholicism and reliable allies of the French.[115]

The man chosen to handle this delicate mission was the Ritter Ludwig von Lebzeltern, formerly a high official in the Habsburg Embassy in the Papal States: in the absence of the ambassador, he had been chargé d'affaires on two occasions. Born in Portugal, he had also served as a diplomat in Madrid and had travelled in Italy extensively. As a man of some religious sensibility, of delicate manners, he had formed a good working relationship with members of the Curia. He was also on terms of friendship with the pope.[116] After the occupation of Rome he had been expelled from the Papal States. On his journey to Vienna he was captured by French troops, who violated his diplomatic immunity by searching his baggage. Here they discovered that he carried a copy of the bull of excommunication against Napoleon. He was interned in Bavaria and only released after the peace of Schönbrunn.[117]

Lebzeltern was loyal to his imperial masters and sympathetic to the pope. His knowledge of Habsburg and papal affairs made him well suited to travel to Savona and meet with Pius. His mission was to see how many of the French demands the pope might be willing to consider. Foreign ministry officials in Paris demanded that he make clear to Pius VII that he would not receive support or assistance from the Austrian monarchy. For Metternich the goal of the mission to Savona was different. The powers of Europe would never accept a pope relegated to the status of mere French client. The Habsburg chancellor thought that, for the time being, the best the pope could hope for was to be transferred to Avignon. Here he would be permitted to meet freely with the College of Cardinals and foreign diplomats.[118] This idea was put to Napoleon. To everybody's surprise, the emperor replied that he was willing to allow the pope to return to Rome. Here he could meet with his cardinals, receive foreign ministers and send nuncios to the courts of Europe. It was accepted that the Papacy would be endowed with independent revenues free from imperial interference. In return, the emperor of the French would remain the sovereign of Rome, and the pope would tacitly accept him as his overlord.[119] This offer was the absolute bottom line for the French. The Papacy could remain spiritually independent in Rome, but could exercise no temporal jurisdiction. To this proposal the Austrians added the release of Cardinal Pacca, the re-establishment of religious orders, a reopening of discussions on the organic laws and a troop reduction in Rome.

Lebzeltern's memoirs, written with the benefit of some hindsight but not intended for publication, reveal that he believed any agreement with Napoleon would be temporary rather than binding. He would urge the pope to acquiesce until he was in a stronger position from which to regain his temporal rights. In the end, accepting Napoleon's offer would free him from Savona and allow him to regain the counsel of the Sacred College.[120] The French emperor meanwhile was unhappy with the choice of Lebzeltern, given that he was a friend of the pope. Would he really present the French offer to Pius in a positive light? Metternich assured him that his agent was a professional, who would obey his instructions to the letter. Champagny, as French foreign minister, presented an official note to Lebzeltern stating the French position and offer for Pius. Metternich made it clear to his agent that Austria could not be bound by this document. As mediators, they would not present the pope with an ultimatum, but rather would listen to his views and present them to Napoleon. On 7 May Metternich issued his own set of instructions to his agent. Although the chancellor was sympathetic to Pius's position, his intransigence had placed the very survival of Catholicism in peril. If the current pontiff died a French prisoner this would lead to an inevitable schism. In such an eventuality the Catholic powers of Europe would find it difficult to repair the damage done to the unity of the church. Pius was urged to accept an unsatisfactory compromise now, in the hope of a better arrangement in the future.

Lebzeltern was to go to Savona. His official mission was to settle Habsburg church affairs, but clearly mediation with France was the true purpose of his journey. This was not to be done in writing, but through informal discussions, preliminaries that would serve as the basis for more formal negotiations. Metternich wanted the pope to know that Napoleon was willing to allow him to return to Rome. He would be spiritually independent in the eternal city, but would lose all temporal sovereignty. Pius could request that a few trusted individuals travel to Savona to advise him, but the Sacred College would remain in Paris for the time being.[121] Duly briefed, Lebzeltern travelled at great speed to Savona. He arrived on 15 May 1810 and immediately headed to the bishop's palace, where he was stopped by the troops guarding the entrances. Despite his diplomatic credentials, nobody could be admitted without being cleared by the commander of the 'papal guard of honour'. At the very moment of his arrival, two Royal Navy frigates hove into view, and the gunners of the citadel, clearly over-excited, started firing their guns at these enemy ships. The British sailors, evidently unperturbed, started playing the tune 'Go to bed, Tom, rise as early as ever you can'.[122] It was a comic and incongruous scene that greeted the Austrian representative.

The commander insisted that, as he had not been informed of Lebzeltern's mission, he would be present during all conversations with the pope. The chevalier replied that this would be unacceptable: he would be discussing affairs relating to the church in Austrian lands, especially the archdiocese of Vienna. If he was not given access, he would send a diplomatic complaint to the French emperor directly. The commander, angrily, persisted in reminding him that he had no orders to admit him. Lebzeltern had appeared out of the blue, claiming to have government authorisation, but how could the commander know without confirmation from Paris? The commander's words clearly showed Napoleon's assurance that the pope was free to see whomever he wished in Savona to be a blatant lie. When Metternich's agent threatened to return immediately to Paris, the commander, in frustration, threw his bicorne hat on the ground and said: 'Damn it, do whatever you want, see the pope for all I care.'[123]

After this stormy interview, the papal *maestro di camera* introduced Lebzeltern into the pope's presence. Pius was much moved after months of isolation to have contact with a diplomat without police surveillance. He inquired after the diplomat's health and thanked the Austrian emperor for taking an interest in his fate. They discussed the deepening crisis at length and the vexations suffered by Pius at Napoleon's instigation. The pope then expressed how pained he was from both a political and religious perspective that Francis had been forced to wed his favourite daughter to Napoleon. The pope regretted that the valiant Austrian troops had not succeeded in defeating the French at Wagram.[124] He believed the current peace was a truce, and blamed Russian weakness for the lamentable situation. Much of the conversation revolved around the pope's pain in learning that the Archduchess Marie-Louise had married an excommunicated soldier of fortune. The pope felt betrayed that his authority had been flouted in this matter.

Feeling that this line of conversation was a cul-de-sac, Lebzeltern started to discuss Napoleon's offers. The pope prayed that these proposals might open the road for reconciliation. He hoped that, at the very least, the Austrian marriage had mellowed his nemesis. The agent spoke of the real danger of a schism that loomed over the church while His Holiness was away from the Holy See. Pius deplored the circumstances, but was serene in his conscience and stressed that he had done his duty. He demanded that he be allowed to communicate freely with all cardinals, bishops and foreign diplomats. During his confinement Pius had not been idle, and had received thousands of petitions. He had replied to 500 of these requests, including some which were quite bizarre. However, with one copyist alone he could not keep up with the burden of work.[125] Isolation had clearly made the pope somewhat manic. He now had the opportunity to vent his frustration.

His interlocutor realised that it was essential to focus on the matter at hand. The conversation turned to Napoleon's devastating plans to move the Holy See to Paris. This deeply distressed the Holy Father, who seemed to enter a state of great agitation. Lebzeltern mentioned Avignon as a possible alternative location, to which Pius replied 'Never!'[126] At this point, Metternich's agent announced that a better alternative was on offer. Austria, the most loyal Catholic power in the world, offered its services to the Papacy at this critical hour. The French emperor's compromise was described in detail, as were its conditions. The pope listened earnestly and replied that he desired nothing more than to return to Rome. He was willing to return to the Quirinal, but he would, and indeed must, continue to protest publicly against the violation of his sovereignty. Lebzeltern lamented that any such protest would inflame Napoleon's anger. All of Europe would realise that Pius had not been deprived voluntarily of his principality. He tacitly urged Pius to forgo his kingdom, in the hope that one day he might recover it.[127]

The pope turned to his interlocutor, his eyes ablaze with passion. He hissed that his conscience impelled him to defend the rights of the Holy See and the Patrimony of Saint Peter. He had sworn to hold these territories and pass them on to his successors. Lebzeltern urged the pope to reconsider his stance. The meaning of his silence would be plain to all of Europe. In order to preserve the spiritual powers of the Papacy he would need to sacrifice the temporal ones for the time being. What would become of Christendom if it remained deprived of its natural leader? Pius, again, stressed that he wanted to return to Rome, but would accept no monies from France. Yielding to hyperbole, the pope proposed to live in the catacombs as his predecessors had done during the first century. There he would rely on donations of food, clothing and shelter from his flock.

Pius stressed that Napoleon was likely to interfere, not only in temporal affairs, but also in spiritual matters. It would be impossible for him as pope to ignore issues like the organic laws or divorce. Lebzeltern suggested, unwisely, that a new Concordat could regulate such issues. In anger, Pius exclaimed that Napoleon could not be relied upon, and that signed treaties were dead letters to him.[128] Furthermore, the pope refused to withdraw his bull of excommunication until the emperor made positive steps to reconcile himself with the church. He was amenable to compromise, but he would not show weakness nor concede the prerogatives of Holy Mother Church. The diplomat begged the Holy Father to reconsider his position for the greater good. As the first meeting ended, Pius promised that, if genuine steps were made towards peace, he would be willing to entertain them.[129]

Two days later, Lebzeltern met with the pope again. Clearly, during this interlude, Pius had had many hours on which to reflect on their initial conversation. His conscience troubled him, and he was more fearful of compromise. Weakness was one of the vices this former Benedictine monk dreaded the most. As pope, human frailty was far more dangerous for him than for an ordinary mortal. He could not give up the rights of the church without imperilling his soul and those of millions of others. Newspaper reports had reached him, as well as letters from Cardinal Fesch, which made him fear that Napoleon was not genuinely in the mood for conciliation. He launched into a frantic tirade, listing the usurpations that the French had visited upon him, and how he, in all circumstances, had been guided by moderation. He was accused of inciting the emperor's subjects to rebel! Nothing could be further from the truth. Had he not ordered even his own devoted subjects not to resist the French invasion of his domains? Exhausted from his fitful outbursts, Pius collapsed into an armchair. He conceded that, if the emperor made some concessions, he would withdraw the bull of excommunication.[130]

Many hours of discussion followed. Slowly, the pope came around to the idea of returning to Rome, without protesting the loss of his sovereignty, in exchange for a guarantee of spiritual independence. According to Lebzeltern's memoirs, Pius even offered to crown Napoleon emperor of the West in Rome. This would demonstrate to the world that he did not contest his legitimacy.[131] Indeed, as noted in the previous chapter (pp. 144–6), this was a scenario which the College of Cardinals had considered as far back as 1806. Slowly, Pius was coming to accept a scenario in which a return to Rome would be possible as long as he would be free to communicate with the church and seek the advice of his cardinals. The request was made that Austria would act as guarantor of this agreement. The pope also demanded, as a sign of good faith, that he be allowed his most faithful courtiers and cardinals to join him in Savona. This gesture would be a starting point for any future progress.[132]

Three days later, in a parting audience, Lebzeltern was given the pope's verbal instructions. These informal talks had established his willingness to explore the emperor's proposal to return to Rome. He was resolved never to do anything that would compromise his conscience or the prerogatives of the church. Pius stressed that he bore Napoleon no rancour, and even forgave him for his mistreatment. He hoped that a future Austrian mediation could solve the outstanding issues. The central sticking-point was that his isolation be ended immediately and that his most trusted counsellors join him in Savona. Lebzeltern kissed the pope's feet as he took his leave of the pontiff and headed to Paris with all speed.[133]

On 29 May 1810 he reached the French capital. He briefed Metternich that the pope was willing to talk and make concessions. The situation seemed promising, but in the space of a few weeks Napoleon's attitude had hardened.

The emperor told Metternich that his agent had merely encouraged the pope to become more stubborn. Some recent papal letters had been leaked from Savona, filled with invectives against the French. The Austrian chancellor stated that the opposite was the case, and indeed the pope had shown himself open to concessions.[134] After this meeting Champagny, as foreign minister, held a number of conferences with Lebzeltern to understand how the crisis with the pope might be resolved. The Austrian agent stressed that all of the emperor's conditions were open for discussion. The starting point for negotiations was that Pius wanted his advisers close to him. Champagny believed this would inevitably lead to an impasse. After all, the emperor would never accept delegates chosen by Pius and, vice versa: the pope would never accept those prelates loyal to Napoleon. Lebzeltern advised that he, as a neutral third party, had been authorised to select a small group of advisers who would go to Savona to counsel the pope.[135]

The foreign minister felt that these discussions in Savona represented some progress, indeed might prove a promising starting point for substantive negotiations. This bubble was soon burst: Napoleon refused to accept Lebzeltern's list of advisers, and insisted that Cardinal Spina and Cardinal Caselli go to Savona. Metternich responded that the emperor well knew that such a solution would never be accepted by the pope.[136] The imperial government felt that the informal discussions initiated by Austria had not broken the impasse, and that there were no grounds to proceed with a formal mediation. Napoleon took Metternich to one side and expressed his conviction that the time was not yet right for making peace with the pope. Further time spent in isolation would persuade Pius to make further concessions. In the end, the Lebzeltern mission to Savona was a dismal failure.

On their return to Paris from their honeymoon, on 1 July 1810 Napoleon and Marie-Louise were invited to a grand reception at the Austrian Embassy at the Hôtel de Montesson.[137] Over 2,000 other guests were also invited. Temporary wooden structures were erected in the gardens to welcome the imperial couple and other dignitaries of both empires. Due to the poor fire-safety standards of the early nineteenth century, the chandeliers had been hung too close to the roof of the wooden pavilion. An inferno was sparked, and the main escape routes blocked by the flames. Napoleon and the imperial family escaped as the situation became dangerous.[138] Then the emperor and his Austrian allies tried to keep the fire under control and save as many people as possible. Though officially only one death was recorded – that of Princess Pauline von Schwarzenberg, the sister-in-law of the ambassador – casualties were probably much higher.[139] All involved were deeply traumatised by this tragic incident. The superstitious wondered if it was an ill omen. Had not the fireworks for Louis XVI's 1770 marriage to Marie-Antoinette resulted in a fire causing the death of 132 people?[140] Certainly, the Habsburg marriage and Austrian alliance did not bring the peace and prosperity that were anticipated. Equally, the rejection of the Lebzeltern mission had left the conflict with the pope unresolved.

# SEVEN

# THE EMPIRE OF GOD
## THE NATIONAL COUNCIL OF 1811

Ecumenical councils have played vital roles in the history of the Christian Church. Through their deliberations they have defined beliefs and reformed the structures of church governance (also known as ecclesiology).[1] Such councils were summoned with some regularity in the ancient and medieval world, assembling hundreds of bishops from across Europe. They were summits at which the key church leaders and theologians debated the pressing issues of the day. In antiquity, some Roman and Byzantine emperors had attended in person, but, by the modern age, monarchs no longer did so. Instead, emissaries and ambassadors were sent by Catholic monarchies to influence deliberations. Since the fifteenth century, the Catholic Church had only held the Council of Trent (1545–63), which lasted for no fewer than eighteen years, and sought to provide a concerted response to the challenge posed by nascent Protestantism. Its theologians defined Catholic beliefs with a clarity and confidence hitherto unprecedented.[2] The canons, or rules, promulgated then saw the pope as the supreme head of the church, greatly strengthening his authority. Yet, the conclusions reached by the council were never universally recognised by the secular authorities. Several Catholic powers also did not accept the outcomes of Trent. For example, the law courts, in *ancien régime* France, refused to register the Tridentine canons and enforce them within the kingdom.[3] Gallicanism argued, for centuries, that it was autonomous from Rome, and that papal decisions needed to be ratified by national councils.

The main reason why popes had been reluctant to summon ecumenical councils relates to the theory of conciliarism, which claims that bishops and priests meeting as a body supersede the authority of the pope. As already discussed (p. 43), in 1414–18, during the Council of Constance, two rival popes were deposed and Martin V was elected to heal the wounds of the Great Western Schism.[4] The principle was enshrined, in this and subsequent councils, that the church, as a body, could regulate its own internal governance without reference to the Papacy. Not surprisingly, since the late Middle Ages, Roman pontiffs had declared such views heretical, and avoided the dangers of summoning such unpredictable assemblies of bishops.[5] It is not surprising that, as the year 1810 drew to a close, Napoleon became fascinated with these councils and their history. They seemed to provide a useful theoretical instrument to bypass the pope's authority. The Gallican Church had used its national councils and prerogatives to resist encroachments from Rome throughout its history. As already mentioned in Chapter 1 (p. 16), the Pragmatic Sanction of Bourges of 1438 had allowed the French church to invest bishops without papal confirmation.[6] This led to a quarrel between Gallicanism and Rome that was only settled in 1516 with the Concordat of Bologna.[7] This agreement, like the one signed in 1801, allowed the kings of France to nominate bishops to vacant sees subject to papal approval. For most of the *ancien régime*, the Bourbon monarchy was involved in cyclical disputes with the Curia over the limits of their respective prerogatives.

The 1680s had witnessed a serious flashpoint in Franco-papal relations. Louis XIV and Innocent XI had become embroiled in a quarrel over church income and property, and this led to an investiture dispute.[8] As a result, Louis XIV's absolutist government had to find ways to sidestep the Papacy. The first solution had been the proclamation of the Four Gallican Articles of 1682.[9] These not only granted the monarch immunity from excommunication, but also stated that the church of France had to ratify any decrees and reforms issued by Rome.[10] In reaction, Innocent XI refused to invest French bishops nominated by the crown. Louis XIV and his ministers found an elegant way around this refusal. According to canon law, when a bishop died, the cathedral chapter, which comprised the senior priests in the diocese, would elect a vicar-capitular to administer the diocese until a new bishop was confirmed. The king now forced chapters throughout France to elect his nominees as vicars-capitular.[11] Although councils, in the past, had forbidden such nominees from being elected vicars-capitular, the French government ignored these rules, and imposed its own candidates on the cathedral chapters. This procedure allowed bishops nominated by the crown to administer their dioceses without papal confirmation. After a decade of wrangling, the Sun King came to an understanding with the Holy See. Gallicanism was reined in, and the Papacy resumed investing new bishops as if nothing had ever happened. In 1693, in a gesture of goodwill, the king went so far as to disavow the Four Articles of 1682 and accepted the pope's authority.[12] After this crisis, the relationship with Rome was much more cordial, with both sides operating in partnership. The last

Gallican National Council was held in Embrun in 1723, and was sanctioned by Innocent XIII. Its purpose was to censure a wayward bishop, who had unwisely supported Jansenism.[13]

The precedents established by the Bourbon monarchy during the last two decades of the seventeenth century were clear and attractive. For Napoleon, they offered practical solutions to the religious crisis, which confronted his vast European empire. He followed Louis XIV's example almost to the letter. The Four Gallican Articles of 1682 (see Appendix), through an imperial decree dated 25 February 1810, were incorporated into French law, and all seminaries in the Empire were ordered to include them into their curricula.[14] The police, meanwhile, were instructed to pursue and seize any publications that contested the legitimacy of Gallicanism.[15] These provisions were also extended to the Kingdom of Italy, even though these territories had little native tradition of ecclesiastical autonomy from Rome. As autumn 1810 approached, the imperial government decided to pilot Louis XIV's solution to the investiture crisis in three dioceses. In Paris, Asti and Florence episcopal candidates were elected vicars-capitular. This would entitle them to administer their diocese until a time when the pope eventually confirmed their appointment.[16]

Cardinal Fesch was offered the archdiocese of Paris. Despite being intimidated and threatened, he refused, arguing that, as archbishop of Lyon, he was already primate of all Gaul, and the most senior prelate in France.[17] During this time, as previously noted (p. 117), Cardinal Maury had opportunistically transferred his allegiance from the Bourbon dynasty to the Empire. His newfound devotion to Napoleon was embarrassing, given his track record as a staunch defender of the *ancien régime*. His former devotion to counter-revolution, and his public denunciation of the Concordat, made his volte-face extremely controversial.[18] He came to be viewed as a turncoat, ready to serve the highest bidder. Cardinal Maury had not been popular as bishop of Montefiascone in central Italy: his flock had been involved in several property disputes against him, while numerous buildings and fields belonging to Maury were vandalised in retaliation for the levying of high rents. When he took his tenants to court, the attacks against his property increased.[19] It is hardly surprising that he wanted to abandon an Italian see, where he was unpopular, to become the archbishop of the capital of the greatest empire on earth. It was a great propaganda victory for the Empire that their most bitter ecclesiastical enemy had now rallied to their eagles. When he accepted the appointment to Paris, the cathedral chapter were scandalised by his willingness to usurp their archdiocese.

At the same time, two French prelates were earmarked for the diocese of Asti and the archdiocese of Florence.[20] These initial appointments were meant to pave the way for a new Gallican episcopate, which was to be entirely subservient to Napoleon's wishes. Although Piedmont and Tuscany had been annexed to France, their populations were Italian-speaking. It showed a decided lack of confidence in the local clergy for French candidates to be sent to head some of the most important Italian dioceses: the imperial administration felt that only Frenchmen could be relied upon to implement energetically the reform policies emanating from Paris.[21] Finding reliable ecclesiastical collaborators in Italy was an uphill struggle for the Empire. Even on the French side of the Alps, the pressure exerted on cathedral chapters to elect such collaborators as vicars-capitular was a public scandal, which did not shine a good light on the government.

Resentment against Napoleon's ecclesiastical reforms had a distinctly Franco-Italian flavour. The ultra-Catholic and royalist opposition, which had been such a thorn in the side of the French Revolutionary government, appeared moribund after the Concordat of 1801. Indeed, by the imperial coronation in 1804 it seemed as if Napoleon had rallied and charmed the enemies of the Revolution to his side.[22] Such appearances were highly deceptive. Priests like the former Jesuit Pio Brunone Lantieri had, for decades, been horrified by what they viewed as the heresies of the Enlightenment. With like-minded friends, he had created secret societies, known as *Amicizie* ('Friendships'), which met regularly to promote 'good' books and counter the evils of modern philosophy.[23] Reactionary, devoted to the Holy See, and fearless, these secret societies had locked horns with radical *philosophes* during the twilight of the eighteenth century.[24] Napoleon's Catholic enemies did not emerge out of nowhere, but were veterans of many campaigns against Enlightenment and Revolution. Like the Grande Armée, they were well-organised, and tended to strike where the enemy least expected. Lantieri's association spread like wildfire throughout north-western Italy and extended as far as Germany and France.

Within France itself, the Catholic royalist movement had gone underground rather than disappearing. Clandestine cells and royalist information networks slowly spread through the country. As religious orders had been dissolved, informal congregations of clergy and laypeople devoted to prayer multiplied throughout Europe. At first glance, their official aim was to rekindle devotion to the Sacred Heart of Jesus, the Virgin Mary and other such devotional icons.[25] The most famous society was the Paris congregation of Sancta Maria Auxilium Christianorum, created by Jean-Baptiste Delpuits in February 1801 with the approval of the capital's archbishop.[26] These highly conservative clerics, many of whom were former Jesuits, taught their lay brethren devotion and submission to the Papacy. On the surface, these congregations appeared to be simple prayer groups, but, beneath their supposedly peaceable aims, they stoked the fires of Catholic fervour.

Their discretion and apparent inertness allowed them to survive unobserved for years. Indeed, they did not catch the imperial police's eye for some time. In 1809 they played a vital role in spreading news across Paris that Napoleon and his administrators had been excommunicated.[27] Their printing presses provided an important source of alternative information, countering the propaganda disseminated by imperial gazettes. From Napoleonic Piedmont, Lantieri published a dissertation in 1811 vindicating the pope's prerogative powers of confirmation over new bishops and denying that these rights could ever be legitimately bypassed.[28] Such publications deeply irritated the Empire's authorities but arresting those responsible proved difficult, especially as these Catholics had organised themselves into cells and congregations that acted autonomously from each other: if one group were arrested, they would be unable to name other conspirators. Such groups were an early example of an organised non-violent resistance movement preaching civil disobedience. Behind the scenes, they kept the flame of opposition to the Empire burning bright, and denounced the persecution of the Papacy.

By February 1810, the lay members of these congregations had created a new conspiratorial organisation: the *Chevaliers de la Foi* ('Knights of the Faith').[29] Its membership was mainly made up of young male *ancien régime* aristocrats, though aided by an impressive female following who provided vital logistical support for their activities. The members were not of the same generation as the émigrés who had fled the Revolution of 1789, but rather were their children. These conspirators were young, energetic, idealistic and imagined themselves to be made of the same metal as the crusading knights of the Middle Ages. Service to the Papacy in this time of persecution became their priority.[30] Unlike their parents, they had little nostalgia for Gallicanism; inspired by their priests, they were imbued with an iron devotion to the Papacy. Such sentiments would have been alien to their parents. Their conspiratorial networks supported the clergy loyal to Rome and prepared some of the groundwork for the restoration of the Bourbon monarchy.[31] They also provided food, fuel and other necessities to the black cardinals throughout their exile.[32] Such agents were ingenious in carrying information across France, hiding cyphered letters in secret compartments in boots and in the brims of hats. The police were baffled as to how they managed to elude their tight surveillance. They spied not only on behalf of Louis XVIII, now in exile in Britain, but also made contact with the pope in Savona.

By September 1810, a complex and high-risk communications network had been established between the clergy of Paris and Pius VII in his exile. Through a network of daring secrets agents, notes and documents were carried back and forth from the Ligurian coast to the French capital, undetected by the imperial postal authorities.[33] Initially messengers travelled from Paris to Lyon. Here at inns, *bouchons*, coach houses and other discreet locations, they met their contacts in order to deliver messages.[34] Italian couriers, recruited by the *Amicizie*, would eventually ferry these notes and fragments to Turin.[35] Here, other agents would decode and reassemble them.

Finally, these messages were delivered to Pius during public audiences in Savona. According to legend, agents would place the notes from Paris in the seams of his cassock when they prostrated themselves to kiss his feet, undetected by his guards. Late in the evening the pope and his secretaries extracted these messages and read them by candlelight. Throughout the small hours, replies were written and addressed to secret apostolic delegates spread throughout the Empire. The pious washerwomen of the episcopal palace also had a role to play in this plot.[36] The secret correspondence that was smuggled out of Savona was hidden in clothing sent to be laundered.[37] The missives were then delivered to secret couriers who carried them to Turin. From there they slowly made their way back to Paris. For the better part of a year, this system allowed the pope to communicate discreetly with his church and the outside world.

By November 1810, a brief from Pius, addressed to Cardinal Maury, was in circulation throughout Paris. The turncoat cardinal was admonished as follows:

> How is it that after having so bravely and eloquently defended the cause of the Catholic Church during the tempestuous times of the French Revolution, you now abandon this same church, especially now that you have been rewarded with its highest honours and dignities? Are you not tied to it by the strictest oaths [of allegiance]? Are you not ashamed and do you not blush in taking sides against us in a struggle that we have undertaken to defend the dignity of the church? Do you care so little for our authority that you defy it

publicly through your behaviour? Do you not owe us obedience and loyalty? The issue which most afflicts us, is that you have sought from a cathedral chapter the administration of an archdiocese [outside your jurisdiction]. You should have imitated the noble example of Cardinal Joseph Fesch, archbishop of Lyon, who was appointed to the same archdiocese of Paris and thought it wise to refuse absolutely the spiritual administration of this church, despite being invited to do so by its chapter.[38]

The letter ended with an exhortation that Maury rethink his actions, and refuse the exercise of any jurisdiction over Paris. As bishop of Montefiascone, his first thoughts should be to provide for the well-being of his own flock in central Italy, and not to interfere in the affairs of other dioceses. The bishops-elect of Florence and Asti were stricken with similar papal interdicts.[39] It was made manifest to the world that the imperial solution of electing appointees as vicars-capitular was illegitimate.

In Paris, the vicar-general of the diocese, the Abbé Paul-Thérèse-David d'Astros, was deeply troubled by the pope's condemnation of Maury. Up to this point, Astros had been a model priest in the eyes of the regime: extremely hard-working, efficient and loyal to the imperial administration, not to mention well-connected with the ministry of religions, building up a close working relationship with its staff. This was hardly a surprise, given that he was a nephew of Portalis, the late minister of religions, and a cousin of the head of the imperial library, an institution which had a role in censoring books and other sensitive publications.[40] Up to 1809, he had often been consulted in relation to ecclesiastical nominations, and played an important role in preparing the Imperial Catechism of 1806.[41] The expulsion of Pius from Rome had troubled his conscience deeply. He was not a natural rebel, but was uncertain of where his loyalties lay in the current crisis.

The election of Maury to the administration of the Paris archdiocese was troubling for many of its priests and canons. Astros, as vicar-general, was given the task of welcoming Cardinal Maury into his new cathedral. This chore was intensely resented. In his address to the cardinal, Astros reminded Maury of his brave opposition to the French Revolution, and expressed his regret about the crisis with Rome. The abbé, through his unenthusiastic tone, made manifest that the archbishop-elect was hardly welcome.[42] As one of the most senior clergymen in the capital, Astros decided to tap into the clandestine network, and sent a letter to Savona asking for papal instructions on how to act.[43] In December, after an interlude of several weeks, he received a papal brief, smuggled out of Savona. Pius commanded him to ignore and countermand any orders issued on Maury's illicit authority.[44]

For the pope, Astros remained the true leader of the cathedral and its chapter. He was to refuse to obey the commands of an archbishop who was a usurper. This brief, condemning Maury's usurpation, was soon printed and circulated amongst the priests of Paris. Bigot, as minister of religions, prepared a report for the emperor, outlining that the pope had not only compromised the authority of the cardinal in Paris, but also the nominees for the dioceses of Asti and Florence. Bigot informed Napoleon that, through a secret network of Catholic activists, Pius had outmanoeuvred the imperial government. The bishops' elections as vicars-capitular had been denounced publicly. Their authority and ability to act was severely compromised.[45] Even from his exile, the pope had been able to sabotage the Empire's administration of the church.

On 1 January 1811, as was traditional, a reception was held in the Tuileries for the great dignitaries of the Empire, providing them with the opportunity to present the emperor and empress with their best wishes for the new year. As the great men of France and their spouses filed past and paid homage to the emperor, the moment arrived for Cardinal Maury to present the members of the Paris chapter. Napoleon inquired who were the cardinals' vicars: he wished to see them. When Maury introduced Astros there was a glacial pause, before the emperor hissed at the abbé that his behaviour was considered deeply suspect by his government. One of Napoleon's legendary verbal assaults followed. He showered Astros with a stream of invective against the pope's stubbornness, and declared him a traitorous priest. As he concluded this tirade, Napoleon grabbed the hilt of his sword and shouted: 'I have a sword at my side, beware!'[46] He then turned his back abruptly in a clear sign that Astros was now in disgrace. The new minister of police, General Anne Jean Marie René Savary, duc de Rovigo, was tasked with the investigation of the secret network and the arrest of those involved. A former aide-de-camp and commander of Napoleon's bodyguard, Savary was supremely loyal but lacked the investigative flair, insinuation and network of informants that the wily Fouché had built up in the ministry over the past decade. Essentially, he was a soldier playing policeman, and found it difficult to grasp the complex information and communication network that the Papacy had at its disposal.[47]

After the reception, Astros was taken aside by the minister and interrogated. In the meantime, a group of policemen ransacked the abbé's residence in search of compromising papers.[48] They found a copy of the bull of excommunication, and secret instructions from an unnamed apostolic delegate (di Pietro, one assumes). It also became clear that, during this time, Astros had been in close contact with Francesco Fontana, the general of the Barnabite Order.[49] This caused enormous embarrassment, as Fontana was considered trustworthy by the imperial regime: as mentioned in the previous chapter (p. 163), he had been co-opted onto the ecclesiastical committee of 1809 to advise the emperor on church affairs. In reality, Fontana had been in covert communication with Cardinal di Pietro, who although now exiled in the town of Semur-en-Auxois, was still able to send letters to important church officials and bishops. Fontana was a double agent at the heart of the imperial capital, doing his best to undermine the governmental policy of bypassing the pope during the investiture crisis. Throughout this time, he had been feeding sensitive government secrets to the Catholic opposition.[50] The police now tried to get their hands on those priests and laypersons involved in the courier network.[51] Both the Abbé Astros and Father Fontana, meanwhile, would spend the next four years as prisoners in the fortress of Vincennes, to the east of Paris.[52]

Many others involved in conspiracy were also imprisoned or exiled. The abbé's cousin, Joseph-Marie Portalis, who oversaw the imperial library and had the authority to censor publications, was very publicly disgraced. When, on 4 January 1811, he attended the Council of State, Napoleon demanded how he dared to show his face after what he had done. For fifteen minutes he showered this official with abuse and claimed that his ingratitude, not to mention his perfidy, were without comparison. Portalis, though stunned, replied that he had never strayed from his duty. The emperor ordered him to leave the council room immediately.[53] The disgrace of Portalis was somewhat unfair. He had not colluded actively in the affair, and had merely been aware of his cousin's activities and contacts with the pope. He would spend some years in exile away from Paris, but was eventually forgiven and recalled to service in June 1813.[54] The opposition of the Parisian cathedral chapter was particularly embarrassing, as most of its members were Gallican in their sympathies. They were hardly inveterate enemies of the Napoleonic Empire. As the crisis deepened, rather than rallying the Gallican establishment, the imperial administration showed an uncanny ability to alienate its ecclesiastical supporters. In 1811, a broadly sympathetic French Church was transformed into a breeding ground for opposition.

Frustrated that Pius, even from the depths of exile, continued to oppose his plans, the emperor decided to prohibit all communication between the pope and the outside world. The government commissioned the head of the Imperial Archives to publish a diatribe against the temporal power of the popes. Historians and pamphleteers were hired for a print campaign to turn the public sphere against the church, which painted the Papacy as the enemy of reason and good government.[55] Napoleon wrote to Prince Borghese on 15 January 1811, informing him that the budget for the papal household in Savona was to be reduced to the bare minimum.[56] Embarrassingly, it now emerged that members of both the papal household and the Gendarmerie were misappropriating funds allocated for the maintenance of the episcopal palace: as the pope refused to personally accept the monies allocated for his care, it was easy for others to embezzle them. It was decided to replace the local commander, who was considered too lax, with Colonel Antoine Lagorce, who was completely dependable and devoted to Napoleon. According to local tradition in Brives-la-Gaillarde, the town where he was born, Lagorce had been a clergyman in earlier life before joining the army and becoming a committed military man.[57] He was divorced, and had left his Catholic faith (if not sentiments) behind him. This soldier was determined to ensure that the pope did not communicate with the outside world.

In mid-January 1811 Chabrol received instructions that at night Pius should be deprived of his quills, writing paper and all books.[58] All his private letters and documents were seized and read.[59] Spyholes were drilled into the walls of the Holy Father's private apartments: one of them overlooked his bed, so that he was always monitored. His household servants were reduced, and his visitors limited, while his valet Morelli was arrested and sent to Genoa for interrogation.[60] Pius was no longer allowed to give public blessings, nor to hold general audiences. A cordon sanitaire of troops surrounded the palace, instructed to grant access only to authorised personnel. The interdict extended to the bishop and canons of Savona, who were now forbidden from speaking with the pope or attending Mass in his private chapel. For the next six months, the pope lived in a state of almost complete isolation. On 14 January, as he took his usual morning stroll in the gardens, gendarmes broke into his bedroom. They tore his mattress to shreds, forced open his desk and removed his breviary. Two months later Lagorce informed his prisoner that he was commanded to confiscate the Ring of the Fisherman, one of the great badges of pontifical office, used by Pius to seal and authenticate his letters. The confiscation of this ring deepened his confinement and inability to communicate with the outside world. Pius's eyes filled with tears and he trembled with indignation as he removed the ring and presented it to Lagorce.[61] Chabrol privately expressed his regret to the pope that it had come to this, but he sheepishly stated that he was only following orders. Pius accepted his torment with resignation, steadfastly refusing to capitulate to these aggressive psychological tactics.

Since the pope's kidnapping, the provisional government of Rome, the Consulta, had finished its task of preparing the local administration for annexation into greater France. On 17 February 1810, the Imperial Senate decreed the incorporation of the Roman departments into the Greater Empire.[62] The former Papal States would be ruled as any other French territory, with prefects overseeing civil administration. The city of Rome would have special status as the second city of the Empire. The decree stated that, in future, the emperors of the French would first be crowned in Notre-Dame, with a second coronation taking place in Saint Peter's Basilica in Rome before the tenth year of their reign expired. The decree also categorically stated that popes would renounce any claims over Rome and swear to do nothing that was contrary to the Four Gallican Articles. It was furthermore declared that these articles were now in force in every part of the Greater Empire. The pope would be provided with several palaces for his use across Europe, and the College of Cardinals was declared an imperial institution.[63]

The decree would make the situation within the former Papal States decidedly tense: few were willing to work with a regime that had usurped the legitimate rights of the Papacy in such a brutal manner. In 1809 the Consulta had been able to find some token collaborators to help them with the administration of these central Italian territories. These radicals who flocked to the French colours were examples neither of competence, probity nor reliability. The former radical *giacobini* and *sbirri* that collaborated with the French in Rome made a very poor impression on the population.[64] In mid-June 1810 all administrators, bishops and priests were ordered to sign their names to an oath of allegiance to the French Empire.[65] Thousands of priests, and most bishops, categorically refused to do so.[66] Some tried to take the modified oath prescribed by the pope in 1808, but it was at the discretion of local authorities to accept this formula or not. As the situation worsened, many priests were deported, some to the Piacentino, a number into the Alps and others shipped to Corsica, where they would spend years of uncomfortable exile being taunted by the local garrison and population.[67]

On his departure from Rome, the pope had delegated his powers over the eternal city to Cardinal di Pietro. When this prelate was himself forcibly transferred to Paris, his authority was automatically delegated to a senior judge of the Roman

Inquisition, Benedetto Fenaja, who immediately urged the clergy to continue resisting the invaders. Unsurprisingly he was quickly arrested and imprisoned in France. Following this, another ecclesiastical judge, Domenico Attanasio, received the powers of apostolic delegate. He would exercise them over Rome for five years, up to 1814.[68] Not as daring as his predecessors, he tried to find alternative phrasings for the oath of allegiance which would spare Roman priests from deportation. For the new prefect of Rome, Camille de Tournon-Simiane, and the mayor of the city, Luigi Braschi-Onesti, duke of Nemi (a nephew of Pius VI), the situation was extremely fraught.[69] For most of their tenure both lamented the lack of engagement they received from the general population, clergy and nobility of the eternal city.

In the Papal States, the French only ever managed to achieve a grudging acquiescence from their newly acquired citizen-subjects. Napoleon's Empire, which claimed to bring progress, enlightenment and civilisation to these provinces, was deeply resented.[70] In turn, the French occupiers complained that, unlike the ancient Romans, modern Italians were lazy, stupid and bigoted: the administrators of the Empire drew much inspiration from imperial Rome, but found little to admire in contemporary Italians. From the vantage point of Paris, decadence, laziness and superstition had created a moribund political culture.[71] Napoleon felt that the accomplishments of his civilisation exceeded those of antiquity, and that Rome needed to be purified after centuries of ecclesiastical government. The pope's subjects resented their new rulers' heavy-handed and condescending manner. The French decidedly failed to win the hearts and minds of the people of central Italy.

Back in Paris, as 1811 progressed, Napoleon decided to seek expert advice on how to proceed. He summoned a second ecclesiastical committee, broadly similar in its membership to that of 1809.[72] Its remit was to advise on two issues:

1. As the pope was not allowed to communicate with the church, would ordinary bishops be permitted to bestow the special dispensations, indults and indulgences that were usually the preserve of the Holy See?
2. As the pope would not confirm the Empire's new bishops, could these candidates receive investiture without papal consent?[73]

The delegates deliberated these questions with some animation; as theologians they felt uncomfortable with any solution that would usurp papal authority. They produced a joint statement in which they lamented the present impossibility of communicating with the pope. They expressed the hope that the clergy would soon be able to correspond with the spiritual head of the church as freely as in the past. Their answer to the first question was straightforward. Although it was regrettable, bishops could, temporarily, exercise some of the powers of the Holy See while the pope remained in Savona.[74] Thus, bishops could bestow special graces until such a time as the pope was released.

The more important question of episcopal investiture was a completely different matter. The Concordat was silent on the issue of what should occur if the Holy See refused to confirm a governmental candidate. Any change to the nomination procedure would require the pope's consent. It was transparent that Pius would never agree to a process of investing new bishops, which might bypass his authority. The ecclesiastical committee advised that the pope could not be ignored. They did feel, however, that a church council of bishops could put pressure on the Holy Father to compromise with the imperial administration.[75]

This was far from what the imperial administration wanted to hear. The members of the committee made it clear that a simple resolution of the current crisis could not be found in canon law. There was no legitimate means of bypassing the authority of a reigning pontiff. Only a national council would have the prestige and authority to exhort Pius to give way. However, summoning such a body held the risk that bishops might create their own agenda, and come to their own independent conclusions. This was something the government wanted at all costs to avoid. The minister of religions and loyal Gallican bishops would need to manage any such council carefully, to ensure that it would support the imperial reform agenda without protest. The risk of this initiative backfiring was considerable. Moreover, the ecclesiastical committee believed that a national council could merely advise the pope, but could not compel him to act against his will. Although perilous, a conciliar solution was becoming the preferred remedy for the imperial government.

On 16 March 1811, the members of the ecclesiastical committee were summoned to the Tuileries. After making them wait, deliberately, for over two hours, the emperor received them.[76] As soon as they were before him, he demanded to know how he could punish a pope who preached rebellion and civil war against his state. The emperor entered his usual routine, listing all he had done for the Catholic Church since coming to power, and describing how the pope had breached the terms of the Concordat. He complained of how Pius had never been sincere about religious peace, and stated that a solution was needed in order to resolve the investiture crisis. When Napoleon finished, he stared intensely at the terrified prelates. He turned suddenly on the elderly Abbé Emery, the director of the seminary of Saint-Sulpice. As already mentioned in previous chapters (p. 108), this learned theologian had been the virtual head of the Gallican Church during the 1790s.[77] He was not easily intimidated on the issue of investiture and was asked to express his opinon. Emery replied that all he could do was refer the emperor to the Imperial Catechism of 1806, which stated, unequivocally, that 'the pope is the visible head of the church'. Even the preamble of the Four Gallican Articles of 1682 reminded all that Rome held pre-eminence over the Catholic world. Although these articles did limit the extent of papal power, they still at their heart recognised the primacy of the pope over the church.[78]

Saint Peter's supremacy was manifest in the Gospels and divine providence. Emery defended the temporal power of popes. He claimed that it guaranteed the spiritual independence of the church. The world had often witnessed spectacular revolutions, in which great empires had arisen and fallen. In the midst of such uncertainty and change the temporal power of the popes had endured. He reminded Napoleon that nothing was eternal, and that even his imperial edifice could one day vanish beneath the waves of history.[79] Stunned, the emperor asked him if he thought that the pope would delegate his power of investiture to metropolitan archbishops (heads of ecclesiastical provinces made up of several dioceses). Emery replied that he believed this to be most unlikely, as it would destroy his authority. The emperor laughed, and turned to the other prelates: 'So you want me to ask the pope for something that is impossible!'[80] Clearly, the director of Saint-Sulpice had made an impression, but this seventy-nine-year-old priest was exhausted by the twin struggles of trying to direct his seminary and the ordeal of advising the government on the investiture crisis. He would die a month later, depriving the French Church of one of the few clergymen the emperor respected.[81]

Four days after this meeting, on 20 March 1811, Empress Marie-Louise gave birth to a Bonaparte-Habsburg male heir. It was a difficult delivery, and Napoleon was deeply moved by his wife's suffering: in a move going against the dynastic mores of the times, which privileged the life of the unborn heir above all else, he instructed the surgeon in attendance to save the mother at all costs.[82] Remarkably for a man who had witnessed the deaths of hundreds of thousands on the battlefield, he found individual pain hard to bear. This birth was not just a private family moment, but also a supremely political turning point: with the birth of a son, the dynasty now had a clear line of direct succession. The crown prince was given the title of king of Rome.[83] (This mirrored the Holy Roman Emperor, whose designated heir had borne the title 'king of the Romans'.) The child was a living symbol that a new Carolingian Empire now covered Europe. On the surface, the years 1810 and 1811 marked the apogee of the Empire. In reality all was very far from well.[84] Spain remained difficult to pacify, and guerrillas soaked the Iberian peninsula in the blood of imperial conscripts.[85]

Religion was in no small measure responsible for inspiring the insurgents who fought against the French.[86] Pius's conscience troubled him deeply: he feared that his example and policies of resistance to the occupier had increased Catholic resistance throughout Europe, which in turn led to violent retaliation from the imperial authorities against those who dared question France's modernising mission. Thousands of priests were persecuted, imprisoned and deported during the French occupation of Rome. The growing crisis unsettled the pope's morale and his physical health. Would his resolve waver after almost two years of exile?[87] After meeting with the ecclesiastical committee, Napoleon decided to send a delegation of Gallican bishops to negotiate with the pope in person. He instructed them to make it clear to Pius that, if he did not confirm new bishops within six months, then the local metropolitan archbishops would be empowered to do so.[88] If he stubbornly continued to refuse to yield, then the bishops had a trump card up their sleeves. They were to inform the pope that a national council of French, Italian and German bishops would meet in Paris in June to discuss and resolve the crisis.[89] The emperor hoped that the threat of conciliarism would panic Pius into submission.

On 30 April 1811 the bishops departed from Paris on their delicate mission.[90] In the emperor's official instructions, these Gallican stormtroopers were authorised to negotiate an end to the investiture crisis in France, but also to discuss the future of the church in those territories annexed to the Empire since 1806.[91] The situation in Germany and Italy needed to be put on a more secure footing for the Empire. If the pope acquiesced, he would receive an annual stipend of 2 million francs; he would be able to reside either in Rome or in Avignon, his spiritual freedom would be guaranteed, and he would be free to receive foreign diplomats without hindrance. If the pope chose to go to Rome, he would have to swear allegiance to the Empire and recognise Napoleon as Charlemagne's successor and legitimate sovereign of the city.[92] The delegation was also armed with a menacing letter, signed by a dozen French bishops, informing the pope that a large national council had been summoned to debate the question of episcopal investiture.

Exhausted by their journey, the bishops reached Savona on 9 May and met with Chabrol to brief him on their mission. The prefect promised to do his utmost to facilitate their talks.[93] By now, twenty-six dioceses were vacant and in need of replacement bishops; it was imperative to persuade the pope to resolve this crisis. The next day Pius VII greeted the bishops warmly and asked them for news of the outside world. He was shocked to learn that two cardinals had died since the beginning of the year. To Chabrol's amazement, the pope did not complain of his confinement and isolation. It would have been pointless: as the pope knew well, these bishops were the emperor's men. He was cordial, but placed little trust in their counsel. Pius became anxious when he was informed that a council had been summoned in Paris for June.[94] He reminded the delegates that only a pope could convene an ecumenical council.

The bishops explained that this gathering was to be national, rather than ecumenical. This qualification seemed to reassure His Holiness a little. When the question of investiture was broached, the pope said that it was impossible for him to confirm any candidates without the advice of the College of Cardinals and other theologians: it would be necessary to verify the worthiness of each candidate from independent sources before proceeding to invest them. Given that the pope was visibly irritated by these initial discussions, the bishops decided to adjourn until the next day.[95] They did not want to overwhelm the pontiff with too much bad news in one sitting.

Chabrol advised the bishops not to engage the pope in reasoned argument, since he would resist them. It was much better to act on the pope's emotional exhaustion and frayed nerves. To achieve this effect, the prefect asked Dr Porta to harass Pius with doubts and exaggerated news from the outside world: Chabrol hoped that a barrage of dispiriting news would force the pontiff to bend to imperial demands. Napoleon had personally instructed the prefect to pay Pius's personal physician the considerable sum of 12,000 francs as a generous gift to keep him on side.[96] The doctor was to torment the pope with Iago-like advice during the delegates' stay in Savona. Porta told Pius that nobody would blame him if he weakened and that indeed the local population would celebrate his liberation. Their joy over the end of the crisis would make the pope a hero in the Catholic world.[97] Pius found such pressure difficult to bear, as he trusted Porta and found him a sympathetic character. Little did he know that his own doctor was working against his best interests.

The second conference with the pope was tense. The bishops informed Pius of the emperor's conditions for his release and return to Rome: he would have to take a Gallican oath and renounce sovereignty over the Papal States. Such stipulations were dismissed as repugnant.[98] The Gallican Declaration of 1682 had been condemned by Pope Alexander VIII and was irrelevant to Rome. Pius would not comment publicly on the Gallican liberties, but neither would he endorse them. Regarding investiture, three months was not enough time for Rome to verify the suitability of candidates. Equally, metropolitan archbishops were not competent to invest bishops without written papal permission. They were subordinate to the pope: if he refused investiture how could such archbishops proceed to invest candidates without his permission? The proposals were thus categorically dismissed. The pope, sensing that things were becoming intolerably tense, invited the bishops to stroll with him in the gardens. Here he spoke amiably to them of his past life as bishop of Imola, and expressed his personal admiration for Napoleon.[99] Pius possessed great personal charm, which disguised his iron determination not to weaken. This second meeting had ended in abject failure, making it seem that the mission's goals were impossible to achieve.

Despite his resolve, the pope's nights were sleepless, reported Dr Porta. The psychological torture exerted against Pius was giving rise to psychosomatic symptoms. He complained of stomach pains, agitation and general malaise. Both prefect and doctor tormented the pope further during daylight hours. They warned Pius, with much exaggeration, that if the National Council in Paris met it would create a schism within the imperial church. They pestered him by foretelling that the bishops would pronounce in favour of the emperor's reforms and reject papal authority. The pope's body language betrayed the anguish that such harassment caused him.[100]

The bishops, during their ten days at Savona, heeded Chabrol's advice, resorting to emotional blackmail. They reminded the pope of the suffering that his decisions had caused to the clergy and laity in Rome. They feared that, if it came to a direct confrontation with the emperor, the Gallican Church might sever its ties with Rome. To increase Pius's sense of isolation, they revealed to him that many cardinals had disobeyed his commands: several of his most trusted servants had socialised with the grandees of the French Empire, and some even attended Mass in the Tuileries. His bull of excommunication had fallen on deaf ears.[101] The bishops, perceiving that Pius had reached breaking point, now tried to press home their advantage. They urged the pope to sign a statement which showed his openness to compromise. Pius refused to put his name to any document. He did, however, verbally accept a note which outlined a series of articles setting out the basis for future negotiations.

This note gave the impression that the pope had yielded major concessions. It stated that the Holy See must confirm all episcopal nominations from Paris within six months; after this deadline, metropolitan archbishops would be automatically empowered to invest imperial candidates.[102] The pope stressed that the power to confirm bishops was the exclusive prerogative of the Papacy and that he would never relinquish it. It was also impossible for him to accept Napoleon's demand to nominate bishops within the former Papal States. He did, however, concede the emperor's right to select candidates for dioceses in Tuscany, Parma and Piacenza. After some days of reflection, the pope wrote a few lines in which he accepted that this note might provide a solution to the conflict with the Empire.[103] If he was freed and given the benefit of counsel, then he would be happy to reopen negotiations.

This informal document was the best outcome the bishops could hope for. Their mission was now at an end. The fact remained that Pius had not signed any document; the note which he had verbally accepted was not legally binding. Nevertheless, they hoped it would suffice to persuade the National Council assembling in Paris that papal approval for Napoleon's solution to the investiture crisis would be forthcoming. On 19 May the imperial delegation began their return journey to Paris.[104] The next morning, Colonel Lagorce found the pope in a state of extreme agitation. He described it as resembling 'semi-inebriation'.[105] The pope now demanded to see Chabrol. When the prefect arrived, he was asked if the bishops had departed: Pius had written a memorandum that needed urgently to be transmitted to the bishops. It came down to this: Pius now categorically denied that he had made concessions on the matter of investiture, and he wanted to make it clear that he would retain full papal authority over any new episcopal appointment. The pope blamed himself: he had faltered, he said, due to weakness.[106] Chabrol wrote to the delegation giving them the bad news that the pope had changed his mind. Their note was now utterly worthless.

On 6 June the bishops arrived back in Paris and wrote a long report to Bigot.[107] They were of the opinion, they wrote, that Pius would reopen the question of investiture under the right circumstances.[108] However, he was unwilling to proceed with discussions so long as he was deprived of writing materials, books and counsel. Furthermore, he would not recognise the legitimacy of the Gallican

Declaration of 1682, which had been condemned by his predecessors. And there was his categorical refusal to ever accept the violation of his sovereignty and the loss of Rome. For Pius, the abolition of the suburbicarian dioceses and other urban benefices, reserved for cardinals, was unacceptable. The emperor's demand to appoint all bishops within former Papal States was not open for discussion. The bishops had to concede that their trip to Savona had been a failure. Later, bulletins by Chabrol attributed the pope's stubbornness to senility and mental illness. This was deeply unfair. Pius VII was sixty-nine years of age, but he remained in full control of his faculties. It took substantial resilience and discipline to resist the pressure exerted by the most powerful monarch in the world. The fate of the church would now be decided in Paris.

The National Council was delayed by several weeks to give the Italian bishops time to cross the Alps.[109] Dalberg, some German prelates, and all of Napoleon's unconfirmed episcopal nominees would also attend.[110] On 9 June 1811 the baptism of the king of Rome took place. Of all the religious ceremonies Napoleon used to cement his dynasty, this was one of the most sumptuous and lavish in terms of expenditure. He wanted to show that his firstborn son would, one day, be the master of Europe. In the morning he received the tributes of the entire diplomatic corps. In the afternoon a solemn cortège of troops and dignitaries accompanied the imperial couple and crown prince to Notre-Dame, where they were greeted by Cardinal Fesch, who would preside over the ceremony. After his son had been baptised Napoléon François, the emperor granted him the Grand Cordon of the Legion of Honour. A *Te Deum* followed; cannon salvos announced the good news to the population of the capital and free concerts created a festive atmosphere. The day ended with Napoleon and Marie-Louise in full regalia attending a special banquet at the Hôtel de Ville.[111]

Even though the Empire faced a grave economic crisis due to the Continental System, and was fighting a difficult war in Spain, Napoleon was resolved to settle his dispute with Pius.[112] 16 June 1811 saw the state opening of the Corps Législatif. It was traditional for a speech to be given from the throne, outlining the legislative programme for the new session. The emperor's radical plans for the Papacy were here discussed with little in the way of tact:

The affairs of religion have all too often been caught up in and sacrificed to the interests of a third-rate power. If half of Europe has separated itself from the church of Rome, one can attribute this to the contradiction which has always existed between the true principles of religion, which are universally valid, against the particular claims and interests that concern a mere corner of Italy. I have put an end to this scandal forever. I have annexed Rome to the Empire. I have given the popes palaces in both Rome and Paris. If they have the interests of religion at heart they will come and reside at the centre of the affairs of Christianity, in the same way as St Peter preferred Rome to the Holy Land.[113]

As the bishops assembled in Paris, they would soon realise just how intolerant their ruler was when confronted by any whiff of ecclesiastical opposition. It must be said that, at the outset, the National Council was not doomed to failure.[114] Many bishops appointed by Napoleon were sympathetic to the Empire's reform programme. They recognised that it was thanks to the 1801 Concordat that Catholicism was again practised freely in France after a decade of revolutionary turmoil. Some found it frustrating that the pope could not come to terms with France's rulers. Soon they realised that Pius had a point, and that Napoleon could be – generally was – intractable.

As the bishops arrived in Paris, Cardinal Fesch invited them to some preliminary meetings in his sumptuous residence on the rue de Montblanc. His nephew had charged him to take control of this church council and direct its deliberations. In many ways 1811 had been a year of family reckoning for Napoleon. His brother Joseph in Spain, Louis in Holland and to an extent his brother-in-law Murat in Naples had disappointed him as rulers of his satellite states. The emperor was beginning to despair of the Bonapartes: he hoped that Fesch would serve him better. The cardinal had taken on the role of family mediator in the previous years, but his indecisiveness and nagging conscience made him unsuited to the task at hand. His nephew wanted results, not theological quibbles. Fesch had many fine qualities, including much humanity and a fine eye for art, but decisive action was not in his character. Throughout this period, he wavered from being a loyal agent of the Empire to being a defender of the Papacy. Such vacillation and temporising were guaranteed to exasperate his far-from-patient imperial master.

During the conferences at Fesch's town house only procedural and ceremonial matters were broached in the first instance.[115] It was beginning to become clear that a number of bishops, especially those of Bordeaux, Ghent and Tournai, were uncomfortable with holding a council while the pope was still a captive.[116] They were hostile to the presence of Napoleon's episcopal candidates, whom they viewed as intruders bereft of any legitimacy. The delayed opening of the council allowed them to concert their opposition to the imperial reform programme. Cardinal Fesch wanted to be made president of the National Council as primate of all Gaul. His colleagues joked that there were older, more prestigious dioceses in France, but eventually acquiesced to his seniority. They knew that the emperor wanted a member of his dynasty to preside over their deliberations.

Maurice de Broglie, bishop of Ghent, emerged as the ringleader of the disgruntled bishops in 1811. The younger son of a dynasty of *ancien régime* dukes and princes, he had initially rallied to the Empire, impressing Napoleon with his moderation.[117] As a member of a great family of the old order that had suffered during the Revolution, he was exactly the sort of prelate the regime wanted to attract to the new episcopate. However, as time progressed, de Broglie's enthusiasm for the imperial system waned considerably. In 1810 he caused grave offence by refusing the Legion of Honour.[118] He was not willing to take the required oath, which would have recognised the legitimacy of the annexation of papal territory. Napoleon was furious at this rebuffal, and stripped him of his title as honorary chaplain to the imperial court. De Broglie, though, was no nostalgic for the Gallican past which had been destroyed by the Concordat; during the 1790s he had learned to look to the Papacy for leadership within the church. His diary, now held in the Vatican Archives, is a unique source for the events of the summer of 1811.[119]

On 17 June 1811, the National Council was opened in a solemn ceremony at Notre-Dame.[120] Nearly 100 bishops processed from the archbishop's palace to the cathedral and entered singing the hymn *Veni creator spiritus* ('Come, Creator Spirit'). The bishop of Troyes preached a sermon that was unimpeachably Gallican in its principles, but still recognised the primacy of Rome over the church.[121] After the Solemn Mass, Cardinal Fesch, as president, proceeded to a rollcall of those present. Each bishop was then required to profess his loyalty to the pope, as prescribed by the canons of the Council of Trent.[122] Napoleon was furious with his uncle, as this oath reminded everyone of the Holy Father's legitimacy. The first session debated whether the emperor's episcopal nominees would be admitted to the council's debates. Some felt their very presence in the cathedral was a scandal. However, after significant debate, they were permitted to observe proceedings, but would not be allowed to vote in the general sessions.[123]

Three days later, Bigot, the minister of religions, gave a speech in which he outlined the emperor's intentions and the agenda to be discussed by the council. The tone of the speech was misjudged and disrespectful, listing the alleged outrages committed by Rome since 1801. Unwisely, it compared Pius VII's reign to the worst excesses of the medieval Papacy: the Curia was accused of plotting the assassination of the emperor and fomenting rebellion.[124] Those who listened to these hysterical words were unimpressed: rather than eliciting the bishops' goodwill, the minister's opening speech alienated many. Essentially, the bishops were commanded to authorise metropolitan archbishops to sidestep Rome and to invest new appointees. All knew that this would lead to a renewed schism worthy of the Civil Constitution of the Clergy of the 1790s. Many Catholics would simply refuse to recognise the imperial candidates as legitimate bishops, and would ignore them.

Fesch recommended the creation of a subcommittee to draw up a formal address to thank Napoleon and to respond to his programme for the council. The bishops elected six delegates to sit on this committee. They were, more or less, evenly balanced between those who supported Napoleon's agenda and those who opposed it. The presence of Maurice de Broglie ensured energetic opposition when it came to any attempt to bypass the pope and usurp his authority. Mismanagement and hesitation on Fesch's part soon meant that he lost control of the council. The committee met from 21 June to 11 July, with the first to speak the Gallican theologian Jean-Baptiste Duvoisin, bishop of Nantes, who was extremely loyal to the Empire. He read a pre-prepared statement of thanks and support for the imperial reform programme.[125] De Broglie was upset: the text made no reference to the pope's prerogatives and it chained the church to the government's whims. Duvoisin made matters significantly worse by revealing that Napoleon had pre-approved his statement.[126] Committee members were furious at such interference, and insisted that they would prepare an independent reply. Pius's unfortunate position and his primacy over the Catholic Church had to feature in the address.

On 25 June 1811, with discussions stalling, the committee of twelve bishops was enlarged. The inclusion of the archbishop of Bordeaux and the bishop of Tournai, known to be tactful critics of the imperial regime, signalled that the bishops would not acquiesce easily to the emperor's desires.[127] The next day, Napoleon sent his grand master of ceremonies, the comte de Ségur, to inform the council that he would receive a delegation of bishops at the Tuileries Palace the following Sunday. It was expected that the representatives of the council would humbly endorse the imperial reforms, and pledge their loyalty to the crown. As it was already Wednesday, the emperor wished to pre-approve the council's address the next day. This caused panic, as the text was far from being finalised. It was decided that Duvoisin's pre-prepared statement would be read to the General Assembly.[128] Its content caused consternation, and during the General Assembly it was picked apart almost line by line by the bishops; all agreed that any address to the emperor on the council's behalf should include a petition for the pope to be freed. There was a categorical rejection of the subservient language used by Duvoisin: his statements that 'the council had assembled in obedience to imperial orders' and that 'the bishops threw themselves at the feet of the emperor' were eliminated. Equally, in the address, all references to the illegitimacy of the bull of excommunication were removed.[129]

Two days of chaotic discussion and debate followed. On 28 June 1811 the council decided to produce a modified version of the address and defer discussion. Ultimately, the release of the pope was the *sine qua non* condition for the bishops. Further discussion was delegated to the committee charged with rewriting the address to Napoleon. That Sunday, the emperor, angry so little progress had been made, cancelled the audience with the council's delegation. During Mass at the imperial court, as a sign of dissatisfaction and contempt, Napoleon and his courtiers ignored several bishops.[130] The committee spent the following days in discussions over whether the council was competent to resolve the investiture crisis. In the end it concluded that, without papal approval, it had no authority to make recommendations over episcopal appointments.[131] Barral, archbishop of Tours, theatrically produced the report on the recent negotiations with Pius in Savona.[132] He hoped to convince his colleagues that Pius was not opposed to their deliberations. This disclosure backfired: the note, summarising the May negotiations in Savona, was unsigned. To make matters worse, the pope had regretted its content and had immediately disowned it. In the aftermath of this, the outraged bishops showed little desire to bypass the pope's authority.

On 5 July Napoleon summoned Fesch to the palace of Saint-Cloud. All too familiar scenes of imperial harassment followed, with the bishops accused of bad faith and betrayal. Fesch interjected that investiture was a prerogative reserved for the Holy See. The emperor erupted: 'Be quiet! What do you know of theology? You are ignorant, where on earth did you learn what you know?'[133] The emperor declared that, if the council refused to implement his reforms, he would empower the prefects in provincial France to nominate parish priests, seminarians and bishops. Napoleon informed his uncle that the ministry of justice had assembled a commission of jurists to draft legislation that would make archbishops criminally liable if they did not invest new bishops within six months.[134] Fesch, showing some courage, replied that no archbishop would ever disrespect the pope by confirming candidates against his will. He warned his nephew that, as archbishop of Lyon, he would choose martyrdom rather than create a breach with the Holy See.[135]

Realising that even his uncle would not do his bidding, Napoleon now became more malleable. Together they produced a decree, in the hope that it would be adopted by the council: this stated that the pope would retain the power to reject candidates in cases of dubious morality or lack of theological education. However, since 1807, Napoleon's candidates had not been refused on these grounds, but rather for political reasons. Investiture had rather been withheld due to diplomatic and temporal matters relating to central Italy.[136] This breached the terms of the Concordat, and the emperor wanted to create a legitimate means of providing bishops for vacant dioceses. It was reiterated that if the pope did not confirm candidates within six months, the metropolitan archbishop would be entitled to do so. He gave a somewhat vague undertaking that the pope's consent would be sought in order to encourage the bishops to approve the decree.[137] Fesch left Saint-Cloud satisfied, believing this was a major concession, and returned to Paris.

The next few sessions of the committee were to be stormy. Its members, initially terrified by Napoleon's threats, saw the decree as a positive step forward. After all, the promise of consulting the pope gave them a glimmer of hope that the council could work in concert with the Holy See. However, de Broglie, supported by other prelates, persuaded the committee that the draft decree contained too many unknown quantities, and that its wording was very slippery. The text gave the impression that the pope's approval was guaranteed. Indeed, the emperor's draft stated simply that an episcopal delegation would be sent to Savona to thank the pope for ending the troubles which afflicted the church. Although the imperial decree was initially approved, after dinner at Cardinal Fesch's residence on 7 July, several bishops changed their minds and retracted their support. This volte-face was to have grave consequences. The committee would not recommend that the imperial decree be ratified by the council at the next general congregation.[138] Effectively, this group of bishops now put itself in direct defiance of the emperor.

Cardinal Fesch travelled again to Saint-Cloud bearing the bad news that his plan had failed. Napoleon seemed remarkably calm, given that the National Council was backfiring. He demanded to know who, among the committee members, were the worst troublemakers, and then intimated that he would dissolve the council. Fesch felt this would be unwise: as the emperor had himself summoned the bishops, sending them home would be perceived as a humiliation.[139]

Napoleon revealed that his ministry of justice was still working on making archbishops criminally liable should they refuse to invest new bishops. He would now await developments. His apparently calm demeanour hid the fact that Napoleon had lost all confidence in his uncle. Never again would Fesch be given his nephew's confidence or favour as in the past: the failure of the early deliberation of the council saw to it that Fesch would enter a period of semi-official disgrace at the imperial court. On 10 July the council met in general session, and the committee advised the bishops to reject the emperor's draft as it stood.[140]

The bishops seemed uncertain of how to proceed and many feared the wrath that would inevitably follow their refusal. They agreed that they could only ratify the emperor's draft decree once it had been approved by Pius. This episcopal rebellion was to be brutally repressed. Two days later, at three in the morning, the imperial police knocked on the doors of de Broglie and his closest associates (the bishops of Tournai and Troyes). All three were arrested and imprisoned in the fortress of Vincennes.[141] The rebel bishops were placed in its *donjon*, deprived of quills, ink, papers and books.[142] Their apartments were searched: in de Broglie's compromising papers criticising the Empire's interference in the spiritual realm were discovered. He had been preparing his opposition for some time.[143] These three prelates would eventually be sent into internal exile and spend several years under house arrest for their open resistance to the emperor. The archbishop of Bordeaux came near to sharing the same fate but, given his advanced age, he was spared imprisonment.[144]

On 10 July 1811, the same day it rejected his draft decree, Napoleon dissolved the National Council. Despite this, the bishops were ordered to remain in the capital.[145] A period of uncertainty followed. Throughout this time, Savary's police carried out an investigation into what had occurred during the council. His agents interrogated bishops and did much to intimidate them. After all, three of their colleagues were already languishing in prison. Significant pressure was now put on the bishops to yield. On 27 July Bigot, minister of religions for France, and Giovanni Bovara, minister of religions for Italy, met with the ninety-three bishops present in Paris.[146] The ministers presented a streamlined decree on the investiture crisis for their approval. This document promised that a delegation from the council would travel to Savona to obtain the pope's approval. Bigot and Bovara did their best to persuade the bishops to accept this new compromise.

Eighty bishops countersigned the decree, while thirteen remained opposed.[147] With these overwhelming numbers the council reopened on 5 August. This time the ministers of religions for France and Italy were present to supervise the bishops' deliberations. With little in the way of debate, a decree that stated the council was competent to deliberate on the investiture crisis, as well as containing five articles bypassing the pope's power of episcopal confirmation, was put forward for sanction. As expected, the final article conceded that a deputation of six bishops would travel to Savona to gain papal approval of the council's decree.[148] When Fesch asked the assembled bishops for their opinion, Cardinal Maury stated that the issue had been discussed at length: there was no need for further debate.[149] A vote followed in which the same thirteen brave bishops refused to ratify the decrees. The vast majority of bishops, however, were cowed into submission. Years later, Cardinal Pacca lamented to a friend who had attended the National Council of 1811 that so many bishops had forgotten their duty: 'Even the best horse sometimes bolts, your eminence,' replied his friend. 'That may be,' said the cardinal, 'but that the entire stable should bolt!'[150]

Although the emperor had, on the face of it, obtained his goal of getting conciliar support for his plan, the truth was that it had backfired. The council had not willingly given its approval, and no fewer than three bishops were in prison due to their opposition. Furthermore, the council's decree was valueless without papal approval. More seriously, the French episcopacy, which had been broadly sympathetic to the Empire, now viewed its political establishment with suspicion. The fallout from 1811 proved that the Concordat had not given birth to a neo-Gallican Church, but rather an ultramontane one that had become reliant on the leadership of Rome.[151] Only a small minority of clerics recognised the imperial claims to supremacy over the pontiff.

Six bishops, prominent members of the National Council with unimpeachably Gallican credentials, were to travel to negotiate with Pius.[152] To their number were added four 'red' cardinals who were known to be pro-imperial.[153] This would allow the pope to receive the counsel he had requested for over two years. On the advice of officials in Rome, it was decided that the pope's confessor and friend, the theologian Francesco Bertazzoli, archbishop of Edessa, would join the deputation to Savona.[154] Although he was known to be an enemy of France, it was hoped that his twenty-five-year friendship with Pius would exert further pressure. Chabrol reiterated that the pope was more likely to yield to emotion than to cold hard reason. This important group of church dignitaries now set out for Savona.

On 16 August 1811, Napoleon sent a letter to the delegation heading to Savona containing clear instructions.[155] The pope was to accept the council's decree without any qualifications or modifications. A joint letter signed by all the bishops of the National Council begged the pope to ratify the fruit of their deliberations.[156] This new method of confirming bishops, which bypassed papal authority, would extend to the entire Empire, including the diocese of Rome.[157] To keep in close contact with the dozen cardinals and prelates sent to the Ligurian coast, Prince Borghese was authorised to give the bishops access to the imperial telegraph service, one of the proudest technological achievements in telecommunications for the Napoleonic establishment.[158] The visual semaphore telegraph, invented by Claude Chappe, had been trialled across the French Empire. By 1812 it extended as far as Venice and Bayonne.[159] It could transmit in a few hours messages that would have taken weeks to be delivered on horseback. (The only drawback was that it could not operate in thick fog or at night.)[160] That the bishops were given access to this technical marvel demonstrated the importance of their mission.

Since 20 May, Pius had spent almost three months in isolation, bereft of news from the outside world.[161] Cardinal Bayanne and Archbishop Bertazzoli were the first to arrive on 29 August.[162] They were admitted into the pope's presence: both immediately burst into tears. Pius was deeply moved, but maintained a calm expression throughout. He was particularly delighted to see his friend Bertazzoli, who was to spend the subsequent days sighing 'God help us all', and commenting on the need to 'obey the government'.[163] Clearly, these delegates, having witnessed the fate of the black cardinals and rebel bishops of the council, were terrified of being struck down by Napoleon's wrath. They were unlikely to stiffen the pope's resolve and encourage opposition. On 2 September the rest of the deputation arrived, and negotiations resumed.[164] Pius was pleased to see the deputation, but, when made aware of the council's decree, he felt that he was being asked to sanction the impossible.

He was upset that there was no mention of the outrages he had had to endure since his kidnapping on 6 July 1809. At this point, the bishops produced the letters written by the council pleading with the Holy Father to help the church emerge from its current predicament. Over the next few days, the pope seemed to accept that the decree might be applied to the French Empire. However, he was upset that it should encompass the former Papal States as well.[165] To recognise that imperial power extended to these territories would be akin to a formal renunciation of papal sovereignty over central Italy. Pius felt that he could not take such a step.

Meeting frequently with his friend Bertazzoli, the pope sensed he could yield in part to the council's decree.[166] He informed the delegates that, in a few days' time, he would write a solemn brief outlining his position. The process of composing this statement was to be laborious; the delegation did their best to simplify its intricate language, reminding the pope that he had to approve the decrees without reservation, alteration or qualification. Initially Pius baulked at these restrictions, but eventually found ingenious ways around them. The brief was addressed to the 'bishops assembled in Paris', not to the emperor.[167] Despite this, he did mention 'our beloved son Napoleon, emperor of the Gauls and king of Italy' several times in the text. Cunningly, Pius portrayed the National Council as if it had operated under his guidance, and made it appear as though they recognised the Papacy's supremacy over the universal church. The brief stated that all future bishops would continue to swear allegiance to the church of Rome as a condition for their confirmation.[168] The decrees could be accepted as exceptional arrangements with the French Empire, but the episcopacy still had to have an ultimate allegiance towards the pope in Rome. The delegation wrote back to Bigot and Fesch, stating that their mission had been a great success. On 20 September the brief was ready for transmission to Paris. Pius wrote a covering letter to the emperor, bestowing his blessing and expressing the hope that, in future, he would use his 'sword' for the good of the church and the protection of religion.[169]

Napoleon received the brief and papal letter while he was touring the northern defences of his empire. His attention had been distracted away from church affairs by a looming conflict with Russia. The alliance achieved at the cost of so much blood at Tilsit in 1807 was on the point of collapse.[170] It was becoming apparent that the tsar and his court were no longer honouring their treaty obligations and that enemy shipping was being allowed into Russian ports in contravention of the Continental System.[171] Napoleon's priorities shifted from the internal administration of his dominions to preparations for a forthcoming campaign.[172]

To Bigot's surprise, the papal brief was deemed unsatisfactory and it was decided not to reply officially to the pope's letter.[173] As the emperor put it, the brief was addressed to his bishops, not to him, and therefore was not his concern.[174] Napoleon planned to make the council's decree a law of the state, and extend its provisions to the former Papal States. However, he realised that this act, without the pope's approval, would lead to a schism. On 1 October 1811 he instructed the minister of religions to allow the bishops of the National Council to return to their dioceses. They were not informed of the papal brief: instead, they were curtly told that the deputation to Savona had been a success. The next step was to demand that the pope immediately confirm all twenty-six bishops appointed by the emperor to vacant dioceses. If Pius agreed, he would be allowed the counsel of additional cardinals, and the deputation would be permitted to continue negotiations in Savona.[175] The papal brief was to be rewritten as a simple and uncomplicated acceptance of the deliberations of the National Council. Essentially, Napoleon wanted to extract a capitulation from Pius as if he had been defeated in battle like Austria or Prussia. In so doing, the emperor managed to snatch defeat from the jaws of victory.

In mid-October the pope was informed of this ultimatum. He was furious, and felt as if he had been played for a fool. He could not give an unqualified acceptance of the conciliar decrees: this would have conceded the emperor's right to nominate bishops for the Papal States. Pius stated that if he was sent some theologians of his choice, who could assuage his conscience, he was willing to enter into negotiations on this issue. France was naturally unwilling to approve any such compromise. By November, the pope's nights became more agitated and he requested that his personal confessor, Father Menocchio, be sent to Savona to assist him.[176] This request was refused. Equally, no black cardinals would be allowed to join him on the Ligurian coast. The issue of the Roman bishoprics became an intractable stumbling block. According to the historian of the church, the comte d'Haussonville, Napoleon was not keen to sign any agreements at this time.[177] Overconfidence had always been his greatest flaw: this time it would prove fatal. A year's campaigning in the east crowned by a decisive victory, alongside the continued exile in Savona, would, hopefully, break Pius's will. Ever since his crushing victory at Austerlitz in 1805, Napoleon had demanded that Pius VII acknowledge his supremacy. The papal failure to accept French suzerainty led to one of the most brutal confrontations between church and state in history. Throughout this crisis the emperor had underestimated the pope deeply. Alone, isolated and ill, Pius would unwaveringly maintain both his dignity and resolve.

In December, the emperor returned to Paris after his tour of the north and his empire's defences in Dutch territory. A special commission of jurists had been charged with the task of rejecting the pope's brief. They decided that the wording of the brief did not explicitly recognise the legitimacy of the National Council, and that the pope's claims to spiritual supremacy were unacceptable.[178] A simple approval of the conciliar decrees that included Rome was vital; the imperial jurists argued that the pope could not exempt his former domains and diocese from this agreement. After all, what was to stop him from doing the same in other areas of the Empire? On 13 December 1811 the cardinals and bishops presented Pius with this extremely bad news. Usually calm, the pope expressed his disgust and said that he refused to be played for a fool.[179] He reminded the cardinals that they had approved the wording of his brief, and that they had led him to believe that an alternative arrangement over the Roman dioceses could be found.

Pius now became cold towards the red cardinals sent to negotiate with him. He realised that they were the emperor's creatures. He also admonished Bertazzoli, his friend, for his weakness in the face of the Empire's demands.[180] Several weeks passed in which the pressure placed on Pius to accept the inevitable produced the opposite effect – although it was not without its human cost: the pope's insomnia and digestive problems worsened. On 24 January 1812, Pius wrote directly to Napoleon, begging him to be reasonable.[181] The emperor's glib reply to the minister of religions was that the pope was responsible for his own misfortunes.[182] Recognising defeat, the deputation sent to negotiate with the pope departed from Savona on 28 January 1812.[183] Although the brief written on 20 September had seemed to settle the investiture crisis, Napoleon's refusal to accept this document meant that a compromise had now become impossible. The emperor's expectation that Pius would renounce implicitly his sovereignty over Rome and its dioceses had proved highly unrealistic.

The events of the National Council of 1811 have been dismissed as doomed to failure from the outset. Such councils, however, have often marked moments of triumphant renewal in the history of the church.[184] This could have been the case in 1811. However, the intimation and pressure exerted by the Empire's secular authorities made this impossible. The hundred or so bishops who met in Paris were never free in their deliberations. As ever, the emperor was a man in a great hurry. Given time, the Gallican loyalists might have been able to forge a compromise solution. But this was never the intention. It was all or nothing. To urge unconditional surrender on Pius was the council's true purpose. As soon as the bishops showed a glimmer of autonomy, its three senior ringleaders were imprisoned.

It is an irony that, rather than strengthening the Empire's grip on the church, the National Council of 1811 catalysed Catholic opposition against Napoleon. Only ecclesiastical turncoats and careerists now remained at Napoleon's side. With such disreputable figures heading the Napoleonic clerical establishment, it is unsurprising that Catholics turned to prelates who had more moral backbone and independence. Pius had shown himself remarkably amenable to finding a shared solution to the issues facing the church, but had refused to be sidestepped. As the year 1812 dawned, Chiaramonti had endured two and a half years of imprisonment and exile. His woes were far from at an end. Napoleon's focus, meanwhile, turned to war.

# EIGHT

# THE LAST CONCORDAT, 1812–13

On 23 June 1812 half a million men, recruited from among twenty nations, crossed the frontier between the Duchy of Warsaw and the Russian Empire.[1] Thus began the largest military invasion of the nineteenth century. All of Europe, under the weight of French hegemony, was coerced into a military adventure whose goal was to disarm Russia militarily and to force her to accept the Continental System. Victory would ensure that any threat from the east would be permanently removed. Simultaneously, the French Admiralty was engaged in a massive naval rebuilding programme. The minister of the navy, Admiral Denis Decrès, aspired to achieve parity with the Royal Navy within one or two years. Revenge for the 1805 Battle of Trafalgar was no longer an impossible dream.[2] Prefects despatched arborists, bearing large callipers, throughout the Empire to measure the circumference of tree trunks, in order to find specimens large enough for the masts of future ships of the line: these were the aircraft carriers of the age of sail, vital if the Royal Navy were to be kept at bay.[3] With Russia and Britain facing the prospect of defeat, Europe seemed poised to fall completely under French hegemony. Not since Charlemagne had the European mainland faced the prospect of becoming a continental empire similar in scale to those of Russia and China.[4]

Despite these signs of outer strength, the domestic situation of the Napoleonic Imperium was far from stable: the years 1810 to 1812 may have marked the apogee of French power, but colossal problems lurked beneath the surface.[5] Economic crises, manufacturing decline and poor grain harvests meant that the Continental System had been relaxed through the Trianon licensing system of 1810, which permitted some merchants to trade with Britain in colonial goods under special conditions and tariffs.[6] Resentment grew across Europe over the heavy yoke of imperial dominion and economic exploitation. This was palpable not just on the furthest fringes of the Empire, but at its core too. Disorder grew to the extent that the Imperial Guard had to be ordered to Normandy to quell grain riots. This province was hardly a far-flung outpost, but was situated a mere 60 miles from the imperial capital. On the peripheries of the Empire, guerrillas, endemic banditry and passive resistance continued unabated.[7] Furthermore, the religious rift with the pope showed no sign of resolution. The emperor hoped that military victory in the east, and the collapse of Britain's economic stranglehold on the continent, would draw attention away from his domestic problems, and break the Catholic Church's will to defy him.

As 1812 dawned in Savona, Pius knew his situation was dire. Half the College of Cardinals was collaborating with Napoleon, and the National Council of 1811 had demonstrated the extreme lengths to which the imperial government was prepared to go to bypass his spiritual authority. After the departure of the cardinals and bishops in February 1812, the pope spent three months in complete isolation. He received regular visits from the prefect Chabrol, who inquired after the pontiff's health and shared whatever news he could.[8] Excluding these daily audiences, Pius was subject to a communications blackout with the outside world. His guard was increased and security doubled. From the Gendarmerie's reports, which have survived in the French National Archives, his guards found their duties intolerably dull. Lagorce was a stern taskmaster: any sentries found asleep on duty were arrested, put on half rations and confined to quarters.[9] Pius's monastic routine of prayers, spiritual exercises and walks in the gardens helped him to pass the hours and avoid despair. As far as prisoners go, he was docile, and unlikely to try to escape. Despite his outward appearance of tranquillity, three years of captivity had marked him considerably. He was no longer the gentle and peaceable man who had been arrested in July 1809. A growing sense of betrayal and isolation had strained his psychophysical health, while irritation and resentment at his treatment were gnawing at him internally. He complained of psychosomatic symptoms. Indeed, his stomach and bladder were constantly inflamed. These afflictions made his nights restless; often he would look off into space and enter a catatonic state. Chabrol was anxious that these altered states of consciousness were signs of an impending mental collapse.

By now in Dresden, Napoleon had not forgotten his prisoner. He wrote to Prince Borghese, the governor of Piedmont, on 21 May 1812: having learned that several Royal Navy vessels had been sighted off the coast of Savona, the emperor concluded that the pope's 'safety' could no longer be assured.[10] Borghese was provided with detailed instructions. Pius was to be transferred to the palace of Fontainebleau, just to the south-east of Paris. In a co-ordinated plan, to be agreed in conjunction with Chabrol, their prisoner was to be moved out of Savona with the utmost speed. He would traverse cities such as Turin, Chambéry and Lyon only by night, in order that the carriages and the distinguished passenger would pass unnoticed. Bertazzoli, archbishop of Edessa and papal chaplain, was to rendezvous with the convoy near Turin and accompany it to Fontainebleau. A brief stopover was planned at the convent hospice of the Mont-Cenis Pass in the Alps, where the pontiff might be afforded some rest and refreshment before resuming the journey northwards.[11] Knowing that Pius's health was precarious, it was thought best that Dr Porta should travel in the same carriage for the entire journey. Lagorce was placed in control of the operation. It is difficult to know whether Napoleon genuinely believed that the British would try to launch an amphibious rescue operation to whisk the pope away from Savona. Regardless, the head of the Catholic Church's presence near Paris would isolate him further from Rome and his ecclesiastical supporters. The imperial government hoped that by increasing the pressure on Pius, by cutting him off from Italy, he would be led at last to break.

The operators of the imperial telegraphic service worked furiously to transmit instructions to Lugo di Romagna, where Bertazzoli was staying.[12] He was ordered to depart in all haste for Turin. Equally top-secret orders were sent to all military outposts along the route ordering them to prepare for the pope's transit and to make arrangements for his security. Savary, as minister of police, despatched two officers of the Elite Gendarmerie of the Imperial Guard, at breakneck speed towards Mont-Cenis.[13] Members of an elite military police unit that was used for delicate missions and special operations, Savary instructed them to dress in civilian clothes and to make sure that ordinary travellers were kept away from the papal convoy. Their mission was to guarantee that the pope passed the Alps in complete secrecy, unobserved by any curious bystanders. An itinerary was also co-ordinated with the imperial postal service to ensure that fresh horses would be available along the route.[14]

It took over two weeks to complete preparations: throughout this time, Pius was kept in the dark as to his fate. At five in the evening, on 9 June 1812, Chabrol arrived at the episcopal palace in Savona. Finding the pope asleep, he waited nervously to deliver the news of his imminent departure. As Chabrol's visits were not an unusual occurrence, Pius had no reason to suspect that anything was awry, but to his surprise, once awake the pontiff was informed by Chabrol that his safety on the Ligurian coast could no longer be guaranteed. Consequently, he was commanded by the emperor to arrange transportation and an escort to transport the Holy Father to the Château de Fontainebleau. Faced with yet another ordeal, backed up by the threat of overwhelming force, Pius expressed his resignation but showed little sign of regret at leaving Savona.[15] Departure was set just after midnight, so that few would witness the pope leaving town.[16]

Chabrol was particularly keen that the prisoner travel incognito: the pope was dressed in a large grey overcoat and a wide-brimmed black hat to conceal his features. His white papal silk slippers were dyed with black ink, while his pectoral cross was cut from his cassock to avoid any danger of recognition. Two transports would form the main body of the convoy, and Lagorce would lead the escort. Just before departure, the doors to the papal carriage were locked from the outside and the curtains lowered. As with his kidnapping in Rome on 6 July 1809, Pius's confinement within his coach made manifest that he was a prisoner, driven away from his native Italy against his will. The first leg of the journey was carried out at a gallop, deeply uncomfortable for all involved. There were only brief pauses at postal stations to change horses and to take on some quick refreshment. Near Turin, as planned, Bertazzoli joined the convoy. Meanwhile, back at Savona, Chabrol created the illusion that the pope was still in his custody. He continued to visit the episcopal palace regularly, while candles were left burning bright through the night.[17] The altar in the papal chapel was dressed as if Mass were still celebrated daily. According to local lore, few were fooled by this charade: word soon spread that the pope had been taken away to an undisclosed location.

After twenty-two hours of constant travel, the convoy reached the foothills of the Alps. Stress and discomfort from the pace of the journey had made the pope gravely ill. His bladder had become severely inflamed and could only pass water with great difficulty, not to mention horrendous pain. By the second day of the journey his urine had turned red, indicating that the situation had worsened considerably. Soon the pope was feverish and showing signs of delirium.[18] In the early hours of 11 June 1812 the convoy reached the convent hospice of Mont-Cenis. This large complex had been built on one of the key alpine mountain passes that acted as a gateway to Italy, its function to offer nourishment, medical assistance and shelter to weary travellers.[19] Often in the past it had been the first checkpoint for armies invading the Italian peninsula; indeed, Napoleon had arrived here riding a mule in 1800 at the start of his second Italian campaign.[20]

The Abbé Gabet, the head of the religious order who ran the hospice, and his deputy, the Abbé Dubois, were commanded to prepare the so-called emperor's bedroom for a distinguished guest.

Meanwhile, the two agents of the Elite Gendarmerie took up strategic positions along the entry points onto the Mont-Cenis Pass: one stayed at the entrance to the hospice, the other travelled to the village of Lanslebourg further down the mountains. Here they took command of the local troops. Orders were sent out that the pass was to be cleared of 800 or so seasonal road workers, casual labourers who had the task of keeping communication between the Empire and Italy open. Commands were also issued to close the road to all ordinary travellers for forty-eighty hours. Soon significant numbers of disgruntled Italian and French travellers started flowing into Lanslebourg, wondering aloud why their journeys were being delayed without explanation.

The pontiff, shivering and pale, alighted from his carriage very unsteadily and was practically carried into the emperor's bedroom. The monks of the hostel of Mont-Cenis fell to their knees, barely able to contain their astonishment when they recognised that the head of the universal church was their mysterious guest. His medical condition gave them deep cause for concern. The situation became so severe that in the early hours of 14 June they gathered to administer the last rites to Pius VII.[21] Lagorce wrote to Prince Borghese, begging not only that they be given permission to stay in Mont-Cenis for some more days but also that medical equipment be sent from Turin with great haste. Dr Porta feared that his patient would not make it through the night and urged that a general surgeon be sought from Turin as a matter of urgency. Borghese, fearing the displeasure of Napoleon in permitting any delay, categorically refused to accept these requests, insisting that the colonel and his captive resume their journey. Lagorce objected: the pope had threatened to throw himself on the side of the road and die if he was not allowed further rest.[22]

Given Pius's failing health, Lagorce decided to consult with Porta and others in the papal household. Porta stated that it was impossible for the pope to continue the journey: it would surely kill him. Technically the only means to relieve Pius's bladder infection would be an operation. Porta advised that Lagorce seek a second opinion from a qualified surgeon. Balthazard Claraz was identified as the local *officier de santé* of the Mont-Cenis Pass. He had medical jurisdiction over all military and civil personnel and travellers going through the area. Claraz, much to his surprise, was now torn from dinner with his family by gendarmes. Nobody was told where he was being taken, only that he had to treat a distinguished passenger. Little did he expect that his patient would be the supreme head of the Catholic Church. To Lagorce's annoyance, Claraz knelt before the pope, revealing that he was a man of devout religious beliefs.[23]

The pope's near-death experience at Mont-Cenis in June 1812 represents one of the great and irresistible 'what ifs' of history. What would have happened had Pius VII died on 14 June? During this time, Savary had been deeply alarmed by reports from Mont-Cenis. He worried that a papal election would be the ultimate result of the attempt to move the pope from Savona to Fontainebleau.[24] One could, with some justification, speculate that a Paris conclave would have taken place in the autumn of that year and that, in all probability, a Napoleonic ecclesiastical collaborator would have been elected pope by the red cardinals. It seems reasonable to suppose that the black cardinals would have refused to attend a papal election, which they would have viewed as illegitimate. Napoleon's successful papal candidate would have been dismissed as an imperial 'antipope', and would only have been recognised within territories under French hegemony. A counter-conclave might have been arranged by cardinals outside the Empire, choosing its own candidate. The spectre of a second great schism of the western church was a real possibility during these dismal days.[25]

According to myth, Pius at this time removed his ring and gave it Bertazzoli, telling him to bestow it upon his legitimate successor.[26] Pius confessed his sins, commended his soul to God and seemed resigned to his death. At this point, Lagorce insisted that Claraz perform an operation to relieve pressure on the patient's inflamed bladder. Essentially, the colonel wanted an early modern version of a catheter to be deployed: this procedure, given the circumstances, would – with its high risk of infection and bleeding – have put the pontiff's life at risk. The surgeon refused to intervene and instead suggested the use of diuretics. In so doing, he probably saved his patient's life.[27] At long last, during the night, the inflammation eased, and the pope was able to get some rest. His condition became less critical and hope returned that he would live through his ordeal.

Unable to refuse his orders from Prince Borghese, and fearful that the increasingly enraged travellers prevented from crossing the mountain pass would riot, Lagorce ordered the pope's entourage to ready themselves for departure. The pontiff's carriage was now modified so that an improvised camp bed could be put in place, allowing the pope to travel in more comfort during the remainder of the journey. Porta and Claraz would alternate in sitting next to the pope and ministering to his medical needs. The Abbé Dubois provided fresh bed linen, a black cassock and a woollen vest to protect the pope from the cold mountain air.[28] Throughout this time, Claraz's family were kept in the dark as to his father's whereabouts, only receiving news that he was heading towards Paris four days later. The pope's entourage and servants were furious at the treatment of their master who had after all been administered the last rites only a few hours before. Their strenuous protests fell on deaf ears. The pope's secretary, Ceregalli, and Dr Claraz wrote detailed accounts of Pius's ordeal.[29] Through an accident of history, these papers were purchased at auction by an Anglican clergyman who donated them to the British Museum.[30] They are now held in the manuscript collection of the British Library. These documents were consulted by a few nineteenth-century historians, but – remarkably – have lain untouched throughout the twentieth century.

On the morning of 15 June, the pope was carried by his household from the Mont-Cenis hospice and placed on the improvised bed in his carriage. The doors were locked, and curtains lowered. Travellers and local residents were again kept away from the Mont-Cenis Pass as the convoy resumed its progress. The journey was uneventful until they had passed Chambéry. Pius VII was starting to feel better and stole some hours of sleep. Claraz administered fresh water and some drops of spirits to fortify the pope. Events at Mont-Cenis had broken the seal of secrecy: word of the pontiff's journey had quickly spread down from the Alps into France. Large crowds of peasants began to line the route, asking for the pope's blessing. In one instance, a nun holding a child and a crucifix approached the carriage. A member of this group was permitted to present the pope with a large bouquet of flowers. The pope weakly gestured his benediction. Given the growing crowds, Lagorce was particularly worried about transiting through Lyon and ordered that the convoy pass through at a gallop. The pope was extremely uncomfortable as the coaches were violently jolted on the uneven paving stones of this great French city. Once clear of the city, the pope, apparently, uttered the cryptic words: 'God forgive him; as for me, I have already forgiven him this!'[31] The journey through Burgundy was less eventful, although Lagorce was annoyed with the pope's household, who leaked their master's identity to the public with little hesitation. At one point the colonel almost came to blows with one of Pius's valets for being too indiscreet.

At noon on 19 June 1812 the carriages pulled into the gate lodge of the Château de Fontainebleau. This dismal journey seemed to be at an end. Lagorce was weary when he dismounted his horse and was greeted by the gatekeeper, Monsieur Ribbe, with the immortal words, 'Who are you and what do you want?'[32] Lagorce explained that he was charged with a special mission directly from the emperor to deliver the pope to Fontainebleau. The gatekeeper informed the bewildered colonel that he had received no such orders: the palace gates would remain closed until he had received instructions from Paris to open them. A furious argument erupted, but the gatekeeper of Fontainebleau was the model officious bureaucrat: without orders he would not take any personal initiative. It was decided to send a courier as fast as possible to Champagny, the intendant of the imperial domains and palaces.[33] The situation had lurched from tragedy to near comedy. Pius was greeted by Ribbe. Offered a guest bedroom in a house nearby, the exhausted pope accepted, and spent the afternoon waiting for a response from Paris. By evening, orders arrived commanding the formidable Monsieur Ribbe to open the gates. The pope was to resume the apartments he had occupied in 1804, when he had come to crown the emperor. These were behind the Cour du Cheval Blanc, commanding a spectacular view over François I's Renaissance gardens. The apartments had been hastily prepared, and the pope's livery used to decorate his rooms.[34]

The next day the imperial ministers travelled to Fontainebleau to present their compliments to the pope. Bigot, the minister of religions, read a short speech welcoming Pius to France, presented his colleagues and then returned to the capital. Government permission had been granted to the red cardinals to form a rump College of Cardinals at Fontainebleau. Pro-imperial bishops were also allowed to request audiences with the Holy Father and pay their respects. Ultimately, the security protocols established at this great Renaissance palace were not as strict as the vexatious regime Pius had endured during his stay at Savona. The pope would spend the next nineteen months in this regal pleasure dome, hidden in the midst of the great forests to the south-east of Paris. In comparison to the grimness of his Ligurian exile, Fontainebleau was a world apart. The palace and its surrounding lands had been part of the royal domain since at least the twelfth century.[35] Four hundred years later, the last Valois kings had decided to transform the defensive castle on this site into a luxurious Italian-Renaissance-style *palazzo*.[36] During this time the Tuscan art historian and theorist Giorgio Vasari had described this site as a 'new Rome'. Three centuries later Vasari's words would prove prophetic. The palace was a magnet for Italian artists and scholars, who used the vast collection of books in the library for study and contemplation.[37]

The château was renowned for its vast surrounding forests, which were filled with game and were a major hunting retreat for the French court in the late autumn. The feast of Saint Hubert (the patron saint of hunting since the ninth century) on 3 November was a major royal festivity.[38] Kings and nobles had charged across the vast domains of this palace chasing game for nearly 600 years. By the eighteenth century the palace comprised over 1,500 rooms and 130 hectares of elaborate gardens.[39] It was among Napoleon's favourite residences, and he had spent lavishly on its restoration. Fine galleries and the elaborate horse-shoe stone staircase facing the Cour du Cheval Blanc made it one of the most sumptuous royal residences in Europe. The emperor had directed that the long gallery of Diana be transformed into a library. Dominated by a gigantic globe mapping the known world, it possessed one of the most impressive private collections of books of the early nineteenth century.[40] Napoleon instructed the marshal of the palace, General Duroc, to encourage the pope to accept French money and to spend lavishly on his upkeep. However, once Pius's health was restored, he resumed the monastic routine of Savona and refused all funds: he did not want to be compromised by accepting largesse from the imperial regime. No matter how beautiful Fontainebleau may have been, it remained a place of exile. The ever vigilant Lagorce was charged with discreetly observing to whom the pope spoke and trying to understand the subjects of conversation amongst the cardinals.

Napoleon, by the end of June, had occupied Vilnius. To his immense frustration the Russian army refused to give him the battle that would decide the outcome of the campaign. From his headquarters the emperor remained well informed of events in Paris. On 29 June he wrote an angry letter to Cambacérès, the archchancellor of the Empire, and his virtual regent:

> It was my wish that the pope always had his doctor with him and that he was treated only by persons who had his full confidence. Thus, nothing could have been worse than sending for this surgeon [Claraz] . . . not to mince words, and no matter how horrible it might be to say, had the pope died, nothing could have given more of a pretext for malice. There is great imprudence and thoughtlessness in this behaviour, not to mention a total lack of tact. If the pope needed a surgeon why not send for one from Turin, chosen by his own household?[41]

(Certainly, Pius did not feel like this towards Claraz, who was sent back to his family on the understanding that he would maintain absolute secrecy. After 1815, the pope would bring him to Rome and make him a papal doctor, as well as rewarding him with membership of the prestigious Order of Saint Gregory the Great. He would remain in the service of the Papacy until his death in the 1840s.)[42]

A week later Napoleon, again from Vilnius, wrote to Empress Marie-Louise in the following terms: 'My friend . . . the pope is at Fontainebleau. Write to him asking for his news when you reach Saint-Cloud, inquire how he is faring and about his health, you can write him a short letter, without however expressing any affection in it. Farewell my friend. It is very hot [here], my affairs go well.'[43] Despite the overconfident tone of this letter, the emperor was well aware that his religious troubles were far from over. An agreement with the pope would have made a great contribution to restoring tranquillity to his vast empire. For the time being, the pursuit of the Russian army continued to consume his attention. On 7 September the French attacked a strongly entrenched Russian force under Field Marshal Mikhail Kutuzov. By the end of the day the Russians had retreated, leaving the road open for the French occupation of Moscow, the ancient capital of Russia.[44]

On 14 September 1812, Napoleon entered Moscow to fanfares and awaited the tsar's offer of peace terms.[45] In the meantime the pope settled into his unhappy routine at Fontainebleau. Although the means at his disposal were greater, Pius did not want to give the impression that his resolve was weakening. He refused to walk in the gardens in the presence of an armed escort of gendarmes and equally stated he would only enter a carriage to return to the Quirinal in Rome.[46] His life was spent mainly in the presence of Bertazzoli and Dr Porta. Although the library in the palace contained over 30,000 books, these mostly dealt with profane subjects. Special permission was given for the pope to contact the Abbé Garnier, the Abbé Emery's successor at the seminary of Saint-Sulpice, to request a large number of learned works on theology and church history.[47] Equally, the penniless author Charles Rémard, who had been imperial librarian at Fontainebleau for some years, did his best to purchase those tomes necessary to the Holy Father's meditations.[48] Gallican bishops tried to test the waters to see if the pope would resume negotiations. Pius replied that without the counsel of the black cardinals and the restoration of his freedom he was not prepared to entertain any discussion.

As the weeks passed in Moscow, the situation became desperate due to lack of supplies.[49] The emperor took the fateful decision on 18 October to retreat. As is well known, this withdrawal turned into catastrophe. A very small portion of the half-million men from twenty nations who had crossed the Neman four months earlier would make it back to the Polish frontier. Meanwhile, Paris was unaware of the extent of the defeat in Russia.[50] The bulletins of the Grande Armée had continued to broadcast reassuring news, as if victory were close.[51]

During the night of 23 October 1812 three officers wearing generals' uniforms approached the barracks of the tenth military cohort of the Paris garrison. The sentry confronted them, demanding the password. They replied 'Conspiracy!'[52] Once admitted they immediately asked to see the commander of the cohort, General Jean Antoine Soulier. Dramatically, they produced a decree from the Senate proclaiming that Napoleon had died in Moscow on 7 October.[53] It further stated that a provisional government under the leadership of the republican General Moreau and other members of his faction was now in control of France.[54] Although surprised, Soulier accepted the document as genuine. He was ordered to arrest Savary, the minister of police: Cambacérès as virtual regent of the Empire also was to be detained, so too was the minister of war along with a long list of other dignitaries.[55] It seemed that night that a bloodless transition from Empire back to Republic was going to occur. Events took a different course when they approached the military governor of Paris in his office. Pierre-Augustin Hulin, well connected and a distinguished soldier, was a proud veteran who had gained his stripes during the wars of the 1790s.[56] He immediately realised that one of the men was not who he claimed to be.

The ringleader was none other than General Claude François de Malet. Born in 1754 into an *ancien régime* aristocratic family from Franche-Comté, they later disowned him for his fanatical devotion to the Revolution. During the 1790s he was promoted to general and was close to Moreau's republican faction; he had disliked Bonaparte from the earliest days of the Brumaire coup.[57] During the Spanish campaign of 1808 he falsely alleged that Napoleon had died, and tried to stage a coup, but it ended in farce. The military commission trying him commuted his death sentence as they felt he was not sane.[58] By 1812 he was living in a sanitorium run by a Dr Dubuisson in Paris. The regime at this asylum was very lax: Malet could walk outside and fraternise with other inmates. During this time he met the abbé Jean-Baptiste Lafon, a member of a congregation from Lyon, who had been interned for spreading the news that Napoleon had been excommunicated by Pius VII.[59] The abbé, in 1811, had also published the pope's letters condemning the bishops appointed to vacant dioceses. In all probability he was linked to the secret society of the *Chevaliers de la Foi*.[60] The abbé was instrumental in encouraging the 1812 conspiracy. It had been he who helped Malet to forge the Senate's decree, and also selected two ultra-Catholic nobles to serve on the provisional government.

Hulin told the soldiers that they had been duped, and that their leader was an impostor. Malet then fired a shot into Hulin's face, smashing his jawbone. By some miracle, the general survived. Once Malet was recognised the game was up, and the military garrison of Paris realised that the senatorial decree was a forgery. Lafon, wisely, made a discreet getaway and disappeared permanently from the pages of history.[61] Within six days, Malet and thirteen other conspirators were court-martialled and executed on the plaine de Grenelle.[62]

On 6 November, news of this attempt to topple the regime reached the imperial headquarters in Russia.[63] Napoleon was furious that in the heat of the moment no one had thought to proclaim his son, the king of Rome, as Napoleon II. The Malet affair of October 1812 exposed just how vulnerable to attack the legitimacy of the Bonaparte dynasty remained. Without Napoleon alive it was unclear whether France would have accepted his infant son as his legitimate heir.[64] As the situation in Russia deteriorated due to an extremely harsh winter and the decimation of his army in retreat, Napoleon felt the need to return to his capital and take the situation under his firm control. At Smorgoni in Lithuania, on 5 December 1812, he bade farewell to his marshals and troops.[65] It was his intention to race back to Paris in order to raise a new army and prepare for a new defensive campaign. Already his German and Habsburg allies were starting to show signs of wavering as the Russian army approached the border with the Duchy of Warsaw.

His confidant, and former ambassador to Saint Petersburg, Armand de Caulaincourt, duc de Vicence, accompanied the emperor.[66] Discussion of the Malet affair was to form a recurring conversation during the long thirteen-day carriage ride back to Paris. Bonaparte's dynastic fears, and his horror of resurgent Jacobinism, were utmost on his mind. As ever, he believed that another military victory would silence his critics and stop the opposition from rallying against his regime. Before midnight on 18 December 1812 Napoleon's carriage, preceded by a military escort, processed beneath the arc du Carrousel in central Paris – this route, under the key ceremonial archway of the French capital, was an honour reserved exclusively for the emperor[67] – before passing through the gates of the Tuileries. Within two days news had spread through the capital that the defeated emperor had returned. During the following weeks, a desperate campaign to raise a new army began.

Napoleon had never faced definitive defeat on the battlefield. His propaganda machine now claimed that the forces of nature might well have destroyed his army in the Russian tundra, but that no human opponent could hope to do the same.

As the process of conscription, assembling armaments and supplies accelerated, Napoleon's thoughts turned to more domestic matters. He knew that before too long he would have to return to the frontline. By springtime, he would need to engage in battle with the Russians in central Europe. There were suspicions, soon to prove true, that his erstwhile Prussian allies were on the brink of defecting. This perilous situation increased rather than diminished Napoleon's desire to find a settlement to his religious woes. In all this time he had not forgotten the pope and, indeed, had discussed his frustrations with Caulaincourt on the long journey back from Lithuania.[68] It was becoming part of Napoleonic dogma that the religious authorities of his empire must acknowledge the supremacy of the secular power. The Jews and Protestants of his lands had been led to do so with relative ease. It was his determination that the Catholic Church should follow suit.[69]

The bishop of Nantes had been despatched in mid-December to discuss with the pope whether he might be ready to reopen discussions. Jean-Baptiste Duvoisin was in many ways the perfect emissary from Napoleon. He had graduated first in his class from the prestigious seminary of Saint-Sulpice, and during the *ancien régime* had held several prestigious benefices, published widely on theology and been vicar-general of Laon when the Revolution erupted in 1789. Like so many, he refused the oath to the Civil Constitution of the Clergy and was forced to emigrate to Britain; his ardent Gallicanism and decision to rally to the Consulate in 1800 put him among the leading candidates for a new diocese after the Concordat was signed.[70] As bishop of Nantes, he worked to reconcile the refractory clergy with constitutional priests, and was a key member of the committees on ecclesiastical affairs and deputations sent to Savona between 1810 and 1812. Napoleon admired his learning and loyalty to the regime. As 1813 loomed, he would be the key intermediary between church and state in the ongoing crisis with the Papacy.

After years of silence, the emperor wrote directly to his prisoner on 29 December 1812:

> Most Holy Father, I hasten to send an officer of my household to Your Holiness so as to express the satisfaction I felt upon learning from the bishop of Nantes that you are in good health, especially as, for a time, I was most

alarmed to hear that you were dangerously ill. The new sojourn of Your Holiness in Fontainebleau will provide the opportunity [for us] to see each other, and it is my heart's desire to tell you that, despite all the events which have taken place, I have always maintained the same friendship for your person. Perhaps we shall achieve the goal so desired by all to end the differences that divide church from state. For my part, I am strongly disposed towards this, and this [outcome] depends completely on Your Holiness. Nevertheless, I pray you to believe that I hold sentiments of great esteem for your person which are independent of [recent] events and circumstances. I pray God, Most Holy Father, that He preserve you for many years, so that you will have the glory of re-establishing the government of the church, so that you can profit and enjoy for a long time [the fruits of] your efforts.[71]

In response the pope selected the Genoese-Roman cardinal Giuseppe Doria Pamphilj as his envoy to compliment Napoleon and thank him for his letter.[72] It is not clear to what extent the pope was aware of recent military and political events, but it is very difficult to believe that news of the defeat in Russia, and the formation of a great anti-French coalition, could have been kept from him. With the Russians approaching eastern Germany the emperor would need allies. For the Catholic Habsburgs and king of Bavaria the fate of the pontiff was going to be a factor in deciding their adherence to the French alliance.[73]

Within days, the same Gallican bishops sent to Savona, now headed by Duvoisin, arrived in Fontainebleau to present new terms for the pope to consider.[74] To everybody's surprise the emperor insisted not only on the same terms as in previous years, but on harsher conditions. Beyond the articles already discussed in Savona three further requests were made:

1. that all future popes before their coronation would swear an oath not to order or execute anything contrary to the Four Gallican Articles;
2. that the pope and his successors would freely select one-third of all cardinals, with the remaining two-thirds to be nominated by the Catholic princes of Europe;
3. that a brief be published in which the pope would condemn the behaviour of the thirteen cardinals who refused to attend the religious wedding of Napoleon and Marie-Louise; in return, the emperor would grant an amnesty to these cardinals, with the exclusion of di Pietro and Pacca.[75]

Unlike the terms of previous draft treaties, the pope was now to reside in France and enjoy a revenue of 2 million francs. Pius was deeply afflicted on learning of these new conditions. He reiterated that he could only consider these articles with the counsel of the entire College of Cardinals. After expressing grave doubts to Duvoisin, he retired in private with Bertazzoli. For the next few days, the pope's agitation grew: his health worsened, and his nights became once more sleepless. Duvoisin hoped, like Chabrol, to catch the pope in a moment of weakness in order to prompt concessions, but this failed to materialise. Lagorce wrote to the minister of religions that the pope's servants had not received their usual Christmas gratifications: the Holy Father had no funds available. The colonel asked if he could use the money at his disposal to compensate the married men in papal service and provide them with new liveries.[76] Pius apparently spent much of his time in Fontainebleau darning his own cassocks, shirts and socks. He refused to accept any funding from the French state, as that would be tantamount to accepting symbolically his subordination to secular power.

On 19 January 1813 the imperial hunt was galloping through the forests of Melun, near Fontainebleau. The hounds were baying for blood, when the emperor suddenly decided to leave the chase and headed southwards. Empress Marie-Louise had also been sent word to make for the palace.[77] Almost nine years had elapsed since Napoleon had first met Pius on 25 November 1804 at the crossroads of Saint-Herem: the moment had now arrived for a second meeting.[78] The emperor was no great lover of hunting. He had created an imperial hunt to adhere to the forms and conventions of traditional kingship, but lacked the Bourbon lust for blood sports.[79] Even when it came to shooting, which Bonaparte preferred, he was not known for being a great marksman. As with the first meeting in 1804, the truth here was that his unexpected and unplanned arrival would avoid the problem of ceremonial delays.

According to Pacca's memoirs, that evening the pope was conversing with the red cardinals when the doors of his salon suddenly opened to reveal Emperor Napoleon. He entered with determination, placed his hands on the pope's shoulders and kissed Pius twice.[80] Both men must have considered how much they had changed physically since their last meeting. Time had been especially unkind to Napoleon, who had grown portly. (It has been speculated that he was suffering from a pituitary illness that was affecting his metabolism.)[81] His thinning hair revealed a tired man, whom the concerns of state had aged prematurely. Chiaramonti had always been slim but not very tall: his sunken cheeks, agitated manner and exhausted face now betrayed a man at the limits of his endurance. They both greeted each other kindly. It was agreed that they would discuss directly the dispute that pitted Empire against Papacy. For five days emperor and pope were locked in secret and apparently animated discussions. Sadly, nobody else was present to record these delicate negotiations. Only Agathon Jean François Fain, the emperor's secretary, was admitted towards the end to make a written record of what had been decided.[82]

The few accounts we have were written long after the event, and thus need to be interpreted with some care: they are hardly first-hand accounts of what was said and debated. It is certainly the case that Napoleon unleashed his fury during the talks: at one point he was heard screaming in anger. The emperor tended to use the same shock tactics that proved so effective on the battlefield in his diplomatic negotiations too. In 1814, the writer Chateaubriand invented the story that the emperor had slapped the pope's face and dragged him by the hair as a way of threatening him into signing an agreement.[83] This story is a fabrication and has rightly been dismissed as such. The Vatican Archives contain a remarkable document written by Bonaventura Gazzola, bishop of Cervia, who was a personal friend of the pope. During his return to the Papal States in 1814, Pius stayed with his friend, and Gazzola asked him if the rumours that Napoleon had struck him were true. Pius replied that only once had the emperor raised his hand, but in a gesture of desperation. (To this the pope had responded with the words: 'Oh! This affair that began as a comedy could end in tragedy!')[84] And in response to a letter from a Flemish nobleman asking if it was true that the pope had been the victim of violence in Fontainebleau, Pius responded unequivocally, on 27 September 1814:

That is false and I ask you to say in my name to all who will talk to you about it that he [Napoleon] never undertook such an excess against my person. However, one day in the heat of the moment when discussing the subject of the renunciation of the Papal States he grabbed me by one of the buttons of my cassock and shook me so strongly, by pulling it, that my entire body stirred. It is probably to this incident that most are referring.[85]

Though the emperor had not actually hit the pope, the interviews and discussions had clearly been deeply confrontational. Napoleon did not go into much detail in the reminiscences he dictated to his loyal followers on Saint Helena, his only comment being that he showed uncharacteristic patience and restraint when dealing with Pius.[86]

The only independent – though not very illuminating – account we have of these meetings comes from Marie-Jacques de Pange. A younger son of an *ancien régime* marquis, he had fled France during the Revolution, but returned in 1799 and gradually rallied to the Napoleonic state. In 1809 he was appointed a chamberlain to the emperor, and a year later was made a count in the imperial peerage. As chamberlain at the time of the interview between pope and emperor he enjoyed privileged access; he was certainly well placed to observe what occurred during these five momentous days. His diary that recorded events at Fontainebleau is disappointing: it is full of exact and mundane details, but, while it chronicles the hours Napoleon and the pope spent in private discussion, it says virtually nothing about the tone and content of the negotiations.[87] The account, however, gives an excellent list of all members of the court and clergy present at Fontainebleau during these days. These negotiations with the pope were a great court occasion: Marie-Louise and the ladies of the imperial court had frequent audiences with him, Napoleon regularly dined late with the cardinals, and musical entertainments were improvised to amuse the imperial and papal court. Perhaps the most unexpected part of Pange's diary is his claim that an agreement was reached on 24 January: the official documents have the signing of the agreement taking place on 25 January 1813. This was probably a slip of the quill. Pange, as chamberlain, was not present at these discussions, and it seems he could not tell what had occurred. Regardless, Napoleon was pleased with the outcome, gifting a bejewelled snuff box emblazoned with his portrait to each of the bishops and cardinals present at Fontainebleau.

Pius VII seems to have been deeply shaken regarding the document he had just signed, which became known as the Concordat of Fontainebleau. Its text contained the following stipulations:

> His Majesty the emperor and king, and His Holiness, wish to put an end to the differences that have arisen between them and resolve several matters and difficulties relating to the church, and have concluded the following articles, which will serve as the basis for a definitive settlement:
>
> Article 1. His Holiness will exercise the pontificate in France and the Kingdom of Italy in the same fashion and in the same forms as did his predecessors.
>
> Article 2. Ambassadors, ministers and chargés d'affaires of those [foreign] powers accredited to the Holy Father and those ambassadors, minister or

chargés d'affaires that the pope will send to foreign powers will enjoy the same immunities and privileges enjoyed by members of the diplomatic corps.

Article 3. The [private] domains that the Holy Father previously owned, and that have not been alienated, will be exempt from all types of taxation: they will be administered by agents or chargés d'affaires. Those which have been alienated, will be replaced to the value of 2 million francs in [annual] revenues.

Article 4. In the six months that will follow the traditional notification of those appointments made by the emperor to [vacant] archdioceses and dioceses of the Empire and Kingdom of Italy, the pope will bestow his canonical investiture, in conformity with the concordats and by virtue of the present indult. The necessary information will be gathered beforehand by the metropolitan. Once the six months have expired without the pope bestowing his investiture, the metropolitan, and in his absence, the most senior bishop of the province, will proceed with the investiture of the episcopal appointee; in this way no diocese will remain vacant for more than one year.

Article 5. The pope will appoint, be it in France, or be it in the Kingdom of Italy, [candidates] to ten dioceses, which will be selected in future negotiations.

Article 6. The six suburbicarian dioceses will be re-established; their [incumbents] will be appointed by the pope. Their existing properties will be returned; and measures will be taken for those properties which have been sold. Upon the death of the bishops of Anagni and Rieti, their dioceses will be subsumed within the aforementioned six dioceses, in conformity with the future negotiations which will take place between His Majesty and the Holy Father.

Article 7. With regard to the bishops of the Papal States who have been forced to leave their dioceses due to present circumstances, the pope will exercise in their favour his right to bestow on them dioceses *in patribus*. They will receive a pension that will equal the revenues they previously enjoyed; and they will be eligible to be appointed to vacant dioceses either in the Empire or Kingdom of Italy.

Article 8. His Majesty and His Holiness, at an opportune moment, will negotiate on the reduction of dioceses in Tuscany and Liguria, and also will enter into discussion on the dioceses that need to be established in Holland and the Hanseatic departments.

Article 9. The propaganda, the penitentiary and the archives will be established in the place of residence of the Holy Father.

Article 10. His Majesty will bestow an amnesty on those cardinals, bishops, priests and laymen who have incurred his disgrace due to recent events.

Article 11. The Holy Father accepts these measures in consideration of the present state of the church, and trusts that His Majesty will accord his powerful protection to the many needs of religion given the [troubled] times in which we live.[88]

After three and a half years of captivity and resistance, Pius VII, facing overwhelming psychological pressure and intimidation, had temporarily capitulated. It was an astonishing feat that he had resisted for so long in solitary confinement. Indeed, that an exhausted and isolated seventy-one-year-old should have eventually complied with the demands of the most powerful empire in Europe was hardly surprising; it must have struck contemporaries as an inevitability. His reserves of determination and resolve had, however, proved remarkable. For over three years he had not surrendered the church's prerogatives, demonstrating an iron will. In January 1813 that will broke, marking the nadir of Pius VII's life and reign.

The Concordat of Fontainebleau enshrined the supremacy of the state over the church. Although not formally expressed therein, the document tacitly accepted the dissolution of the Papal States. Many of these concessions had been agonisingly difficult for Pius to swallow, but the issue that most troubled him was Article 4, which, basically, sanctioned the provisions made by the National Council of 1811.[89] Under its terms, metropolitan archbishops now shared power of investiture with popes. The prerogative to confirm and invest all Catholic bishops had been one of the most jealously guarded rights of the Papacy; this concession was by far the most disturbing. Equally painful was the agreement's implicit surrender of the Papacy's temporal power in central Italy. In a very disingenuous letter, dictated to Duvoisin on the evening of 25 January, Napoleon reassured Pius that the text drawn up at Fontainebleau dealt only with spiritual matters, and that the sovereignty of Rome and the Papal States would be discussed at a later stage.[90] At the very least the emperor had agreed that the black cardinals would be released and allowed to join the pope in Fontainebleau.

For Catholics the only consolation to be found in the text was that it implied that its articles constituted preliminaries for a more formal and extended negotiation to be held at some future date. Pius's agreement had been extracted on the understanding that its terms be kept secret. Napoleon, however, had no intention of letting his great diplomatic victory against the church pass unnoticed. The empress was instructed to write immediately to her father, Francis I of Austria, with the happy news.[91] Her letter announced that peace with the church had been re-established through a solemn agreement with the pope; Marie-Louise stressed – a little disingenuously – how happy the pope seemed with the agreement, adding that it resolved once and for all the long-drawn-out crisis in the relationship between church and state.

At the same time, Savary issued orders that the black cardinals be released and allowed to return to Paris.[92] Cardinal Pacca, who had been languishing in the grim and forbidding alpine fortress of Fenestrelle, was especially glad when he received news that his harsh and insalubrious confinement was over. Cardinal Fesch had been one of the last cardinals to reach Fontainebleau. He had quarrelled violently with his nephew after the National Council of 1811. By 1813 there were few members of his family with whom the emperor was on speaking terms; indeed, only the empress and his Beauharnais stepchildren provided some domestic solace. All of the Bonapartes on whom Napoleon had showered kingdoms, titles, vast wealth and political authority had deeply disappointed him in their failure to administer their realms as efficiently as him. When Fesch had been made the virtual head of the Gallican Church Napoleon had expected him to follow his orders and to promote the interests of the Empire. His uncle, however, had shown himself torn between his priestly vocation and family loyalty. His sympathy for Pius VII and his quibbles over the National Council had done much to alienate him in the emperor's affections. To make matters worse, a letter from the cardinal expressing solidarity with the pope's plight in Savona had been intercepted by the imperial police in 1812.[93] In response, Napoleon had threatened his uncle with imprisonment in the fortress of Fenestrelle, and removed his annual 300,000-franc emolument he received as coadjutor archbishop of Regensburg.[94] Once seen as the natural head of the Gallican Church, Fesch was now decidedly in disgrace. The threat of imprisonment and this reduction in his revenues frightened Fesch into submission. When he met with the pope in 1813 the cardinal kept a low profile, quickly returning to his archdiocese of Lyon in order to avoid being drawn into the unfolding drama.[95] He and his nephew never fully reconciled their differences, although Fesch was no ingrate: when the wheels of fortune turned against the Empire he did his best to support his emperor.

On 13 February 1813 the text of the Concordat of Fontainebleau was approved by the Imperial Senate.[96] The next day Napoleon proceeded in great fanfare to the state opening of his parliaments. From the throne, he gave the traditional speech, setting out the state of his Empire and the challenges it faced. He admitted that, although unvanquished in Russia by any army or general, his forces had been defeated by the elements. As ever, Britain was blamed for the new coalition forming in the north of Europe. The emperor used the speech to announce that this situation would soon require a new German military campaign. He did, however, bring some good news for the deputies of the Corps Législatif: 'I have signed directly with the pope a Concordat that puts an end to the differences which sadly had arisen within the church. The French dynasty reigns and will reign in Spain. I am satisfied with the conduct of all my allies. I will never abandon them; I will maintain the integrity of their states. The Russians will [be forced to] return to their dreadful climate.'[97] As ever, the emperor announced that the continuing war would require great sacrifices in terms of taxation and manpower. The publication of the Concordat in both French and Italian was one of the few pieces of good news that Napoleon was able to give to the peoples of his empire. Its publication and dissemination shocked the pope, however. Its public announcement backfired badly, leading Pius to deeply regret signing the document.

Several black cardinals criticised openly the terms of the Concordat of 1813.[98] This strained Chiaramonti even further, and, to many, he seemed to be approaching a nervous breakdown. After three years in his prison fortress, Cardinal Pacca had now returned to the pope. He was shocked by what he saw. The pope had lost much weight; he was pale, his eyes sunken into his skull. His gaze was transfixed and, at times, he appeared catatonic.[99] Napoleon wanted to create the appearance that Pius was pleased with the Concordat, and that a renewed papal court was slowly forming in Fontainebleau. A large detachment of servants from the imperial household was assigned to attend to the pope's every need. The ever-present Lagorce was ordered to abandon his gendarme's uniform and to wear instead the silk suit with gold braid of an imperial chamberlain.[100] Every effort was made to give the false impression that the pope was no longer a captive, but resided voluntarily at the heart of the French Empire.

Cardinal Consalvi, former secretary of state and one of Pius's most trusted advisers, who had been in the political wilderness for many years, now decided to intervene. As a trained lawyer he was ideally suited to counsel the pope. He advised that a clear solution presented itself under the present crisis. As the Concordat of Fontainebleau merely constituted preliminaries for future, more detailed, negotiations, the pope could easily retract his consent in an open letter to the emperor.[101] The cardinals advised that none of Napoleon's nominated bishops should be confirmed, and that no monies from the French government should be accepted.[102] When it was learned that the terms of the Concordat had been published throughout the Empire, both red and black cardinals agreed that a letter of retraction had to be written and sent to the emperor. The pope had to be careful in doing this undetected. His daily celebration of Mass had become quite an event in Fontainebleau: ordinary members of the public were allowed into the imperial chapel to witness Pius VII celebrate the divine mysteries. While the pope was at Mass, agents of the government would search all the drawers in his apartments and examine all his papers.[103] Essentially, the regime continued to mistrust the pope and his entourage.

Given that it was so difficult to act unobserved, not to mention that the pope's health had taken another turn for the worse, it took him over a month to produce the retraction. This was an extremely long and detailed document, its tone and content excruciating. Over several pages, signed and dated 24 March 1813, the pope blamed his age, infirmities and weakness for his having mistakenly consented to sign the articles presented by Napoleon on 25 January. In a series of questions, he asked: how could a pope renounce the primacy of Saint Peter over all bishops? How could the pope allow others to invest episcopal candidates? Equally, how could the pontiff allow so many bishops in the Papal States to be deposed without just cause? Finally, how could the pope renounce his temporal sovereignty? He was not the owner of the Papal States, but merely their custodian. He knew his letter would cause the emperor pain, but did not want to endanger his immortal soul by ratifying a document so damaging for the church. The letter ended by expressing his openness to resuming negotiations with the emperor in order to find a mutually satisfactory settlement.[104] He stressed ominously that, as successor to Saint Peter, there were limits to the concessions he could grant.

The letter did not come as a complete surprise to Napoleon. He had already been warned on 9 March that some cardinals had turned the pope against the Concordat.[105] Furthermore, the bulls of investiture for Napoleon's episcopal candidates had failed to materialise. This did not bode well for the agreement coming into force. On learning of the pope's letter, Napoleon said to an aide-de-camp: 'The tsar finds it convenient to have a holy synod under his tight grip and that [institution], or something similar, would suit France even better as things stand!'[106] The emperor immediately wrote to Bigot informing him that the strictest secrecy was to be maintained surrounding the pope's retraction. All bishops at Fontainebleau were to return to their dioceses to celebrate Easter. The only exceptions were to be the bishops of Nantes and Trier. As counsellors of state, they were to head to Paris and advise the government. Napoleon also wanted all French bishops and cardinals to write to Pius urging him to enact the Concordat of 1813. This was imperative now that this agreement was incorporated as a law of the state by the Imperial Senate. For the French Empire, the terms agreed at Fontainebleau were beyond dispute. For Bigot, the minister of religions, the only solution was to appoint an imperial commissioner to negotiate further with the pope. The best candidate for the position was Duvoisin.[107]

Retribution was not long in being visited on the papal household. The servants and officers of the imperial household sent to attend to the pope were recalled to Paris, leaving Pius with the few attendants who had accompanied him into exile in 1809. In the small hours of 5 April 1813, a police agent burst into Cardinal di Pietro's bedroom. He had been marked out as the key troublemaker who had inspired the pope's retraction of the Concordat. Exemplary punishment was to be meted out to deter further resistance. Given no time to dress, he was sent back into exile in Auxonne.[108] The imperial wrath was also directed at the existing episcopate. After their concerted opposition to the National Council of 1811, the bishops of Ghent, Troyes and Tournai had been forced to resign their sees. Around this time, Napoleon appointed successors to take over their dioceses, replacing them with Bonapartist loyalists. As in the past, the pope steadfastly refused to confirm these candidates. As the spring of 1813 began to blossom it was clear that the so-called Concordat of Fontainebleau had been a stillbirth. The pope and the black cardinals continued to oppose the French emperor's designs.

Religious matters, however, became a secondary consideration as the French Empire embarked on the Saxon Campaign of 1813. Its outcome was hardly a foregone conclusion, as Napoleon was able to field an enormous force of 800,000 troops on the German, Italian and Spanish fronts.[109] In May he personally commanded armies of conscripts that gave a bloody nose to Russo-Prussian forces arrayed against him at the battles of Lutzen and Bautzen. However, due to a crippling lack of cavalry these became pyrrhic victories, and the allies lived to fight another day. Regardless, orders were given that a solemn *Te Deum* be sung in all the churches of the Empire to give thanks to the Lord God of Hosts for providing victory on the battlefield.[110] With both sides exhausted by the fighting of these early months, a truce was called at Pläswitz on 4 June. It would last until 10 August. The Habsburg Empire offered to mediate between the warring parties, and on 26 June at the Marcolini Palace in Dresden, Metternich, the Austrian chancellor, presented the French Empire with the allies' peace terms.[111] Essentially, the extent of French territory was to be severely limited and its hegemony in Germany dissolved. The position of Italy remained open for future negotiation, and no specific proposals were discussed in this Habsburg mediation.

Napoleon was indignant at these terms, and over several hours showered Metternich with abuse and insults, asking him if he was on the payroll of the British. Historians have criticised Napoleon for being unreasonable in his demands, and portrayed the Austrian mediation as generous in its promises.[112] There is much truth in this: Bonaparte failed to grasp the precariousness of his situation. If the mediation failed, Austria had given a commitment to join the coalition against the French. For Napoleon, the vital issue was that the peace offer presented at Dresden had not been endorsed by the British government.[113] If the French accepted this peace deal there was no guarantee that London would cease naval operations and the military offensive in Spain. It was unclear whether France's most determined enemy would accept the outcome of these negotiations. As Metternich left his interview with the French emperor, he sighed the words: 'Sire, you are lost.'

Negotiations continued for another six weeks, but to no avail. At this time the Belgian aristocrat Count Paul van der Vrecken and the priest Tomasso Bernetti (the nephew of Cardinal Brancadoro) became secret agents for the Papacy.[114] On 24 July 1813 these trusted Catholics succeeded in transmitting a letter from Pius VII to Francis I of Austria. Pius demanded the complete restitution of the Papal States. He reminded the Habsburg sovereign that the church had never formally renounced or accepted the loss of its central Italian principality. Equally, all ecclesiastical states beyond Italy would need to be restored. Pius also offered to send a negotiator to join the peace talks.[115] It is by no means clear how the European powers felt at this stage about the issue of restoring ecclesiastical states. Italy was a secondary theatre in comparison to the main military offensive in Germany. It seemed unlikely that secular princes were keen to see the power of the church restored to its full extent in central Europe.

The position of the Catholic Church and its temporalities could only be broached once the tide of the war had turned in the coalition's favour. When hostilities resumed, the Austrian mediation having ended in failure, the Habsburgs joined the allies in the campaign to stop the French Empire. For the first time in many years, Napoleon was outnumbered and battling against the odds.

As the war in Saxony began anew, Jacques-Louis de La Brue de Saint-Bauzille had been appointed to the diocese of Ghent. Having served as vicar-general in Malines and possessing some knowledge of the Belgian context, the charismatic La Brue was considered loyal to the regime. (Two of his three nephews had died fighting in Spain.) On 22 July 1813 the cathedral chapter in Ghent elected him their vicar-capitular, as had been the practice elsewhere in the Empire.[116] La Brue wanted to celebrate his appointment with a Solemn Mass on 25 July. When he appeared in full episcopal dress, the students of the local seminaries stood up and left the cathedral in protest, to great public scandal.[117] It was clear that, as he had not received papal confirmation, they considered him an intruder in their diocese.[118] On being made aware by Bigot of events in Ghent, Napoleon felt that these protesting seminary students needed to be punished, as an example to the rest of the Empire.[119]

From his imperial headquarters in Saxony Napoleon now wrote a series of heated letters, commanding that dire retribution be visited on these rebellious students. On the emperor's orders, they were expelled from the seminary and their exemption from conscription rescinded.[120] The prefect of the department of Lys was instructed to order that they be called up for immediate active service in the ongoing military campaign. Even when the very future of the Empire seemed in doubt, Napoleon's reprisals against ecclesiastical opposition were ruthless. The young seminarians of Ghent were drafted into an artillery brigade that was directed towards the River Wesel to fight the allies: almost fifty swiftly perished from disease while serving under the Tricolour.[121] The theologians and professors of Ghent who had instigated their rebellion against the emperor were all sent to prison in France.[122] The religious vocation of these seminarians and the freedom of their professors were sacrificed for political expediency. The theology professors of the seminary of Tournai were meanwhile taken into custody and forced to swear an oath to uphold the Four Gallican Articles (see Appendix) in order to forestall any opposition.[123]

In the face of overwhelming odds, Napoleon was able to inflict a serious reverse on the Austrian Army under Prince Karl Philipp zu Schwarzenberg at Dresden on 26 and 27 August.[124] In this battle the French emperor showed himself still capable of the energy and genius of his early years. General Joseph Radetzky von Radetz, the Austrian chief of staff, was among the chief architects of a new strategy to defeat the French emperor known as the Trachenberg Plan.[125] This prescribed that the allies would avoid engaging Napoleon in direct battle but, instead, would focus their offensive actions on individual marshals commanding French corps, with the aim of significantly weakening the Grande Armée to the point that even Napoleon's military brilliance could not hope to vanquish the overwhelming odds stacked against him. Throughout August and September France's marshals suffered a series of catastrophic reverses.[126]

Napoleon decided to occupy a strong defensive position around the town of Leipzig, which permitted his men potentially to ford the Pleiße and the Parthe rivers. This would allow him to attack each of the allied armies separately and resume the offensive. The allies, instead of waiting for an assault, decided to concentrate all their forces on this French defensive line. On 16 October 1813 the Battle of the Nations began: its outcome would determine the Napoleonic Wars. For three days over half a million men fought to decide the future of Europe. The world would have to wait until the First World War to witness again such massive armies inflicting horrendous carnage on each other. On 18 October, realising he could no longer hold Leipzig, Napoleon ordered a retreat. The army was withdrawing in good order until a nervous corporal blew up a bridge on the River Elster too early, leaving over 30,000 men stranded on the wrong side.[127] They were to become allied prisoners. Soon the Bavarians, Württembergers and Saxons abandoned their alliance with the French. The defeat at Leipzig, unlike the Russian disaster, was so severe that it was impossible for Napoleon to rebuild his army as he had to a large extent exhausted his pool of available conscripts. The French Empire had clearly lost the war.

On 9 July 1813 Duvoisin died in Nantes. According to legend, one of his last acts before dying was to write to Napoleon begging him to release the pope from captivity.[128] As things started collapsing around him, Napoleon instructed Bigot to order public prayers for victory and sermons instilling patriotic fervour to be preached throughout the Empire and Kingdom of Italy. The question of the pope's fate and the restoration of the Papal States, as the French Empire crumbled, remained of great importance and a potential bargaining chip in future peace negotiations. As Napoleon retreated from Germany and prepared to defend

France from invasion, he renewed his attempts to reach an agreement with Pius, which would allow the pope to return to Rome. One of the Empress Marie-Louise's ladies-in-waiting, the Countess Anna Pieri Brignole Sale, the daughter-in-law of one of the last doges of Genoa and a niece of Cardinal Consalvi, sought a series of audiences with the pope in November.[129] As a pious noblewoman who was at the same time a Napoleonic loyalist, it was hoped she might persuade Pius and his cardinals to open peace negotiations.

The pope, however, rejected these overtures, stating that he was unprepared, given the unstable military and diplomatic situation, to enter any negotiations. The same resolve that had guided his resistance to Napoleon in Savona was rekindled in the coming months. The once open-minded bishop of Imola, who had preached in 1797 that democracy and Christianity were not mutually exclusive, had by now transformed into a much more neurotic and stubborn reactionary pope. Given his ordeals and close encounters with death, it is easy to understand how this metamorphosis had come to pass. The Concordat of 1801, and his accommodation with Napoleon, had become his bitterest regret.[130]

# NINE

# CHRISTIANITY RESTORED
## THE PAPAL RETURN TO ROME AND THE
## HUNDRED DAYS, 1814–15

By the winter of 1813 the new Carolingian Empire, created by Napoleon at the cost of so much blood and misery, was collapsing at a staggering speed. Central Europe and Spain had been lost irretrievably. Metropolitan France was poised for invasion and northern Italy, under Viceroy Eugène de Beauharnais, was preparing to meet an allied offensive led by the Habsburg field marshal Heinrich von Bellegarde.[1] What shape post-Napoleonic Europe would assume was uncertain. The French Empire would not go down without a fight. In late October the allies had presented generous peace terms to Paris, known as the Frankfurt proposals, which would have allowed France to retain its natural frontiers, namely, the Rhine, Alps and Pyrenees.[2] There was the added advantage that, unlike the mediation put forward at Dresden in June 1813 (see above, p. 246), the Frankfurt proposals were underwritten by Britain. Napoleon would have been wise to accept this offer, but alas, he had little wish to see his empire dismembered. He also feared that a disadvantageous peace would stoke the fires of domestic opposition and rebellion.[3] He decided instead to temporise and see if better terms might be negotiated. General Caulaincourt, now French plenipotentiary for the peace talks, was to explore if members of the Bonaparte clan would be allowed to keep their crowns. That Eugène de Beauharnais be allowed to succeed the emperor as ruler of northern Italy was among the hypotheses explored. The French rejection of the Frankfurt proposals demonstrated that Napoleon was not willing to relinquish control over his empire and satellite states easily.[4]

Given such obstinacy, the allies were forced to withdraw their offer, and the fighting continued. Italy's future hung precariously in the balance. So too did the fate of the Papal States, which had not been decided by the great powers. Since its mediation, six months previously, Austria had set itself the goal of restoring Pius VII to his throne. How this was to be achieved remained nebulous.[5] Cynically, the French realised that there might be benefits to restoring Pius to his diocese in

Rome. They hoped that his return would sow discord and division among the allies: it was well known that the Papacy would demand a full restoration to the *status quo ante* of 1789, and that this might upset the coalition's post-war plans. In December 1813 Étienne Fallot de Beaumont, bishop of Piacenza, was summoned by the imperial government. Appointed emissary to Fontainebleau, he was now to explore under which terms the pope would accept his restoration.[6]

Fallot had been born into a noble family in the papal enclave of Avignon, north of Provence, in 1750. He was thus a subject of the pope. As an aristocrat, he rose swiftly through the ranks of the First Estate but, in 1789, was forced to emigrate to Rome. Towards the end of the 1790s he had been among the first prelates to return to France. In Marseille he became a close friend to the Clary family. The daughters of this prosperous merchant clan would provide brides for both Joseph Bonaparte and Jean-Baptiste Bernadotte, a former Napoleonic marshal and crown prince of Sweden; Fallot was thus a friend to both the queen of Spain and crown princess of Sweden. A reliable Gallican bishop who was considered a safe pair of hands, it was known he would fully implement imperial policies within his diocese without hesitation. He was therefore posted to Piacenza, a region which had experienced mass rebellion against the French in 1805 and 1806. Only an enlightened Frenchman could fight Italian superstition and backwardness, which had bred such dissent amongst the locals.[7]

It was for this reason that he had been present during the negotiations at Savona. He had advised the imperial government on its religious problems for some time. For Napoleon he was the ideal candidate to offer this olive branch. The cardinals and Curia, however, distrusted him deeply as an imperial collaborator. After meeting with Minister of Religions Bigot and Secretary of State Maret in their respective ministries, he travelled to Fontainebleau to seek an audience with the pope. Fallot was received on 19 December 1813, and exchanged Christmas greetings with Pius.[8] He gave assurances that the government might be willing to allow the pontiff's return to Rome: Pius replied that he was unwilling to negotiate while he remained a prisoner. He and his cardinals were aware that the war was going badly for the Empire, and they felt the moment for compromise had passed. With the pontiff refusing to open any discussions, Fallot's first meeting ended in complete failure.

Meanwhile, events in Italy had taken a decided turn for the worse. Reports reached Paris that the emperor's brother-in-law Joachim Murat and sister

Caroline, the king and queen of Naples, were engaged in secret negotiations with Austria.[9] On 11 January 1814 a treaty of alliance was signed between Murat and the Habsburg monarchy.[10] In return for 30,000 Neapolitan troops joining the coalition, the king of Naples would be allowed to retain his throne, with the promise of some territorial gains at the expense of the southern fringes of the Papal States.[11] On 19 January Murat entered Rome at the head of his army. Soon his troops occupied central Italy, and the Neapolitans established provisional administrations within the papal territories to replace the French. Murat's real intentions in 1814 remain controversial. He was desperately trying to salvage what he could of Napoleonic Italy, and started playing a dangerous double-game, which would end in disaster a year later (see below, pp. 276–8). Deliberately slow in joining Field Marshal Bellegarde's allied forces, he simultaneously opened secret negotiations with Eugène de Beauharnais with a view to sharing post-Napoleonic Italy amongst themselves.[12] Now that the Neapolitans were in control of the Papal States, the question emerged: were they going to return these provinces to the pope?

This family betrayal hit Napoleon hard; he never forgave Murat for his treason. It now became imperative to return the pope to Italy, as his presence in Rome would thwart Murat's plans and sow discord among the allies. On 19 January Fallot again travelled to Fontainebleau to meet with Pius VII.[13] This time he had written instructions and full powers to negotiate.[14] He had been ordered to tell Pius that the allies had concluded a secret treaty, which allowed the king of Naples to annex Rome and most of central Italy; the ministers hoped this lie would put renewed pressure on the pope to give way. The draft peace treaty Fallot had brought with him promised to return the Papal States to Pius. It was unclear whether the Marche and Umbrian provinces annexed to the Kingdom of Italy would be returned: these were not mentioned in the text.

Furthermore, the draft specified several additional conditions. These mainly dealt with papal property sold during the annexation, the preservation of French churches in Rome and the matter of those Romans who had collaborated with the Empire: they would be allowed to resettle in France.[15] Fallot's written instructions stated that, if the pope accepted the treaty, he was to press for the confirmation of all bishops nominated to vacant dioceses by the emperor. Pius received the offer with disdain: he would only negotiate after his return to Rome. He expected that all that was rightfully his would be given back immediately, including Avignon and the Comtat Venaissin in Provence.[16] As mentioned in

Chapter 1 (p. 27), these territories had been annexed unilaterally by French revolutionaries in 1790.[17] This insistence on the restitution of all papal territory showed that Pius now wanted to capitalise on his advantage. Following the advice of Cardinal Pacca and Cardinal Consalvi, the pope categorically stated that the return of his principalities was merely an act of justice and therefore not subject to any bargaining.

Fallot's mission was an act of desperation. The imploding Napoleonic Empire sought a settlement with a pope whom it had held prisoner for almost five years. Discussions were shipwrecked on Pius's understandable refusal to compromise as events turned in his favour. For him, papal sovereignty was a question of principle and a guarantee of the church's spiritual independence, not a mere bargaining chip. Colonel Lagorce, who by now knew his prisoner well, sought to replace Fallot as the government's negotiator.[18] However, the ministers in Paris did not feel that anything could be gained by more talks. On 22 January 1814 two large postal coaches entered the Cour du Cheval Blanc in the palace of Fontainebleau.[19] Lagorce informed the pope that he would depart for Rome the next day. Celebrations were cut short by the news that no cardinals were to be allowed to join Pius on the journey. Only Bertazzoli, archbishop of Edessa, the omnipresent Dr Porta and two valets would accompany the convoy.[20] The next day, after Solemn Mass, the pope exhorted the College of Cardinals to remain united and not to negotiate with the French government. They swore continued obedience, and some shed tears as the pope blessed them as he entered his coach. Behind him he left secret written instructions for them to follow.[21] The cardinals were, under no circumstances, to associate with Napoleonic prelates appointed to vacant dioceses; they were also instructed not to attend any public events, and not to recognise the king of Rome in any way.

Four days later, the sixteen cardinals in Fontainebleau were ordered to vacate the palace immediately, without escort, with the exceptions of Pacca and Consalvi. Napoleon held these two prelates responsible for the pope's refusal to sanction Fallot's peace initiative.[22] In a final act of pique, they were ordered into exile in the towns of Uzès and Béziers in the south of France.[23] Here they would restlessly await the fall of the Empire. Their exile was a refusal to accept the inevitable as events accelerated.[24] During the Congress of Châtillon of 3–7 February 1814, Napoleon was offered a final peace settlement: under the coalition's new terms, France was to be reduced to its 1792 frontiers. Importantly, all parties agreed that the pope was to be restored to Rome; the extent of papal territory in central Italy would be decided later. Initially, the French emperor was tempted to accept these terms, but, as was ever his way, he later decided to stake everything on battle. Despite being desperately outnumbered, during a six-day campaign he attacked the Prussian army to his north and won an unexpected string of victories.[25] Unwisely, Napoleon decided to press his temporary advantage by demanding more territory. On 19 March peace negotiations collapsed, and the allies became convinced that deposing the French emperor was the only means of guaranteeing peace.[26] The Habsburg emperor, Francis I, meanwhile, sent a diplomatic note to Napoleon demanding the release of Pius VII.[27]

As the allies closed on Paris, Empress Marie-Louise, as regent, and the king of Rome took the fateful decision to flee. On 28 March they headed towards Blois, with government ministers following them.[28] Three days later, after a half-hearted defence, the garrison of Paris capitulated to allied forces. The tsar, the Habsburg emperor and the king of Prussia entered the French capital in triumph.[29] On 1 April 1814, Talleyrand, fearing anarchy and wishing to save the situation, convened a meeting of the rump Imperial Senate. After heated debate, Napoleon was deposed as emperor of the French in absentia, with the Senate's decree accusing Bonaparte of trampling on the freedoms of his citizens and condemning him for his refusal to seek peace.[30] Events now moved to Fontainebleau, where Napoleon had retreated with the remnants of his army. After several tense stand-offs with his marshals and generals, Napoleon realised that all was lost.[31] He abdicated in favour of his son as Napoleon II, but the allies refused to accept this stipulation. On 6 April the emperor of the French renounced his throne unconditionally. Five days later another treaty was signed. This allowed Napoleon to retain the title of emperor, and made him the sovereign of the small island of Elba off the coast of Tuscany.[32]

Unable to face this bitter humiliation, the fallen Bonaparte attempted suicide on the night of 12 April. The poison he drank, however, had lost its potency and just made him violently ill.[33] His first period of exile was to be much less harsh than the one he had imposed on Pius in Savona. On Elba he would remain sovereign, receive a generous pension and have a personal guard of 1,000 loyal troops.[34] According to legend, as the fallen emperor travelled through Provence to embark on the ship bound for Elba, his carriage crossed that of Cardinal Consalvi, who had been liberated from exile in Béziers. Napoleon, seeing the cardinal, nodded at him, and expressed his admiration for the formidable secretary of state who had defied him for so long: 'That man, who never became a priest, is the best priest of the lot.'[35] Indeed, Consalvi was among the last cardinals of the modern world not to have taken holy orders. The story is apocryphal, but it is just possible that these great adversaries did cross each other's paths. The allies would live to regret the decision to send Napoleon to Elba. He remained uncomfortably close to Europe, and free to cause mischief.[36] Meanwhile, in Italy, news of his abdication led to riots in Milan and other cities of the satellite kingdom. Eugène de Beauharnais was reluctantly forced to surrender to Bellegarde on 26 April 1814.[37] Murat, for his part, showed little sign of wishing to evacuate the Papal States, especially the rich Legations of Romagna. The inhabitants of this region had been loyal to Napoleon and had no desire to return to papal rule after two decades of effective imperial administration.[38]

As these events unfolded, Pius's own journey back to Italy had been tortuous. Lagorce was ordered to deliver his captive to Savona, but he was to head deep into the French interior and take an extremely long time to reach the Ligurian coast.[39] The reason behind this impractical route is unclear, but perhaps Napoleon did not want to release his captive too quickly in case he needed to use him as a trump card in the ongoing peace negotiations. Pius's journey took him to the west, then south into Guyenne, and then eastwards through Languedoc and Provence before finally crossing the Alps into Liguria.[40] The minister of police had ordered that all major cities be avoided, and that the pope should travel incognito under the title of bishop of Imola (his old diocese before his election as pope). It was a badly kept secret: all the way along the route priests and loyal Catholics turned out in enormous numbers to receive a papal blessing.

En route Lagorce bonded with the pontiff and displayed a more humane side. By coincidence the papal convoy passed the town of Brive-la-Gaillarde in Corrèze, the colonel's birthplace. He asked if Pius might be willing to meet his family, to which the reply was 'yes'; not only that, but Pius blessed Lagorce's elderly – and surprised – Catholic mother. A night was spent at the local inn and the Lagorce family were given a Pontifical set of rosary beads as thanks for the hospitality received.[41] Unlike during the previous journey in 1812, progress was leisurely, and the pope was allowed to rest. On 7 February, at the town of Orgon in Provence, crowds turned out to celebrate the convoy's transit. Pius was greeted by the jubilant municipality, clergy and people.[42] Bands played music along the route, decorations were put up and a dais erected to receive Pius in pomp. This was in marked contrast to when, weeks later, on 25 April 1814, Napoleon passed through the town on his way into exile; the enraged population surrounded the fallen emperor's carriage and tried to lynch him.[43] The contrast between the jubilation over the pope's transit and the attack on the fallen emperor could not have been greater. Angrily, Napoleon swore that, if he ever returned, he would raze the town to the ground.[44]

Scenes of rapturous applause and triumph greeted the papal convoy on the road from Nice to the Ligurian coast. On 17 February the coaches pulled into Savona, where they resumed temporary residence in the episcopal palace which had been Pius's prison for almost three years.[45] (Chabrol, however, was no longer present: he had been transferred to serve as prefect of Paris in the aftermath of the Malet affair (see above, pp. 233–4). He was a deeply efficient administrator and would govern the French capital, excluding a brief interruption during the Hundred Days, until 1830.)[46] Lagorce's letters to the minister of (as 8 other cases) police made it clear that he believed the situation was now extremely delicate: one signal from the pope might launch a holy war against the remainder of the French forces in Italy. Indeed, the colonel was fearful that he and his gendarmes might be lynched by local people.[47] Enthusiasm for religion had become intertwined with anti-French feeling. Lagorce would spend a further month in Savona awaiting developments. After the Congress of Châtillon, Napoleon had accepted the Habsburg request that the pope be freed, writing to Savary on 10 March 1814 commanding that Lagorce take Pius towards Parma. There he would release his prisoner to the Austro-Neapolitan army.[48]

Lagorce sent a final report to the ministry of police, in which he described the historic handover on 25 March. The papal convoy had been directed beyond Parma to the banks of the Taro river, which marked the frontline dividing the forces loyal to Eugène de Beeauharnais from the Austro-Neapolitans led by Field Marshal Bellegarde. Lagorce was greeted by Nikolaus, Count Esterházy, commander of a regiment of Hussars, who had been sent to receive the pope and escort him to safety. Pius blessed Lagorce and bid him farewell. According to legend, Pius gifted the colonel his carriage and a grey mare named Cocotte, two of the few luxuries he had been allowed to take from Rome in July 1809.[49]

Lagorce was to prosper in his later career. During his eighteen months at Fontainebleau he had not dedicated his time to guarding his prisoner exclusively; he had also been busy networking. On his return to France, in August 1814 he married the daughter of the mayor of Fontainebleau. He was now a wealthy man: his new wife brought him a dowry of 100,000 francs. He bought the château of Gironville in Gâtinais, south of Paris, where he retired to enjoy the life of a country squire. Eventually he became mayor of the local town and tried his hand at politics with mixed results. In 1842 he died of an apoplectic fit after learning that former friends were to field a mayoral candidate to oppose him in the forthcoming elections. Lagorce, like so many officers of the Gendarmerie, had a truly adventurous career.[50]

Now a free man after nearly five years, Pius was granted full sovereign honours by the Austro-Neapolitan soldiers. He was to spend his first night of freedom in the state apartments of the Farnese ducal palace in Parma. His next stop was Bologna, where on 31 March he had an audience with the king of Naples.[51] This was an unpleasant meeting, at which Murat advised the pope not to return to Rome: he surprised Pius with a petition signed by the most eminent Roman citizens, demanding that in future a secular prince should rule them rather than the pope.[52] Pius took the petition and, without glancing at it, threw it into a nearby brazier. 'Now, I take it,' he said, 'nothing opposes our return to Rome?'[53] Murat had exaggerated the ill feeling towards the pope in Rome, which was felt by French collaborators rather than the population at large. After this fraught encounter, the papal entourage headed for the pope's former diocese of Imola. Flowers, dignitaries and cheering crowds lined his route to fête their former bishop in triumph.

Fully restored to power, he decided that his next stop would be his birthplace of Cesena. He returned to the Chiaramonti *palazzo*, the ancestral seat of his family, and took some time to organise his restoration. Here a miniature papal court began to materialise, and Pius tried to resume the governance of the church as best as he could. One of the first matters to consider was an urgent letter from Cardinal Fesch and Letizia Bonaparte, Napoleon's mother. Now exiled from France, they beseeched the Holy Father to be allowed to make Rome their place of exile.[54] Generously, this request was granted. On 4 May 1814, Pius issued the so-called 'triumphant brief', in which he announced to the people of the Papal States his imminent return to his capital city. He proclaimed:

> If due to military considerations we cannot as yet resume the exercise of our sovereignty over all the ancient lands possessed by the church, we do not doubt that we shall resume [said exercise]; we trust not only in our sacred

rights (to which this act is not intended to be prejudicial) but also in the enlightened justice of the victorious allied monarchs, from whom we have already received particular and consoling reassurances.[55]

The document went on to warn:

> We declare to our peoples, that, if amongst them there are those who are guilty of whatever betrayal, it is to our sovereign authority alone that belongs the right to examine said guilt and to judge the extent of it and apportion punishment. We ask all to be obedient sons, and not to usurp any authority, but remain subordinate to the laws and to the will of their common father.[56]

Five years of captivity had marked Chiaramonti. His personality had changed from one of affability to paranoia. It is part of the argument of this book, unlike most other histories of the period, that Pius returned to his state with far less peaceable intentions than most scholars have attributed to him; instead, he felt a decided bitterness towards those priests and former subjects who had betrayed him. His physical exhaustion had led to neuroses and an inability to compromise or trust others, a marked contrast to his personality on the eve of his election as pope. Half a decade of imprisonment and confinement had sapped his tolerance and his patience.

Cardinals and prelates had been hastening to Cesena to rally to Pius. The most important cleric to arrive was Annibale della Genga (who would succeed Pius as Leo XII in 1823). As previously mentioned, he had been nuncio to several German courts, and had thwarted Napoleon's attempts to negotiate a German Concordat for the Confederation of the Rhine. On 7 May he was appointed extraordinary nuncio to the newly restored Louis XVIII of France. He had a dual mission to fulfil in Paris. Its nature was decidedly reactionary: first, to establish good relations with the restored Bourbon regime and, second, to open negotiations with the allied powers for the return of church territories throughout Europe.[57] His instructions warned of the diplomatic perils and snares that awaited him. The key question was this: would the allies recognise the treaty of Tolentino as valid and, in consequence, cede the Legations of Ferrara, Bologna and Ravenna to the Habsburg emperor?

Antonio Aldini, a native of Bologna and formerly Napoleon's secretary of state for the Kingdom of Italy, was lobbying the allied monarchs not to return these territories to papal rule.[58] Della Genga was told that it was imperative that no formal negotiations be opened with Murat, who was ruling over much of central Italy. The church feared his expansionist aims, and declared that his occupation was illegitimate. Equally important was that Louis XVIII be asked to return the Vatican Archives to Rome as soon as possible; these still languished in the now defunct Imperial Archives in Paris.[59] There was also irritation that the Charter of 1814 (the new constitution of France), granted by Louis to his subjects, enshrined liberty of the press and freedom of conscience. Della Genga was instructed to protest against this, and to see if the church could be returned to its privileged *ancien régime* pre-eminence.

Four days after the departure of della Genga, Consalvi arrived from Béziers. He was most upset with the reactionary line taken in the papal instructions given to the extraordinary nuncio to Paris.[60] After discussions with Pius, Consalvi was reappointed secretary of state and given fresh instructions: he was to intercept della Genga and replace him. During Consalvi's mission abroad, Pacca was to act as pro-secretary of state and maintain diplomatic relations with Europe's powers. For Consalvi, the priority was to rescue and improve the Concordat of 1801.[61] He was to negotiate with Louis XVIII and explore if those anticlerical laws present in the organic articles might be repealed. Furthermore, it was expected that Consalvi would track down the last surviving *ancien régime* bishops who had refused to resign their dioceses between 1801 and 1803. He was to put pressure on them to accept the pope's exhortation to relinquish their sees: Pius wanted to end the schism with the Petite Église, which had refused to accept the provisions of the Concordat.[62] Consalvi felt that the full implementation of the 1801 Concordat was the only means of restoring religious peace to France. It was hoped that Louis XVIII could make this compromise work in a way that Napoleon had failed to do. The restitution of Avignon and the Papal Legations was of secondary importance to these spiritual negotiations.

Consalvi was authorised to visit both London and Vienna or wherever the allies might hold a peace conference. As the scholar Roberto Regoli notes, della Genga wanted to turn the clock back to before 1789, while Consalvi wished to make the Concordat, which he had negotiated in good faith in July 1801, work efficiently. Two opposing and antithetical world views were exposed in these divergent set of diplomatic instructions.[63] Consalvi, from 1814 to 1823, was to be one of the few moderate and progressive voices within the Roman Curia. For the cardinal, compromise with modernity was legitimate. Della Genga's condemnation of the liberty of press and freedom of conscience was not taken forward. These issues had already been resolved in 1801. For Consalvi, his mission to Paris was to reboot the Concordat, not to abrogate it. The following year would mark the most crucial moment in his diplomatic career.

At the same time, it was imperative for Pius to regain control of his capital. From Rome he could raise a formal protest against Murat's occupation of his principality. Having departed Cesena, the pope stopped on his way southwards in Ancona and then headed to the shrine of the miraculous Madonna of Loreto, where he gave thanks for his deliverance.[64] Outside Rome he stopped in Villa Giustiniani.[65] Here he received greetings from two monarchs Napoleon had deposed. Charles IV of Spain and Maria Luisa of Bourbon, former queen of Etruria, embraced the pope warmly: Pius received their wishes with benevolence, and they exchanged tales of their woes. The Habsburg diplomat Ludwig von Lebzeltern was also at Villa Giustiniani, having joined the papal entourage a few weeks previously (Francis I had appointed him as his extraordinary minister to the papal court); he had not seen the pope since his unsuccessful mission in Savona in 1810.[66] This stopover 5 miles outside Rome must have seemed like the famous scene from Proust's *Time Regained*. The pope met an extraordinary cast of characters who had played leading roles in the drama that had pitted the French Empire against the Papacy. Meeting these notables must all at once have released an explosion of unpleasant memories for the ageing pontiff. From Pius's perspective, his return to Rome was a direct manifestation of divine providence. After putting him to the test, God was now reinstating him to his capital.

On 27 May 1814 the papal cortège approached the Milvian Bridge and Chiaramonti finally caught sight of his beloved eternal city. As noted in Chapter 5 (p. 151), this had been the site of Constantine's conversion to Christianity, and had been where the French invasion of Rome began in February 1808.[67] Now, the pope was to regain control of his kingdom at the very spot where he had lost it six years previously. Growing crowds hailed the convoy as it passed, a demonstration of the great enthusiasm felt by many for the pope's imminent return. For over fifty months Pius had not seen Rome. His joy and excitement were uncontainable. He changed into his full pontifical robes and entered a ceremonial golden state carriage, which had been restored for the occasion. Cardinal Pacca, who had spent most of these years in the formidable fortress of Fenestrelle, rode next to him. Instrumental in the restoration of Pius in 1814, he had not forgotten the humiliations and privations to which he had been subjected. As the papal carriage entered the city, a large group of men unlimbered its horses. These seventy-two youths, from some of the most important families of Rome, proceeded to pull the coach with their bare hands as a sign of their joy and submission to the pope.

The first stop was Saint Peter's Basilica where the jubilation would reach its zenith. In the mother church of the Catholic world the pope knelt in adoration before the Blessed Sacrament and gave thanks for his deliverance from his long ordeal. At the foot of the *scala regia* he was met by King Victor Emmanuel I of Sardinia, who prostrated himself and kissed the pope's slippers.[68] The Savoy dynasty had been forced to leave Piedmont in 1798; Victor Emmanuel was to preside over one of the most reactionary restorations in Europe.[69] He was considered one of the most loyal sovereigns and collaborators of the Papacy. Reviving Catholicism was one of his foremost priorities; in his territories all Napoleonic reforms were wiped clean, and, as in the Papal States, the Jews were returned to Turin's Ghetto.[70] He was to be an important character in the story of Pius's restoration over the coming months. Taking his leave of the Sardinian king, Pius VII appeared in Saint Peter's Square wearing the papal tiara and was carried on the *sedia gestatoria* to the enthusiastic acclamation of the Roman citizenry. This was the true moment of glory for the pope, and probably the high point of his eventful pontificate. He had prevailed over his enemies, and had regained control over his principality. Movingly, Pius next visited the crypt of the basilica, where he knelt in silent prayer before the tomb of Saint Peter.

Then began the final and most poignant part of the journey. His carriage was dragged up the Quirinal hill to the very palace from which General Radet had kidnapped him on that fateful night of 5–6 July 1809. According to eye-witness accounts, Pius shed tears of joy on entering the courtyard of his residence. During these years imperial architects had been busy at work in transforming the monastery-palace of the popes into a sumptuous neoclassical residence for the second city of the French Empire.[71] The new frescos that decorated the ceilings were decidedly pagan in design, and some of the Roman deities represented on the ceiling bore an unnerving resemblance to Napoleon. Walls had been knocked down, ceremonial galleries created, and a study built in the former music room, which had a commanding view of the eternal city. From there Bonaparte had expected to cast his gaze over the city of the Caesars which he had conquered. It is strange to contemplate that the man who had interfered so grossly in the life of

Rome and the church would never set foot in the eternal city. Even now that he was vanquished, his presence, and the legacy of his policies, haunted Pius's return.

Although the tone was one of jubilation and celebration, the immediate actions of the pope were not, as it might have been expected, to issue a general amnesty and seek to forget past misdeeds. Quite the reverse was the case: although violent retribution was avoided, traitors were sought out in order that they might be punished. On 24 May 1814, three days before his triumphal entry into his capital, Pius had commanded Cardinal Pacca to create a special commission of inquiry. It was given the wordy title of the 'Special congregation charged with the general investigation into all disorders that occurred in the recent and very painful events with special reference to clergymen, be they secular, or regular, both in Rome and within the Papal States in order to advise His Holiness on appropriate actions to be undertaken'. Generally known as the *Congregazione dei disordini* ('Congregation for Disorders'), it was made up of five cardinals, a theologian and Archbishop Bertazzoli, and would probe those who had collaborated with the French during the occupation of Rome.[72] The congregation held twenty-one sittings from June 1814 to January 1816, with its investigations also extending into the dioceses of Florence and the patriarchate of Venice. The French imperial authorities had evacuated Rome very precipitously: in so doing they left behind a trail of detailed records. The congregation knew exactly who had paid taxes to the French, accepted public office, and facilitated the imperial government. Furthermore, there were papers relating to the five bishops and 2,000 priests who had, despite a papal injunction, directly collaborated with the French. Any priests who had celebrated Mass, sung *Te Deums* for Napoleonic victories, or feasted on Saint Napoleon's feast day, had to justify their conduct in writing to this commission of inquiry.[73]

On 5 July 1814, the Congregation for Disorders issued a printed set of instructions to the civil and criminal authorities of the Papal States, listing ten typologies of ecclesiastical collaboration.[74] These were recorded in descending order of gravity, and recommendations were made for chastisement commensurate with the offence. They make for decidedly odd reading to modern eyes. The 'intent' by the collaborator, and the extent of coercion faced, were the key issues under investigation. Those who had interacted with the French under the threat of overwhelming force or violence were judged much less guilty than those who had collaborated with ideological commitment to the Empire's modernising agenda. Measuring intent is very difficult: one needs to penetrate the psychology and mindset of the accused. The congregation operated more as father-confessors than as prosecutors in their investigation. They wanted to save the souls of Napoleonic collaborators from the torments of eternal damnation. Those guilty of collaboration could purge their sins by a full confession of their grievous misdeeds. Indeed, in all cases the clergy involved had to print full retractions of their oaths of allegiance to the French government and had to publicly (not to mention humiliatingly) admit their past disloyalty to the pope.[75] In more serious cases priests would be deposed from their parishes and offices.

The extent to which some top-tier elites had collaborated was embarrassing. The chief librarian of the Vatican was deeply implicated with the French authorities.[76] So too were most of the faculty and professors of La Sapienza University.[77] Even some seminaries had compromised themselves by teaching the Four Gallican Articles.[78] There was also the instance of a disloyal papal master of ceremonies, who had enthusiastically guided the French through the apartments of the Quirinal Palace days after the pope had been kidnapped.[79] Although an exact number is difficult to ascertain, it is likely that around 2,000 individuals appeared before the Congregation. Its findings into collaboration with the Napoleonic authorities in Rome still await a full and scholarly analysis by historians. Pius was determined to mete out exemplary punishment to those who had collaborated with the French Empire; this was especially the case with Cardinal Maury, who was in Paris when the Empire collapsed. His appointment as archbishop of the French capital had never been confirmed by the pope, and so was now null and void.

On 12 May 1814, Maury published a rather pathetic pamphlet, in which he tried to justify his conduct.[80] He appealed to Gallican principles and claimed he was unaware of the papal brief condemning his appointment to the archdiocese of Paris. Several prelates immediately refuted these lies. The Abbé Astros had now been released from the fortress of Vincennes after four years of imprisonment. As the cardinal's former vicar-general, he knew only too well that Maury was lying, and demolished his argument in print.[81] The Bourbons also bore a grudge against Maury: he had abandoned their cause for Bonaparte. He was ordered to leave the kingdom in all haste and return to his diocese of Montefiascone in Lazio. Unbeknownst to Maury, Pius had already suspended him from all ecclesiastical functions. Wishing to face the music directly, the cardinal decided to head for Rome, where he arrived on 19 June.[82]

Here he received a withering note from Cardinal Pacca, curtly telling him that he was forbidden from visiting the Quirinal and from attending any papal solemnity. A year later, during the Hundred Days, he was arrested and confined in Castel Sant'Angelo, the citadel of Rome. A special commission was set up to try the traitorous cardinal.[83] When he requested that his confinement be relaxed, Pius refused, but consented to Maury being allowed a few inches of tepid bathwater to help with his arthritis.[84] The cardinal was persuaded, eventually, to resign his diocese, and spent the rest of his days in isolation in a convent near the Quirinal.[85] He was the most high-profile Napoleonic collaborator of the period to be punished.

Consalvi reached Paris during the summer of 1814. His initial talks were far more difficult than anticipated. The restored French royal court was under the influence of several *ancien régime* bishops who had refused to resign in 1801: their loyalty to the Bourbons was unwavering, and they felt bitter towards those who had adhered to the Napoleonic settlement. They wanted to abrogate the Concordat and restore the old Gallican Church.[86] Especially important in this faction was Alexandre Angélique de Talleyrand-Périgord, the titular archbishop of Reims, and uncle to Napoleon's former foreign minister. Unlike his nephew Charles Maurice, he had remained loyal to Louis XVIII and encouraged the Petite Église to resist the Concordat.[87] It was also his plan to crown the newly restored king at Reims in June 1815 (a privilege jealously guarded by the archbishops of that city since the early Middle Ages). Consalvi made it clear that the Holy See might be willing to modify the boundaries of dioceses and even reappoint *ancien régime* bishops to any vacancies, but that the validity of the agreement made in 1801 was beyond dispute.[88]

The Petite Église's hope that the pope might repudiate the agreement he had entered into with the first consul a decade earlier was unrealistic. The supreme pontiff had every right to exhort bishops to resign: if they refused, he could deprive them of their dioceses. Little by little, the restored Bourbons were forced to concede that there was little hope of abrogating the Concordat (they would eventually try and fail to negotiate a new Concordat in 1817). During this time, the allies concluded a peace treaty with France on 30 May 1814. The first treaty of Paris was generous. Its terms allowed the French to return to the frontiers of 1792, and some Caribbean colonies were restored.[89] Disappointingly for the church, the former papal enclaves of Avignon and the Comtat Venaissin remained French. There was no provision made to compensate the pope for their loss. To make matters worse, the Louvre and other museums were to retain all the art and treasures looted by Napoleon's armies in Italy.[90] Consalvi protested against the agreement and refused to underwrite it.

Article 32 of the treaty specifically mentioned that the fate of the rest of Europe would be decided in the coming months at a congress to be held at Vienna.[91] In the meantime, the tsar, the king of Prussia and the Austrian chancellor, Metternich, travelled to London to celebrate their victory against Napoleon with the prince regent, the future George IV. In light of this, Consalvi requested that the British ambassador in Paris issue him with a passport for the United Kingdom. It was imperative that the pope's emissary be present so that he could begin discussions on the restoration of all papal territory in central Italy. His journey to England would be extremely sensitive: before leaving Cesena, Consalvi had been instructed by the pope to lobby the British government on behalf of Catholics in the United Kingdom.[92] Ever since the reign of William and Mary penal laws had been in force, curtailing the civil rights of those British subjects loyal to the pope in Rome.[93] Attempts were made to improve the position of non-Anglicans in Britain: however, such efforts proved contentious.[94] In 1780 mass violence, resulting in over 500 deaths, had exploded during the Gordon Riots over the issue of Catholic relief in the United Kingdom.[95] Ever since this disturbing episode, politicians had had to tread carefully. Bills, brought before Parliament in 1805 and 1813, proposed extending full civil rights to Catholics in the United Kingdom.[96] In return it was expected that the British monarch would be given the right to veto Catholic episcopal candidates whose loyalty was suspect. This condition bitterly divided Catholic opinion in the British Isles.

Matters were further complicated by the fact that, from 1810 to 1814, Cardinal di Pietro had been unable to exercise his office as prefect of the congregation for the Propaganda Fide, the institution which oversaw all of the missionary activities of the Catholic Church. Its aim was to spread the Roman faith throughout the world and it possessed jurisdiction over the reconversion of Britain to Catholicism.[97] Giovanni-Battista Quarantotti, a secretary, administered this important congregation during di Pietro's exile in France.[98] In February 1814 Quarantotti had issued a complicated rescript concerning Britain. This stated that the British Parliament was entitled to issue punitive measures that would prevent Catholics from any subversive activities against the United Kingdom's government and the Anglican Church. Rome would accept such measures if they were accompanied by an amelioration in the condition of Catholics in England and

Ireland. The English press, somewhat acrobatically, interpreted this to mean that Rome would accept a veto by the British monarchy over Catholic episcopal appointments in the United Kingdom.[99] Irish Catholics were furious with this apparent concession, seeing it as an unwarranted intrusion into their faith. Doubts emerged as to whether Quarantotti had the authority to issue such a rescript, given that the pope had not yet been released from his captivity.[100]

It was in this fraught context that Consalvi's twenty-six-day mission to Britain took place. Consalvi decided to do his best, and let his naturally Anglophilic tendencies direct his behaviour. His tall slim frame, elegant facial features and Roman nose endeared him to the British public, and the cardinal was received in some of the most important houses and clubs in London society.[101] On 1 July he joined the diplomatic corps to be introduced to the prince regent by Foreign Secretary Lord Castlereagh at Carlton House. In his report to Cardinal Pacca he described how differently Anglican bishops dressed from Roman prelates, and was intrigued by a deputation from the House of Lords and House of Commons that had come to witness the audience. The prince regent opened with a few words of welcome. He stated that never was there 'a pope more saintly, heroic, great or courageous, nor could any man add greater lustre to the Roman Church than Pius VII had done'.[102] Consalvi reported that he was deeply moved by these words of admiration for the pope's bravery during his captivity. The cardinal replied to the prince regent, thanking Britain for her powerful support and key role in toppling Napoleon. Consalvi also begged the prince of Wales to support the restoration of the Papal States, with the prince regent responding that this was certainly an important objective of the allied powers: it would be something to be taken forward at the forthcoming peace congress.

More trivially, the cardinal spoke of the objects left to the prince regent by the will of Cardinal York, the last Jacobite pretender to the British throne, who had died in 1807.[103] The prince expressed glee at receiving these mementos and objects from the final heir of the Stuart dynasty. (Later, as George IV, he would pay a large portion of the subscription raised to fund a funerary monument dedicated to England's exiled Stuart kings. This tribute, sculpted by Antonio Canova, is still located inside Saint Peter's Basilica. It is a remarkable compliment paid by the Hanoverian dynasty to the Stuarts they had supplanted in 1714.)[104] During the audience, the prince regent could not contain his curiosity about more trivial matters. He expressed sartorial admiration for the cardinal's crimson robes, and in particular for his red silk stockings. The great British portraitist of the age, Sir Thomas Lawrence, was meanwhile impressed by Consalvi's noble and dignified features. Two years later, he travelled to Rome where he asked the cardinal and the pope to sit for him for two striking portraits that are an explosion of reds and crimsons. Today they hang in the Waterloo Gallery at Windsor Castle.[105] Appropriately, Consalvi's likeness hangs amongst the generals and statesmen who contributed to Napoleon's fall.

Consalvi's final days in London were spent with Foreign Secretary Castlereagh in more formal discussions. Having already agreed the issue with Metternich, the British government promised to support, in principle, the restoration of the Papal States. The key, and yet unknown, point on the agenda was the return of the Papal Legations, which had been surrendered in the treaty of Tolentino in 1797. Further uncertainty was added by the fact that Murat's Neapolitan troops occupied the Marche. Most European powers, especially Bourbon France, were very unhappy with Murat's continued reign in Naples, and it was hoped that developments would allow for his dethronement. For his part, Castlereagh requested that Consalvi support Britain's goal to abolish the slave trade. He exhorted the cardinal to assist him in putting pressure on the other powers at the forthcoming congress to achieve this humanitarian aim. Consalvi broadly agreed, and reiterated the Papacy's repeated condemnations of slavery during the early modern period, but quibbled that he was going to need formal instructions before making any commitment on this issue (subsequently Pacca wrote in official endorsement of Britain's abolitionist agenda).[106] Finally, the Quarantotti rescript was discussed at length. On this document, the cardinal was unable to comment officially, as there was no bill for Catholic emancipation or relief under consideration in Parliament. Consalvi, however, believed that the Holy See might allow new Catholic bishops in the United Kingdom to take an oath of allegiance to the British monarchy; after all, similar arrangements were in place in other European countries.

The meetings in London had been very amicable, and Consalvi had impressed all who had met him with his charm, moderation and gentle manners. However, very soon afterwards Pacca wrote from Rome stating that it was impossible for the Curia to accept that Catholic prelates swear loyalty to an Anglican monarch, shattering any détente with Protestant Britain.[107]

Equally, the Irish politician Daniel O'Connell and others in the Catholic Association, which campaigned for emancipation, accused Consalvi, with very little evidence, of having sold them out to the Protestant ascendancy.[108] They made cheap jibes about the fact that Consalvi, although a cardinal, had never been ordained a priest, in effect accusing him of being a scheming opportunist.[109]

Consalvi's mission to London achieved few results for the Catholic population of the British Isles; the struggle for civil emancipation would only finally be resolved in 1829.[110] However, Consalvi had secured Castlereagh as an ally at the Congress of Vienna. Throughout his absence from Rome, it was becoming clear that the cardinal and the Curia had distinctly different views of the world. The cardinal wanted to compromise, and create a healthy working relationship with the emerging post-Napoleonic international order; the Curia wished to resurrect as much of the ecclesiastical *ancien régime* as possible. The view from Rome was reactionary and unrealistic: many of the changes wrought by the Revolution and Napoleon were irreversible. Consalvi knew this, and he wanted to reconstruct the church so that it would be stronger and prepared to face the challenges of modernity.

Back in the eternal city, Cardinal Pacca during his tenure as pro-secretary of state was committed to extreme reactionary measures. He ordered that time in the Papal States be returned to the antiquated 'Italian-hour' or *ora boema* system of measuring time from the modern 'ultramontane hour' introduced by the French.[111] The Italian-hour system was complex: unlike in the French time-keeping system, which began every day at midnight, according to *ora boema* the new day began at dusk, and the hours were separated into half-hour segments measuring day and night hours. Given that sunsets occur at different times during the year, the beginning of each new day varied according to the season. To make matters worse, Pacca's Rome was the only European state to employ this archaic system.[112] The Papacy was now literally in a different time zone to the rest of Europe.

Other controversial policies soon emerged. Among the first acts that Pius VII promulgated on his return to Rome was to revive the Jesuit order: on 7 August 1814 he issued the bull *sollicitudo omnium ecclesiarum*, which resurrected Saint Ignatius of Loyola's Society of Jesus.[113] Clement XIV had been forced by the Catholic powers of Europe to abolish this controversial order in 1773 for a series of extremely complex theological, political and colonial reasons.[114] The Jesuits had fallen foul of the ongoing struggle between church and state. Their loyalty to the pope, their worldliness and their near monopoly of secondary-school education allowed them to be depicted as the stormtroopers of a theocratic order.[115] And, with government during the eighteenth century increasingly deemed to be the business of secular authorities, the Jesuits fell victim to a campaign to curb the church's temporal power.[116] Napoleon had always had a revulsion against the Jesuits and had persecuted congregations inspired by the spiritual exercises of Saint Ignatius of Loyola.[117]

Despite all this, pockets of Jesuit communities had survived in Russia and Sicily.[118] From these small numbers, the Society of Jesus would experience a remarkable regeneration during the nineteenth century.[119] The re-establishment of the Jesuits was something of a public relations disaster for the church. It gave the appearance that the pope and the Curia were viciously reactionary. Conspiracy theories would abound in France and Italy of secret Jesuit cabals and plots aimed at plunging the world into obscurantism and clerical reaction.[120] These were of course untrue, and exaggerated the power of the Jesuits, who, after fifty-one years of proscription, were barely able to make ends meet. The message that came from the Curia during the first months of the restoration seemed reactionary and anti-liberal. Indeed, the re-establishment of the Holy Inquisition in Spain and Rome struck contemporaries as deeply disturbing.[121] It was certainly a sign that, after Napoleon's attempt to remove all ecclesiastical interference from the political realm, the Catholic Church was reasserting its authority with confidence. In doing so it confirmed the worst fears of liberals and progressives.

As Consalvi made his way to Vienna, the Catholic Church seemed to be developing a personality disorder. Several theologians and officials who had suffered under the French occupation were now developing policies that ran counter to the negotiations undertaken in Paris and London. The black and red cardinals heartily resented each other, and were often reduced to factional in-fighting.[122] With this unhelpful situation prevailing at home, Consalvi realised he faced very delicate negotiations for the restoration of the Papal States in central Italy. Up to now, he had received expressions of sympathy from the English, French, Russian and Habsburg governments, but little else: no undertaking for the return of the Legations or the Marche had been formalised. Indeed, there was no commitment whatever from Murat to surrender the enclaves of Benevento and Pontecorvo, in Campania, back to papal control. There was a real danger of Consalvi going into the congress with nothing and leaving with the same.

As the Italian historian Adolfo Omodeo argued decades ago, the cardinal secretary of state had a consistent and clear-sighted approach to diplomacy.[123] He believed that the Papal States needed to relinquish any medieval hankerings for supremacy over the great powers of Europe. Pontiffs, meanwhile, should avoid at all costs acting as mediators in the disputes that pitted the states of Europe against one another: indeed, becoming embroiled in the temporal struggles of princes had often damaged the spiritual mission of Catholicism in the medieval and early modern period. Consalvi had a very modern appreciation of neutrality, which he believed would be the church's sole means of survival in a world of rapacious great powers. He had tried to persuade Napoleon to accept the Holy See's neutrality in 1806 but his attempt had failed spectacularly (see above, p. 143).[124] After 1814, neutrality could only endure if it was guaranteed by the great powers.[125] In the long run, the volatile geopolitical context in Italy proved unfavourable. The Papal States were located, unhelpfully, right in the middle of the peninsula.

Their alliance with Murat gave rise to suspicions that the Habsburgs wanted to create an anti-French coalition within the peninsula. For his part, Louis XVIII was determined to use all his influence to see his cousin, King Ferdinand IV, restored to his Neapolitan domains. The Holy See was caught in the middle of two competing powers whose respect for its neutrality was now wavering. On 2 September 1814, Consalvi reached the Habsburg capital. Six days later he had a preliminary two-hour meeting with Metternich.[126] The Austrian chancellor frankly informed Consalvi that, given Italy's unstable situation, the fate of the Legations was not settled. They were being used as a bargaining chip between Murat and the Bourbons of Naples. In order to secure peace and stability in Italy, the church would need to be flexible. Consalvi was urged to say nothing about Avignon, nor, for the time being, make any specific demands. The only good news that Metternich let slip was that it was now his policy to transfer Napoleon from Elba to a 'safer' location.[127]

On 11 September, the pope's extraordinary envoy had an audience with the Emperor Francis I of Austria.[128] It was a stormy meeting, in which the monarch did not conceal his irritation with the pope, who some weeks before had sent a bishop to administer the vacant patriarchate of Venice without consulting the Habsburg authorities who now militarily occupied the city. Francis felt that this was a violation of his regal prerogatives, and an unwarranted extension of papal authority into his domains. When it came to the Legations, he stated that the pope should not pin too many hopes on their return.[129] He would not annex them to his Italian domains, but the northern bank of the Po river would remain under Austrian control. Consalvi gloomily noted that this implied that at least one third of Ferrara's territory would be annexed to Austria.[130] There was also some disheartening talk of the former French empress, Marie-Louise, being given the government of the Legations instead of Parma.[131]

The tensest moment in the audience was reached when the emperor complained that the episcopal nominations process was too slow: his candidates could only assume the administration of their dioceses once bulls of confirmation had come back from Rome, a lengthy process. Francis seemed to transmute into Napoleon when he angrily protested that this was antiquated and unnecessary.[132] Consalvi left the audience dejected and fearful that a new investiture crisis might be brewing with the Habsburg monarchy over appointments to vacant dioceses. To his surprise, Francis had also leapt to the defence of Cardinal Maury and other bishops appointed by Napoleon during the pope's captivity: the Habsburg emperor believed that the church's persecution of bishops who had collaborated with the French went against the spirit of the age and that Pius was stirring up trouble.[133] The irritation and antagonism of the emperor are difficult to explain. Francis was a lugubrious individual, and not disposed to cheerfulness. The validity of his daughter's marriage to Napoleon was highly controversial within the church, and this irritated him, especially as, from his perspective, the death of the former empress Joséphine de Beauharnais on 29 May 1814 had settled the issue once and for all.[134] One suspects that the Habsburgs, as the senior Catholic dynasty in Europe, viewed the Papacy as a client state. Papal neutrality would pose dilemmas when it came to Austria's aspirations for hegemony in Italy.[135]

Further difficulties soon emerged: the duke of Campochiaro, Murat's minister in Vienna, now tried to sow discord among the allies. He offered a return of the Legations on the proviso that the pope recognised his master as the legitimate king of Naples.[136] Given the instability of the situation, Consalvi thought it best not to commit to this step. Pacca reported from Rome that it was known that Murat had ambitions over Italy. There had been Neapolitan contacts with Napoleon on Elba, but for what purpose it was unclear.[137] To complicate matters futher, the French Bourbons had chosen Talleyrand, Napoleon's former foreign secretary, now prince of Benevento, as their representative at the congress. This apostate and married bishop remained a deep embarrassment for the church. Furthermore, he technically retained sovereignty over the papal enclave of Benevento, which Napoleon had annexed and gifted to him in 1806.[138] As ever, Talleyrand played a complex game. Campochiaro had promised he could retain full rights over Benevento if he could persuade the pope to recognise Murat; this went against Talleyrand's instructions from Louis XVIII, which were to seek the return of his Bourbon cousins to the throne of Naples.[139]

Talleyrand's venality deeply scandalised Consalvi and confirmed his prejudices. The prince hinted to the cardinal that if he were compensated richly for the loss of Benevento he would use his influence for the restoration of the Marche, the Legations and the papal enclaves of Campania. His price, though, would be in the millions of francs.[140] Unhelpfully, Talleyrand had the annoying habit of asking probing, not to mention embarrassing, questions. For example: what was Consalvi's official status? Was he authorised to endorse and underwrite any agreements reached at the congress? Would he be invited to join the powerful committee of eight, which included all the great powers? Essentially, what did his title of extraordinary envoy mean? These were all questions that Consalvi had hoped not to be asked, as he had no wish to provide answers.[141] They proved a decided irritant for the pope's chief negotiator.

Consalvi's commitment to neutrality aimed to prevent the Holy See from being dragged into negotiations as a potential guarantor for any treaty. He did not want the church to become an international arbiter or mediator in future disputes.[142] It was not his intention to sign any document, or compromise the pope, by entering into a system of alliances. Although this was consistent with Consalvi's vision of international relations, it may have been a mistake. An international agreement recognising papal neutrality would have been extremely beneficial for Pius VII. Agreements like this would, eventually, emerge throughout the nineteenth century in relation to Belgium, Holland, Switzerland and Sweden.[143] The neutralisation of minor states, recognised by the great powers, was one of the hallmarks of international stability after 1814.

Realising that the situation was in flux, and that nothing was certain, through October and November Consalvi embarked on a renewed campaign to win over the allies' hearts and minds. He had established a relationship of mutual respect with the British foreign secretary, Castlereagh, in London, and dined with him regularly. Equally, he was well treated by the Prussian delegation. The volatile and religiously zealous Tsar Alexander I was impressed with the cardinal, and negotiations began for a potential Romanov visit to Rome.[144] The latter months of 1814 were essentially exercises in cultural diplomacy, in order to garner goodwill, with Consalvi attending the festivities and entertainments of the Habsburg capital to lobby for the restoration of the Papal States. The man he successfully stopped in his tracks was Count Antonio Aldini, Napoleon's former Italian minister, who had travelled to Vienna to lobby on behalf of the Legations. He was granted an audience with Metternich to beg that Ferrara, Ravenna and Bologna be annexed by the Austrian monarchy.[145] Aldini presented the chancellor with a draft constitution for these territories, but Consalvi, in private discussion with the Austrian chancellor, counteracted this move by promising that, if the Legations were returned to Pius, an amnesty would be agreed, and that former Napoleonic officials would not be purged from the administration.[146] This undertaking was eventually formalised in writing.

Meanwhile, on the island of Elba, Napoleon was settling into his new principality.[147] Although Elba lay only a few miles off the coast of Tuscany, it was part of the Corsican diocese of Ajaccio. Canon Giuseppe Arrighi was the vicar-general who administered the island on the bishop's behalf. His surprise must have been great when he became unofficial imperial chaplain in Bonaparte's miniature kingdom. Shortly after the emperor's arrival, he presided over a solemn *Te Deum* in the church of the Santissimo Sacramento in Portoferraio (the principality's insular capital). Ominously, Napoleon usurped the episcopal throne and dais by sitting on it during the ceremony; indeed, a letter in the Vatican Archives reveals that the church authorities were appalled by Arrighi's loyalty to Napoleon and the way in which he had rallied to the emperor without hesitation.[148]

Not all clergymen on the island were pliant court clerics. Don Assunto Bartolini, parish priest of Capolivieri, although outwardly subservient, was not pleased with the emperor's heavy hand. Although the Elbans had been given a constitution and an ambitious programme of public works had begun, they were taxed more heavily than ever before.[149] According to local legend, Bartolini encouraged his fellow citizens to engage in a tax strike. Napoleon threatened to arrest the priest and bombard Capolivieri, but was dissuaded from doing so by a mysterious woman. Although this story is apocryphal, Elban frustration over taxation was not: even during his exile Napoleon did manage to antagonise some of the clergy in his miniature kingdom.[150] Even here he viewed priests as potential fomenters of opposition, and kept them under surveillance. On the surface it appeared as if the emperor was taking a deep interest in the affairs of his new island kingdom. Domestically he appeared to be bedding down and settling into the lifestyle of a minor Italian prince. The British commissioner, Sir Neil Campbell, sent to keep an eye on Napoleon, felt so confident of the emperor's good intentions that he frequently absented himself from the island to enjoy the feminine delights to be found in Livorno.[151]

As Napoleon acclimatised to life on Elba, in Naples Murat saw in the new year in spectacular fashion. Caroline of Brunswick, the wife of the prince regent of the United Kingdom and technically the princess of Wales, was visiting the city. Although she had long been estranged from the prince regent it was decided to fête her as a heroine. A great masked ball was held at the Casino Reale di Chiatamone, the grand eighteenth-century lodge on the bay of Naples facing the medieval Castel dell'Ovo.[152] Wearing the costume of a Spanish grand lady, Caroline danced the night away with Murat and his entourage, who were disguised as British tars. The carefree and bacchanalian atmosphere belied the reality: the future of the kingdom was very uncertain.

In Vienna, after much disagreement about the future of Poland and Saxony, the allies were beginning to resume their unity of purpose. Consalvi's irritation with Talleyrand's interference in the affairs of the Holy See grew, especially as the French delegation had publicly derided the Papacy's refusal to ratify the first treaty of Paris and accept the loss of Avignon and the Comtat Venaissin.[153] On 11 February 1815, Consalvi wrote to Pacca that he had dined next to Metternich at a lavish dinner hosted by the duke of Wellington, who had now replaced Castlereagh as the British envoy to the congress.[154] During this banquet the chancellor talked at length about the Papal States' predicament. He promised that Austria would formally demand that Murat evacuate the Marche. Talleyrand insisted that the king of Naples be deposed. At the same time, he argued that the enclaves of Benevento and Pontecorvo in Campania should not be returned to the pope. A few days later, at another function, Talleyrand overreached himself by suggesting that, if the Legations were returned to the Papacy, then Consalvi would need formally to accept the loss of Avignon. The cardinal's reply was dry: 'I shall leave here naked as I arrived without the Legations, but I will not cede anything nor sign anything.' A surprised Talleyrand impertinently observed that 'when the cardinal gets angry, he is even more delightful [than usual]', then turned his back and left.[155]

The allied powers were growing to admire Consalvi's consistency. However, they were worried about the prospect of instability on the Italian peninsula. Murat was an erratic presence; he would be a source of volatility in future. On 25 February 1815, a top-secret despatch was sent to Pacca. In it, Consalvi informed him that Metternich had a message exclusively for the eyes of the pope: the coalition had decided that Murat's days were numbered, and his refusal to evacuate the Marche had sealed his fate.[156] Castlereagh had agreed to encourage Parliament to disavow the armistice with Naples: within three months hostilities would resume. Metternich believed that this would push Murat to attempt a military adventure in which he would appeal to the Italian people to rise up to gain their independence and unity. He would proclaim himself king, thus giving the allies a pretext to declare war.[157] As it happened, these complex diplomatic double dealings proved unnecessary.

On the evening of 26 February 1815 Napoleon embarked on a small flotilla of ships and departed Elba.[158] His destination was unknown, but the papal consuls in Livorno and Florence sent alarming reports that Naples must be his ultimate objective.[159] Five days later, Pacca ordered the authorities in Frosinone, Rieti, Terracina and Subiaco to stand on high alert. They were warned to brace themselves for an imminent Neapolitan invasion.[160] At the same time, Letizia and Pauline Bonaparte, having departed from Elba, landed in Castagneto in Maremma. They quickly headed towards Rome, where they were interviewed by the authorities. They confirmed that Napoleon was heading for France, not Naples. Their baggage was searched, but no compromising documents were found, apart from a list of the French emperor's underwear which he had packed for his return journey to France.[161]

Over the next few weeks conflicting reports emerged. It was the sort of climate in which rumours blossomed. In one report, Napoleon had been arrested by General Miollis, the former governor of Rome.[162] In another, Marshal André Masséna, a veteran of many campaigns, had ambushed and captured him.[163] Clearly, nobody was quite sure about the reality of the situation. On 19 March, after mass defections and mutinies within the French armies, Napoleon returned to the Tuileries Palace in triumph. The Bourbons were forced to flee and take refuge in Ghent.[164] Worryingly for the church, Napoleon's radical supporters chanted neo-Jacobin slogans. They wanted to hang priests from lampposts and punish the church. The allied powers in Vienna did not wait to learn the outcome of Napoleon's flight from Elba. On 13 March they had issued a joint declaration proclaiming 'Buonaparte' an outlaw and an enemy of humanity.

News of the so-called 'Flight of the Eagle' caused massive excitement in Naples.[165] Fearing, with some justification, that Austria would attack, Murat decided to launch a pre-emptive strike and seek a reconciliation with Napoleon. Austrian forces in Ancona began a withdrawal in the face of the Neapolitan offensive, and were forced to retreat behind the Rubicon. Near Cesena, the first shots were fired in this Austro-Neapolitan conflict.[166] Further reinforcements were being hurried from Campania through the Marche. Murat himself travelled quickly to command these troops. Pacca, fearful of a Neapolitan invasion and occupation, informed Pius VII of the critical situation that was developing in central Italy.[167] He advised an immediate flight to Genoa, where the pope could place himself under the protection of the pious king of Sardinia Victor Emmanuel I. Reluctantly, Pius agreed: he had little wish to become a prisoner again. The government of Rome was entrusted to a *giunta* (junta) tasked with administrating the city, while Cardinal di Pietro would exercise the pope's spiritual authority in his absence.[168]

On 22 March, during Holy Week, Pius left the eternal city discreetly in a carriage and headed for Viterbo. He was soon joined by most of the College of Cardinals and the diplomatic corps accredited to the Holy See. (Cardinal Fesch, reappointed by his returning uncle as ambassador to the Holy See, was left behind: the church refused to recognise his position.)[169] Over the next few days, the flight accelerated along the Tuscan coast. From Livorno, the papal entourage headed for Sarzana, a town on the Ligurian border (and ironically the place where the Bonaparte clan had originated).[170] Here a difficult decision had to be made as to how to continue the journey: the roads ahead were mountainous and difficult. Fishermen at Lerici offered the pope their feluccas (wooden sailing boats) to transport him swiftly to Genoa. Cardinal Pacca was concerned, as he had heard that Barbary pirates had secret bases in the coves around Portofino.[171] He despaired of what might happen if these Muslim corsairs captured the Holy Father. Luckily for all, the journey by felucca was uneventful, the weather serene, and the papal entourage disembarked at Genoa on 3 April 1815, where he was greeted by the jubilant people of the city.[172]

In the meantime, Murat occupied Bologna: his troops soon entered Modena and its Habsburg-Este duke took flight. In Vienna, Ottavio Mormile, duke of Campochiaro, Murat's minister at the congress, delivered a formal protest to the allied ministers, in which Murat claimed he was the victim of an aggression and expressed his willingness to honour the Austrian alliance as long as his position in Naples was formally guaranteed.[173] His troops did not occupy Rome, and he wrote to the pope complaining that his flight had been unnecessary. Murat also stated, disingenuously, that he had no expansionist aims.[174] Very little was left for Pius to do in Genoa, except await military and diplomatic developments.

Curiously, he expressed the desire to return to Savona. He had promised the Virgin Mary that if he were ever freed from captivity he would return. It was his intention to travel to the sanctuary of the Nostra Signora della Misericordia in the valley of Saint Bernard, north of Savona (see Chapter 6, pp. 166–7).[175] In doing so, the pope was continuing the process of reconnecting with grassroots Catholicism. Sanctuaries dedicated to Marian piety and worship would become increasingly important during the nineteenth century, and the coming decades would witness a remarkable Catholic revival after decades of revolution.[176] On 8 May the pope reached Savona with his suite. The population gave him a hero's welcome with cheers, fanfares and floral wreaths, and he returned to the episcopal palace, where he had been held prisoner for nearly three years. Sudden cannon salvos announced the arrival of Victor Emmanuel I; Pius decided to take the brief walk to the cathedral square to greet the king in person. In the middle of the town square of Savona the king knelt before the pontiff.[177] The next day, an impressive cortège of royal carriages travelled the tortuous roads to the sanctuary of Nostra Signora della Misericordia. Here, Pius lifted a gold crown onto the head of the statue of the Madonna to the general jubilation of the crowds.

On the other side of the Alps, Napoleon was busy trying to restore his imperial regime. Very few bishops rallied to his colours after his return from Elba. Fallot was among the few prelates who presided over the *Champ de mai* ceremony, which saw the returning emperor, in full regalia, proclaiming a new liberal constitution, the *Acte additionel*. In reality, his return to power was the result of a military coup: Napoleon now presided over a deeply divided French nation. As Talleyrand once joked: 'You can do almost anything with bayonets apart from sit on them.'[178] It was not just a question of friends of the Revolution versus its enemies: the situation, in 1815, was much more complicated than this caricatured simplification allows. Between the supporters of the restored French Bourbons and the radical neo-Jacobins lay a moderate swathe of opinion whose ultimate loyalty remained uncertain.[179]

Ever since the Consulate, Napoleon had distrusted Jacobins and extreme republicans.[180] He was, however, forced to recall former Jacobins like Fouché and Lazare Carnot into his administration.[181] Although the emperor personally wanted to defuse the situation and avoid radical anticlericalism, there is some evidence that not all his supporters were of the same mind. The Vatican Archives contain letters from the clergy in the Lyonnais region complaining of arrests and intimidation after Napoleon's return.[182] There are also records in the National Archives in Paris relating to priests arrested or kept under surveillance between April and June 1815.[183] In Burgundy in particular, hot-headed Bonapartist mayors gleefully arrested parish priests whose loyalty to the Bourbons had been manifest in the preceding months (after Napoleon's fall in June the Bourbons had ordered an inquiry into priests inconvenienced during the Hundred Days so that they could be compensated for their loyalty).[184] Priests linked to the *Chevaliers de la Foi* and the anti-imperial resistance movement also fled France for England. Radical priests who in the future would assume importance, such as the Lamennais brothers, bided their time in London during Napoleon's return.[185] Regardless of his own conciliatory inclinations, the emperor continued to sow division in the religious landscape of France.[186] Indeed, he continued to write to Bigot about troublesome priests and even ordered that the bishop of Soissons resign for not attending the *Champ de mai* ceremony.[187]

The Bonapartist adventure did not take long to unravel. After a strategic retreat, on 2 May 1815 Murat met the Austrian forces of General Bianchi near the town of Tolentino (the very place where the Papal States had ceded the Legations to the French Republic in 1797). During the two-day battle the fate of Italy hung in the balance. The outcome was a catastrophic defeat for Murat.[188] On 12 May, in an act of extreme desperation, the king of Naples issued the Rimini Proclamation (falsely backdated to 30 March 1815). Its tone was stirring:

> Italians! The hour has come in which you must fulfil your destiny. Providence calls you finally to become an independent nation. From the Alps to the straits of Sicily only one cry can be heard: 'The independence of Italy!' . . . I call all the brave around me to fight. I call to me all those who have meditated deeply on the interests of their fatherland, to prepare and draw up a constitution and laws that will govern forever a happy Italy, an independent Italy.[189]

This text, despite its appeal to patriotism, elicited little response from the Italian population. No insurrection proved forthcoming, dooming the enterprise to complete failure.[190] Murat fled to Corsica disguised as a Danish sailor; he was eventually captured and executed by firing squad in October.[191] On 20 May, the Austrians and Neapolitans signed the treaty of Casalanza, an armistice which laid the fundamental groundwork for a Bourbon restoration in southern Italy.[192]

With the defeat of Murat, the biggest hurdle to the restoration of the Papal States had been overcome. In Vienna Consalvi wasted little time. The negotiations remained delicate, as the evacuation of papal territories by the occupying Austrian forces was slow. Pacca, from Genoa and Turin, sent panicked despatches to

Vienna, demanding the immediate return of all territories.[193] Away from Rome, the College of Cardinals was terrified that the allied powers might use their military victory at Tolentino as a springboard to expand into Italy at the expense of the Papal States. Consalvi, on 12 June, sent the despatch they had desired for so long.[194] The allied powers had confirmed, through the final act of the Congress of Vienna, that the Papacy would see the return of nearly all papal territory. The Legations, the Marche and even the enclaves in Campania would all be returned. Only Avignon, the Comtat Venaissin and the north bank of the Po near Ferrara were lost. The allies would return the Legations on condition of a general amnesty for all who had worked for the French; they also demanded that the pope establish an efficient administration, and that there would not be any purge of officials. Pacca very grudgingly accepted these conditions.[195] Talleyrand, to pour salt into the wound, received a king's ransom in compensation for Benevento. The Holy See and king of the Two Sicilies paid 1,200,000 francs to indemnify Talleyrand for a territory he had never legitimately possessed.[196] Furthermore, the Neapolitan exchequer was forced to transfer a further 120,000 francs for revenues that Murat had withheld from Talleyrand during 1814 and 1815. The former bishop of Autun was a remarkable political survivor.

Six days later the official consummation of the final act of Vienna was sealed. On 18 June 1815, on the bloody fields of Waterloo, the last hopes for a Napoleonic restoration crumbled to dust.[197] Decisively defeated, the emperor of the French abdicated for a second time and fled into exile, hoping to reach the United States.[198] His ability to trouble the Catholic Church, to inconvenience the pope, was now at an end. Rome would become the place of exile for his mother Letizia, sister Pauline, and Cardinal Fesch, who refused steadfastly to resign his archdiocese of Lyon.[199] Lucien Bonaparte, Napoleon's more rebellious brother, also moved to Rome, and was given the title of prince of Canino by Pius VII.[200] Napoleon's return from Elba left a heavy burden of bloodshed and war reparations on the French nation, with the second treaty of Paris returning France to her 1790 boundaries.[201] This time the art looted from Italy had to be returned. The famous sculptor Antonio Canova was sent to Paris to ensure that all paintings and statues were identified and packed appropriately in preparation for shipment.[202] The Vatican Archives were also finally returned to Rome at the expense of the French government. (Several boxes 'fell off the back of a cart' during the journey: today former parts of the Vatican Archives have found their way into the library of Trinity College Dublin and other libraries across the world. The files of the legation of Cardinal Caprara were never returned and remain in Paris to this day.[203] The Napoleonic Empire certainly did much damage to the Vatican Archives. Many gaps and disordered files have their origin in the Napoleonic period.)[204]

Pius now decided to make a leisurely return from Genoa. Just before reaching Rome the pope asked to stop at Radicofani.[205] Here, he and his entourage visited the room where he had been detained after his kidnapping from Rome on 6 July 1809. Pacca and Pius spent two hours in contemplation, reflecting on how much their fate had changed since those dark days. They were now returning once more to the Papal States in triumph. On 7 June 1815, after thanking the provisional *giunta* which had governed Rome during his absence, the pope returned to the Quirinal Palace. By the end of the month, Consalvi was back in his office as secretary of state. The scene was now set for the stand-off that would develop between the cardinal secretary's reforming tendencies and the Curia's steadfast refusal to countenance change. As the pontiff ailed, his ability and desire to accept reform waned. Regardless, June 1815 was the moment when the intertwined story of Napoleon and Pius VII came to an end. Their paths henceforth would diverge, and follow different routes.

# CONCLUSION
## THE EMPEROR'S GHOST

Saint Helena is a tropical island, no more than 50 square miles in size. Perched on the Mid-Atlantic Ridge dividing two tectonic plates, during the age of sail it was one of four volcanic isles that became vital entrepôts for military and commercial shipping in the South Atlantic. Discovered by the Portuguese in the sixteenth century, the island was named after Constantine the Great's mother, Helena Augusta, a leading light in the conversion of Rome to Christianity.[1] By the early nineteenth century it was governed by the British East India Company, and had a significant African slave population, and a growing influx of Chinese migrant workers. During the Napoleonic Wars it had become an important base for resupplying East Indiamen and the Royal Navy's operations against Spanish South America and the Dutch Cape Colony.[2]

Not even the greatest romantic author could have imagined that the man who had dominated European politics for nearly two decades would be imprisoned on this isolated rock.[3] This remarkable exile, after his failure to flee to America, added considerably to Napoleon's mystique, not to mention bestowing upon him an aura of martyrdom. This remote banishment of a ruler blamed for ten years of uninterrupted carnage, and now permitted to live out his final days in contemplation, remains without parallel. It must have seemed a fitting punishment for the emperor who had imprisoned the pope for almost five years. It was a strange coincidence that Pius and Napoleon both spent almost the same length of time in exile. Their fates, though, went in opposite directions. The pope was now enjoying a triumphant restoration, whereas Bonaparte was plagued by endless boredom. Subsequent admirers portrayed the stricken emperor as a fallen Prometheus on a desert island, persecuted for bringing light and knowledge to humanity. Apologists presented him as dignified in his ordeal, and resigned to his fate.[4] The truth is certainly more complex, and less edifying.[5] Those who followed their emperor on his final journey, and who would record his reminiscences, had mixed feelings about sharing in his exile. No one had a more extreme reaction than the wife of General Henri-Gatien Bertrand, who on hearing the news that their ship was heading for Saint Helena tried to jump out of a porthole in a clumsy suicide attempt.[6]

In some respects, the prison regime meted out to Napoleon was lax in comparison to the constant surveillance under which Pius had been kept in Savona and Fontainebleau. The commissioners sent by the allied powers to keep watch on the exiled emperor kept their distance, never meeting in person with their captive.[7] To escape the depressing reality of banishment, court etiquette was enforced rigidly at Longwood House, Napoleon's island home, as if it were the Tuileries Palace in Paris. The stiff formality of court ceremony was the only means of ensuring that the strain of enforced idleness did not overwhelm his followers.[8] It provided them with a routine and allowed these courtiers to maintain a respectful distance from the emperor.[9] The greatest similarity between Napoleon and Pius's exiles was that both were unable to communicate with the outside world.

It was the allies' firm resolution that Napoleon would never trouble the peace of Europe again. Unlike with his exile on Elba, this time they would be successful in their aim of isolating the emperor from his lost empire. The biggest vexation Napoleon faced was not British insults, nor material privations, but rather tedium, which proved an invincible enemy on Saint Helena.[10] During his reign, Napoleon had presided over dozens of battles, supervised countless reforms and written almost 40,000 letters. In his final years, his only escape was conversation in which he explored the memories of his remarkable reign. His loyal retinue tried their best to alleviate his *ennui* by creating a routine whereby the emperor could dictate his memoirs and relive his glorious past. Saint Helena was where Napoleon fashioned his legacy and told his version of history.[11] The brutality of imperial rule and the atrocity of war were softened by the team of 'spin doctors' who fashioned a Napoleonic cult on the island.[12]

Although the memoirs dictated directly by Napoleon focused on his Italian and Egyptian campaigns and the Hundred Days, his followers recorded other thoughts and recollections.[13] One aspect of his exile that has been neglected is that Napoleon did spend significant time reflecting on religion, and more specifically on Catholicism.[14] The interminable hours of boredom and his worsening health led to discussions about human nature. Did the body have a soul? Was there life after death? What was religion's role in society? There is debate as to whether Napoleon was an atheist, agnostic or deist.[15] In 1840 Robert-Augustin Antoine de Beauterne published a remarkable compilation entitled *Conversations religieuses de Napoléon* ('Religious Conversations of Napoleon').[16] It purported to collect, and reorder, all of the emperor's pronouncements on religion recorded during his exile on Saint Helena. A second edition was quickly published, just in time for the repatriation of Napoleon's ashes to France.[17] Beauterne was a fervent Catholic from an aristocratic family of great huntsmen. Indeed, legend had it that his most famous ancestor had killed the fabled Beast of Gévaudan, which had preyed on virgin shepherdesses in the mid-eighteenth century.[18] His own father had held the ceremonial title of imperial crossbowman. Peculiarly, Beauterne had set himself the acrobatic literary aim of reconciling the French Empire with Catholicism.

In this edition of conveniently reordered reminiscences, a highly religious emperor emerged, one who regularly attended Mass, believed in the efficacy of the sacraments and argued that Catholicism was superior to all other religions. It was almost as if Napoleon had become the leader of the great religious revival of the nineteenth century. In these pages Beauterne achieved what had seemed unimaginable: the Christianisation and almost the canonisation of Napoleon. Perhaps even more stupefying was the revelation of the emperor's secret admiration for the early Papacy and its ability to convert the Roman Empire. It was clear to many that this astounding portrayal had been accomplished through some questionable editorial practices. Not only was Beauterne highly selective in his quotations, but he possessed a disturbing tendency to improve on the emperor's words and draw conclusions that nobody else, even those present on Saint Helena, had dared to make.[19] An appendix containing letters between Beauterne, Cardinal Fesch and the survivors of the exile on Saint Helena added a veneer of credibility to his work. It is true that Napoleon had retained a mild sense of religiosity throughout his life, but this was deeply compromised by his enlightened education and innate scepticism. To portray him as a romantic Catholic with a fervent admiration for Jesus Christ was to stretch reality to breaking point. Regardless, Beauterne's book went into multiple editions and was something of a publishing sensation in the nineteenth century.

The reality was far more nuanced than these cuttings and pastings allowed. The problem was that those who shared Napoleon's exile depicted his attitude to religion in conflicting ways in their many published accounts of their time on Saint Helena.[20] The grand marshal of the palace, General Bertrand, and General Gaspard Gourgaud, the emperor's last aide-de-camp, portrayed an agnostic and cynical Napoleon when it came to religious faith. As revolutionary soldiers brought up on decades of revolutionary propaganda, they had little time for God.[21] Unsurprisingly, they made their master share their disdain for spirituality in their description of his last years of exile. The imperial chamberlains Emmanuel de Las Cases and Charles Tristan de Montholon meanwhile gave a much more complex representation of religious debate at Longwood House, depicting Napoleon as displaying great admiration for Christianity and the power of religion over human society: Christianity was particularly admirable in its ability to codify ethics and maintain public order. Perhaps more unpredictably, Bonaparte expressed deep admiration for Muhammad's creation of not just a global faith, but a new political order in the Middle East. Certainly, common to all the narratives is Napoleon's obsession with religion's ability to structure society, establish laws, public order and bestow political legitimacy. In some accounts he praised Christianity, and in particular Catholicism, as the most effective religion in the world, but accounts do not agree on this aspect of his conversations.

There was some surprise when Napoleon expressed a belief in the afterlife. Yet his was not a Catholic understanding of the final judgement.[22] There was little discussion of sin, redemption and salvation. Rather, for the emperor, how people were to remember him would represent his immortality. He would live on in his reforms, administrative system and law codes. The survival of his soul struck him as possible, but did not trouble him unduly.

Back in Europe, the monarchs he had fought for over a decade troubled themselves little about their captive. Unexpectedly, Pius VII was the exception, and took some interest in the fate of his former tormentor. In response to the pleas of Letizia Bonaparte and Cardinal Fesch that their son and nephew's suffering should be eased, he wrote to the prince regent requesting that the conditions of Napoleon's exile on Saint Helena be alleviated. Since 1815 Letizia had become obsessed with her son's exile, and this was taking its toll on her mental health. She had been in touch with a mystic, apparently in the pay of the Habsburgs, who had temporarily convinced her that her son had ascended into heaven like Jesus and the Virgin Mary.[23] Cardinal Fesch decided to allow her flight into fantasy and not to disabuse her of this absurd belief. He knew that it provided an escape from the pain of reality. As already noted, when it came to the Bonapartes in his realm Pius showed himself magnanimous. He pleaded in favour of the very man who had persecuted him unremittingly for five years.

In September 1819 the pope's intercession bore some fruit in the form of three new arrivals to Saint Helena, Corsicans all, who had been selected by Letizia and Fesch to join the imperial entourage. Dr Francesco Antonmarchi was to minister to Napoleon's failing health. Towards the end of the exiled emperor's life, in a codicil to his last will and testament, the good doctor was left '20 francs to buy a rope to hang himself with' – hardly a sign of gratitude, let alone of satisfaction at the medical care he had received.[24] The other two arrivals were priests who were well-known to Napoleon's mother. The abbés Angelo Vignali and Antonio Buonavita were to care for the emperor's soul. Some historians have dismissed these clergymen, perhaps a little hastily, as non-entities.[25] It is true that, after many years as a missionary in South America, and recently having suffered a stroke, Buonavita was hardly an ideal choice. However, he had served in the imperial chapel on Elba, and was known to the emperor. The person of Angelo Vignali is much more difficult to decipher, as he has left so few traces in history. In most images depicting Napoleon's deathbed he is portrayed with his back turned: as no artist ever met him, one assumes they had nothing to draw upon in order to paint his face. The chamberlain Montholon described him as having savage features, but this description is hardly helpful.

With the arrival of these priests the celebration of Mass did become a regular activity of the exiled court of Saint Helena from 1819 to 1821. This practice mirrored the rhythms of the court of the Tuileries, where Sunday High Mass was part of court ceremony.[26] It is beyond dispute that Vignali became the imperial chaplain on Saint Helena, a role for which he was not entirely prepared. These final two years coincided with a rapid worsening of Napoleon's health. The stomach cancer which probably killed his father, and which would ravage his Bonaparte siblings, relentlessly took hold of the exiled emperor. On 21 April 1821 Napoleon asked Vignali to prepare an altar in a room next to his bedroom, to expose the Blessed Sacrament and say daily masses. Knowing he was close to the end, he instructed Vignali to intone the prayers for the dying. Eight days later he summoned his chaplain in the dead of night and asked to be alone with him for several hours. The memoirs of those present differ in terms of times and dates, but all agree that, as Napoleon reached his end, he spent significant time with his chaplain.[27] Although there were no direct witnesses, it is highly likely that Napoleon gave a deathbed confession to Vignali. If this was indeed the case, reconciling one of Catholicism's greatest enemies with the church must have been daunting. As the sacrament of confession is an absolute secret, no one will ever know the contents of Napoleon's final confession, and whether specifically he regretted his treatment of Pius VII. According to the scholar Marie Courtemanche, the Abbé Vignali kept a journal while on Saint Helena.[28] This precious document alas has been lost or deliberately destroyed. It alone could have shed light on Napoleon's dying thoughts and state of mind. On 3 May, Vignali was summoned to administer the last rites; Napoleon, due to the terminal cancer that was ravaging his body, was apparently unable to receive communion. At 5.45 p.m. on 5 May 1821 Napoleon gave a long sigh and left the world of the living.[29] He was buried in the Valley of the Willows on Saint Helena, where he remained until his body was exhumed in 1840 and brought back to France in triumph for solemn reburial in the chapel of the Invalides in Paris.[30]

News of Napoleon's death took almost two months to reach Europe. It elicited curiosity, rather than controversy, when it appeared in the newspapers.[31] His former foreign minister, Talleyrand, dismissively exclaimed: 'It is no longer an event, it's just a bit of news.'[32] On the other hand, romantics and poets wrote odes to the deceased emperor and kept his memory alive.[33] Further south, in the eternal city, Pius betrayed little emotion when Consalvi informed him of the death of his former captor. He ordered that no public events or demonstrations be permitted in Rome to mark the deposed emperor's death. The only exception made was for the votive masses offered in his memory by Letizia Bonaparte and Cardinal Fesch. Secretly, the pope closed his doors for three days and personally celebrated Mass in the chapel of the Quirinal, in memory of the man who had signed the Concordat of 1801.[34] On this occasion, the pope wanted to be a model of forgiveness and magnanimity. In death only the virtues of Bonaparte were remembered, and not his persecution of the church.

By 1821, Pius knew his own time on earth was drawing to a close. Four years previously, while staying at his summer palace in Castel Gandolfo, overlooking Lake Albano, the pope had asked not to be disturbed during some quiet meditation. When getting out of bed, he had collapsed, spending several hours on the ground before his servants heard his faint cries for help.[35] Pius was now very frail: this unexplained illness left him bedridden for six weeks. The situation was so grave that discreet preparations for a conclave began. Louis XVIII in Paris requested a list of all cardinals who would participate in any forthcoming conclave. Pius, however, confounded all by making an astonishing recovery. Yet, it was clear that he was no longer quite himself: he now needed assistance in walking from one room to another. From here on he would increasingly delegate administrative and temporal matters to his most trusted cardinals.[36] On 6 July 1823, exactly the fourteenth anniversary of his kidnapping by Radet, Chiaramonti slipped in his study and broke his thigh.[37] This time there was little hope that he would make a full recovery from his injury. Exactly a week later the basilica of Saint Paul outside the Walls caught fire and was severely damaged.[38] The destruction not only of one of Rome's most important churches, but also the shrine that contained the relics of the apostle Paul, was considered a bad omen. On 19 August Pius drifted in and out of consciousness; he apparently murmured the words 'Savona' and 'Fontainebleau' several times. The next day, at five in the morning, Pius VII died, thus ending a long pontificate of twenty-three years and five months.[39] Initially he was buried in the Vatican crypt while the College of Cardinals commissioned the great Danish sculptor Bertel Thorvaldsen to prepare a funerary monument for him. This was constructed inside Saint Peter's Basilica and completed in 1831.[40] His remains were translated to this marble extravaganza and remain there to this day.

Pius VII had been elected at the nadir of Catholicism's fortunes, and had struggled to govern the church entrusted to his stewardship. During his five years as Napoleon's prisoner, he must have often wondered whether he would succeed or fail in safeguarding the independence of the Papacy. After 1814 he resumed his principality and set in motion a process of Catholic renewal which allowed the church to experience remarkable spiritual regeneration through the nineteenth century.

The emperor and the pope had inherited a European world in which religion and politics had been plunged into a period of bitter conflict. Both had come to power at the culmination of a process, the origins of which lay in the Enlightenment reforms of the eighteenth century and which the French Revolution had catalysed. Despite their best intentions in seeking to end the strife between church and state, their ultimate legacy was to exacerbate the divisions rather than to heal them. Pius and Napoleon, in spite of their shared Italian heritage, simply did not understand each other: the Benedictine monk and revolutionary general could not find sufficient common ground to ensure a lasting peace. Their failure to create a modern partnership between church and state was to have lasting consequences in the century that followed their deaths.

The revolutions that erupted in the 1820s, 1830s and 1840s, like those of the 1790s, sought to undermine the church's power and independence. In 1848 revolutionaries took control of the eternal city and, showing few qualms about firing cannons at the gates of the Quirinal, chased Pius IX out of his capital in their bid to replace theocracy with a modern administrative state.[41] Yet for all this revolutionary radicalism there was a sense that the state had a role in funding and supervising religion. Many Europeans continued to share Napoleon's belief in the utility of religion and its role in legitimating power. If Napoleon III, who reigned from 1848 to 1870, learned anything from his uncle, that lesson was not to alienate the church. During the Second Empire, the Concordat of 1801 was respected and made to work in a manner that had proved impossible a half-century earlier.[42] As argued throughout this book, Napoleon's conflict with the church was about supremacy and ultimate power. The emperor wished to create a subordinate church that served the state and was socially useful. That is why the French law on the separation of church and state, passed in 1905, marked a sharp departure from Napoleonic precedent.[43] With this legislation Émile Combes's deeply anticlerical government rescinded the Napoleonic Concordat of 1801 and cut any residual links with the church of Rome. Henceforth the Catholic Church would become a private institution without state support.[44] This shift marked the beginning of modern secularism, often described using the French term *laïcité*, which by severing all links between religion and public life moved radically away from the more hybrid solutions proposed by the French Revolution and Napoleon.[45]

This book's interpretation differs considerably from the vast nineteenth-century historiography analysing Pius VII and Napoleon's tempestuous relationship. Catholic scholars and historians saw decided parallels between their own reality at the turn of the twentieth century and the older battles against the Revolution and Napoleon. When they wrote multi-volume histories of the church during the Revolution and Empire, they painted events in messianic colours as a struggle between good and evil. The French emperor became an Antichrist who heralded modern secularism and atheism: such writers had a remarkable talent for vilifying Napoleon and painting him as the embodiment of the godless modern secularising state. While the erudite research of these scholars, who scoured the archives of Europe, is admirable, the same cannot be said of their conclusions, which were inevitably compromised by the political battles of their present. Although some comparisons might be drawn between Napoleon and the radical secularists of the early twentieth century, there were important differences between them. As this book has shown, the emperor may have revealed himself to be deist on Saint Helena, but he was neither anti-religious nor even anti-Catholic in his outlook. In his lifetime he never sought a separation of church and state. Such an approach would have been antithetical to his controlling and centralising tendencies. He wanted priests to be priests and not politicians. This book breaks new ground by rejecting outdated accounts of the emperor's conflict with the pope, which accuse him of being a secularist *avant la lettre*. Admittedly the French Empire did eradicate monasteries and convents throughout Europe, not to mention abolish both the Roman and Spanish inquisitions. Yet it is vital to understand that anticlericalism is not the same thing as modern secularism. Napoleon wanted to refashion the Catholic Church into a subservient state-sponsored cult that promoted imperial and enlightened values. In this he was a child of the Enlightenment, sharing its distrust of a First Estate greedy for temporal power.

What made conflict inevitable was that at its heart the church headed by Pius VII remained an *ancien régime* institution, committed to its political autonomy from the state. The Curia was willing to collaborate in some measure with the French Empire, but not at the expense of its spiritual independence. The Catholic magisterium could not countenance divorce, nor bow to other social reforms. Although it sounds distinctly odd to modern ears, it must be borne in mind that the pope's principality in central Italy was seen as the ultimate guarantee of the church's independence and prosperity. Pius VII's defence of his kingdom provided the leitmotif for the history of Catholicism during the remainder of the nineteenth century. He created a template, followed by his successors, viewing sovereignty and theocratic government as unrenounceable. What Napoleon had failed to do, Italian nationalism, with the breach of Porta Pia and the annexation of Rome to the nascent unitary state in 1870, accomplished.[46]

Perhaps the most surprising aspect of the conflict between emperor and pope was that it strengthened the spiritual power of the Papacy. Article 3 of the Concordat of 1801 (relating to the removal of *ancien régime* bishops) and the failure of neo-conciliarism in 1811 backfired badly against Napoleon. They produced the unintended consequence of heightening the pope's spiritual authority and increasing his control over the Catholic hierarchy. After 1815 Pius could technically remove prelates from their dioceses as he saw fit. At the same time most bishops in Europe came to accept (some very grudgingly) that church councils were subordinate to the chairmanship of the pope. Thus the most remarkable and paradoxical legacy of the Napoleonic crisis was that in depriving the Papacy of its temporal power it led to its undisputed and infallible mastery over the Catholic world. This was something nobody could have foreseen in 1801, let alone during the National Council of 1811. The Empire's meddling with Gallicanism and conciliarism was to be its final undoing. Though this movement for local ecclesiastical autonomy staggered moribund into the nineteenth century, the Catholic future was ultramontane.[47] In the post-Napoleonic world, national churches turned to Rome for leadership and forsook local traditions of autonomy.

This book is the first extended analysis of the conflict between Pius VII and Napoleon in English. It is an archivally based study that has sought to avoid the nineteenth-century tendency of partisanship in this forgotten but fascinating episode in the history of the politics of religion. It has been my purpose in these pages to understand the Empire's decision to imprison the pope. Anachronistic interpretations that try to paint Pius VII's ordeal in terms of secularism versus theocracy have been avoided. Napoleon and Pius inherited a bitter conflict between state and church from the French Revolution: despite their attempts to find peace they only intensified the struggle, rather than defusing it. Despite the emperor's determination to make the Papacy yield to his will, the church resisted such pressure with vehemence. Through a careful sifting of the evidence in the Vatican Archives and other manuscript repositories, a new picture emerges of the church preparing for Napoleon's invasion of the Papal States: with Pius a prisoner a clandestine network of ecclesiastical resistance bitterly fought against the French occupiers. The failure to find an accommodation with the church did not determine the fall of Napoleon's empire. However, when the emperor faced military defeat on all fronts his mistreatment of Pius meant that he had few friends to defend his regime. Whatever else the legacy of Napoleon's relationship with the pope may have been, this book certainly reveals that it was a public relations disaster: it contributed immensely to the creation of a Napoleonic black legend that dismissed the French emperor as a secularising anti-Christ. Without doubt the Napoleonic experience made the church deeply distrustful of modern states. Indeed, memories of the failure to reach an entente with Napoleon and of his kidnapping of Pius VII would haunt the Vatican well into the early twentieth century, and perhaps beyond.[48]

# APPENDIX
## THE FOUR GALLICAN ARTICLES OF 1682

There are people who wish to destroy and undermine the foundations of the decrees and liberties of the Gallican Church, that our ancestors defended with zeal, through the holy canons and traditions of our fathers. Others, with the pretext of defending it [Gallicanism], have the audacity to deny the primacy of Saint Peter and the Roman pontiffs, whose authority is instituted of Jesus Christ. They encourage disobedience to this authority and diminish the majesty of the Holy Apostolic See which is respected in all the nations where the true faith of the church is taught and its unity treasured. Heretics, for their part, do everything in their power to undermine this authority, which upholds peace within the church, by preaching that it is damaging to kings and society in general. They use this ploy to divide simple souls from communion with the church. Wishing to remedy these ills, our archbishops and bishops, assembled in Paris by the king's command, together with the other ecclesiastical deputies who represent the Gallican Church, have judged it appropriate, after mature deliberation, to issue the following regulations and declare:

### I.

That Saint Peter and his successors, the vicars of Jesus Christ, and all the church, have received from God power over spiritual things, and all that concerns salvation, but not over temporal nor civil matters. Jesus Christ himself taught us that: 'My kingdom is not of this world'; and elsewhere that one should: 'Render therefore unto Caesar the things which are Caesar's; and unto God the things that are God's'. These are confirmed in the unalterable and unshakeable precept of the apostle Saint Paul which states: 'Let every soul be subject unto the higher powers. For there is no power but of God: the powers that be are ordained of God. Whosoever therefore resisteth the power, resisteth the ordinance of God'. We declare in consequence, that kings and sovereigns are not subject to any ecclesiastical power instituted of God, that in temporal matters they cannot be deposed directly nor indirectly by the authority of the keys of the church, and that their subjects cannot be released from the submission and obedience they owe to their [sovereigns], nor be freed from their oaths of allegiance, and that this doctrine so necessary for public tranquillity is no less advantageous for the church than it is for the state. It must be inviolably followed, in keeping with the word of God, the traditions of the Holy Fathers and the example of the saints.

## II.

That the plenitude of the powers held by the Holy Apostolic See, and by the successors of Saint Peter, the vicars of Jesus Christ, on spiritual matters is limited by the decrees of the Holy Ecumenical Council of Constance, promulgated in its fourth and fifth sessions, approved by the Holy Apostolic See and confirmed in the practice of all the church and the Roman pontiffs; that [these decrees] have been observed religiously at all times by the Gallican Church remain in force and virtue; and that the church of France does not approve the opinion of those who attack these decrees or who weaken them by alleging that their authority is not well established, or that they are not in force, or that they merely refer to the time of the [Great] Schism.

## III.

In this way the exercise of Apostolic Power must be limited according to the canons established by the Spirit of God and respected by all; that all the rules, customs and constitutions received in the kingdom [of France] and in the Gallican Church owe their force and virtue to the traditions of our fathers which remain unshakeable; and that it is to the credit of the Holy Apostolic See that these laws and customs, established with the consent of this respectable see and of the churches, remain in force without alteration.

## IV.

Although the pope holds the primatial power over questions of faith, and his decrees regard all churches and each church in particular, however his power is not absolute, unless the church's consent is given.

We have decreed to send to all the churches in France and to all bishops that preside over them, under the authority of the Holy Spirit, these maxims which we have received from our fathers, so that we all may say the same things, and that we may all share the same sentiments and follow the same doctrine.
[Signed by thirty-six bishops]

# ENDNOTES

## ABBREVIATIONS

| | |
|---|---|
| AD de l'Indre et Loire | Archives départementales de l'Indre et Loire (Tours) |
| AD du Rhône | Archives départementales du Rhône (Lyon) |
| AN | Archives nationales de France (Paris) |
| AP | *Archives parlementaires de 1787 à 1860*, 1ère série & 2ème série, ed. M.J. Madival and M.E. Laurant, 89 vols (Paris, 1867–96) |
| ASMi | Archivio di Stato di Milano (Milan) |
| ASV | Archivio segreto vaticano |
| BL Add. Ms | British Library, Additional Manuscript (London) |
| Boulay | Alfred, comte Boulay de la Meurthe, *Documents sur la négociation du Concordat et sur les autres rapports de la France avec le Saint-Siège en 1800 et 1801*, 6 vols (Paris, 1891–1905) |
| fasc. | fascicolo |
| NAP NOUV CORRES | Fondation Napoléon (ed.), *Napoléon Bonaparte. Correspondance générale*, 15 vols (Paris, 2004–18) |

## INTRODUCTION: A SLEEPLESS NIGHT IN THE ETERNAL CITY, 1809

1. Franco Borsi, Chiara Briganti, Marcello del Piazzo, Vittorio Gorresio and Giovanni Spadolini, *Il Palazzo del Quirinale* (Rome, 1973); and Maria Natoli and Maria Antonietta Scarpati (eds), *Il Palazzo del Quirinale. Il mondo artistico a Roma nel periodo napoleonico*, 2 vols (Rome, 1989); Francesco Colalucci, *Il Quirinale. L'immagine del palazzo dal Cinquecento all'Ottocento* (Rome, 2002).
2. Étienne Radet, *Mémoires du général Radet, d'après ses papiers personnels et les archives d'état* (Saint-Cloud, 1892), pp. 162–3.
3. Louis Madelin, *La Rome de Napoléon. La domination française à Rome de 1809–1814* (Paris, 1906), pp. 235–6; and ASV, Segreteria di Stato, Epoca Napoleonica, Italia 7, fasc. 17, 24 fols, account of the pope's kidnapping on 6 July 1809. When this narrative was composed is unclear; it seems to have been hitherto unpublished. It places the blame for Pius VII's arrest squarely on traitors and renegades. Furthermore, it alleges that French preparations for the assault on the Quirinal were far from discreet in contrast to Radet, *Mémoires*. Indeed this account makes it seem as if the pope was prepared for the worst. I suspect this was an official account written on the pope's return in 1814 after an official investigation into the events of 5–6 July 1809.
4. Radet, *Mémoires*, pp. 172–7.
5. Bernardine Melchior-Bonnet, *Napoléon et le pape* (Paris, 1958), p. 124.
6. Radet, *Mémoires*, p. 178.

7. Madelin, *La Rome de Napoléon*, pp. 237–8.
8. Henri de Mayol de Lupé, *La captivité de Pie VII, d'après des documents inédits*, 2 vols (Paris, 1916), I, pp. 169–70.
9. Radet, *Mémoires*, pp. 180–1.
10. Bartolomeo Pacca, *Mémoires du cardinal B. Pacca sur le pontificat de Pie VII traduits sur l'édition Italienne d'Orvieto de 1843 par M. Queyras*, 2 vols (Paris, 1860), I, pp. 187–8.
11. Alexis-François Artaud de Montor, *Histoire du Pape Pie VII, par M. le chevalier Artaud, ancien chargé d'affaires de France à Rome, à Florence et à Vienne*, 2 vols (Paris, 1836), II, p. 221; and in ASV, Segreteria di Stato, Epoca Napoleonica, Italia 7, fasc. 17, no. 1, fol. 16, report on papal abduction.
12. Radet, *Mémoires*, pp. 181–3.
13. Pacca, *Mémoires*, I, pp. 187 and 190.
14. Ibid., p. 189.
15. Madelin, *La Rome de Napoléon*, p. 239.
16. Pacca, *Mémoires*, I, p. 248.
17. Silvio Balloni, *Pio VII a Firenze e in Toscana. I cinque viaggi di papa Chiaramonti dal 1804 al 1815* (Cesena, 2019), pp. 98–109.
18. Ibid., pp. 251–2.
19. Mayol de Lupé, *La captivité de Pie VII*, I, p. 217.
20. Pacca, *Mémoires*, I, pp. 252–3.
21. Joseph-Antoine Angeli, *Élisa Bonaparte* (Paris, 2016).
22. Melchior-Bonnet, *Napoléon et le pape*, pp. 129–31.
23. Mayol de Lupé, *La captivité de Pie VII*, I, pp. 242–55.
24. Henri Ponchon, *L'incroyable saga des Torlonia. Des monts du Forez aux palais Romains* (Paris, 2005), pp. 114–94.
25. David Chandler, *The Campaigns of Napoleon* (London, 1993), pp. 663–736.
26. NAP NOUV CORRES, no. 21,562, Schönbrunn, 18 July 1809, IX, p. 885.
27. NAP NOUV CORRES, no. 21,289, Schönbrunn, 19 June 1809, IX, pp. 745–6.
28. Radet, *Mémoires*, pp. 203–38.

## CHAPTER 1: GOD AND REVOLUTION: FRANCE IN TURMOIL, 1789–99

1. Michel Vergé-Franceschi, *Histoire de Corse. Le pays de la grandeur* (Paris, 1996), pp. 341–52; and Thadd E. Hall, *France and the Eighteenth-Century Corsican Question* (New York, 1971).
2. Michel Vergé-Franceschi, *Napoléon. Une enfance corse* (Paris, 2009), pp. 216–21.
3. Ibid., pp. 265–6.
4. Marie Courtemanche, *Napoléon et le sacré. Une vie spirituelle, une politique religieuse* (Paris, 2019), p. 25.
5. Vergé-Franceschi, *Napoléon. Une enfance corse*, pp. 223–55.
6. Thierry Lentz, *Joseph Bonaparte* (Paris, 2016), pp. 40–8.
7. Philip Dwyer, *Napoleon: The Path to Power, 1769–1799* (London, 2007), pp. 26–32.
8. Courtemanche, *Napoléon et le sacré*, p. 47.
9. Jules-Marie Gendry, *Pie VI. Sa vie, son pontificat (1717–1799)*, 2 vols (Paris, 1906), I, pp. 1–24.
10. Jean Leflon, *Pie VII*, vol. I, *Des abbayes bénédictines à la papauté* (Paris, 1958), pp. 4–5.
11. Ibid., pp. 7–12.
12. Ibid., pp. 12–15.
13. Ibid., chs 2–3.
14. William Doyle, *Jansenism* (Basingstoke, 1999), passim; and for the broader implication of this movement see Dale K. Van Kley, *Reform Catholicism and the International Suppression of the Jesuits in Enlightenment Europe* (London, 2018).

15. Ulrich L. Lehner, *The Catholic Enlightenment: The Forgotten History of a Global Movement* (Oxford, 2016), esp. ch. 1.
16. David Sorkin, *The Religious Enlightenment: Jews, Christians, and Muslims from London to Vienna* (Princeton, NJ, 2011); and Jeffrey D. Burson and Ulrich L. Lehner (eds), *Enlightenment and Catholicism in Europe: A Transnational History* (Notre Dame, IN, 2014).
17. Peter Gay, *Voltaire's Politics: The Poet as Realist* (Princeton, NJ, 1959), pp. 259–72.
18. John Robertson, *The Case for the Enlightenment: Scotland and Naples 1680–1760* (Cambridge, 2007), pp. 1–44.
19. Geoffrey Ellis, 'Religion according to Napoleon: The limitations of pragmatism', in Nigel Aston (ed.), *Religious Changes in Europe, 1650–1914* (Oxford, 1997), pp. 235–55; p. 235.
20. C.B.A. Behrens, *Ancien Régime* (London, 1989); and William Doyle, *The Old European Order, 1660–1800* (Oxford, 1993).
21. Nigel Aston, 'The Established Church', in William Doyle (ed.), *The Oxford Handbook of the Ancien Régime* (Oxford, 2012), pp. 285–301.
22. Marc Bloch, *The Royal Touch: Monarchy and Miracles in France and England* (London, 1989); and Jeffrey W. Merrick, *The Desacralisation of the French Monarchy in the Eighteenth Century* (London, 1990), pp. 1–26.
23. Noël Valois, *Histoire de la Pragmatique Sanction de Bourges sous Charles VII* (Paris, 1906).
24. Robert Knecht, *Francis I* (Cambridge, 1982), pp. 51–65.
25. Joseph Bergin, *Crown, Church and Episcopate under Louis XIV* (London, 2004), pp. 232–60.
26. Francis Oakley, *The Conciliarist Tradition: Constitutionalism in the Catholic Church 1300–1870* (Oxford, 2003).
27. René Taveneaux, *Le catholicisme dans la France Classique, 1610–1715*, 2 vols (Paris, 1994), II, p. 322.
28. Doyle, *Jansenism.*
29. Dale K. Van Kley, *The Religious Origins of the French Revolution, from Calvin to the Civil Constitution, 1560–1791* (London, 1996), esp. ch. 5.
30. Alexander Dupilet, *Le cardinal Dubois. Le génie politique de la régence* (Paris, 2016); Guy Chaussinand-Nogaret, *Le cardinal Fleury. Le Richelieu de Louis XV* (Paris, 2002); and Joseph Perrin, *Le cardinal de Loménie de Brienne, archevêque de Sens. Ses dernières années, episodes de la Revolution* (Paris, 1898).
31. John McManners, *Church and Society in Eighteenth-Century France*, 2 vols (Oxford, 1998), I, pp. 192–8.
32. David Bien, *The Calas Affair: Persecution, Toleration and Heresy in Eighteenth-Century Toulouse* (London, 1979); and Christian Petr, *François-Jean Lefebvre, chevalier de La Barre, voyou de qualité* (Paris, 2007).
33. Jonathan Israel, *Democratic Enlightenment: Philosophy, Revolution and Human Rights 1750–1790* (Oxford, 2011), pp. 336–48.
34. Paula Hyman, *The Jews of Modern France* (Los Angeles, 1998), pp. 1–15; Philippe Joutard, 'The Revocation of the Edict of Nantes: End or renewal of French Protestantism?', in Menna Prestwich (ed.), *International Calvinism, 1541–1715* (Oxford, 1985), pp. 339–68; Zosa Szajkowski, 'Protestants and Jews of France in fight for emancipation, 1789–1791', *Proceedings of the American Academy for Jewish Research*, vol. 25 (1956), pp. 119–35.
35. McManners, *Church and Society*, I, p. 177; and Nigel Aston, *Religion and Revolution in France, 1780–1804* (Basingstoke, 2000), pp. 215–17.
36. McManners, *Church and Society*, I, p. 122.
37. Ibid., p. 98.
38. Ibid., pp. 141–50.
39. Nigel Aston, *The End of an Élite: The French Bishops and the Coming of the Revolution* (Oxford, 1992), pp. 1–29.
40. McManners, *Church and Society*, I, p. 216.
41. Ibid., pp. 335–6.
42. Derek Beales, *Prosperity and Plunder: European Catholic Monasteries in the Age of Revolution 1650–1815* (Cambridge, 2003), pp. 85–6.

43. McManners, *Church and Society*, I, chs 17–18.
44. Ibid., pp. 476–80 and 492–4.
45. Ibid., pp. 476–86.
46. Beales, *Prosperity and Plunder*, pp. 104–5.
47. McManners, *Church and Society*, I, p. 478.
48. P.M. Jones, *Reform and Revolution in France: The Politics of Transition, 1774–1791* (Cambridge, 1995), pp. 107–38.
49. Geoffrey Adams, *The Huguenots and French Opinion, 1685–1787: The Enlightenment Debate on Toleration* (Waterloo, Ontario, 1991), pp. 295–306.
50. William Doyle, *The Oxford History of the French Revolution*, 2nd edn (Oxford, 2002), pp. 86–111.
51. Gilbert Shapiro and John Markoff, *Revolutionary Demands: A Content Analysis of the Cahiers de Doléances of 1789* (Stanford, CA, 1998), pp. 1–13.
52. McManners, *Church and Society*, II, pp. 726–32.
53. Timothy Tackett, *Becoming a Revolutionary: The Deputies of the French National Assembly and the Emergence of a Revolutionary Culture (1789–1790)* (Princeton, NJ, 1997), pp. 24–7.
54. Michael Hayden, *France and the Estates General of 1614* (Cambridge, 1974), pp. 88–94.
55. John McManners, *The French Revolution and the Church* (London, 1982), p. 1.
56. Ambrogio A. Caiani, *Louis XVI and the French Revolution, 1789–1792* (Cambridge, 2012), pp. 202–3.
57. Doyle, *The Oxford History of the French Revolution*, pp. 102–6.
58. Jean-Denis Bredin, *Sieyès. La clé de la Revolution française* (Paris, 1988).
59. William H. Sewell, *A Rhetoric of Bourgeois Revolution: The Abbé Sieyès and What Is the Third Estate* (London, 1994), pp. 66–108.
60. Emmanuel-Joseph Sieyès, *Political Writings: Including the Debate between Sieyès and Tom Paine in 1791*, ed. Michael Sonenscher (London, 2003), pp. 136–42 and 151–4.
61. Whether this meant that the church had renounced its independent corporate identity was unclear: see John McManners, *The French Revolution and the Church* (London, 1982), p. 21.
62. Doyle, *The Oxford History of the French Revolution*, pp. 109–11.
63. Georges Lefebvre, *The Great Fear of 1789: Rural Panic in Revolutionary France* (London, 1989).
64. Michael P. Fitzsimmons, *The Remaking of France: The National Assembly and the Constitution of 1791* (Cambridge, 1994), part 1.
65. Lynn Hunt, *Inventing Human Rights: A History* (New York, 2007), pp. 119–45.
66. David Andress (ed.), *The Oxford Handbook of the French Revolution* (Oxford, 2015), p. 357.
67. Michael P. Fitzsimmons, *The Night the Old Regime Ended: August 4, 1789 and the French Revolution* (University Park, PA, 1998), pp. 47–92.
68. McManners, *The French Revolution and the Church*, pp. 27–30.
69. Ibid., p. 31.
70. Tackett, *Becoming a Revolutionary*, pp. 267–73.
71. Jean-Joseph-François Poujoulat, *Le cardinal Maury. Sa vie, ses œuvres* (Paris, 1859).
72. McManners, *The French Revolution and the Church*, p. 38.
73. Malcolm Crook, 'Citizen bishops: Episcopal elections in the French Revolution', *Historical Journal*, vol. 43, no. 4 (2000), pp. 955–76.
74. McManners, *The French Revolution and the Church*, pp. 47–60.
75. Euan Cameron, *The European Reformation* (Oxford, 1991).
76. Aston, *The End of an Élite*, pp. 245–6.
77. Timothy Tackett, *Religion, Revolution, and Regional Culture in Eighteenth-Century France: The Ecclesiastical Oath of 1791* (Princeton, NJ, 1986), chs 7–8.
78. Edward James Kolla, 'The French Revolution, the Union of Avignon, and the challenges of national self-determination', *Law and History Review*, vol. 31, no. 4 (2013), pp. 717–47.
79. McManners, *The French Revolution and the Church*, p. 59.
80. Caiani, *Louis XVI and the French Revolution*, p. 95.
81. Timothy Tackett, *When the King Took Flight* (Cambridge, MA, 2003), pp. 41, 101–2.

82. René Picheloup, *Les ecclésiastiques français émigrés ou déportés dans l'état pontifical, 1792–1800* (Toulouse, 1972).

83. T.C.W. Blanning, *The Origins of the French Revolutionary Wars* (London, 1986), p. 122.

84. McManners, *The French Revolution and the Church*, pp. 64–5.

85. Rodney Allen, *Threshold of Terror: The Last Hours of the Monarchy in the French Revolution* (London, 1999).

86. McManners, *The French Revolution and the Church*, p. 67.

87. David Jordan, *The King's Trial: Louis XVI versus the French Revolution* (Los Angeles, CA, 2004).

88. Jacques Godechot, *The Counter-Revolution: Doctrine and Action 1789–1804* (Princeton, NJ, 1981), pp. 201–30.

89. Jean-Clément Martin, *La Vendée et la Révolution* (Paris, 2007), pp. 86–107.

90. Michel Vovelle, *The Revolution against the Church* (Columbus, GA, 1991); and idem, *Religion et révolution. La déchristianisation de l'an II* (Paris, 1976).

91. Alain Corbin, *Village Bells: Sound and Meaning in the Nineteenth-Century French Countryside* (Oxford, 1999), pp. 3–44.

92. AP, LXXIV, p. 550.

93. Sanja Perovic, *The Calendar in Revolutionary France: Perceptions of Time in Literature, Culture, Politics* (Cambridge, 2012), pp. 110–17.

94. Ibid., pp. 117–24.

95. Matthew Shaw, *Time and the French Revolution: The Republican Calendar, 1789–Year XIV* (Woodbridge, 2011), chs 4–5; and Noah Shusterman, *Religion and the Politics of Time: Holidays in France from Louis XIV through Napoleon* (Washington, DC, 2010), chs 5–6.

96. David Andress, *The Terror: Civil War in the French Revolution* (London, 2005), pp. 239–42.

97. Christopher M. Greene, 'Alexandre Lenoir and the Musée des monuments français during the French Revolution', *French Historical Studies*, vol. 12, no. 2 (1981), pp. 200–22.

98. Joseph F. Byrnes, *Priests of the French Revolution: Saints and Renegades in a New Political Era* (University Park, PA, 2014), pp. 101–2.

99. Claire Cage, *Unnatural Frenchmen: The Politics of Priestly Celibacy and Marriage, 1720–1815* (Charlottesville, VA, 2015), pp. 130–65.

100. Robert Palmer, *Twelve Who Ruled: The Year of Terror in the French Revolution* (Princeton, NJ, 1941), esp. pp. 3–21.

101. Peter McPhee, *Robespierre: A Revolutionary Life* (London, 2012), pp. 174–6.

102. Jonathan Smyth, *Robespierre and the Festival of the Supreme Being: The Search for a Republican Morality* (Manchester, 2016), p. 24.

103. Andress, *The Terror*, pp. 310–11.

104. Colin Jones, 'The overthrow of Maximilien Robespierre and the "indifference" of the people', *American Historical Review*, vol. 119, no. 3 (2014), pp. 689–713.

105. Bronisław Baczko, *Ending the Terror: The French Revolution after Robespierre* (Cambridge, 1994).

106. McManners, *The French Revolution and the Church*, pp. 118–19.

107. Ibid., pp. 108–10.

108. Martyn Lyons, *France under the Directory* (Cambridge, 1975), pp. 105–7.

109. Rodney Dean, *L'abbé Grégoire et l'Église constitutionnelle après la Terreur, 1794–1797* (Paris, 2008).

110. Lyons, *France under the Directory*, pp. 108–9.

111. McManners, *The French Revolution and the Church*, pp. 128–9.

112. Paul W. Schroeder, *The Transformation of European Politics, 1763–1848* (Oxford, 1994), p. 167.

113. Barnabà Chiaramonti, *Omelia del cittadino cardinal Chiaramonti vescovo d'Imola al popolo della sua diocesi nel giorno del santissimo Natale l'anno MDCCXCVII* (Florence, 1859), passim.

114. E.E.Y. Hales, *Revolution and Papacy* (Indianapolis, IN, 1966), pp. 91–103.

115. Howard G. Brown, *Ending the French Revolution: Violence, Justice, and Repression from the Terror to Napoleon* (Charlottesville, VA, 2008).

116. Suzanne Desan, *The Family on Trial in Revolutionary France* (Los Angeles, CA, 2006), p. 94.
117. Michael Broers, *Napoleon: Soldier of Destiny* (London, 2014), pp. 202–29.
118. Juan Cole, *Napoleon's Egypt: Invading the Middle East* (Basingstoke, 2007), passim.

## CHAPTER 2: ELECTING THE POPE IN VENICE, 1799–1800

1. Christopher Duffy, *Eagles over the Alps* (London, 1999).
2. Cole, *Napoleon's Egypt*.
3. Gérard Pelletier, *Rome et la Révolution française. La théologie et la politique du Saint-Siège devant la Révolution française (1789–1799)* (Rome, 2004), pp. 460–1; and ASV, Archivio Concistoriale, Serie Conclavi 86, no. 357, ordres des cérémonies qui seront observé à la sépulture du Pape Pie VI.
4. ASV, Archivio Concistoriale, Serie Conclavi 87, no. 6, copy of Spina's letter to College of Cardinals, Delfinato 29 agosto 1799.
5. Timothy Blanning, *The French Revolutionary Wars, 1787–1802* (London, 1996), pp. 230–8.
6. Brown, *Ending the French Revolution*, pp. 21–118.
7. Nina Burleigh, *Mirage: Napoleon's Scientists and the Unveiling of Egypt* (London, 2007).
8. Broers, *Napoleon: Soldier of Destiny*, pp. 203–29.
9. Isser Woloch, *Napoleon and His Collaborators: The Making of a Dictatorship* (New York, 2002), pp. 36–65; and Patrice Gueniffey, *Bonaparte, 1769–1802* (Cambridge, MA, 2015), pp. 577–600.
10. Malcolm Crook, 'The uses of democracy: Elections and plebiscites in Napoleonic France', in Maire Cross and David Williams (eds), *The French Experience from Republic to Monarchy, 1792–1824: New Dawns in Politics, Knowledge and Culture* (New York, 2000), pp. 58–71.
11. Emmanuel de Waresquiel, *Talleyrand. Le prince immobile* (Paris, 2003), p. 283.
12. Enrico Celani, 'I preliminari del Conclave di Venezia', *Archivio della Società romana di storia patria*, vol. 36 (1913), pp. 486–95.
13. Mario Casaburi, *Fabrizio Ruffo. L'uomo, il cardinale, il condottiero, l'economista, il politico* (Soveria Mannelli, 2003); and Francesco Leoni, *Storia della Controrivoluzione in Italia (1789–1859)* (Naples, 1975), pp. 92–6.
14. Michael Broers, *Napoleon's Other War: Bandits, Rebels and Their Pursuers in the Age of Revolutions* (Oxford, 2010), pp. 59–68.
15. Robin Anderson, *Pope Pius VII (1800–1823)* (Rockford, IL, 2001), p. 31.
16. Dwyer, *Napoleon: The Path to Power*, pp. 291–6 and 314–15.
17. Giovanni Vian, 'La Chiesa veneziana nei mesi del Conclave', *Studi veneziani*, no. 43 (2002), pp. 299–308.
18. Alberto Melloni, *Il Conclave: Storia dell'elezione del Papa* (Bologna, 2005).
19. Sergio Baldan, *Il Conclave di Venezia: L'elezione di Papa Pio VII, 1 dicembre 1799–14 marzo 1800* (Venice, 2000).
20. They were health-and-safety-conscious nevertheless; firefighters and a reservoir of water were present at the Conclave at all times. ASV, Archivio Concistoriale, Serie Conclavi 83, no. 80, 16 novembre 1799, macchine idrauliche.
21. Tracy Elizabeth Cooper, *Palladio's Venice: Architecture and Society in a Renaissance Republic* (London, 2005), pp. 109–46; Patricia Fortini Brown, *Venetian Narrative Painting in the Age of Carpaccio* (London, 1990), p. 70; and ASV, Archivio Concistoriale, Serie Conclavi 83, nos 45–6, camera per lo scrutino da fissarsi nel coro d'inverno.
22. Marzieh Gail, *The Three Popes: An Account of the Great Schism* (New York, 1969).
23. Pelletier, *Rome et la Révolution française*, pp. 491–8; and Davy Marguerettaz, 'Il Conclave di Venezia e l'elezione di Pio VII', *Benedictina. Rivista del Centro storico benedettino italiano*, vol. 64, no. 2 (2017), pp. 255–94.
24. Miles Pattenden, *Electing the Pope in Early Modern Italy, 1450–1700* (Oxford, 2017), pp. 46–55.
25. Artaud de Montor, *Histoire du Pape Pie VII*, I, pp. 63–72.

26. John Martin Robinson, *Cardinal Consalvi, 1757–1824* (London, 1987), pp. 1–31; and ASV, Archivio Concistoriale, Serie Conclavi 83, no. 2, registro di tutto cio che è stato scritto da me Ercole Consalvi dopo la mia destinazione all'impiego di Pro Segre. Del S. Collegio in Venezia nell'occasione del Conclave in seguito alla morte del Sommo Pontefice Pio Sesto accaduto nel Delfinato il di 29 Agosto 1799.

27. Gabriel Seguí Vidal, 'El cardenal Despuig y la Santa Sede', *Analecta sacra tarraconensia*, vol. 16, no. 1 (1944), pp. 201–12.

28. ASV, Archivio Concistoriale, Serie Conclavi 84, nos 33–5, letters to Louis XVIII informing him of the death of Pius VI and the Venice Conclave.

29. Jacques de Saint-Victor, *La première Contre-Révolution, 1789–1791* (Paris, 2010), pp. 408–15 and 434–70.

30. Ludwig von Pastor, *The History of the Popes, from the Close of the Middle Ages, Drawn from the Secret Archives of the Vatican and Other Original Sources*, 40 vols (Hertford, 1952), XXXIX, pp. 441–2 and 468–71.

31. Charles van Duerm, *Un peu plus de lumière sur le Conclave de Venise et sur les commencements du pontificat de Pie VII (1799–1800). Documents inédits extraits des archives de Vienne* (Paris, 1896), pp. v–x.

32. Henry Dietrich Fernández, 'The Patrimony of St Peter: The Papal Court at Rome *c.* 1450–1700', in John Adamson (ed.), *The Princely Courts of Europe: 1500–1750* (London, 1999), pp. 141–63.

33. Emiliana Ricci, *Palazzo Braschi. Storia ed architettura di un edifico settecentesco* (Rome, 1989).

34. Antonio Menniti Ippolito, *Il tramonto della Curia nepotista. Papi, nipoti e burocrazia curiale tra XVI e XVII secolo* (Rome, 1999).

35. ASV, Archivio Concistoriale, Serie Conclavi 86, no. 233, diario de Novendiali celebrati nella chiesa patriarcale e primaziale di S. Pietro in Castello di Venezia ne giorni 23 a 31 Ottobre per suffragar l'anima di NS Pio VI POM.

36. Tommaso Gallarti-Scotti, 'Il Conclave del 1800', in *La civiltà veneziana nell'età romantica* (Florence, 1961), pp. 7–9.

37. Karl. A. Roider, *Baron Thugut and Austria's response to the French Revolution* (Princeton, NJ, 1987), pp. 3–80.

38. Giorgio Vaccarino, *Torino attende Suvaro, aprile–maggio 1799* (Turin, 1971), pp. 160–8.

39. Ibid., pp. 292–327.

40. Antoine Ricard (ed.), *Correspondance diplomatique et mémoires inédits du cardinal Maury (1792–1817)*, 2 vols (Lille, 1891), I, p. 273.

41. Van Duerm, *Un peu plus de lumière*, p. 40.

42. Dries Vanysacker, 'Giacinto Sigismondo Cardinal Gerdil (1718–1802): Enlightenment as cultural and religious achievement', in Burson and Lehner (eds), *Enlightenment and Catholicism in Europe*, pp. 89–123.

43. Van Duerm, *Un peu plus de lumière*, p. 41

44. Leflon, *Pie VII*, pp. 557–66.

45. Ibid., pp. 570–5.

46. Alberto Lumbroso, *Ricordi e documenti sul Conclave di Venezia 1800* (Rome, 1903), p. 39.

47. Ricard (ed.), *Correspondance diplomatique*, I, pp. 278–9.

48. Ercole Consalvi, *Mémoires du cardinal Consalvi,* 2 vols (Paris, 1866), I, pp. 242–5.

49. Van Duerm, *Un peu plus de lumière*, p. 72.

50. ASV, Archivio Concistoriale, Serie Conclavi 83, nos 1–387, Consalvi's mainly administrative correspondence on heating and building maintenance of the monastery of San Giorgio Maggiore.

51. Van Duerm, *Un peu plus de lumière*, pp. 97–101.

52. Leflon, *Pie VII*, p. 576.

53. Van Duerm, *Un peu plus de lumière*, pp. 188–90.

54. Cardinal Antonelli's candidates were himself, Valenti, Giovanetti, Archetti and Livazzani; Cardinal Albani's were himself, Calcagnini, Honorati, Borgia and Chiaramonti. This was the

first time Chiaramonti was seriously considered as a contender: Ricard (ed.), *Correspondance diplomatique*, I, pp. 328–35.

55. Van Duerm, *Un peu plus de lumière*, pp. 210–11.
56. Ricard (ed.), *Correspondance diplomatique*, I, pp. 344–5.
57. In fact he lived a further eight years, dying at the venerable age of eighty-two in 1808.
58. The Savoyard Cardinal Gerdil, who was well into in his eighties, was proposed as a compromise candidate. He met with Herzan's firm resistance: his court had instructed him that the subject of the Savoyard monarchy must be excluded: van Duerm, *Un peu plus de lumière*, pp. 213–24.
59. He received as many as twenty-four votes: Marguerettaz, 'Il Conclave di Venezia', p. 282.
60. Ricard (ed.), *Correspondance diplomatique*, I, p. 355.
61. Van Duerm, *Un peu plus de lumière*, p. 220.
62. Consalvi, *Mémoires*, I, pp. 263–70.
63. Ibid., pp. 263–64.
64. Ibid., p. 19.
65. According to the historian Jean Leflon, the mystery man was most likely the Milanese Cardinal Antonio Dugnani, who had been the last apostolic nuncio to France before the Revolution. According to Leflon, Dugnani had been persuaded by Despuig to seek support for Chiaramonti's candidature from Mattei's supporters: Leflon, *Pie VII*, pp. 580–1. Others suggest the mystery man was Maury, but his correspondence with Louis XVIII makes this unlikely (see note 66 below). According to Marguerettaz, 'Il Conclave di Venezia', pp. 284–6, Consalvi's memoirs are unreliable. In the end, the Conclave elected Pius VII through exhaustion rather than through a grand pre-arranged strategy of the part of Consalvi and the Braschi clan.
66. Ricard (ed.), *Correspondance diplomatique*, I, pp. 351–3.
67. Van Duerm, *Un peu plus de lumière*, pp. 232–3.
68. Ibid., pp. 233–4.
69. Ibid., p. 236.
70. Consalvi, *Mémoires*, I, pp. 283–5.
71. Thierry Lentz, *Le grand Consulat (1799–1804)* (Paris, 1999), p. 204.
72. According to Consalvi's memoirs, two younger unnamed cardinals, in the deep of night, plotted to wreck the election but failed miserably: Consalvi, *Mémoires*, I, p. 284.
73. Ibid., p. 286.
74. Melchior-Bonnet, *Napoléon et le pape*, p. 16.
75. Van Duerm, *Un peu plus de lumière*, p. 272.
76. Sergio Becerra II, *The Papal Tiara: The Authority and Power of the Pope* (self-published, 2013).
77. Ibid., p. 6.
78. Consalvi, *Mémoires*, I, p. 289.
79. Van Duerm, *Un peu plus de lumière*, p. 323.
80. Ibid., p. 325.
81. Derek Beales, *Joseph II*, 2 vols (Cambridge, 2009), II, pp. 214–38.
82. Van Duerm, *Un peu plus de lumière*, pp. 402–3.
83. Ibid., pp. 392–3.
84. Ibid., pp. 401–6.
85. Consalvi, *Mémoires*, I, pp. 304–6.
86. Van Duerm, *Un peu plus de lumière*, pp. 543–5.
87. Ibid., pp. 592–6.
88. Lentz, *Le grand Consulat*, pp. 219–41.
89. Chandler, *The Campaigns of Napoleon*, pp. 270–86.
90. Ibid., pp. 286–8.
91. Bernard Gainot and Bruno Ciotti (eds), *Marengo. 14 juin 1800* (Paris, 2010), esp. pp. 1–10.
92. Schroeder, *The Transformation of European Politics*, pp. 208–11.
93. Van Duerm, *Un peu plus de lumière*, pp. 594–5.
94. Augustin Theiner, *Histoire des deux concordats de la République française et de la République cisalpine*, 2 vols (Paris, 1869), I, pp. 63–5.

95. Pietro Stella, *Il giansenismo in Italia. Il movimento giansenista e la produzione libraria* (Rome, 2006), pp. 77 and 122.

96. Olwen Hufton, 'The reconstruction of a church, 1796–1801', in Gwynne Lewis and Colin Lucas (eds), *Beyond the Terror: Essays in French Regional and Social History 1794–1815* (London, 1983), pp. 21–52.

97. Theiner, *Histoire des deux concordats*, p. 68.

98. Jean Morvan, *Le soldat impérial (1800–1814)*, 2 vols (Paris, 1904), II, pp. 506–17.

99. Ricard (ed.), *Correspondance diplomatique*, I, pp. 461–79.

100. Robinson, *Cardinal Consalvi*, p. 57.

101. Ellis, 'Religion according to Napoleon'.

102. For an excellent comparative study, see William Roberts, 'Napoleon, the Concordat of 1801, and its consequences', in Frank Coppa (ed.), *Controversial Concordats: The Vatican's Relations with Napoleon, Mussolini, and Hitler* (Washington, DC, 2012), pp. 34–80.

## CHAPTER 3: DIVISIONS HEALED? THE CONCORDAT OF 1801

1. Reynald Secher, *A French Genocide: The Vendée* (Notre Dame, IN, 2003), passim; and cf. Martin, *La Vendée et la Révolution*, pp. 61–85.

2. See an excellent review article by Hugh Gough, 'Genocide and the Bicentenary', *Historical Journal*, vol. 30 (1987), pp. 977–88.

3. Jean-Clément Martin, *La guerre de Vendée (1793–1800)* (Paris, 2014); and Patrick Buisson, *La grande histoire des guerres de Vendée* (Paris, 2017).

4. Godechot, *The Counter-Revolution*, pp. 202–14.

5. Jean Leflon, *Étienne-Alexandre Bernier. Évêque d'Orléans (1762–1806)*, 2 vols (Paris, 1938), I, pp. 89 and 100–1.

6. Émile Gabory, *Les guerres de Vendée* (Paris, 2009), pp. 307–9.

7. Leflon, *Étienne-Alexandre Bernier*, I, p. 101.

8. Ibid.

9. Ibid., pp. 1–5.

10. John McManners, *French Ecclesiastical Society under the Ancien Régime: A Study of Angers in the Eighteenth Century* (Manchester, 1960), pp. 129–62.

11. Timothy Tackett, 'The west in France in 1789: The religious factor in the origins of the Counterrevolution', *Journal of Modern History*, vol. 54, no. 4 (1982), pp. 715–45.

12. Leflon, *Étienne-Alexandre Bernier*, I, pp. 10–11.

13. Lentz, *Le grand Consulat*, p. 200.

14. Leflon, *Étienne-Alexandre Bernier*, I, pp. 15–20.

15. Jean-Marie Augustin, *Le faux évêque de la Vendée* (Paris, 1994), pp. 242–53.

16. Leflon, *Étienne-Alexandre Bernier*, I, pp. 25–7.

17. Jean-Clément Martin, *Blancs et bleus dans la Vendée déchirée* (Paris, 1986), p. 89.

18. Leflon, *Étienne-Alexandre Bernier*, I, pp. 36–8.

19. Ibid., pp. 39–40.

20. Ibid., pp. 62–8.

21. Brown, *Ending the French Revolution*, pp. 241–5.

22. Leflon, *Étienne-Alexandre Bernier*, I, pp. 73–9.

23. During this time, he was in secret negotiations with Rome to obtain the title of 'apostolic vicar', a title which would have given him supreme spiritual jurisdiction in the west of France. Although this attempt to become the pope's spiritual ambassador failed, throughout this time Bernier remained a force to be reckoned with in the Angevin region: ibid., pp. 78–9.

24. Lentz, *Le grand Consulat*, pp. 199–201

25. Leflon, *Étienne-Alexandre Bernier*, I, p. 103.

26. Stuart J. Woolf, *Napoleon's Integration of Europe* (London, 1991), pp. 109–10.

27. Leflon, *Étienne-Alexandre Bernier*, I, pp. 103–4.

28. Ibid., pp. 104–15.

29. Patrick Huchet, *Georges Cadoudal et les Chouans* (Bordeaux, 1997), p. 317.

30. Lentz, *Le grand Consulat*, pp. 229–36.
31. Philip Dwyer, *Talleyrand* (London, 2002), pp. 12–45.
32. Boulay, III, pp. 225–37.
33. Alfred Boulay de la Meurthe, *Histoire de la négociation du Concordat de 1801* (Paris, 1920), pp. 78–83.
34. ASV, Francia Epoca Napoleonica 15, fasc. 10, nos 5–6, personnel file di Pietro.
35. ASV, Francia Epoca Napoleonica 9, fasc. 1, Trattive Vercelli, esp. no. 10, Antonelli letter, 14 July 1800.
36. Ricard (ed.), *Correspondance diplomatique*, I, pp. 461–79.
37. Jean Thiry, *Le Concordat et le Consulat à vie* (Paris, 1956), pp. 36–9.
38. Boulay, III, pp. 566–84; and originals in ASV, Francia Epoca Napoleonica 9, fasc. 1, nos 258–98.
39. Thomas F. Mayer, *Reginald Pole: Prince and Prophet* (Cambridge, 2000), pp. 252–301.
40. Boulay, III, pp. 597–629.
41. C. Piola Caselli, 'Il Cardinale C.F.C. nel periodo servita, napoleonico, e di Maria Luigia', *Rivista storica svizzera*, vol. 26 (1976), pp. 33–86.
42. Boulay, I, pp. 113–15.
43. Ibid., p. 114; and ASV, Francia Epoca Napoleonica 11, fasc. 5, no. 35r, resignation of bishops.
44. W.H.C. Frend, *The Early Church: From the Beginning to 461* (London, 1965), pp. 198–208; David Benedict, *The History of the Donatists* (London, 1875), pp. 43–61.
45. Boulay, I, p. 123.
46. Ibid.
47. Ibid., pp. 122–4.
48. Ibid., p. 119.
49. André Latreille, 'Le gallicanisme ecclésiastique sous le Premier Empire, vers le Concile national de 1811', *Revue historique*, vol. 194, no. 1 (1944), pp. 1–22.
50. Austin Gough, *Paris and Rome: The Gallican Church and the Ultramontane Campaign, 1848–53* (Oxford, 1986), passim.
51. Bernard Plongeron, 'Face au Concordat 1801, résistances des évêques anciens constitutionnels', *Annales historiques de la Révolution française*, no. 337 (2004), pp. 85–115.
52. Boulay, I, pp. 127–9.
53. Thierry Lentz, *Nouvelle histoire du Premier Empire*, 4 vols (Paris, 2007), III, pp. 265–88.
54. Boulay, III, pp. 653–5.
55. Ibid., pp. 654–5.
56. Lentz, *Nouvelle histoire du Premier Empire*, III, pp. 114–18.
57. Boulay, III, p. 666.
58. Plongeron, 'Face au Concordat 1801, résistances des évêques', p. 87.
59. Ibid., p. 91.
60. Louis Madelin, *Histoire du Consulat et de l'Empire*, 16 vols (Paris, 1939), VI, pp. 44–59.
61. Gueniffey, *Bonaparte*, pp. 750–5.
62. Jean Thiry, *La machine infernale* (Paris, 1952), pp. 31–54.
63. Boulay, I, p. 161.
64. Ibid., III, pp. 675–8.
65. Thiry, *La machine infernale*, p. 167.
66. Jean Lorédan, *La machine infernale de la rue Nicaise (3 nivôse an IX)* (Paris, 1924), pp. 56–7.
67. Emmanuel de Waresquiel, *Fouché. Les silences de la pieuvre* (Paris, 2014), pp. 323–34.
68. Lorédan, *La machine infernale*, pp. 57–9.
69. Waresquiel, *Fouché*, pp. 326–8.
70. Marguerite Parenteau, *Pierre-Marie Desmarest. Chef de la police secrète de Napoléon* (Paris, 2009).
71. Lorédan, *La machine infernale*, pp. 68–98.
72. Lentz, *Le grand Consulat*, pp. 268–71.
73. Boulay, I, pp. 253, 320–2 and 328–9.

74. ASV, Francia Epoca Napoleonica 11, fasc. 5, no. 57, letter Spina to Bernier, expressing relief that Napoleon has escaped the assassination attempt unharmed, Paris, 26 December 1800.

75. Boulay, I, p. 173.

76. Ibid., pp. 272–3.

77. Ibid., pp. 272–7.

78. Ibid., p. 282; and ibid., III, p. 686.

79. Boulay de la Meurthe, *Histoire de la négociation du Concordat*, pp. 302–4 and 317.

80. ASV, Francia Epoca Napoleonica 7, fasc. 6, Preparativi Invasione 1801.

81. Boulay, I, pp. 351–3.

82. Ibid., II, p. 58.

83. Schroeder, *The Transformation of European Politics*, pp. 210–30.

84. Boulay de la Meurthe, *Histoire de la négociation du Concordat*, pp. 264–5.

85. Ibid., pp. 317–20.

86. Ibid., pp. 333–4.

87. Boulay, II, pp. 136–9.

88. Ibid., pp. 143–5.

89. Colin Morris, *The Papal Monarchy: The Western Church from 1050 to 1250* (Oxford, 1989), chs 4, 9 and 21; Menniti Ippolito, *Il tramonto della Curia nepotista*, pp. 127–58; and R. Belvederi, *Il papato di fronte alla Rivoluzione e alle conseguenze del Congresso di Vienna (1775–1846)* (Bologna, 1965), pp. 22–6.

90. Thierry Lentz (ed.), *Quand Napoléon inventait la France* (Paris, 2008), pp. 116–19 and 154–6; and Jean Bourdon, *Napoléon au Conseil d'état* (Paris, 1963).

91. Thierry Lentz (ed.), *Napoléon et le droit* (Paris, 2017).

92. Lentz, *Nouvelle histoire du Premier Empire*, III, pp. 58–84.

93. Lynn Hunt, *Politics, Culture and Class in the French Revolution* (Los Angeles, 1984), pp. 44–7.

94. Pasquale Villani, 'François Cacault decano dei diplomatici francesi in Italia durante la rivoluzione', *Studi storici*, vol. 42, no. 2 (2001), pp. 461–501.

95. Boulay de la Meurthe, *Histoire de la négociation du Concordat*, pp. 281–2; and Giustino Filippone, *Le relazioni tra lo Stato pontificio e la Francia rivoluzionaria. Storia diplomatica del trattato di Tolentino*, 2 vols (Milan, 1961–67).

96. Thiry, *Le Concordat et le Consulat à vie*, p. 58.

97. Boulay, II, pp. 201–2.

98. Linda Frey and Marsha Frey, '*Proven Patriots': The French Diplomatic Corps, 1789–1799* (St Andrews, 2011), pp. 14, 17, 62, 103 and 104; online at https://research-repository. st-andrews.ac.uk/handle/10023/1881 (accessed 22 September 2020).

99. Boulay, II, pp. 201–2.

100. Ibid., VI, pp. 1–11.

101. Ibid., II, pp. 268–74.

102. Ibid., pp. 212–16.

103. Perovic, *The Calendar in Revolutionary France*; and ASV, Francia Epoca Napoleonica 10, fasc. 1, Concordato 1801, no. 39r.

104. Boulay, II, p. 459.

105. Ibid., pp. 394–9.

106. Ibid., pp. 395–6.

107. Valois, *Histoire de la Pragmatique Sanction de Bourges*.

108. Boulay, II, p. 397.

109. Ibid., p. 403.

110. Ibid., pp. 419–22.

111. Ibid., p. 455.

112. Ibid.

113. ASV, Francia Epoca Napoleonica 11, fasc. 9, no. 5, order to Cacault to withdraw to Florence.

114. Thiry, *Le Concordat et le Consulat à vie*, pp. 65–6.

115. Robinson, *Cardinal Consalvi*, p. 66.

116. Boulay, II, pp. 484–6.

117. Consalvi, *Mémoires,* vols I and II.
118. Ibid., I, pp. 348–9.
119. Ibid., p. 350.
120. Ibid., p. 354.
121. Waresquiel, *Talleyrand. Le prince immobile,* p. 298.
122. Plongeron, 'Face au Concordat 1801, résistances des évêques', p. 90.
123. Roberto Regoli, *Ercole Consalvi. Le scelte per la chiesa* (Rome, 2006), pp. 288–304.
124. Ibid.
125. Boulay, IV, p. 94.
126. Ibid., III, p. 201.
127. Consalvi, *Mémoires,* I, p. 385.
128. Ibid., pp. 387–8.
129. Ibid., p. 393.
130. Courtemanche, *Napoléon et le sacré,* pp. 254–9.
131. Boulay, III, p. 215.
132. Regoli, *Ercole Consalvi,* pp. 304–11.
133. Consalvi, *Mémoires,* I, pp. 411–19.
134. Ibid., pp. 412–13.
135. Regoli, *Ercole Consalvi,* p. 313.
136. ASV, Francia Epoca Napoleonica 11, fasc. 3, Ratifica Convenzione luglio 1801.
137. Boulay, III, pp. 478–87.
138. ASV, Francia Epoca Napoleonica 9, fasc. 2, Ratificazione agosto 1801, Voti Cardinali, no. 188, 11 agosto 1801.
139. Regoli, *Ercole Consalvi,* pp. 314–15; and ASV, Francia Epoca Napoleonica 9, fasc. 2, votes of 11 August 1801.
140. Boulay, III, pp. 408–9.
141. Lentz, *Nouvelle histoire du Premier Empire,* III, pp. 107–26.
142. Irene Collins, *Napoleon and His Parliaments, 1800–1815* (London, 1979), p. 56.
143. Ibid., pp. 62–3.
144. Boulay, V, pp. 343–91.
145. Ibid., pp. 390–1.
146. Collins, *Napoleon and His Parliaments,* p. 70.
147. Boulay, V, pp. 313–27.
148. Philippe Boutry, *Souverain et pontife. Recherches prosopographiques sur la Curie romaine à l'âge de la restauration (1814–1846)* (Rome, 2002), pp. 340–1 and 472–4.
149. Leflon, *Étienne-Alexandre Bernier,* II, pp. 1–12.
150. ASV, Francia Epoca Napoleonica 11, fasc. 7, nos 34–5, return of remains of Pius VI.
151. Gendry, *Pie VI,* II, pp. 447–53.
152. Ibid., pp. 447–59.

## CHAPTER 4: CROWNING CHARLEMAGNE: NAPOLEON'S CORONATION, 1802–05

1. John D. Grainger, *The Amiens Truce: Britain and Bonaparte, 1801–1803* (Woodbridge, 2004).
2. Lentz, *Nouvelle histoire du Premier Empire,* I, pp. 324–5.
3. Thierry Lentz, 'La proclamation du Concordat à Notre-Dame le 18 avril 1802', in Jacques-Olivier Boudon (ed.), *Le Concordat et le retour de la paix religieuse* (Paris, 2008), pp. 95–112, esp. pp. 101 and 110.
4. Alfred Boulay de la Meurthe, *Histoire du rétablissement du culte en France (1802–1805)* (Tours, 1915), pp. 198–201.
5. Mayer, *Reginald Pole,* pp. 252–301.
6. ASV, Segreteria di Stato, Epoca Napoleonica, Francia 18, fasc. 4, Facoltà al Legato 1801.

7. Agostino Theiner, *Storia di Clemente XIV scritta sopra documenti inediti degli archivi segreti del Vaticano*, 3 vols (Milan, 1855), II, pp. 415–25.

8. Lentz, 'La proclamation du Concordat à Notre-Dame', pp. 100 and 110.

9. François-Auguste Chateaubriand [François-René de Chateaubriand], *Génie du christianisme, ou Beautés de la religion chrétienne*, 1802, 5 vols (Paris, 1802).

10. AN, AF IV 1044, dossier 2, no. 65, Rapport sur la situation de l'église de Notre-Dame et de l'archevêché, 19 germinal an X [9 April 1802].

11. Antoine Pierre Marie Gilbert, *Description historique de la Basilique métropolitaine de Paris* (Paris, 1821), pp. 141–51.

12. Lentz, 'La proclamation du Concordat à Notre-Dame', pp. 102–3.

13. Lentz, *Le grand Consulat*, pp. 331–54; and Philip Mansel, *The Eagle in Splendour: Napoleon I and His Court* (London, 1987), pp. 9–34.

14. Boulay, V, p. 564; Louis-François de Bausset, *Notice historique sur son éminence monseigneur le cardinal de Boisgelin archevêque de Tours* (Paris, 1804); Frédéric de Berthier, *L'Homme du Concordat. Le cardinal de Boisgelin, sa vie, son œuvre, sa famille, 1732–1804* (Paris, 2010), pp. 191–227.

15. Boulay, V, p. 635.

16. Ellis, 'Religion according to Napoleon'; and Antoine Casanova, 'Matérialismes, expériences historiques et traits originaux des élaborations philosophiques de Napoléon Bonaparte', in Natalie Petiteau (ed.), *Voies nouvelles pour l'histoire du Premier Empire. Territoires, pouvoirs, identités* (Paris, 2003), pp. 253–81.

17. Courtemanche, *Napoléon et le sacré*, p. 45.

18. Lentz, 'La proclamation du Concordat à Notre-Dame', p. 110.

19. Ruth Steiner and John Caldwell, 'Te Deum?', in Stanley Sadie (ed.), *The New Grove Dictionary of Music and Musicians* (London, 1980), vol. 18, p. 643.

20. J.-G. Prod'homme and Frederick H. Martens, 'Napoleon, music and musicians', *Musical Quarterly*, vol. 7, no. 4 (1921), pp. 579–605; p. 587.

21. Lentz, 'La proclamation du Concordat à Notre-Dame', p. 111.

22. Delmas remained out of favour until he offered his services to the Empire after the Russian disaster. He died during the disastrous Battle of Leipzig in October 1813: Guillaumin, *Les derniers républicains. Pichegru, Simon, Delmas, Monnier, le lion amoureux* (Paris, 1905), p. 135.

23. ASV, Segreteria di Stato, Epoca Napoleonica, Francia 3, fasc. 19, no. 34, versione stampata breve tam multa.

24. David Hudson, 'The "nouvelles ecclésiastiques", Jansenism, and Conciliarism, 1717–1735', *Catholic Historical Review*, vol. 70, no. 3 (1984), pp. 389–406.

25. ASV, Segreteria di Stato, Epoca Napoleonica, Francia 4, fasc. 1, Lettere des 14 Vescovi a Londra, nos 11–80, Mémoires des évêques résidents à Londres qui n'ont pas donné leur démission.

26. ASV, Segreteria di Stato, Epoca Napoleonica, Francia 3, fasc. 9, Dismissioni per Diocesi, Vescovo Duca di Langres, nos 1–10.

27. ASV, Segreteria di Stato, Epoca Napoleonica, Francia 3, fasc. 3, Dismissioni per Diocesi, nos 13 and 15, Béziers.

28. ASV, Segreteria di Stato, Epoca Napoleonica, Francia 3, fasc. 12, Dismissioni per Diocesi, Vescovo di Pamiers ed Arcivescovo Duca di Parigi, no. 1; and fasc. 13, Dismissioni per Diocesi, Vescovo di la Rochelle, nos 10 and 28–33.

29. ASV, Segreteria di Stato, Epoca Napoleonica, Francia 3, fasc. 1, Dismissioni, nos 38, 41 and 122.

30. ASV, Segreteria di Stato, Epoca Napoleonica, Francia 4, fasc. 4, Voti sulle Dimissioni de Vescovi, nos 14 and 26; and Camille Latreille, *L'opposition religieuse au Concordat de 1792 à 1803* (Paris, 1910).

31. By 1804, of the ninety surviving bishops of the Gallican Church, fifty-two had resigned and thirty-eight refused: Bernard Plongeron, *Des résistances religieuses à Napoléon (1799–1813)* (Paris, 2006), p. 89.

32. Jacques-Olivier Boudon, *Napoléon et les cultes. Les religions en Europe à l'aube du XIXème siècle, 1800–1815* (Paris, 2002), pp. 171–5.

33. Jany Rouger, Jean-Louis Neveu et al., *La Petite Église, deux siècles de dissidence* (Parthenay, 1991); Victor Bindel, *Histoire religieuse de Napoléon*, 2 vols (Paris, 1940), II, pp. 147–95; and for the Lyonnais see AN, F7 6376, Petite Église de Lyon; a determined campaign of police intimidation and interrogation took place there.

34. Jacques-Olivier Boudon, 'La reconstruction des diocèses en 1802', in idem (ed.), *Le Concordat et le retour*, pp. 135–49, esp. p. 138; and Simon Delacroix, *La réorganisation de l'Église de France après la Révolution 1801–1809*, vol. I, *Les nominations d'évêques et la liquidation du passé* (Paris, 1962), pp. 254–81 and 294–300; and for Bernier notes and the individual files on candidates to the episcopacy, see AN, AF IV 1044, dossier 1, nominations.

35. Plongeron, *Des résistances religieuses*, pp. 151–84.

36. Joseph Othenin Bernard de Cléron, comte d'Haussonville, *L'Église romaine et le Premier Empire, 1800–1814*, 5 vols (Paris,1864–79), I, pp. 201–4.

37. ASV, Segreteria di Stato, Epoca Napoleonica, Francia 14, fasc. 10, Ritrattazioni Clero Costituzionale, nos 1–37.

38. ASV, Segreteria di Stato, Epoca Napoleonica, Francia 10, fascs 5–6, Nota de nuovi AV e V di Francia li quali non hanno chiesto le bolle Apostoliche di conferma della canonica loro istituzione [lists the constitutionals]; and ASV, Segreteria di Stato, Epoca Napoleonica, Francia 13, fasc. 3, Clero Costituzionale, nos 77–92, di Pietro rapporto sui vescovi costituzionali.

39. Boulay de la Meurthe, *Histoire du rétablissement du culte*, pp. 268–73.

40. ASV, Segreteria di Stato, Epoca Napoleonica, Francia 8, fasc. 2, Lettere a Napoleone, nos 163–73.

41. ASV, Segreteria di Stato, Epoca Napoleonica, Francia 8, fasc. 2, Lettere a Napoleone, nos 167–9 and 285–8.

42. Theiner, *Histoire des deux concordats*, I, pp. 484–513.

43. ASV, Segreteria di Stato, Epoca Napoleonica, Francia 8, fasc. 2, Lettere a Napoleone, no. 285.

44. Jean Leflon, 'Le clergé de second ordre sous le Consulat et le Premier Empire', *Revue d'histoire de l'Église de France*, vol. 31, no. 18 (1945), pp. 97–119; and Bindel, *Histoire religieuse de Napoléon*, I, pp. 111–24.

45. Jean-Edmé-Auguste Gosselin, *Vie de M. Emery*, 2 vols (Paris, 1861–62), II, pp. 339–444.

46. Roger Price, *Religious Renewal in France, 1789–1870: The Catholic Church between Catastrophe and Triumph* (Basingstoke, 2018), pp. 113–53.

47. ASV, Segreteria di Stato, Epoca Napoleonica, Francia 4, fasc. 9, no. 1, Réflexions sur le mode actuel de réunion des prêtres constitutionnels a l'unité de l'Église catholique.

48. Leflon, 'Le clergé de second ordre', p. 106; Charles Ledré, *Le cardinal Cambacérès, archevêque de Rouen (1802–1818). La réorganisation d'un diocèse français au lendemain de la Révolution* (Paris, 1943), pp. 414–19; and AN, F7 6376, Petite Église de Lyon.

49. ASV, Segreteria di Stato, Epoca Napoleonica, Francia 10, fasc. 7, Giuramento Belgio; fasc. 9, Voti Giuramento 1802; and fasc. 10, Formule di Giuramento.

50. Cf. Cage, *Unnatural Frenchmen*, pp. 130–65.

51. Leflon, 'Le clergé de second ordre', p. 105.

52. Vovelle, *Religion et révolution*, pp. 108–44.

53. The most notorious examples were Dominique Lacombe, Claude Lacoz, Claude-François-Marie Primat and Jean-Pierre Saurine: ASV, Segreteria di Stato, Epoca Napoleonica, Francia 24, fasc. 6, Vescovi Costituzionali.

54. Étienne DeJean, *Un préfet du Consulat. Jacques Claude Beugnot* (Paris, 1907), pp. 351–77.

55. For an excellent case study see Gérard Bouchard, *Le village immobile. Sennely en Sologne au XVIIIème siècle* (Paris, 1971); and Judith Devlin, *The Superstitious Mind: French Peasants and the Supernatural in the Nineteenth Century* (London, 1987).

56. Jean-Clément Martin, *Dictionnaire de la Contre-Révolution* (Paris, 2011), esp. pp. 213–19.

57. Latreille, 'Le gallicanisme ecclésiastique sous le Premier Empire'.

58. Boudon, *Napoléon et les cultes*, pp. 111–21 and 185–201; and Pierre Birnbaum, *L'aigle et la synagogue. Napoléon, les Juifs et l'état* (Paris, 2007).

59. ASV, Segreteria di Stato, Epoca Napoleonica, Italia 10, fasc. 1, Soppressione Ordini Religiosi Piemonte.
60. Ugo Da Como, *I Comizi nazionali in Lione per la costituzione della Repubblica italiana,* 5 vols (Bologna, 1935), II/1, p. 213.
61. ASV, Segreteria di Stato, Epoca Napoleonica, Italia 19, fasc. 1, Concordato Italiano, no. 28; and Daniele Arru, *Il Concordato italiano del 1803* (Milan, 2003), pp. 72–94; Theiner, *Histoire des deux concordats,* II, pp. 261–3.
62. ASV, Segreteria di Stato, Epoca Napoleonica, Italia 19, fasc. 1, Concordato Italiano, no. 28.
63. Teresa Muzzi, *Vita di Ferdinando Marescalchi, patrizio bolognese* (Rome, 1932), pp. 133–6.
64. Haussonville, *L'Église romaine et le Premier Empire,* I, pp. 537–8.
65. Arru, *Il Concordato italiano,* pp. 47–72.
66. ASV, Segreteria di Stato, Epoca Napoleonica, Italia 19, fasc. 2, part 1, Concordato Italiano, no. 3, Bernier mémoire sur le Concordat italien.
67. Nino del Bianco, *Francesco Melzi d'Eril. La grande occasione perduta, gli albori dell'indipendenza nell'Italia napoleonica* (Milan, 2002), pp. 204–13.
68. ASV, Segreteria di Stato, Epoca Napoleonica, Italia 19, fascs 1–3, Concordato Italiano.
69. ASV, Segreteria di Stato, Epoca Napoleonica, Italia 19, fasc. 3, part 1, no. 2, di Pietro riflessioni progetto Parigino Concordato Italiano, April 1803.
70. ASV, Segreteria di Stato, Epoca Napoleonica, Italia 19, fasc. 3, part 2, no. 27, Caprara to Consalvi, 2 September 1803, report on his meeting with Napoleon on Monday 29 August 1803. Ferdinando Marescalchi, the foreign minister of the Italian Republic, and his deputy Jacobj were also present at this meeting.
71. ASV, Segreteria di Stato, Epoca Napoleonica, Italia 19, fasc. 1, no. 23, brief anon. observations on Italian Concordat; and Arru, *Il Concordato italiano,* pp. 457–73.
72. Vittoria Princi, 'Militarised cities? Housing and garrisoning the French Empire's troops in the Napoleonic Kingdom of Italy', DPhil thesis, University of Oxford, 2021, ch. 4.
73. Arru, *Il Concordato italiano,* pp. 504–5.
74. ASV, Segreteria di Stato, Epoca Napoleonica, Italia 19, fasc. 5, Post Concordat, no. 6, di Pietro report on Melzi's organic laws, 26 January 1804.
75. ASV, Segreteria di Stato, Emigrati Rivoluzione Francese; a remarkable archival series which has yet to be studied in any great depth.
76. Elizabeth Sparrow, *Secret Service: British Agents in France, 1792–1815* (Woodbridge, 1999), pp. 120–4; and Michael Drury, *William Wickham, Master Spy* (Abingdon, 2009), pp. 93–7.
77. Ricard (ed.), *Correspondance diplomatique,* II, pp. 207–27.
78. André Latreille, *Napoléon et le Saint-Siège (1801–1808): L'ambassade du cardinal Fesch à Rome* (Paris, 1935), pp. 219–50.
79. ASV, Segreteria di Stato, Ministri Esteri 31, fasc. 1, Vernègues Carte, Filza 1, 17 August 1797–21 December 1803.
80. Paul Pierling, *La Russie et le Saint-Siège. Études diplomatiques V. Catherine II – Paul Ier – Alexandre Ier,* 2nd edn (Paris, 1912), pp. 372 and 401–51.
81. ASV, Segreteria di Stato, Ministri Esteri 28, Consalvi to Cassini on Vernègues's arrest, 26 December 1803.
82. ASV, Segreteria di Stato, Ministri Esteri 28, Cassini to Consalvi to demand international arbitration, 15 March 1804.
83. Consalvi, *Mémoires,* II, pp. 327–47, esp. p. 345.
84. ASV, Segreteria di Stato, Ministri Esteri 30, fasc. 1, rapporto 14 Floreale Anno 12 un'ora dopo mezzo giorno, 31 December 1803–12 May 1804.
85. Pierling, *La Russie et le Saint-Siège,* pp. 444–51.
86. Guy-Edouard Pillard, *Fontanes. Prince de l'Esprit* (Hérault, 1990), pp. 158–9; and Marcello Simonetta and Noga Arikha, *Napoleon and the Rebel: A Story of Brotherhood, Passion, and Power* (Basingstoke, 2011), pp. 72–5.
87. Huchet, *Georges Cadoudal et les Chouans,* pp. 339–54.

88. Lentz, *Nouvelle histoire du Premier Empire*, I, pp. 43–5; and Tim Clayton, *This Dark Business: The Secret War against Napoleon* (London, 2018), pp. 255–91.
89. Jean-Paul Bertaud, *Le duc d'Enghien* (Paris, 2001), pp. 369–90.
90. Philip Dwyer, 'Napoleon and the foundation of the Empire', *Historical Journal*, vol. 53, no. 2 (2010), pp. 339–58.
91. Lentz, *Nouvelle histoire du Premier Empire*, I, pp. 20–2; and Waresquiel, *Fouché*, pp. 387–404.
92. Ibid., p. 21.
93. Pierre Leuregans, 'Louis XVI. "Empereur des Français"', *Revue historique de droit français et étranger*, vol. 44 (1966), pp. 248–61.
94. Robert Morrissey, *Charlemagne and France: A Thousand Years of Mythology* (Notre Dame, IN, 2003), pp. 250–65.
95. Thierry Lentz (ed.), *La proclamation de l'Empire* (Paris, 2002), pp. 24–9.
96. Ibid., pp. 63–9.
97. Lentz, *Nouvelle histoire du Premier Empire*, I, pp. 25–6.
98. Annie Jourdan, 'Conclusion: The Napoleonic Empire in the age of revolutions – The contrast of two national representations', in Michael Broers, Peter Hicks and Agustín Guimerá (eds), *The Napoleonic Empire and the New European Political Culture* (Basingstoke, 2012), pp. 313–26, esp. pp. 316–20.
99. Malcolm Crook, 'The plebiscite on the Empire', in Alan Forrest and Philip Dwyer (eds), *Napoleon and His Empire: Europe, 1804–1814* (Basingstoke, 2007), pp. 16–28.
100. Ricard (ed.), *Correspondance diplomatique*, I, pp. 316–17.
101. Jean-Paul Bertaud, *Les royalistes et Napoléon* (Paris, 2009), pp. 203–56.
102. David Chanteranne, *Le sacre de Napoléon* (Paris, 2004), pp. 43–7.
103. Monza Ozouf, *Festivals and the French Revolution* (Cambridge, MA, 1991).
104. Schroeder, *The Transformation of European Politics*, pp. 257–76.
105. ASV, Segreteria di Stato, Epoca Napoleonica, Francia 5, fasc. 1, Incoronazione Napoleone, no. 1, Pio VII to Napoleon, 30 May 1804.
106. Rosamond McKitterick, *Charlemagne: The Formation of a European Identity* (Cambridge, 2008), p. 292.
107. Michael Rowe, *From Reich to State: The Rhineland in the Revolutionary Age, 1780–1830* (Cambridge, 2003) pp. 153–5.
108. Chanteranne, *Le sacre de Napoléon*, pp. 66–72.
109. Lauren Johnson, *Shadow King: The Life and Death of Henry VI* (London, 2019).
110. ASV, Segreteria di Stato, Epoca Napoleonica, Francia 5, fasc. 2, Viaggio del Papa, nos 25–35, Braschi opinion on journey.
111. It makes uncomfortable reading, with our modern sensitivities, but the church only accepted inter-faith dialogue after the Second Vatican Council (1962–65). Liberalising individual conscience was anathema to Catholic teaching: John W. O'Malley, *What Happened at Vatican II?* (Cambridge, MA, 2008).
112. ASV, Segreteria di Stato, Epoca Napoleonica, Francia 5, fasc. 1, Incoronazione Napoleone, no. 46, Consalvi to Caprara, 2 September 1804.
113. Beales, *Joseph II*, II, pp. 214–38.
114. These included several cardinals: Antonelli, Bayanne, Braschi, Borgia, Caselli and di Pietro. Fesch was part of the group too, but a supernumerary, being French ambassador.
115. ASV, Segreteria di Stato, Epoca Napoleonica, Francia 5, fasc. 1, Incoronazione Napoleone, no. 53, Consalvi to Caprara describing General Caffarelli's arrival in Rome, 6 October 1804.
116. ASV, Segreteria di Stato, Epoca Napoleonica, Francia 5, fasc. 6, Viaggio Pio VII Parigi, nos 1–26, list of convoys.
117. ASV, Segreteria di Stato, Epoca Napoleonica, Francia 5, fasc. 6, Viaggio Pio VII Parigi, no. 28, itinerary in Italy.
118. Consalvi, *Mémoires*, II, pp. 393–423.
119. Jean-Marc Ticchi, 'Le vicaire du Christ en France: Pie VII en voyage pour le couronnement de Napoléon Ier', *Archivum historiae pontificiae*, vol. 43 (2005), pp. 139–55; and AD du

Rhône, 1F, Papiers Fesch, 1F 96, Voyage de Pie VII à Paris pour le Couronnement, Fesch to Napoleon, Turin, 22 brumaire an XIII [13 November 1804].

120. Ticchi, 'Le vicaire du Christ en France', p. 145.

121. Jean-Paul Lyonnet, *Le cardinal Fesch, archevêque de Lyon*, 2 vols (Paris, 1841, I, pp. 348–9; and Antoine Ricard, *Le cardinal Fesch, archevêque de Lyon (1763–1839)* (Paris, 1893), pp. 116–18.

122. Christophe Beyeler et al., *Le pape et l'empereur. La réception de Pie VII par Napoléon à Fontainebleau, 25–28 novembre 1804* (Paris, 2004).

123. Jean-Marc Ticchi, *Le voyage de Pie VII à Paris pour le sacre de Napoléon, 1804–1805* (Paris, 2013), pp. 99–101; and Charles-Éloi Vial, *Le grand veneur de Napoléon Ier à Charles X* (Paris, 2016), pp. 132–3.

124. Lentz, *Nouvelle histoire du Premier Empire*, I, pp. 85–7.

125. Anne Jean Marie René Savary, *Mémoires du duc de Rovigo pour servir à l'histoire de l'empereur Napoléon*, 8 vols (Paris, 1829), II, pp. 111–12.

126. Erasmo Pistolesi, *Vita del sommo pontefice Pio VII*, 4 vols (Rome, 1824), I, p. 207.

127. Ticchi, *Le voyage de Pie VII à Paris*, pp. 238–52.

128. Ibid., pp. 128–31.

129. Ticchi, 'Le vicaire du Christ en France', p. 147.

130. ASV, Segreteria di Stato, Epoca Napoleonica, Francia 5, fasc. 7, Talleyrand request for laicisation and refusal of permission to marry; AN, F19 1909, dossier 1, Talleyrand; and Louis Madelin, *Talleyrand* (Paris, 1944), pp. 125–30 and 153–5.

131. Leflon, *Étienne-Alexandre Bernier*, II, pp. 200–7.

132. Lentz, *Joseph Bonaparte*, pp. 147–8, 176–7, 191 and 242.

133. Henri Welschinger, *Le pape et l'empereur, 1804–1815* (Paris, 1905), pp. 29–31.

134. Lentz, *Nouvelle histoire du Premier Empire*, I, p. 86.

135. Chanteranne, *Le sacre de Napoléon*, p. 96.

136. Jean Tulard, *Le sacre de l'empereur Napoléon. Histoire et légende* (Paris, 2004), pp. 14–20.

137. Ellis, 'Religion according to Napoleon'; and Broers, *Napoleon: Soldier of Destiny*, pp. 425–30.

138. Lentz, *Nouvelle histoire du Premier Empire*, I, p. 84.

139. Todd Porterfield and Susan L. Siegfried, *Staging Empire: Napoleon, Ingres, and David* (University Park, PA, 2007), pp. 91–136.

140. AN, AF IV 1045, dossier 1, no. 64, Camilla Illari to Napoleon, Avignon, 29 August 1804.

141. Nicolas Roze, 'Vivat in aeternum', 1804; listen online at https://www.youtube.com/watch?v=7DtvA6nn6P4 (accessed 24 September 2020).

142. Chanteranne, *Le sacre de Napoléon*, pp. 125–28.

143. Ibid., chs 5–6; and Lentz, *Nouvelle histoire du Premier Empire*, I, pp. 90–8.

144. Artaud de Montor, *Histoire du Pape Pie VII*, II, pp. 25–36.

145. Gemma Betros, 'Napoleon and the revival of female religious communities in Paris, 1800–1814', *Studies in Church History*, vol. 44 (2008), pp. 185–95.

146. ASV, Segreteria di Stato, Epoca Napoleonica, Francia 13, fasc. 12, Missioni Francesi.

147. ASV, Segreteria di Stato, Ministri Esteri 31, fasc. 2, 21 December 1804–13 April 1805, pope asks that Vernègues be released from the Temple prison, 21 December 1804.

148. Artaud de Montor, *Histoire de la vie et du pontificat du Pape Pie VII*, II, pp. 25–42.

149. NAP NOUV CORRES, no. 9,483, Paris, 11 nivôse an XIII [1 January 1805], V, p. 20.

150. Leflon, *Étienne-Alexandre Bernier*, II, pp. 223–38.

151. Ticchi, *Le voyage de Pie VII à Paris*, p. 130.

152. E.E.Y. Hales, *The Emperor and the Pope: The Story of Napoleon and Pius VII* (New York, 1961), pp. 70–1.

153. ASV, Segreteria di Stato, Epoca Napoleonica, Italia 19, fascs 3–4, private correspondence of Pius VII: many letters to Scipione Chiaramonti.

154. Ambrogio A. Caiani, 'Ornamentalism in a European context? Napoleon's Italian coronation, May 1805', *English Historical Review*, no. 132 (2017), pp. 41–72.

## CHAPTER 5: A NEW BABYLONIAN CAPTIVITY: THE FRENCH
## ANNEXATION OF ROME, 1805–09

1. Carol Berkin, *Wondrous Beauty: Betsy Bonaparte, the Belle of Baltimore who Married Napoleon's Brother* (New York, 2014); and Patrick Le Carvèse, 'Jérôme Bonaparte, officier de Marine', *Napoleonica. La revue*, no. 26 (2016), pp. 21–100. Decades later, in a bizarre twist of fate, Betsy's widowed sister-in-law Marianne was to remarry Richard Wellesley, the duke of Wellington's elder brother. The Pattersons of Baltimore would represent the closest family tie between the two rival commanders at Waterloo.

2. AN, F19 1905, Patterson dossier; and ASV, Segreteria di Stato, Epoca Napoleonica, Francia 8, fasc. 2, Lettere a Napoleone, nos 428–37, on Patterson annulment, 9 September 1805.

3. ASV, Segreteria di Stato, Epoca Napoleonica, Francia 8, fasc. 16, Codice Napoleonico, no. 16, di Pietro opinion on extension of code to Italy; Jennifer Ngaire Heuer, *The Family and the Nation: Gender and Citizenship in Revolutionary France, 1789–1830* (Ithaca, NY, 2005), pp. 127–42; and June K. Burton, *Napoleon and the Woman Question: Discourses of the Other Sex in French Education, Medicine and Medical Law, 1799–1815* (Lubbock, TX, 2007), p. 148.

4. Jacques-Olivier Boudon, *Le roi Jérôme, frère prodigue de Napoléon* (Paris, 2008), pp. 78–86.

5. Ibid., pp. 92–8.

6. Eric F. Goldman, *Charles J. Bonaparte, Patrician Reformer: His Early Career* (Baltimore, MD, 1943).

7. ASV, Segreteria di Stato, Epoca Napoleonica, Francia 8, fasc 2, Lettere a Napoleone, nos 428–37, on Patterson annulment, 9 September 1805.

8. Boudon, *Le roi Jérôme*, pp. 155–75.

9. Henri Welschinger, *Le divorce de Napoléon* (Paris, 1889).

10. Latreille, 'Le gallicanisme ecclésiastique sous le Premier Empire'.

11. Michael Broers, *Napoleon: The Spirit of the Age, 1805–1810* (London, 2018), pp. 9–52.

12. Albert Vandal, *Napoléon et Alexandre Ier. L'alliance russe sous le Premier Empire*, 3 vols (Paris, 1906), I, pp. 56–111; Thierry Lentz, 'Napoléon et Charlemagne', in idem (ed.), *Napoléon et l'Europe* (Paris, 2005), pp. 11–30.

13. Frank J. Coppa, *The Modern Papacy since 1789* (Harlow, 1998), chs 1–6.

14. A.D. Wright, *The Early Modern Papacy: From the Council of Trent to the French Revolution, 1564–1789* (Harlow, 2000), chs 5 and 7; Morris, *The Papal Monarchy*.

15. Michael Broers, *The Napoleonic Empire in Italy, 1796–1814: Cultural Imperialism in a European Context?* (Basingstoke, 2005), pp. 101–21.

16. Morrissey, *Charlemagne and France*, pp. 250–65.

17. Latreille, *Napoléon et le Saint-Siège*, pp. 434–47

18. AD du Rhône, 1F, Papiers Fesch, 1F 50, Lettres Meuron Ancône 1805–1806, Meuron to Fesch, report on arrival of troops in Ancona, 18 and 21 October 1805.

19. ASV, Segreteria di Stato, Epoca Napoleonica, Francia 24, fasc. 17, riflessioni sulle diverse note del governo Francese 1806, no. 1, on the violation of Ancona and passage of French troops.

20. Artaud de Montor, *Histoire du Pape Pie VII*, II, pp. 108–11.

21. Latreille, *Napoléon et le Saint-Siège*, pp. 442–7.

22. Andrew Wheatcroft, *The Enemy at the Gate: Habsburgs, Ottomans and the Battle for Europe* (New York, 2010).

23. AD du Rhône, 1F, Papiers Fesch, 1F 21, Correspondance Diplomatique de Fesch an XII à 1806, fol. 535, to prince of Saxe-Coburg-Gotha, 5 January 1806.

24. AD du Rhône, 1F, Papiers Fesch, 1F 21, Correspondance Diplomatique de Fesch an XII à 1806, fol. 564, to Count Johann Emanuel Khevenhüller-Metsch, 6 February 1806; and NAP NOUV CORRES, no. 11,345, Paris, 30 January 1806, VI, p. 67.

25. Casaburi, *Fabrizio Ruffo*, pp. 180–1.

26. NAP NOUV CORRES, no. 11,267, Paris, 7 January 1806, VI, p. 31.

27. Patricia Sorel, *Napoléon et le livre. La censure sous le Consulat et l'Empire* (Rennes, 2020), pp. 121–9.

28. Broers, *Napoleon: The Spirit of the Age*, p. 227.

29. Lentz, *Joseph Bonaparte*, pp. 260–1.

30. Ibid., pp. 274–81; and Jacques Rambaud, *Lettres inédites ou éparses de Joseph Bonaparte à Naples (1806–1808)* (Paris, 1911), pp. 84–95.

31. Lentz, *Joseph Bonaparte*, pp. 282–8.

32. Giuseppe Galasso (ed.), *Storia d'Italia*, vol. XV/1, *Il Regno di Napoli. Il Mezzogiorno angioino e aragonese (1266–1494)* (Turin, 1992); and Norman Housely, *The Italian Crusades: The Papal-Angevin Alliance and the Crusades against Christian Lay Powers, 1254–1343* (Oxford, 1982).

33. Girolamo Lioy, 'L'abolizione dell'omaggio della Chinea', *Archivio storico per le provincie napoletane* (1882), vol. 7, pp. 263–92, 497–530 and 713–75; ASV, Segreteria di Stato, Epoca Napoleonica, Italia 7, fasc. 36, Chinea; and fasc. 20, responsio ad protestationem Chinea, 1795.

34. Daniello Maria Zigarelli, *Storia di Benevento* (Naples, 1860); and 'Pontecorvo' entry, in Gaetano Moroni (ed.), *Dizionario di erudizione storico-ecclesiastica da San Pietro sino ai nostri* (Rome, 1852), vol. 54, pp. 94–104.

35. David Armando, 'La feudalità nello Stato pontificio alla fine del Settecento', *Studi storici*, vol. 45, no. 3 (2004), pp. 751–84, esp. pp. 764–5; and Belvederi, *Il papato di fronte alla Rivoluzione*, pp. 30–3.

36. ASV, Segreteria di Stato, Epoca Napoleonica, Francia 8, fasc. 17, Giuseppe re di Napoli; ASV, Segreteria di Stato, Epoca Napoleonica, Francia 13, fasc. 13, Chiusura porti agli inglesi, nos 11–16; and ASV, Segreteria di Stato, Epoca Napoleonica, Francia 24, fasc. 17, riflessioni sulle diverse note del governo Francese 1806, no. 2, di Pietro reflections on violation of papal territory and recognition of Joseph.

37. ASV, Segreteria di Stato, Epoca Napoleonica, Francia 8, fasc. 2, Lettere a Napoleone, nos 485–6, protest against annexation of Benevento and Pontecorvo, 21 June 1806.

38. Latreille, *Napoléon et le Saint-Siège*, pp. 491–3.

39. Ibid., pp. 501–6.

40. Filiberto Agostini, *La riforma napoleonica della chiesa nella Repubblica e nel Regno d'Italia 1802–1814* (Vicenza,1990), pp. 170–1 and 192–7.

41. In May 1806 this led the French to send a Franco-Neapolitan force to occupy Civitavecchia, the main papal port: ASV, Segreteria di Stato, Epoca Napoleonica, Francia 19, fasc. 3, Trattative 1806–1807, no. 10, protest against occupation of Civitavecchia, 14 June 1806.

42. Katherine B. Aaslestad and Johan Joor (eds), *Revisiting Napoleon's Continental System: Local, Regional and European Experiences* (Basingstoke, 2015), esp. Introduction, chs 1–2 and 6.

43. Francis II became Francis I of Austria after 1806, given the end of the Holy Roman Empire: Peter H. Wilson, 'The meaning of empire in central Europe around 1800', in Alan Forrest and Peter H. Wilson (eds), *The Bee and the Eagle: Napoleonic France and the End of the Holy Roman Empire, 1806* (Basingstoke, 2009), pp. 22–41; and Joachim Whaley, *Germany and the Holy Roman Empire*, 2 vols (Oxford, 2012), II, pp. 636–44.

44. Peter H. Wilson, *The Holy Roman Empire* (London, 2016), pp. 645–54.

45. Sadly there is no English or French biography of Dalberg; Germanophone readers can turn to Herbert Hömig, *Karl Theodor von Dalberg: Staatsmann und Kirchenfürst im Schatten Napoleons* (Paderborn, 2011), esp. 307–23.

46. Leflon, *Étienne-Alexandre Bernier*, II, p. 238.

47. Hömig, *Karl Theodor von Dalberg*, pp. 399–470.

48. Alexis-François Artaud de Montor, *Histoire du Pape Léon XII*, 2 vols (Paris, 1843), I, pp. 10–14.

49. Leflon, *Étienne-Alexandre Bernier*, II, pp. 326–32.

50. André Latreille, *Le Catéchisme impérial de 1806* (Paris, 1935), pp. 71–104.

51. John Bossy, 'The Counter-Reformation and the people of Catholic Europe', *Past & Present*, no. 47 (1970), pp. 51–70.

52. John W. O'Malley, *Trent: What Happened at the Council* (Cambridge, MA, 2013), pp. 263–5.

53. Jacques-Benigne Bossuet, *Catéchisme du diocèse de Meaux* (Paris, 1687).

54. ASV, Segreteria di Stato, Epoca Napoleonica, Francia 7, fasc. 1, Catechismo Imperiale, preliminary approval, 31 March 1806.

55. ASV, Segreteria di Stato, Epoca Napoleonica, Francia 7, fasc. 1, Catechismo Imperiale, no. 48, Voto segretario sant'uffizio.

56. ASV, Segreteria di Stato, Epoca Napoleonica, Francia 7, fasc. 1, Catechismo Imperiale, nos 57–9, Toni de Miavi opinion on prayers for Napoleon.

57. Latreille, *Le Catéchisme impérial*, pp. 80–2.

58. Broers, *Napoleon: The Spirit of the Age*, pp. 226–7; and Jean-Paul Lyonnet, *Histoire de Mgr d'Aviau du Bois-de-Sanzay, successivement archevêque de Vienne et Bordeaux*, 2 vols (Paris, 1847), II, pp. 538–53.

59. ASV, Segreteria di Stato, Epoca Napoleonica, Francia 17b, fasc. 1, carte relative alla San Napoleone; and Marco Emanuele Omes, 'La festa di Napoleone. Sovranità, legittimità e sacralità nell'Europa francese, Repubblica/Impero francese, Repubblica/Regno d'Italia, Regno di Spagna, 1799–1814', PhD thesis, Co-tutelle Scuola Normale Superiore Pisa/Sorbonne Université Paris IV, 2019, passim.

60. Sudhir Hazareesingh, *The Saint-Napoleon: Celebrations of Sovereignty in Nineteenth-Century France* (Cambridge, MA, 2004), pp. 2–21.

61. H. Perrin de Boussac, *Un témoin de la Révolution et de l'Empire. Charles Jean-Marie Alquier (1752–1826)* (La Rochelle, 1983), esp. pp. 33–88 and 193–222.

62. Although nineteenth-century French historians have questioned Consalvi's minutes, they ring true. After all, five years after this audience, the national council threatened by Fesch was indeed convened to bypass the pope's authority: Latreille, *Napoléon et le Saint-Siège*, p. 515; and idem, 'Le gallicanisme ecclésiastique sous le Premier Empire'.

63. Pistolesi, *Vita del sommo pontefice Pio VII*, II, pp. 35–6; and Consalvi, *Mémoires*, II, pp. 481–9.

64. Artaud de Montor, *Histoire de la vie et du pontificat du Pape Pie VII*, II, pp. 138–57.

65. ASV, Segreteria di Stato, Epoca Napoleonica, Francia 20, fasc. 3, Trattative 1806–1808, no. 6, Casoni to Caprara, 19 July 1806.

66. ASV, Segreteria di Stato, Epoca Napoleonica, Francia 13, fasc. 13, Chiusura porti agli inglesi, nos 51–4, undated memoranda.

67. ASV, Segreteria di Stato, Epoca Napoleonica, Francia 13, fasc. 13, Chiusura porti agli inglesi, no. 69, Mgr Arezzo, archbishop of Seleucia summoned by Napoleon in Berlin on 9 November 1806; and M.J. Rouët de Journel, *Nonciatures de Russie d'après les documents authentiques. Nonciature d'Arezzo (1802–1806)*, 2 vols (Rome, 1922).

68. ASV, Segreteria di Stato, Epoca Napoleonica, Italia 10, fasc. 40, untitled, no. 3, domande sulla possibile occupazione degli stati pontefici.

69. ASV, Segreteria di Stato, Epoca Napoleonica, Italia 10, fasc. 40, untitled, no. 4, di Pietro voto.

70. Ibid.

71. ASV, Segreteria di Stato, Epoca Napoleonica, Francia 8, fasc. 10, Eugène de Beauharnais Correspondance, nos 2–46, documents on Venetian sees and problems; and subsequently fasc. 12, Lettere di Eugenio a Pio VII, nos 1–5, 7 and 8–17.

72. Anon., *Serie de' documenti sulle vertenze insorte fra la Santa Sede ed il governo francese*, 6 vols (Rome, 1833), II, pp. 165–6 and 169–75; ASV, Segreteria di Stato, Epoca Napoleonica, Francia 12, fasc. 14, Trattative con Napoleone 1807, no. 9, Cardinal Casoni to Bovara, Italian minister of religions, 11 October 1806.

73. H.E.J. Cowdrey, *Pope Gregory VII, 1073–1085* (Oxford, 1998), pp. 91–166.

74. ASV, Segreteria di Stato, Epoca Napoleonica, Francia 20, fasc. 3, Trattative 1806–1808, passim esp. Risposta IX .

75. Artaud de Montor, *Histoire du Pape Pie VII*, II, pp. 169–71.

76. ASV, Segreteria di Stato, Epoca Napoleonica, Francia 13, fasc. 14, Trattative 1807, nos 19 and 21, report from Caprara and letter from Casoni on Napoleon's demand Bayanne be sent to negotiate.

77. ASV, Segreteria di Stato, Epoca Napoleonica, Francia 20, no. 13, Champagny to Bayanne, 21 September 1807.

78. Vincent J. Pitts, *Henry IV of France: His Reign and Age* (Baltimore, MD, 2009), pp. 317–30; and Roland Mousnier, *L'assassinat d'Henri IV, 14 mai 1610* (Paris, 1979).

79. AN, F19 6287, on Jesuits or *pères de la foi*, whom Napoleon persecuted all the way into Poland.

80. ASV, Segreteria di Stato, Epoca Napoleonica, Francia 20, fasc. 3, Trattative 1806–1808, Champagny to Bayanne, 21 September 1807.

81. Madelin, *La Rome de Napoléon*, p. 179.

82. ASV, Segreteria di Stato, Epoca Napoleonica, Francia 20, fasc. 3, Trattative 1806–1808, no. 14, draft treaty of alliance, November 1807.

83. Ibid.

84. ASV, Segreteria di Stato, Epoca Napoleonica, Francia 13, fasc. 14, Trattative Missione Bayanne 1807, no. 55, Bayanne advised to capitulate, 7 November 1807.

85. Broers, *Napoleon: The Spirit of the Age*, pp. 278–345.

86. Charles J. Esdaile, *Fighting Napoleon: Guerrillas, Bandits and Adventurers in Spain, 1808–1814* (London, 2004); and Gabriel H. Lovett, *Napoleon and the Birth of Modern Spain*, 2 vols (New York, 1965).

87. R. Fantini, 'Due cardinali napoleonisti. Caselli, vescovo di Parma, e Oppizzoni, arcivescovo di Bologna', *Aurea Parma*, vol. 53 (1969), pp. 153–64; and Francesco Gasparolo, 'Il cardinale Caselli', *Rivista di storia e d'arte della provincia di Alessandria*, vol. 21 (1912), pp. 129–36.

88. Maurizio Tagliaferri (ed.), *Il cardinale Carlo Oppizzoni, tra Napoleone e l'Unità d'Italia* (Rome, 2015); and Ambrogio A. Caiani, 'Collaborators, collaboration and the problems of empire in Napoleonic Italy: The Oppizzoni Affair, 1805–1807', *Historical Journal*, vol. 60, no. 2 (2017), pp. 385–407.

89. Ibid., p. 403.

90. Roberto Regoli, 'Il cardinale Oppizzoni e il pontificato di Pio VII', in Tagliaferri (ed.), *Il cardinale Carlo Oppizzoni*, pp. 111–34.

91. ASV, Segreteria di Stato, Epoca Napoleonica, Francia 12, fasc. 15, Oppizzoni Missione, nos 17 and 21, reports from Caselli and Oppizzoni.

92. ASV, Segreteria di Stato, Epoca Napoleonica, Francia 20, fasc. 3, Trattative 1806–1808, nos 18 and 20, Casoni to Bayanne, 3 and 28 December 1807.

93. ASV, Segreteria di Stato, Epoca Napoleonica, Francia 20, fasc. 3, Trattative 1806–1808, nos 26 and 27, angry meeting with Napoleon and departure of Bayanne, 7–11 January 1808.

94. AN, F19 1919, dossier 4, Concordat d'Allegmagne.

95. Ibid.

96. Henri Auréas, *Un général de Napoléon. Miollis* (Paris, 1961).

97. Antoine Ricard, *Mgr de Miollis, évêque de Digne* (Paris, 1893).

98. Antonio Cretoni, *Roma giacobina* (Rome, 1971).

99. David Potter, *Constantine the Emperor* (Oxford, 2013), pp. 137–44.

100. ASV, Segreteria di Stato, Epoca Napoleonica, Italia 6, fasc. 11, Voti proposta dalla Francia 1808, no. 35, Resta to Casoni, 2 February 1808.

101. ASV, Segreteria di Stato, Epoca Napoleonica, Italia 6, fasc. 12, Invasione di Roma 1808, no. 8, Colli to Casoni, 2 February 1808.

102. Ibid.

103. Madelin, *La Rome de Napoléon*, pp. 186–7.

104. Ibid., p. 181.

105. Melchior-Bonnet, *Napoléon et le pape*, p. 103.

106. Anon., *Serie de' documenti sulle vertenze insorte*, III, pp. 29–31.

107. Boutry, *Souverain et pontife*, pp. 371–2.

108. Jeannine Charon-Bordas, *Inventaire des Archives de la légation en France du cardinal Caprara (1801–1808)* (Paris, 1975); and Anon., *Serie de' documenti sulle vertenze insorte*, III, pp. 149–53.

109. Madelin, *La Rome de Napoléon*, p. 184.

110. ASV, Segreteria di Stato, Epoca Napoleonica, Italia 9, fasc. 20, no. 1, list of Cardinals ordered to leave, 23 March 1808.

111. ASV, Segreteria di Stato, Epoca Napoleonica, Italia 7, fasc. 2, Allocuzione 16 marzo 1808.

112. ASV, Segreteria di Stato, Epoca Napoleonica, Italia 7, fasc. 2, Allocuzione 16 marzo 1808, nos 31–4, refusal to join French Federation.

113. ASV, Segreteria di Stato, Epoca Napoleonica, Italia 7, fasc. 3, Decreto annessione Marche al Regno d'Italia Napoleonico.

114. ASV, Segreteria di Stato, Epoca Napoleonica, Italia 7, fasc. 7, Marche, no. 24, Copia d'istruzione trasmessasi ai vescovi delle Marche, 22 May 1808.

115. ASV, Segreteria di Stato, Epoca Napoleonica, Italia 9, fasc. 21, Invasione 1808, no. 4, Gabrielli to foreign courts protest against his arrest in Rome, 17 June 1808.

116. Pacca, *Mémoires*, I, pp. 5–21.

117. Lentz, *Joseph Bonaparte*, pp. 345–55.

118. John Edwards, *Inquisition* (Stroud, 1999), pp. 159–75; and Francisco Bethencourt, *The Inquisition: A Global History, 1478–1834* (Cambridge, 2009), pp. 416–48.

119. Luis Barbastro Gil, *El episcopado español y el alto clero en la Guerra de la Independencia, 1808–1814* (Alicante, 2013), esp. ch. 3.

120. Gérard Dufour, *Juan Antonio Llorente, el factótum del Rey Intruso* (Zaragoza, 2014).

121. Jean-Antoine Llorente, *Histoire critique de l'Inquisition d'Espagne. Depuis l'époque de son établissement par Ferdinand V jusqu'au règne de Ferdinand VII*, 4 vols (Paris, 1817).

122. Cf. Henry Kamen, *The Spanish Inquisition: An Historical Revision* (London, 1997), pp. 305–20.

123. Broers, *Napoleon: The Spirit of the Age*, pp. 307–45.

124. Gunther Eyck, *Loyal Rebels: Andreas Hofer and the Tyrolean Uprising of 1809* (Washington, DC, 1986).

125. Melchior-Bonnet, *Napoléon et le pape*, pp. 116–35.

126. ASV, Segreteria di Stato, Epoca Napoleonica, Italia 9, fasc. 18, Truppe Pontificie, nos 1–3, Colonel Fries and Count Ercoli letters.

127. ASV, Segreteria di Stato, Epoca Napoleonica, Italia 9, fasc. 21, Invasione 1808, no. 2, Gabrielli to Lefebvre, 7 April 1808; and no. 3, Gabrielli to Lefebvre protesting against decision to imprison those wearing new papal cockade, 9 April 1808.

128. Maddalena Spagnolo, *Pasquino in piazza. Una statua a Roma tra arte e vituperio* (Rome, 2019).

129. P. Romano, *La satira nella Roma napoleonica* (Rome, 1936), p. 39.

130. Madelin, *La Rome de Napoléon*, pp. 189–91.

131. Broers, *The Napoleonic Empire in Italy*, pp. 127–32.

132. ASV, Segreteria di Stato, Epoca Napoleonica, Italia 9, fasc. 17, Allocuzione Pio VII, condemnation by Pius VII of the civic guard, 24 August 1808.

133. ASV, Segreteria di Stato, Epoca Napoleonica, Italia 7, fasc. 9, Guardia Civica, nos 1–3, Pacca protests against civic guard, esp. Piperno.

134. Ibid.

135. Madelin, *La Rome de Napoléon*, pp. 188–9.

136. ASV, Segreteria di Stato, Epoca Napoleonica, Italia 9, fasc. 21, Invasione 1808, no. 2, Gabrielli to Lefebvre, 7 April 1808.

137. Madelin, *La Rome de Napoléon*, p. 192; and Pacca, *Mémoires*, pp. 137–43.

138. Haussonville, *L'Église romaine et le Premier Empire*, II, pp. 346–62.

139. Lyonnet, *Le cardinal Fesch*, II, pp. 143–9; and Ricard, *Le cardinal Fesch*, pp. 223–43.

140. Ricard (ed.), *Correspondance diplomatique*, II, pp. 364–83.

141. Madelin, *La Rome de Napoléon*, pp. 195–6.

142. Romano, *La satira nella Roma napoleonica*, pp. 30–40.

143. David I Kertzer, *The Popes against the Jews: The Vatican's Role in the Rise of Modern Anti-Semitism* (New York, 2002), ch. 3; Carla Nardi, *Napoleone e Roma. Dalla Consulta romana al ritorno di Pio VII (1811–1814)* (Rome, 2005), pp. 63–6; and Abraham Berliner, *Storia degli Ebrei di Roma. Dall'antichità allo smantellamento del Ghetto* (Rome, 2000).

144. Margaret Murata and Lorenzo Bianconi, 'Il carnevale a Roma sotto Clemente IX Rospigliosi', *Rivista italiana di musicologia*, vol. 12, no. 1 (1977), pp. 83–99; esp. p. 85.

145. Filippo Clementi, *Il carnevale romano nelle cronache contemporanee* (Rome, 1939), pp. 78–9 and 146.

146. ASV, Segreteria di Stato, Epoca Napoleonica, Italia 7, fasc. 20, Annessione di Roma, no. 14, decree annexing Rome, Imperial Headquarters, Vienna, 17 May 1809.

147. Pacca, *Mémoires*, I, p. 178.
148. Anon., *Documenti officiali relativi alle questioni esistite tra S.S. il sommo pontefice Pio VII e il governo francese, sotto l'impero di Napoleone con la bolla di scomunica contro il detto governo e le istruzioni in proposito date da S.S. ai Vescovi ed ai fedeli* (Vion, 1814), pp. 81–96, esp. 93–4; and for a modern reissue see Ugo Bellocchi (ed.), *Tuttle le encicliche e i principali docmenti pontifici emanti dal 1740* (Vatican, 1994), II, p. 385.
149. ASV, Segreteria di Stato, Epoca Napoleonica, Italia 7, fasc. 12, Caprano parere sul dubbio se il papa possa scomunicare i sovrani; fasc. 13, no. 3, Pacca dubbi sulla scomunica, 10 June 1809; and fasc. 14, draft bull of excommunication.
150. Bergin, *Crown, Church and Episcopate*, pp. 232–60.
151. ASV, Segreteria di Stato, Epoca Napoleonica, Italia 7, fasc. 13, no. 3, Pacca dubbi sulla scomunica, 10 June 1809, essentially believes the pope has authority from Council of Trent to excommunicate secular rulers.
152. Carla Nardi, *Napoleone e Roma. La politica della Consulta romana* (Rome, 1989), chs 1–3.
153. Melchior-Bonnet, *Napoléon et le pape*, pp. 116–35.
154. Anon., *Serie de' documenti sulle vertenze insorte*, IV, pp. 214–16.
155. Natoli and Scarpati (eds), *Il Palazzo del Quirinale*.

## CHAPTER 6: ONE WEDDING AND THIRTEEN BLACK CARDINALS, 1809–10

1. Pacca, *Mémoires*, I, pp. 284–5.
2. Mayol de Lupé, *La captivité de Pie VII*, I, pp. 267–91.
3. Claudio Costantini, *Storia d'Italia*, vol. IX, *La Repubblica di Genova nell'età moderna*, ed. Giuseppe Galasso (Turin, 1978), esp. ch. 4; and in English, Steven A. Epstein, *Genoa and the Genoese, 958–1528* (Chapel Hill, NC, 2001), esp. ch. 2.
4. Teofilo Ossian De Negri, *Storia di Genova* (Florence, 2003).
5. Thomas Allison Kirk, *Genoa and the Sea: Policy and Power in an Early Modern Maritime Republic, 1559–1684* (Baltimore, MD, 2013), esp. ch. 4.
6. Vergé-Franceschi, *Napoléon. Une enfance corse*, p. 231.
7. Riccardo Mandelli, *Notturno dal Bosforo. Sanremo 1923–1926. L'esilio di Mehmet VI Vahideddin, ultimo sultano dell'Impero Ottomano* (Macerata, 2009); and Philip Mansel, *Constantinople: City of the World's Desire, 1453–1924* (London, 1995), pp. 407–11.
8. Ian Verstegen (ed.), *Patronage and Dynasty: The Rise of the Della Rovere in Renaissance Italy* (Kirksville, MO, 2007).
9. Giovanni Assereto and Marco Doria (eds), *Storia della Liguria* (Rome, 2007), ch. 3.
10. Costantini, *La Repubblica di Genova*, pp. 501–5.
11. ASV, Segreteria di Stato, Epoca Napoleonica, Italia 16, fasc. 5, Diocesi Diverse, nos 12 and 15, di Pietro report on Maggioli.
12. Domenico Martinengo and Francesco Martinengo, *Pio VII in Savona. Memorie storiche* (Turin, 1888), pp. 37–8.
13. Mayol de Lupé, *La captivité de Pie VII*, I, p. 330.
14. For the scientific background of the expedition, see Burleigh, *Mirage*; and Christian Marbach, 'Chabrol, X 1794, de la politique à la lave de Volvic', *Bulletin de la Sabix*, vol. 52 (2013), pp. 105–6.
15. Marie-Vic Ozouf-Marignier, 'Administration, statistique, aménagement du *territoire:* l'itinéraire du préfet Chabrol de Volvic, 1773–1843', *Revue d'histoire moderne et contemporaine*, vol. 44, no. 1 (1997), pp. 19–39.
16. AN, F1bl 157 13, nos 7–56, Chabrol de Volvic personnel file.
17. Mayol de Lupé, *La captivité de Pie VII*, I, pp. 321–4.
18. ASV, Archivio Concistoriale, Serie Conclavi 86, no. 178, Dottor Carlo Porta Romano uno dei Medici Primarj del venerabile ed apostolico arci-ospedale di S Spirito.
19. Mayol de Lupé, *La captivité de Pie VII*, I, p. 470.
20. Ibid., pp. 490–6.

21. Henry Chotard, *Le pape Pie VII à Savone, d'après les minutes des lettres du général Berthier au prince Borghèse* (Paris, 1887).
22. NAP NOUV CORRES, no. 21,979, Schönbrunn, 5 September 1808, IX, p. 1,121.
23. Cristina Gamberini, Enrica Grasco and Giovanni Farris, *Palazzo vescovile di Savona, appartamenti di Papa Pio VII* (Genoa, 2015).
24. Giovanni Farris, *Studi, documenti e articoli su Pio VII* (Savona, 2010), pp. 13–28.
25. ASV, Segreteria di Stato, Epoca Napoleonica, Italia 1, Italia 2, Italia 3, Italia 4, Italia 5 and Italita 14 (esp. fasc.1 filled with a rich collection of petitions addressed to Pius VII in Savona).
26. Mayol de Lupé, *La captivité de Pie VII*, I, p. 339.
27. D. Baldassarre d'Emilio, *Storia dell'apparizione di N.S. della misericordia in Savona* (Naples, 1838).
28. Giovanni Farris, *Studi e documenti su Pio VII* (Savona, 2012), pp. 79–82.
29. Nicholas Atkin and Frank Tallett, *Priests, Prelates and People: A History of European Catholicism since 1750* (Oxford, 2003), pp. 85–128.
30. Mary Heimann, 'Catholic revivalism in worship and devotion', in Sheridan Gilley and Brian Stanley (eds), *The Cambridge History of Christianity*, vol. 8, *World Christianities* c. *1815–c. 1914* (Cambridge, 2006), pp. 70–83.
31. Giovanni Farris, *Atti per l'Inquisitio su Pio VII* (Savona, 2013).
32. Antonio Verico, 'The miracle of Pope Pius VII "levitating" at Mass on 15 August 1811' (1811), after Vincenzo Gozzini; British Museum, museum no. 1869,0410.1352; view online at https://www.britishmuseum.org/collection/object/P_1869-0410-1352 (accessed 24 September 2020).
33. Mayol de Lupé, *La captivité de Pie VII*, I, pp. 366–7.
34. AP, 2ème série, X, pp. 322–4.
35. Mayol de Lupé, *La captivité de Pie VII*, I, pp. 417–18.
36. On the death of Portalis, see Jean-Luc Chartier, *Portalis. Père du Code Civil* (Paris, 2004), pp. 380–5.
37. Gosselin, *Vie de M. Emery*, 2 vols (Paris, 1862), pp. 236–43.
38. Jean Leflon, *La crise révolutionnaire, 1789–1846* (Paris, 1949), pp. 256–8.
39. Ibid.
40. AN, AF IV 1046, dossier 3, Bigot orders cardinals to head for Paris, 10 October 1809.
41. AN, AF IV 1046, dossier 3, no. 77, Bigot to Miollis, order to transfer Dataria and Penitenzieria to Reims, 13 December 1809.
42. Victor Bindel, *Le Vatican à Paris (1809–1814)* (Paris, 1942), pp. 135–53; and more recently Andreina Rita, *Biblioteche e requisizioni librarie a Roma in età Napoleonica* (Vatican City, 2012).
43. Lucie Favier, *La mémoire de l'état. Histoire des Archives nationales* (Paris, 2004), pp. 85–105; and Marcel Chappin, 'Un mostro nell'Archivio segreto vaticano. Il fondo Epoca Napoleonica come problema archivistico', in Ambrogio Piazzone (ed.), *Studi in onore del cardinale Raffaele Farina. Studi e testi 477–478* (Vatican City, 2013), pp. 135–46.
44. AN, AF IV 1047, dossier 1, no. 25, Bigot to Napoleon, 16 January 1810; and no. 68, Bigot to Napoleon, 23 May 1810, on Father Altieri hiding archival documents and precious tomes, burial of material in gardens; Jean Mauzaize, 'Le transfert des Archives vaticanes à Paris sous le Premier Empire', *Bulletin de l'Association des archivistes de l'Église de France*, vol. 8 (1977), pp. 3–14; and Maria Pia Donato, 'La conquista della memoria. Napoleone, Galileo e gli Archivi dell'Impero', in *Galilæana: Journal of Galilean Studies*, vol. 10 (2013), pp. 187–200.
45. AN, AF IV 1047, dossier 1, no. 25, plan générale pour les affaires du clergé.
46. Kate Williams, *Josephine: Desire, Ambition, Napoleon* (London, 2013); and Jacques-Olivier Boudon (ed.), *Sous l'empire de Joséphine, 1763–1814* (Paris, 2015).
47. Lentz, *Joseph Bonaparte*, pp. 146–51 and 189–93.
48. Broers, *Napoleon: Soldier of Destiny*, pp. 214–15.
49. Adolphe Thiers, *Histoire du Consulat et de l'Empire*, 21 vols (Paris, 1851), XI, pp. 561–5.
50. Carola Oman, *Napoleon's Viceroy: Eugène de Beauharnais* (New York, 1966), pp. 284–93.
51. Roderick Phillips, *Untying the Knot: A Short History of Divorce* (Cambridge, 1991), pp. 121–3; and Clémence Zacharie, 'La femme dans le code civil de 1804', in Jacques-Olivier Boudon (ed.), *Napoléon et les femmes* (Paris, 2013), pp. 55–68.

52. Welschinger, *Le divorce de Napoléon*, pp. 94–7.

53. Ibid., pp. 87–104.

54. Marie-Pierre Rey, *Alexander I: The Tsar who Defeated Napoleon* (DeKalb, GA, 2012), pp. 199–200.

55. Vandal, *Napoléon et Alexandre Ier*, II, pp. 168–97.

56. Welschinger, *Le pape et l'empereur*, pp. 29–31.

57. AN, AF IV 1046, dossier 3, no. 69, di Pietro statement di Casa, 21 October 1809.

58. Welschinger, *Le divorce de Napoléon*, pp. 123–39.

59. Boudon, *Le roi Jérôme*, pp. 78–86; AN, AF IV 1046, dossier 3, Bigot to Napoleon, 11 February 1809; Haussonville, *L'Église romaine et le Premier Empire*, III, pp. 198–202; and Lyonnet, *Histoire de Mgr d'Aviau du Bois-de-Sanzay*, II, pp. 558–61.

60. Welschinger, *Le divorce de Napoléon*, pp. 127–33.

61. Ibid., p. 130.

62. Ibid., pp. 140–6.

63. Ibid., pp. 143–4.

64. Ibid., pp. 154–5.

65. Ibid., pp. 161–2.

66. Ibid., p. 164.

67. Ibid., pp. 165–70.

68. Ibid., p. 172.

69. Ricard, *Le cardinal Fesch*, pp. 245–59.

70. Welschinger, *Le divorce de Napoléon*, pp. 188–97.

71. Andrew Wheatcroft, *The Habsburgs: Embodying Empire* (London, 1996), p. 242; and Laurence Chatel de Brancion (ed.), *Cambacérès. Mémoires inédits*, 2 vols (Paris, 1999), II, pp. 326–8.

72. John Hardman, *The Life of Louis XVI* (London, 2016), pp. 31–5.

73. Thomas E. Kaiser, 'Who's afraid of Marie-Antoinette? Diplomacy, Austrophobia and the queen', *French History*, vol. 14, no. 3 (2000), pp. 241–71.

74. Schroeder, *The Transformation of European Politics*, pp. 5–52.

75. Diarmaid MacCulloch, *Reformation: Europe's House Divided 1490–1700* (London, 2004), chs 4–5.

76. Latreille, 'Le gallicanisme ecclésiastique sous le Premier Empire'.

77. Emmanuel de Lévis-Mirepoix, *Un collaborateur de Metternich. Mémoires et papiers de Lebzeltern* (Paris, 1949), pp. 116–19.

78. Charles-Éloi Vial, *Marie-Louise* (Paris, 2017), chs 1–2.

79. Welschinger, *Le divorce de Napoléon*, p. 199.

80. Vial, *Marie-Louise*, chs 4–5.

81. Frédéric Hulot, *Le maréchal Berthier* (Paris, 2007), ch. 11.

82. Ruth Kleinman, *Anne of Austria, Queen of France* (Columbus, OH, 1985), pp. 20–3.

83. Welschinger, *Le divorce de Napoléon*, pp. 215–24.

84. Broers, *Napoleon: The Spirit of the Age*, p. 441.

85. Waltraud Maierhofer, 'Maria Carolina, Queen of Naples: The devil's grandmother fights Napoleon', in idem, Gertrud M. Rösch and Caroline Bland (eds), *Women against Napoleon: Historical and Fictional Responses to his Rise and Legacy* (Frankfurt, 2007), pp. 57–78, esp. p. 58.

86. Michel Lacour-Gayet, *Joachim et Caroline Murat* (Paris, 1996), pp. 186–7.

87. David Chanteranne, 'Les cérémonies du mariage', in Thierry Lentz (ed.), *1810. Le tournant de l'Empire* (Paris, 2010), pp. 37–50.

88. Pacca, *Mémoires*, II, pp. 284–337.

89. Bindel, *Le Vatican à Paris*, p. 36.

90. Geoffroy de Grandmaison, *Napoléon et les cardinaux noirs (1810–1814)* (Paris, 1895), p. 30.

91. AN, AF IV 1047, dossier 1, no. 30, renseignements sur les cardinaux étrangers qui se trouvent à Paris, 4 February 1810.

92. Ibid.

93. Grandmaison, *Napoléon et les cardinaux noirs*, pp. 31–2.

94. Hausonville, *L'Église romaine et le Premier Empire*, III, pp. 275–7; and Consalvi, *Mémoires*, II, p. 176.

95. Umberto Beseghi, *I tredici cardinali neri* (Florence, 1944), p. 56.

96. Grandmaison, *Napoléon et les cardinaux noirs*, p. 33.

97. AN, AF IV 1047, dossier 1, no. 99, Bigot to Napoleon, 21 June 1810.

98. Grandmaison, *Napoléon et les cardinaux noirs*, pp. 33–5.

99. Beseghi, *I tredici cardinali neri*, pp. 63–4.

100. Grandmaison, *Napoléon et les cardinaux noirs*, p. 37.

101. Broers, *Napoleon: The Spirit of the Age*, p. 443.

102. Florence Austin-Montenay, *Saint-Cloud. Une vie de château* (Paris, 2005).

103. Consalvi, *Mémoires*, II, pp. 202–5.

104. Jean-Philippe Garric, *Percier et Fontaine. Les architectes de Napoléon* (Paris, 2012); and Charles Percier and Pierre-François Fontaine, *Empire Stylebook of Interior Design: All 72 Plates from the 'Recueil de Décorations Intérieures'* (Mineola, NY, 1991).

105. Beseghi, *I tredici cardinali neri*, pp. 76–81.

106. Grandmaison, *Napoléon et les cardinaux noirs*, p. 42; and Dominique-Georges-Frédéric Dufour de Pradt, *Les quatre concordats, suivis de considérations sur le gouvernement de l'église en général, et sur l'Église de France en particulier depuis 1515*, 3 vols (Paris, 1818), II, pp. 439–40.

107. Consalvi, *Mémoires*, II, pp. 209–10.

108. Caiani, 'Collaborators, collaboration and the problems of empire'.

109. Grandmaison, *Napoléon et les cardinaux noirs*, p. 48.

110. Beseghi, *I tredici cardinali neri*, p. 88.

111. AN, AF IV 1047, dossier 1, nos 40–1, Bigot to Napoleon, 8 April 1810, and copy of cardinals' declaration.

112. AN, AF IV 1047, dossier 1, no. 57, Bigot to Napoleon, 10 May 1810.

113. Beseghi, *I tredici cardinali neri*, pp. 106 and 125–31.

114. Welschinger, *Le pape et l'empereur*, pp. 122–32.

115. Lévis-Mirepoix, *Un collaborateur de Metternich*, p. 143.

116. Ibid., pp. 12–45.

117. Ibid., pp. 88–103.

118. Ibid., p. 139.

119. Prince Richard Metternich, *Memoirs of Prince Metternich 1773–1815*, 5 vols (New York, 1970), II, pp. 403–8.

120. Lévis-Mirepoix, *Un collaborateur de Metternich*, p. 145.

121. Ibid., pp. 153–5.

122. Ibid., p. 154.

123. Ibid., p. 157.

124. Ibid., p. 158.

125. Mayol de Lupé, *La captivité de Pie VII*, I, p. 531.

126. Lévis-Mirepoix, *Un collaborateur de Metternich*, p. 167.

127. Ibid., p. 169.

128. Ibid., pp. 171–2.

129. Welschinger, *Le pape et l'empereur*, pp. 128–31.

130. Lévis-Mirepoix, *Un collaborateur de Metternich*, p. 173.

131. Ibid., p. 180.

132. Metternich, *Memoirs*, II, pp. 412–13.

133. Lévis-Mirepoix, *Un collaborateur de Metternich*, pp. 182–6.

134. Metternich, *Memoirs*, II, pp. 414–18.

135. Lévis-Mirepoix, *Un collaborateur de Metternich*, pp. 192–4.

136. Ibid., p. 196.

137. Christian Fileaux, 'Drame à l'ambassade d'Autriche', in Lentz (ed.), *1810. Le tournant de l'Empire*, pp. 51–60.

138. See also Michael Broers, *Napoleon: The Famous Delinquent* (New York, forthcoming), Introduction.

139. Fileaux, 'Drame à l'ambassade d'Autriche', p. 57.

140. Antonia Fraser, *Marie-Antoinette: The Journey* (London, 2001), pp. 76–7.

CHAPTER 7: THE EMPIRE OF GOD: THE NATIONAL COUNCIL OF 1811

1. Hans Küng, *Structures of the Church* (New York, 1982), esp. ch. 7.
2. Ronnie Po-Chia Hsia, *The World of Catholic Renewal, 1540–1770*, 2nd edn (Cambridge, 2005), pp. 10–25; Robert Bireley, *The Refashioning of Catholicism, 1450–1700: A Reassessment of the Counter-Reformation* (Basingstoke, 1999), pp. 45–69; O'Malley, *Trent*; and Robert Bireley, 'Redefining Catholicism: Trent and beyond', in Ronnie Po-Chia Hsia (ed.), *The Cambridge History of Christianity*, vol. 6, *Reform and Expansion, 1500–1660* (Cambridge, 2014), pp. 145–61.
3. Thomas Crimando, 'Two French views of the Council of Trent', *Sixteenth Century Journal*, vol. 19, no. 2 (1988), pp. 169–86.
4. J.H. Smith, *The Great Schism 1378: The Disintegration of the Papacy* (London, 1970).
5. Oakley, *The Conciliarist Tradition*.
6. Valois, *Histoire de la Pragmatique Sanction de Bourges*.
7. Jules Thomas, *Le Concordat de 1516. Ses origines, son histoire au XVIe siècle*, 3 vols (Paris, 1910).
8. Bergin, *Crown, Church and Episcopate*, pp. 232–60.
9. See Appendix.
10. Aimé-Georges Martimort, *Le gallicanisme* (Paris, 1976).
11. Bergin, *Crown, Church and Episcopate*, pp. 245–53.
12. Pierre Blet, 'Louis XIV et le Saint-Siège à la lumière de deux publications récentes. Le conflit de la régale. La fable de l'excommunication secrète. La réconciliation de 1693', *Archivum historiae pontificiae*, vol. 12 (1974), pp. 309–37.
13. Jean Carreyre, *Le Concile d'Embrun (1727–1728)* (Bordeaux, 1929), esp. pp. 28–62.
14. Plongeron, *Des résistances religieuses*, p. 287; and Pistolesi, *Vita del sommo pontefice Pio VII*, III, p. 69.
15. AN, F7, Police Générale, 3021, dossier 7, réponses à circulaire relative aux ouvrages renfermant des maximes contraires à la déclaration du clergé de 1682 (1810).
16. Pierre-Étienne Guillaume, *Vie épiscopale de Mgr Antoine-Eustache Osmond, évêque de Nancy* (Nancy, 1862), pp. 564–602; and Boudon, *Napoléon et les cultes*, pp. 282 and 287.
17. Ricard, *Le cardinal Fesch*, pp. 227–30.
18. Ricard (ed.), *Correspondance diplomatique*, II, pp. 303–25 and 364–406.
19. ASV, Segreteria di Stato, Epoca Napoleonica, Italia 17, fasc. 2, Maury 1794–1805, nos 33–44, on the plucky peasants of Corneto and their attacks on Maury's property.
20. They were François-André Dejean and Antoine Eustache d'Osmond: Archives de l'archevêché de Lyon, 2 Episcopat de Mgr Fesch 1802–1840, 2 II 15, Pièces remises par le ministre des cultes, nos 73–81, dossier archevêché de Florence; and nos 82–9, dossier évêché d'Asti.
21. Michael Broers, *The Politics of Religion in Napoleonic Italy: The War Against God, 1801–1814* (London, 2002), pp. 86–99.
22. Bertaud, *Les royalistes et Napoléon*, pp. 203–31.
23. Candido Bona, *Le 'Amicizie'. Società segrete e rinascita religiosa, 1770–1830* (Turin, 1962), pp. 265–300.
24. Darrin M. MacMahon, *Enemies of the Enlightenment: The French Counter-Enlightenment and the Making of Modernity* (Oxford, 2002), pp. 3–16.
25. Guerrino Pelliccia and Giancarlo Rocca (eds), *Dizionario degli istituti di perfezione*, 10 vols (Milan, 1974–2003), VIII, pp. 310–14.
26. Geoffroy de Grandmaison, *La Congrégation* (Paris, 1889), p. 19.
27. Bona, *Le 'Amicizie'*, pp. 283–300; and Grandmaison, *La Congrégation*, pp. 97–119.
28. Bona, *Le 'Amicizie'*, p. 298.
29. Guillaume de Bertier de Sauvigny, *Le comte Ferdinand de Bertier (1782–1864) et l'énigme de la Congrégation* (Paris, 1948), pp. 49–87.
30. Bertaud, *Les royalistes et Napoléon*, pp. 247–56.
31. Bertier de Sauvigny, *Le comte Ferdinand de Bertier*, pp. 87–146.
32. Ibid., pp. 58–61.
33. AN, AF IV 1048, dossier 1, Affaire d'Astros, sans date, rapport à SM sur l'affaire d'Astros; and Guillaume de Bertier de Sauvigny, 'Un épisode de la résistance catholique sous le Premier Empire. L'affaire d'Astros', *Revue d'histoire de l'Église de France*, vol. 35 (1949), pp. 49–58.

34. AN, AF IV 1048, dossier 1, Affaire d'Astros, communication with Savona, undated; probably a report by Savary describing the secret network; and Antoine Lesta, *Histoire secrète de la congrégation de Lyon* (Paris, 1967), pp. 167–228, esp. pp. 188–92.

35. Bona, *Le 'Amicizie'*, pp. 283–300.

36. ASV, Segreteria di Stato, Epoca Napoleonica, Italia 15, fasc. 3, Savona, no. 6, Catena delle Persone per mezzo delle quali passavano le notizie e pieghi da Parigi a Savona.

37. Martinengo and Martinengo, *Pio VII in Savona*, p. 125.

38. Mayol de Lupé, *La captivité de Pie VII*, II, p. 52.

39. Anon., *Serie de' documenti sulle vertenze insorte*, V, pp. 59–66.

40. Paul Droulers, 'L'abbé d'Astros et l'expérience religieuse du Premier Empire', *Gregorianum*, vol. 29, no. 2 (1948), pp. 252–87.

41. Latreille, *Le Catéchisme impérial*, pp. 46–51.

42. Haussonville, *L'Église romaine et le Premier Empire*, III, pp. 456–7.

43. Bertier de Sauvigny, 'Un épisode de la résistance catholique sous le Premier Empire', pp. 53–4.

44. Anon., *Serie de' documenti sulle vertenze insorte*, V, pp. 66–71.

45. Plongeron, *Des résistances religieuses*, pp. 279–90.

46. Haussonville, *L'église romaine et le Premier Empire*, III, pp. 464–6.

47. Thierry Lentz, *Savary. Le séide de Napoléon* (Paris, 2001), pp. 237–307.

48. Savary, *Mémoires du duc de Rovigo*, V, pp. 92–5.

49. AN, AF IV 1048, dossier 1, Affaire d'Astros, interrogation Fontana, 3 January 1811; and Marco Ranica, *L'intransigenza nella Curia. Il cardinale Francesco Luigi Fontana (1750–1822)* (Rome, 2019), pp. 193–226.

50. Ibid.

51. AN, AF IV 1048, dossier 1, Affaire d'Astros, nos 9–11, arrest of priests and others involved.

52. Paul Droulers, *Action pastorale et problèmes sociaux sous la monarchie de Juillet chez Mgr d'Astros, archevêque de Toulouse, censeur de Lamennais* (Paris, 1954), p. 25.

53. Lentz, *Nouvelle histoire du Premier Empire*, II, pp. 120–1.

54. 'Portalis, Joseph Marie' entry, in Guy Caplat, Isabelle Havelange, Françoise Huguet and Bernadette Lebedeff-Choppin (eds), *Les inspecteurs généraux de l'Instruction publique. Dictionnaire biographique 1802–1914* (Paris, 1986), pp. 560–1.

55. Pierre Daunou, *La puissance temporelle des papes, et l'abus qu'ils ont fait de leur ministère spiritual*, reprint (Paris, 2007).

56. NAP NOUV CORRES, no. 25,694, Paris, 15 January 1811, X, p. 1,112.

57. Louis de Nussac, 'Le colonel Antoine Lagorsse (1770–1842), gardien de Pie VII', *Bulletin de la Société scientifique, historique et archéologique de la Corrèze*, vol. 46, no. 1 (1924), pp. 97–122; pp.193–226.

58. Haussonville, *L'Église romaine et le Premier Empire*, III, pp. 481–6.

59. NAP NOUV CORRES, no. 25,768, Paris, 25 January 1811, X, p. 1,144.

60. Mayol de Lupé, *La captivité de Pie VII*, II pp. 101–7.

61. Haussonville, *L'Église romaine et le Premier Empire*, III, pp. 484–5.

62. AP, 2ème série, X, p. 595; and Nardi, *Napoleone e Roma. La politica della consulta romana*, pp. 183–99.

63. Ibid.

64. Broers, *The Napoleonic Empire in Italy*, pp. 127–32.

65. AN, AF IV 1047, dossier 1, no. 96, decree on oath in Rome, 8 June 1810, and nos 121–2, Bigot to Napoleon, 14 July 1810.

66. AN, AF IV 1047, dossier 1, no. 98, Degerando to Bigot, 6 June 1810; and nos 104–8, summary and numbers of priests refusing the oath.

67. Jean Destrem, 'Déportations de prêtres sous le Premier Empire', *Revue historique*, vol. 11, no. 2 (1879), pp. 331–88.

68. Domenico Rocciolo, 'Clero e vicariato di Roma nel periodo napoleonico, note per una ricerca', *Roma moderna e contemporanea*, vol. 2, no. 1 (1994), pp. 125–38.

69. Jacques Moulard, *Le comte Camille de Tournon*, 3 vols (Paris, 1926–32), esp. vol. 2; and Gaetano Moroni, *Dizionario di erudizione storico-ecclesiastica da S. Pietro sino ai nostri giorni*, 103 vols (Venice, 1840), VI, pp. 97–9.

70. Michael Broers, 'Noble Romans and regenerated citizens: The morality of conscription in Napoleonic Italy, 1800–1814', *War in History*, vol. 8, no. 3 (2001), pp. 249–70.

71. Broers, *The Napoleonic Empire in Italy*, pp. 217–44.

72. Cardinal Caselli, as a loyalist, was added to its membership, as was the prelate Dominique Dufour de Pradt. De Pradt had been an imperial chaplain, and was on close terms with some of the highest court officials in the Empire. A highly political animal, the abbé was the worst sort of 'quisling' careerist that periodically emerged from the Catholic clergy. Napoleon himself had described him in far from glittering terms: 'a profound hypocrite, possessing neither the morals nor the mindset of his estate, he delivers himself easily to the type of intrigues which one day will lead him to the scaffold': NAP NOUV CORRES, no. 21,987, Schönbrunn, 5 September 1809, IX, p. 1,129. The emperor had nominated him to the vacant archdiocese of Malines in Belgium. Therefore, the Abbé de Pradt had a vested interest in urging his colleagues to comply with the imperial will. Throughout his service during the Empire he showed himself to be a pliant and unctuous clerical client of Napoleon: Émile Dousset, *L'abbé de Pradt. Grand aumônier de Napoléon* (Paris, 1959), pp. 73–106.

73. Leflon, *La crise révolutionnaire*, pp. 261–3.

74. Louis Mathias de Barral, *Fragmens relatifs à l'histoire ecclésiastique des premières années du dix-neuvième siècle* (Paris, 1814), pp. 181–228.

75. Ibid., pp. 198–228.

76. Haussonville, *L'Église romaine et le Premier Empire*, IV, pp. 80–3.

77. Jean Leflon, *Monsieur Emery*, 2 vols (Paris, 1944), I, pp. 392–432.

78. Ibid., II, pp. 523–32.

79. Haussonville, *L'Église romaine et le Premier Empire*, IV, pp. 89–90.

80. Ibid., p. 90.

81. Leflon, *Monsieur Emery*, II, pp. 533–46.

82. Henri Welschinger, *Le roi de Rome (1811–1832)* (Paris, 1902), pp. 12–15.

83. Jean Tulard, *Napoléon II* (Paris, 1996), passim.

84. Lentz (ed.), *1810. Le tournant de l'Empire*, passim.

85. Esdaile, *Fighting Napoleon*; and Jean-Marc Lafon, *L'Andalousie de Napoléon. Contre-insurrection, collaboration et résistances dans le midi de l'Espagne, 1808–1812* (Paris, 2007).

86. Barbastro Gil, *El episcopado español y el alto clero*, pp. 53–86.

87. Pistolesi, *Vita del sommo pontefice Pio VII*, III, pp. 51–68.

88. Barral, *Fragmens relatifs à l'histoire ecclésiastique*, pp. 254–61.

89. Ibid., p. 261.

90. These included trustworthy Gallican stormtroopers like the archbishop of Tours and the bishops of Nantes and Trier. The bishop of Faenza was also instructed to join them as soon as possible. He was known to Pius, and would help soften the blow.

91. NAP NOUV CORRES, no. 26,820, Saint-Cloud, 24 April 1811, XI, pp. 220–1.

92. Barral, *Fragmens relatifs à l'histoire ecclésiastique*, p. 260.

93. Mayol de Lupé, *La captivité de Pie VII*, II, pp. 205–11.

94. Haussonville, *L'Église romaine et le Premier Empire*, IV, p. 125.

95. Ibid., pp. 133–7.

96. Mayol de Lupé, *La captivité de Pie VII*, II, p. 146.

97. Ibid., p. 210.

98. Haussonville, *L'Église romaine et le Premier Empire*, IV, p. 135.

99. Ibid., pp. 138–41.

100. Mayol de Lupé, *La captivité de Pie VII*, II, p. 221.

101. Ibid., pp. 207–8.

102. Barral, *Fragmens relatifs à l'histoire ecclésiastique*, pp. 328–30.

103. Ibid.

104. Haussonville, *L'Église romaine et le Premier Empire*, IV, pp. 158–65.

105. Mayol de Lupé, *La captivité de Pie VII*, II, p. 217.

106. Ibid., p. 218.

107. Barral, *Fragmens relatifs à l'histoire ecclésiastique*, pp. 305–13.

108. The bishops believed at this stage that an addendum to the concordats would be the best solution to solve the crisis: ibid.

109. ASMi, Culto Parte Moderna 2540, dossier 2, Concili e Sinodi; NAP NOUV CORRES, no. 26,846, Saint-Cloud, 26 April 1811, XI, p. 234; and Alberto Rossetti, *Giornale, ossia memorie relative al Concilio Nazionale convocato in Parigi colla circolare dell'imperatore e re Napoleone 25 aprile 1811* (Venice, 1844).

110. Hömig, *Karl Theodor von Dalberg*, pp. 498–502.

111. Welschinger, *Le roi de Rome*, ch. 2.

112. Lentz, *Nouvelle histoire du Premier Empire*, II, pp. 75–105 and 165–200.

113. AP, 2ème série, XI, p. 71.

114. Ambrogio A. Caiani, 'The *Concile national* of 1811: Napoleon, Gallicanism and the failure of neo-Conciliarism', *Journal of Ecclesiastical History*, vol. 70, no. 3 (2019), pp. 546–64.

115. Antoine Ricard, *Le Concile national de 1811* (Paris, 1894), pp. 119–24.

116. Joseph Lenfant, 'Maurice de Broglie, évêque de Gand, 1766–1821', *Revue d'histoire de l'Église de France*, vol. 76 (1931), pp. 312–47; Gabriel Van den Gheyn, *Maurice prince de Broglie, XIXe évêque de Gand* (Ghent, 1923); and Lyonnet, *Histoire de Mgr d'Aviau du Bois-de-Sanzay*, II, pp. 610–23.

117. Lenfant, 'Maurice de Broglie', pp. 314–18.

118. Ibid., pp. 325–6.

119. ASV, Segreteria di Stato, Epoca Napoleonica, Francia 6, fasc. 7, Journal de Mgr de Broglie, nos 6–26, journal; published in part in Haussonville, *L'Église romaine et le Premier Empire*, IV, pp. 431–86.

120. Anon., *Cérémonial du Concile national de Paris tenu l'an 1811* (Paris 1811).

121. Étienne-Antoine Boulogne, *Sermons et discours inédits de M. de Boulogne, évêque de Troyes*, 3 vols (Ghent, 1827), III, pp. 338–73.

122. AN, AF IV 1047, dossier 2, nos 31–2, report from Bigot to Napoleon on ecclesiastical oath.

123. Welschinger, *Le pape et l'empereur*, p. 201.

124. AN, AF IV 1047, dossier 2, no. 74, imperial address.

125. Ricard, *Le Concile national de 1811*, pp. 158–60; Haussonville, *L'Église romaine et le Premier Empire*, IV, pp. 258–61; and AN, AF IV 1047, dossier 2, nos 32–3, esprit du concile (police reports on the bishops).

126. Ricard, *Le Concile national de 1811*, pp. 171–4.

127. Ibid., p. 177.

128. Ibid., pp. 182–90.

129. Ibid., pp. 194–7.

130. Haussonville, *L'Église romaine et le Premier Empire*, IV, p. 285.

131. Ibid., p. 286.

132. AD de l'Indre et Loire, 1J1290, rapport de Mgr l'archevêque de Tours sur la députation envoyée à Savone au mois de mai 1811; copies of this are also contained in the archiepiscopal archives of Lyon.

133. Haussonville, *L'Église romaine et le Premier Empire*, IV, p. 325.

134. AN, AF IV 1047, dossier 2, no. 44, rapport de la commission présidée par S.E. le grand juge et chargée de proposer un projet touchant l'institution canonique des évêques; and no. 45, a long undated draft piece of legislation signed by Cambacérès.

135. Haussonville, *L'Église romaine et le Premier Empire*, IV, pp. 324–6.

136. Ricard, *Le Concile national de 1811*, pp. 226–30.

137. Ibid., pp. 230–1.

138. Ibid., pp. 231–8.

139. Haussonville, *L'Église romaine et le Premier Empire*, IV, pp. 339–42.

140. Ricard, *Le Concile national de 1811*, pp. 239–44.

141. AN, F7 6567, papers seized from the bishops of Ghent, Tournai and Troyes, esp. Broglie Gand folder.

142. Archives de l'archevêché de Lyon, 2 Episcopat de Mgr Fesch 1802–1840, 2 II 16, Concile 1811, arrestations.

143. Archives de l'archevêché de Lyon, 2 Episcopat de Mgr Fesch 1802–1840, 2 II 16, Concile 1811, duc de Rovigo (police) transmet à Fesch deux rapports sur les écrits trouvés chez eux, 1 August 1811; and AN, F7 6567, papers seized from the bishops: folders marked Hirn Tournai and Boulogne Troyes.

144. Savary, *Mémoires du duc de Rovigo*, V, pp. 161–7.

145. Archives de l'archevêché de Lyon, 2 Episcopat de Mgr Fesch 1802–1840, 2 II 15, Concile de 1811, lettre du ministre des Cultes, 10 July 1811, le décret de dissolution du Concile.

146. AN, AF IV 1047, dossier 2, nos 48–52, Bigot and Bovara's tallies of bishops for and against the decree; ASMi, Culto Parte Moderna 2540, dossier 2, Concili e Sinodi, Eugène orders Bovara to Paris, 8 June 1811.

147. Ibid.; embarrassingly, the bishop of Digne, the brother of General Miollis, the military governor of Rome, refused to endorse the decree: Ricard, *Le Concile national de 1811*, pp. 254–5.

148. Archives de l'archevêché de Lyon, 2 Episcopat de Mgr Fesch 1802–1840, 2 II 15, Concile de 1811, lettre du ministre des Cultes, 29 July 1811, le projet de décret à soumettre au Pape.

149. Ricard, *Le Concile national de 1811*, pp. 262–3.

150. Ibid., p. 283.

151. Latreille, 'Le gallicanisme ecclésiastique sous le Premier Empire'.

152. Amongst them was de Pradt, who made a very bad impression on all with his desperate desire to please the emperor in all matters: de Pradt, *Les quatre concordats*, II, pp. 506–23.

153. AN, AF IV 1048, dossier 2, nos 123–4, report by de Gérando.

154. Giovanni Baldini and Vittorio Tampieri (eds), *Francesco Bertazzoli. Primo cardinale di Lugo nel 250° della nascita* (Lugo, 2004), pp. 56–63.

155. NAP NOUV CORRES, no. 28,181, Saint-Cloud, 16 August 1811, XI, p. 845; and no. 28,213, Saint-Cloud, 17 August 1811, XI, p. 860.

156. Barral, *Fragmens relatifs à l'histoire ecclésiastique*, pp. 338–44.

157. Mayol de Lupé, *La captivité de Pie VII*, II, pp. 280–1.

158. For earlier instructions, see NAP NOUV CORRES, no. 26,845, Saint-Cloud, 26 April 1811, XI, pp. 233–4; and Mayol de Lupé, *La captivité de Pie VII*, II, p. 282.

159. Marc Gocel, *La télégraphie aérienne*, 2 vols (Florange, 2011).

160. Jean-Claude Quennevat (ed.), 'Napoléon et les télécommunications', special issue of *Souvenir napoléonien*, no. 280 (1975).

161. René Boudard, 'La mission du préfet Chabrol, "geôlier" de Pie VII, à Savone 1809–1812', *Revue de l'Institut Napoléon*, vol. 112 (1969), pp. 181–8.

162. AN, AF IV 1047, dossier 1, no. 98, Degerando to Bigot, 6 June 1810; and Haussonville, *L'Église romaine et le Premier Empire*, V, pp. 10–14.

163. Mayol de Lupé, *La captivité de Pie VII*, II, p. 287.

164. Haussonville, *L'Église romaine et le Premier Empire*, V, pp. 40–1.

165. Ibid., p. 42.

166. Mayol de Lupé, *La captivité de Pie VII*, II, pp. 293–9.

167. Barral, *Fragmens relatifs à l'histoire ecclésiastique*, pp. 346–62.

168. Mayol de Lupé, *La captivité de Pie VII*, II, pp. 299–305.

169. Haussonville, *L'Église romaine et le Premier Empire*, V, pp. 58–9.

170. Vandal, *Napoléon et Alexandre Ier*, III, pp. 192–226.

171. Alexandre Tchoudinov, 'Russia and the Continental System: Trends in Russian historiography', in Aaslestad and Joor (eds), *Revisiting Napoleon's Continental System*, pp. 56–60.

172. Dominic Lieven, *Russia against Napoleon: The Battle for Europe, 1807 to 1814* (London, 2010), esp. ch. 4.

173. NAP NOUV CORRES, no. 28,744, Antwerp, 30 September 1811, XI, pp. 1,089–90.

174. Mayol de Lupé, *La captivité de Pie VII*, II, pp. 312–14.

175. Haussonville, *L'Église romaine et le Premier Empire*, V, pp. 74–8.

176. Ibid., pp. 89–90.

177. Ibid., pp. 100–3. Haussonville believed that Napoleon wanted to return victorious from Russia and impose his will on Pius the following year.

178. Mayol de Lupé, *La captivité de Pie VII*, II, pp. 339–43.
179. Haussonville, *L'Église romaine et le Premier Empire*, V, pp. 111–13.
180. Ibid., p. 115.
181. Mayol de Lupé, *La captivité de Pie VII*, II, pp. 357–9.
182. Ibid., pp. 360–4.
183. Haussonville, *L'Église romaine et le Premier Empire*, V, pp. 131–4.
184. John O'Malley, *When Bishops Meet: An Essay Comparing Trent, Vatican I, and Vatican II* (Cambridge, MA, 2019), passim.

## CHAPTER 8: THE LAST CONCORDAT, 1812–13

1. Broers, *Napoleon: The Famous Delinquent*, ch. 5.
2. Nicola Todorov, *La Grande Armée à la conquête de l'Angleterre. Le plan secret de Napoléon* (Paris, 2016).
3. Ibid., pp. 87–93.
4. Paul Kennedy, *The Rise and Fall of the Great Powers: Economic Change and Military Conflict from 1500–2000* (London, 1988), pp. 3–38; and Dominic Lieven, *Empire: The Russian Empire and Its Rivals from the Sixteenth Century to the Present* (London, 2003).
5. Lentz (ed.), *1810. Le tournant de l'Empire*; and Charles-Éloi Vial, *15 août 1811. L'apogée de l'Empire?* (Paris, 2019).
6. Gavin Daly, 'Napoleon and the "City of Smugglers", 1810–1814', *Historical Journal*, vol. 50, no. 2 (2007), pp. 333–52; and François Crouzet, *L'économie britannique et le Blocus continental* (Paris, 1987).
7. Esdaile, *Fighting Napoleon*.
8. AN, F19 1926, Chabrol's reports, fol. 390 onwards; and AN, F7, 6530, Plaq1 Savona, esp. fol. 65 onwards.
9. AN, 33 AP 40, B Mission à Savone, rapports journaliers sur le service de garde du palais du Saint Père.
10. NAP NOUV CORRES, no. 30,651, Dresden, 21 May 1812, XII, pp. 593–4.
11. Mayol de Lupé, *La captivité de Pie VII*, II, pp. 378–91.
12. Baldini and Tampieri (eds), *Francesco Bertazzoli*, pp. 60–3.
13. They were called Hallouin and Garbet: Mayol de Lupé, *La captivité de Pie VII*, II, pp. 396–8.
14. AN, 33 AP 40, B Mission à Savone, Estafettes.
15. Martinengo and Martinengo, *Pio VII in Savona*, pp. 266–8.
16. Welschinger, *Le pape et l'empereur*, p. 339.
17. Martinengo and Martinengo, *Pio VII in Savona*, p. 267.
18. Mayol de Lupé, *La captivité de Pie VII*, II, p. 413.
19. Louis Bouvier, 'Le Mont-Cenis. Souvenirs de voyage', *Revue des deux mondes*, vol. 87 (1888), pp. 908–21.
20. Elisabeth Foucart-Walter, 'Paul Delaroche et le thème du *Passage du Saint-Bernard par Bonaparte*, Musée du Louvre, département des peintures', *Revue du Louvre et des musées de France?*, nos 5–6 (1984) pp. 367–84; Stephen Bann, *Paul Delaroche: History Painted* (London, 1997).
21. BL Add. MS 8390, Traslazione di Pio VII nel Castello di Fontainebleau, fols 19–35, esp. fol. 27.
22. Mayol de Lupé, *La captivité de Pie VII*, II, p. 404.
23. BL Add. MS 8389, fols 23–7, Claraz narrative.
24. Savary, *Mémoires du duc de Rovigo*, V, pp. 287–8; Mayol de Lupé, *La captivité de Pie VII*, II, p. 413; and Haussonville, *L'Église romaine et le Premier Empire*, V, pp. 163–4.
25. Smith, *The Great Schism*.
26. One can only speculate that this must have been returned to the pope since its confiscation the previous year: Mayol de Lupé, *La captivité de Pie VII*, II, p. 415.
27. BL Add. MS 8389, fols 23–7, Claraz narrative.
28. BL Add. MS 8389, fols 29–30, letter from Dominique Dubois of the Mont-Cenis hospice, undated.

29. BL Add. MS 8390, Traslazione di Pio VII nel Castello di Fontainebleau, fols 19–35.

30. Anon., *List of Additions made to the Collections in the British Museum in the Year MDCCCXXXI* (London, 1831), pp. 8–9.

31. BL Add. MS 8389, fols 23–7, Claraz narrative.

32. Haussonville, *L'Église romaine et le Premier Empire*, V, p. 165.

33. Ibid., pp. 165–6.

34. Christophe Beyeler (ed.), *Pie face à Napoléon. La tiare dans les serres de l'Aigle. Rome, Paris, Fontainebleau 1796–1814* (Paris, 2015), pp. 177–213.

35. Monique Berger and Jean-Claude Polton, *Château et forêt de Fontainebleau* (Lausanne, 2010), pp. 5–13.

36. Robert J. Knecht, *The French Renaissance Court, 1483–1589* (London, 2008), pp. 161–7.

37. Marc Hamilton Smith, 'La première description de Fontainebleau', *Revue de l'art*, no. 91 (1991), pp. 44–6; p. 45.

38. Philippe Salvadori, *La chasse sous l'Ancien Régime* (Paris, 1996), pp. 193–224.

39. Jean-François Hebert and Thierry Sarmant, *Fontainebleau. Mille ans d'histoire de France* (Paris, 2017), pp. 181–245.

40. Beyeler (ed.), *Pie face à Napoléon*, pp. 186–7.

41. NAP NOUV CORRES, no. 31,058, Vilnius, 29 June 1812, XII, p. 782.

42. Bernard Demotz and François Loridon, *1000 ans d'histoire de la Savoie. La Maurienne* (Chambéry, 2008), p. 372.

43. NAP NOUV CORRES, no. 31,169, Vilnius, 8 July 1812, XII, p. 837.

44. Adam Zamoyski, *1812: Napoleon's Fatal March on Moscow* (London, 2005), ch. 13.

45. Lieven, *Russia against Napoleon*, pp. 212–14.

46. Mayol de Lupé, *La captivité de Pie VII*, II, pp. 426–8.

47. Beyeler (ed.), *Pie face à Napoléon*, pp. 186–7.

48. Ibid.

49. Lentz, *Nouvelle histoire du Premier Empire*, II, pp. 301–6.

50. David Markham, *Imperial Glory: The Bulletins of Napoleon's Grande Armée* (London, 2003), pp. 244–314.

51. Thierry Lentz, *La conspiration du général Malet. 23 octobre 1812, premier ébranlement du trône de Napoléon* (Paris, 2012), pp. 153–8.

52. Henri Dourille, *Histoire de la conspiration du général Malet, 1812* (Paris, 1840), p. 36.

53. Paschal Grousset, *La conspiration du général Malet d'après les documents authentiques* (Paris, 1869), pp. 105–8.

54. Ibid.

55. Savary, *Mémoires du duc de Rovigo*, V, pp. 7–11; and Frédéric Bluche, *Septembre 1792. Logiques d'un massacre* (Paris, 1986), ch. 2.

56. Lentz, *La conspiration du général Malet*, pp. 192–201.

57. Grousset, *La conspiration du général Malet*, pp. 23–6.

58. Lentz, *La conspiration du général Malet*, pp. 120–7.

59. Antoine Lestra, *Histoire secrète de la congrégation de Lyon. De la clandestinité à la fondation de la propagation de la foi* (Paris, 1967), p. 223.

60. Bertier de Sauvigny, *Le comte Ferdinand de Bertier*, pp. 39–47 and 63–4.

61. Ibid., p. 63.

62. Lentz, *La conspiration du général Malet*, pp. 224–30.

63. Armand de Caulaincourt, *Memoirs of General de Caulaincourt, Duke of Vicenza, 1812–1813* (London, 1935), pp. 327–34.

64. Ibid., pp. 552–5.

65. Munro Price, *Napoleon: The End of Glory* (Oxford, 2014), p. 5.

66. Caulaincourt, *Memoirs*, passim.

67. Lentz, *Nouvelle histoire du Premier Empire*, II, p. 343.

68. Caulaincourt, *Memoirs*, pp. 580–3.

69. Ibid.

70. Jacques-Olivier Boudon, *Les élites religieuses à l'époque de Napoléon. Dictionnaire des évêques et vicaires généraux du Premier Empire* (Paris, 2002), pp. 138–9; and Émile Gabory, *Un grand évêque oublié. Mgr Duvoisin, évêque de Nantes, aumônier de l'impératrice Marie Louise* (Nantes, 1947), pp. 9–43.

71. NAP NOUV CORRES, no. 32,169, Paris, 29 December 1812, XII, pp. 1,322–3.

72. Mayol de Lupé, *La captivité de Pie VII*, II, p. 433.

73. Haussonville, *L'Église romaine et le Premier Empire*, V, pp. 209–10.

74. These included Ruffo, Dugnani and Bayanne.

75. Welschinger, *Le pape et l'empereur*, p. 350.

76. AN, AF IV 1048, dossier 4, Lagorce to Bigot de Préameneu, 17 January 1813.

77. Haussonville, *L'Église romaine et le Premier Empire*, V, p. 221.

78. Savary, *Mémoires du duc de Rovigo*, II, pp. 111–12.

79. Vial, *Le grand veneur*, pp. 37–160.

80. Pacca, *Mémoires*, II, p. 98.

81. James Kemble, *Napoleon Immortal: The Medical History and Private Life of Napoleon Bonaparte* (London, 1959).

82. Haussonville, *L'Église romaine et le Premier Empire*, V, p. 223.

83. François-René de Chateaubriand, *De Buonaparte et des Bourbons et de la nécessité de se rallier à nos princes légitimes pour le bonheur de la France et celui de l'Europe* (Paris, 1814), p. 12.

84. 'Oh! L'affare ha cominciato in commedia e vuol terminare in tragedia!': ASV, Segreteria di Stato, Epoca Napoleonica, Francia 6, fasc. 10, Memoria Mgr Gazzola Concordato di Fontainebleau, fol. 85. This phrase almost entirely reprises the dialogue invented in Alfred de Vigny, *Servitude et grandeur militaires* (Paris, 1864), pp. 244–61, esp. pp. 255 and 258.

85. Paul Verhaegen, 'Le comte Paul van der Vrecken, 1777–1868. Biographie et notes concernant l'histoire religieuse des Pays-Bas', *Publications de la Société historique et archéologique dans le duché de Limburg*, T.XXX (1893), pp. 98–146; p. 122.

86. Emmanuel de Las Cases, *Mémorial de Sainte-Hélène* (Paris, 1968), pp. 420–4.

87. Antoine Sutter, 'Choses vues en Janvier 1813 au Concordat de Fontainebleau par Jacques de Pange, chambellan de l'empereur Napoléon', *Mémoires de l'Académie de Metz*, série VI, T. VII (1979), pp. 61–77.

88. Anon., *Collection des lois, sénatus-consultes, décrets impériaux et avis du Conseil d'état relatif aux cultes, publiés depuis le Concordat jusqu'au 1er janvier 1813* (Paris, 1813), pp. xx–xxi.

89. Haussonville, *L'Église romaine et le Premier Empire*, V, pp. 237–9.

90. Mayol de Lupé, *La captivité de Pie VII*, II, pp. 445–6; and Haussonville, *L'Église romaine et le Premier Empire*, V, pp. 529–30.

91. Jean de Bourgoing, *Le cœur de Marie-Louise. Marie-Louise, impératrice des Français, 1810–1814. Lettres et documents oubliés et inédits* (Paris, 1938), pp. 111–12.

92. Grandmaison, *Napoléon et les cardinaux noirs*, p. 167.

93. Ricard, *Le cardinal Fesch*, p. 299.

94. Ibid.

95. Lyonnet, *Le cardinal Fesch*, II, pp. 457–64.

96. AP, 2ème série, XI, pp. 217–19.

97. Ibid., p. 222.

98. These included di Pietro, Gabrielli and Litta: Grandmaison, *Napoléon et les cardinaux noirs*, pp. 168–70.

99. Pacca, *Mémoires*, II, pp. 103–6.

100. Mayol de Lupé, *La captivité de Pie VII*, II, p. 452.

101. Welschinger, *Le pape et l'empereur*, pp. 365–6.

102. Pacca, *Mémoires*, II, pp. 111–14.

103. Mayol de Lupé, *La captivité de Pie VII*, II, pp. 466–7.

104. Ibid., pp. 455–61.

105. AN, AF IV 1048, dossier 4, fols 24–5, Bigot de Préameneu to Napoleon, 9 March 1813.

106. Welschinger, *Le pape et l'empereur*, p. 377.

107. Lagorce's reports from this time are similarly negative. He also advised asking the pope to appoint a cardinal to negotiate with the proposed commissioner as the only way out of the emerging impasse: AN, AF IV 1048, dossier 4, fol. 26, draft decree for appointment of an imperial commissioner; and fols 32–4, proposal to nominate an imperial commissioner.

108. Mayol de Lupé, *La captivité de Pie VII*, II, pp. 467–9.

109. Francis Loraine Petre, *Napoleon's Last Campaign in Germany, 1813* (London, 1912).

110. For an example, see Joseph Fesch, *Mandement de S.A.É. monseigneur le cardinal Fesch, archevêque de Lyon, primat des Gaules, qui ordonne un* Te Deum *pour la victoire de Lutzen soit chanté, et que des prières soient faites pour obtenir la continuation de la protection divine sur l'empereur des Français et ses armées* (Lyon, 1813).

111. Munro Price, 'Napoleon and Metternich in 1813: Some new and some neglected evidence', *French History*, vol. 26, no. 4 (2012), pp. 482–503.

112. Price, *Napoleon: The End of Glory*, pp. 71–88; Schroeder, *The Transformation of European Politics*, pp. 459–76; and Wolfram Siemann, *Metternich: Strategist and Visionary* (Cambridge, MA, 2019), pp. 320–60.

113. Price, 'Napoleon and Metternich', p. 492.

114. Artaud de Montor, *Histoire du Pape Pie VII*, II, p. 343; and Verhaegen, 'Le comte Paul van der Vrecken', pp. 105–7.

115. Mayol de Lupé, *La captivité de Pie VII*, II, pp. 487–9.

116. AN, AF IV 1048, dossier 4, fol. 66, letter from La Brue de Saint-Bauzille to the prefect of Escaut, Antoine Desmousseaux de Givré, Ghent, 26 July 1813.

117. AN, AF IV 1048, dossier 4, fol. 67, report from La Brue de Saint-Bauzille to Bigot de Préameneu, Ghent, 26 July 1813.

118. AN, F7 8369 A, Séminaires de Gand et Tournai 1813, Gand dossier.

119. AN, AF IV 1048, dossier 4, fols 70–1, report from Bigot de Préameneu to Napoleon, 2 August 1813.

120. NAP NOUV CORRES, no. 35,756, Dresden, 6 August 1813, XIV, p. 308; no. 35,771, Dresden, 7 August 1813, XIV, pp. 315–16; and no. 35,894, Dresden, 14 August 1813, XIV, pp. 379–80.

121. Joseph van der Moere, *Récit de la persécution endurée par les séminaristes du diocèse de Gand en 1813 et 1814 à Wezel, à Paris, etc., précédé d'un coup-d'œil sur l'histoire de l'église dans ses rapports avec ce diocèse de 1800 à 1814* (Ghent, 1863).

122. AN, F7 6526, list of prisoners released; the release of the professors and seminarians of Ghent and Tournai would have to await the fall of the Empire.

123. AN, F7 8369 A, Séminaires de Gand et Tournai 1813, Tournai dossier.

124. Price, *Napoleon: The End of Glory*, pp. 111–34.

125. Alan Sked, *Radetzky: Imperial Victor and Military Genius* (London, 2010), pp. 30–42.

126. Lentz, *Nouvelle histoire du Premier Empire*, II, pp. 458–69.

127. Price, *Napoleon: The End of Glory*, pp. 151–2.

128. Haussonville, *L'Église romaine et le Premier Empire*, V, pp. 288–9.

129. Artaud de Montor, *Histoire du Pape Pie VII*, II, p. 345.

130. Michael V. Leggiere, *The Fall of Napoleon: The Allied Invasion of France* (Cambridge, 2007), pp. 42–62.

## CHAPTER 9: CHRISTIANITY RESTORED: THE PAPAL RETURN TO ROME AND THE HUNDRED DAYS, 1814–15

1. Reuben John Rath, *The Fall of the Napoleonic Kingdom of Italy, 1814* (New York, 1975), pp. 45–61.

2. Leggiere, *The Fall of Napoleon*, pp. 42–62.

3. Price, *Napoleon: The End of Glory*, pp. 176–85.

4. Ibid., pp. 168–9.

5. Alan Reinerman, *Austria and the Papacy in the Age of Metternich*, 2 vols (Washington, DC, 1979), I, pp. 6–7.

6. Artaud de Montor, *Histoire du Pape Pie VII*, II, pp. 346–50.
7. Boudon, *Les élites religieuses*, pp. 143–4; Broers, *The Politics of Religion in Napoleonic Italy*, pp. 90–9; and Doina Pasca Harsanyi, 'Brigands or insurgents? Napoleonic authority in Italy and the Piacentino counter-insurrection of 1805–06', *French History*, vol. 30, no. 1 (2016), pp. 51–76.
8. Haussonville, *L'Église romaine et le Premier Empire*, V, pp. 307–8.
9. Albert Espitalier, *Napoleon and King Murat* (London, 1912), pp. 297–335; and Lacour-Gayet, *Joachim et Caroline Murat*, pp. 249–62.
10. Jean-Baptiste Capefigue, *Le Congrès de Vienne et les traités de 1815, précédé et suivi des actes diplomatiques* (Paris, 1863), pp. 83–7.
11. Lacour-Gayet, *Joachim et Caroline Murat*, pp. 260–1.
12. Domenico Spadoni, *Milano e la congiura militare nel 1814 per l'indipendenza Italiana*, 3 vols (Modena, 1936), I, pp. 18–21.
13. AN, AB XIX 4496, dossier 4, fol. 3, duc de Bassano to Fallot de Beaumont, 19 January 1814.
14. AN, AB XIX 4496, dossier 4, fols 3–4, Projet de Traité.
15. Ibid.
16. AN, AB XIX 4496, dossier 4, fols 20, Fallot de Beaumont to duc de Bassano, draft letter for the pope, 20 January 1814.
17. Kolla, 'The French Revolution, the Union of Avignon, and the challenges of national self-determination'; and idem, *Sovereignty, International Law, and the French Revolution* (Cambridge, 2017), pp. 84–120.
18. Haussonville, *L'Église romaine et le Premier Empire*, V, pp. 547–50.
19. Mayol de Lupé, *La captivité de Pie VII*, II, pp. 501–2.
20. Ibid.
21. Ibid., p. 503; Pacca, *Mémoires*, II, pp. 166–9.
22. Grandmaison, *Napoléon et les cardinaux noirs*, pp. 191–9.
23. Pacca, *Mémoires*, pp. 170–1; and Grandmaison, *Napoléon et les cardinaux noirs*, p. 198.
24. Price, *Napoleon: The End of Glory*, pp. 187–204.
25. Chandler, *The Campaigns of Napoleon*, pp. 964–76.
26. Albert Sorel, *L'Europe et la Révolution française*, 8 vols (Paris, 1904), VIII, p. 307.
27. Pierre Feret, *La France et le Saint-Siège sous le Premier Empire, la restauration et la monarchie de juillet*, 2 vols (Paris, 1911), II, p. 376.
28. Charles-Éloi Vial, 'Marie-Louise régente', in Patrice Gueniffey and Pierre Branda (eds), *1814. La campagne de France* (Paris, 2016), pp. 287–97.
29. Marie-Pierre Rey, *1814. Un tsar à Paris* (Paris, 2014), pp. 159–71.
30. John P.T. Bury, 'The end of the Napoleonic Senate', *Cambridge Historical Journal*, vol. 9, no. 2 (1948), pp. 165–89; and Pierre Serna, *La République des girouettes. 1789–1814 et au-delà. Une anomalie politique. La France de l'extrême centre* (Paris, 2005), pp. 149–58.
31. Price, *Napoleon: The End of Glory*, pp. 232–44.
32. Capefigue, *Le Congrès de Vienne et les traités de 1815*, pp. 148–51.
33. Price, *Napoleon: The End of Glory*, p. 241.
34. Vincenzo Mellini, *L'isola d'Elba durante il governo di Napoleone I* (Florence, 1914), pp. 112–37; and Mark Braude, *The Invisible Emperor: Napoleon on Elba from Exile to Escape* (London, 2018).
35. Robinson, *Cardinal Consalvi*, p. 99; and Dorothy Margaret Stuart, *Dearest Bess: The Life and Times of Lady Elizabeth Foster afterwards Duchess of Devonshire, from Her Unpublished Journals and Correspondence* (London, 1955), p. 213.
36. Pierre Branda, *La guerre secrète de Napoléon. Île d'Elbe, 1814–1815* (Paris, 2014), pp. 231–9.
37. Rath, *The Fall of the Napoleonic Kingdom of Italy*, pp. 124–6.
38. Giorgio Cencetti, *Le tre legazioni. Antonio Aldini e il Congresso di Vienna* (Bologna, 1935).
39. Melchior-Bonnet, *Napoléon et le pape*, pp. 332–4.
40. Gian Michele Gazzola, *Pio VII prigioniero a Cuneo. Cronache ed avvenimenti locali attorno al suo passaggio nel 1809*, 2 vols (Cuneo, 2011), I, p. 19.
41. Nussac, 'Le colonel Antoine Lagorsse', pp. 216–19.

42. Ibid., pp. 202–3.
43. Price, *Napoleon: The End of Glory*, pp. 245–6; and Friedrich Ludwig von Waldburg-Truchsess, *Nouvelle relation de l'itinéraire de Napoléon, de Fontainebleau à l'île d'Elbe, rédigé par le comte de Waldbourg-Truchsess, commissaire nommé, par SM le roi de Prusse pour l'accompagner*, 2nd edn (Paris, 1815), pp. 23–6.
44. Nussac, 'Le colonel Antoine Lagorsse', p. 202.
45. AN, F7 6530, Plaq1 Savone, fol. 36, report by prefect of Montenotte, Anton Brignole Sale, 17 February 1814.
46. AN, F1bl 157 13, Chabrol de Volvic dossier.
47. Welschinger, *Le pape et l'empereur*, pp. 422–3; and Nussac, 'Le colonel Antoine Lagorsse', pp. 205–7.
48. NAP NOUV CORRES, no. 38,476, Chavignon, 10 March 1814, XV, p. 389.
49. Nussac, 'Le colonel Antoine Lagorsse', p. 216.
50. Ibid., pp. 218–24.
51. Mayol de Lupé, *La captivité de Pie VII*, II, p. 520.
52. Artaud de Montor, *Histoire de la vie et du pontificat du Pape Pie VII*, II, pp. 354–5.
53. Ibid., p. 354.
54. Mayol de Lupé, *La captivité de Pie VII*, II, p. 521.
55. Anon., *Il rapimento da Roma e viaggio di S.S. Pio VII gloriosamente regnante. Bolla di scomunica contro Buonaparte ed altri documenti relativi, e suo proclama datato da Cesena il 4 maggio 1814* (Milan, 1814), p. 91.
56. Ibid., p. 92.
57. Samuele Giombi, 'Leone XII (Annibale della Genga Sermattei). Per un profilo biografico a partire dalla recente storiografia', in Gilberto Piccinini (ed.), *Il pontificato di Leone XII. Restaurazione e riforme nel governo della chiesa e dello stato* (Genga, 2011), pp. 29–44; p. 34.
58. Cencetti, *Le tre legazioni*, pp. 3–9.
59. Phillip Cuccia, 'Controlling the archives: The requisition, removal, and return of the Vatican Archives during the age of Napoleon', *Napoleonica. La revue*, no. 17 (2013) pp. 66–74.
60. Regoli, *Ercole Consalvi*, p. 338.
61. Ibid., pp. 339–45.
62. Latreille, *L'opposition religieuse au Concordat*; and idem, *Après le Concordat. L'opposition de 1803 à nos jours* (Paris, 1910), pp. 125–69.
63. Regoli, *Ercole Consalvi*, pp. 339–45.
64. Pistolesi, *Vita del sommo pontefice Pio VII*, II, pp. 35–6; and Consalvi, *Mémoires*, 2 vols (Paris, 1866), III, p. 193.
65. Mayol de Lupé, *La captivité de Pie VII*, II, p. 524.
66. Lévis-Mirepoix, *Un collaborateur de Metternich*, pp. 313–21.
67. Feret, *La France et le Saint-Siège sous le Premier Empire*, p. 384; Artaud de Montor, *Histoire du Pape Pie VII*, II, pp. 357–8; Mayol de Lupé, *La captivité de Pie VII*, II, pp. 524–5; Philippe Boutry, 'Traditions et trahisons. Le retour de Pie VII à Rome, 19 mars–24 mai 1814', in Yves-Marie Bercé (ed.), *La fin de l'Europe napoléonienne, 1814. La vacance du pouvoir* (Paris, 1990), pp. 203–18.
68. Mayol de Lupé, *La captivité de Pie VII*, II, p. 525.
69. Michael Broers, 'The Restoration in Piedmont-Sardinia, 1814–1848: Variations on reaction', in David Laven and Lucy Riall (eds), *Napoleon's Legacy: Problems of Government in Restoration Europe* (Oxford, 2000), pp. 151–64.
70. Filippo Ambrosini, *L'ombra della restaurazione. Cospiratori, riformisti e reazionari in Piemonte e Liguria, 1814–1831* (Torino, 2002), pp. 199–200.
71. Marina Natoli, 'Raffaele Stern e l'allestimento degli appartamenti imperiali al Quirinale', in Natoli and Scarpati (eds), *Il Palazzo del Quirinale*, I, pp. 1–82; Susanna Pasquali, 'Raffaele Stern, 1774–1820', in Angela Cipriani, Gian Paolo Consoli and Susanna Pasquali (eds), *Contro il barocco. Apprendistato a Roma e pratica dell'architettura civile in Italia, 1780–1820* (Rome, 2007), part V, pp. 120–6; and Garric, *Percier et Fontaine*.

72. ASV, Congregazione Particolate Disordini, 20 boxes: Lajos Pásztor catalogue in archives.

73. ASV, Congregazione Particolare Disordini 1–2 contain many lists of priests who compromised with the Napoleonic regime.

74. ASV, Congregazione Particolare Disordini 9, Istruzione 1814, fols 136–53.

75. For a good example see ASV, Congregazione Particolare Disordini 4.

76. ASV, Congregazione Particolare Disordini 1, fol. 177, Sacerdote Angelo Battaglini Canonico, Santa Maria in Via Lata, Primo Conservatore ossia custode della Biblioteca Vaticana.

77. ASV, Congregazione Particolare Disordini 1, fol. 372, Indice delle Dichiarazioni particolari dell Universita della Sapienza e de Maestri Religionari; and ASV, Congregazione Particolare Disordini 2, fol. 161, list of professors of La Sapienza.

78. ASV, Congregazione Particolare Disordini 2, fol. 163, retraction of Collegio Romano, 1 May 1814.

79. ASV, Congregazione Particolare Disordini 4, fol. 41, Notizie sulla Condotta di vari prelate Palatini e altri sogetti ecclesiastici e laici e nota de castighi ad essi inflitti d'ordine di SS; and fol. 42, lists of personae non gratae.

80. Jean-Sifrein Maury, *Mémoire pour le Cardinal Maury* (Paris, 1814).

81. Paul-Thérèse-David d'Astros, *De l'abus de cette maxime que l'usage abroge la loi ou l'on traite. 1. Du pouvoir des évêques nommés. 2. Des administrations capitulaires des évêques nommés. 3. De la révocabilité des vicaires capitulaires* (Paris, 1814).

82. Ricard (ed.), *Correspondance diplomatique*, II, pp. 502–8.

83. ASV, Segreteria di Stato, Epoca Napoleonica, Italia 17, fascs 4–5, Maury affair.

84. ASV, Segreteria di Stato, Epoca Napoleonica, Italia 8, fasc. 41, Maury affair, 1815, no. 15, Maury to be allowed tepid baths, 30 June 1815; and no. 17, medical report on Maury bladder inflammation, 26 June 1815; see also fasc. 42.

85. Ricard (ed.), *Correspondance diplomatique*, II, pp. 512–16.

86. Latreille, *Après le Concordat*, pp. 125–69; and Antoine Roquette, *Le Concordat de 1817. Louis XVIII face à Pie VII* (Paris, 2010), pp. 15–46.

87. Regoli, *Ercole Consalvi*, pp. 346–72.

88. Ibid., pp. 368–71.

89. Schroeder, *The Transformation of European Politics*, p. 509.

90. Dorothy Mackay Quynn, 'The art confiscations of the Napoleonic Wars', *American Historical Review*, vol. 50, no. 3 (1945), pp. 437–60; and Christopher M.S. Johns, *Antonio Canova and the Politics of Patronage in Revolutionary and Napoleonic Europe* (London, 1998), pp. 171–94.

91. Capefigue, *Le Congrès de Vienne et les traités de 1815*, p. 170.

92. Robinson, *Cardinal Consalvi*, pp. 102–4.

93. Colin Haydon, 'Religious minorities in England', in H.T. Dickinson (ed.), *A Companion to Eighteenth-Century Britain* (Oxford, 2002), pp. 241–51.

94. Maureen Wall, *The Penal Laws, 1691–1760* (Dundalk, 1961); and Sean J. Connolly, *Religion, Law, and Power: The Making of Protestant Ireland, 1660–1760* (Oxford, 1992), pp. 263–313.

95. Ian Haywood and John Seed (eds), *The Gordon Riots: Politics, Culture and Insurrection in Late Eighteenth-Century Britain* (Cambridge, 2012).

96. Grayson M. Ditchfield, 'The parliamentary struggle over the repeal of the Test and Corporation Acts, 1787–1790', *English Historical Review*, no. 89 (1974), pp. 551–77; Oliver MacDonagh, 'The politicization of the Irish Catholic bishops, 1800–1850', *Historical Journal*, vol. 18, no. 1 (1975), pp. 37–53; and Margaret Ó hÓgartaigh, 'Catholic politics in early nineteenth-century Ireland', *Seanchas Ard Mhacha: Journal of the Armagh Diocesan Historical Society*, vol. 23, no. 1 (2010), pp. 185–200.

97. Peter Guilday, 'The Sacred Congregation de Propaganda Fide, 1622–1922', *Catholic Historical Review*, vol. 6, no. 4 (1921), pp. 478–94.

98. He came from a dynasty of Roman missionaries, who saw the church's mission as universal, and one that should be extended to every corner of the globe. In order to achieve this goal, the Quarantotti family had been arch-pragmatists who believed allowances should be made for local conditions. During the eighteenth century, the artist Marco Benefial painted a remarkable portrait of the Quarantotti family. Some of its members were depicted in their ecclesiastical

robes, while others wore Asiatic and Chinese dress representing the peoples to whom they had travelled to preach and spread the Catholic faith. The painting can be seen today in the Galleria Bernini in Rome: Kees van Dooren, 'The drawings of Marco Benefial', *Master Drawings*, vol. 46, no. 1 (2008), pp. 61–90, esp. p. 72.

99. Antonia Fraser, *The King and the Catholics: The Fight for Right, 1829* (London, 2018), pp. 78–80.

100. To complicate matters further, as a canon of the Lateran Basilica, Quarantotti had taken the oath of loyalty to the French Empire in 1810. He soon came under investigation by Cardinal Pacca's Congregation for Disorders. He was removed from the Propaganda Fide and retracted the oath sworn to the French. By 1816 he had made sufficient amends, and Pius VII elevated him to cardinal: Boutry, *Souverain et pontife*, pp. 453–4.

101. Robinson, *Cardinal Consalvi*, pp. 106–9.

102. Alessandro Roveri, *La missione Consalvi e il Congresso di Vienna*, 3 vols (Rome, 1976), I, p. 165.

103. Walter W. Seton, 'The relations of Henry Cardinal York with the British government', *Transactions of the Royal Historical Society*, vol. 2 (1919), pp. 94–112; and Roveri, *La missione Consalvi*, I, pp. 166–7.

104. Johns, *Antonio Canova*, pp. 160–3.

105. Michael Levey, *Sir Thomas Lawrence: The Artist* (London, 2005), pp. 222–34.

106. Roveri, *La missione Consalvi*, I, pp. 170–2 and 224–5; and Joel S. Panzer, *The Popes and Slavery* (New York, 1996).

107. Roveri, *La missione Consalvi*, I, pp. 172–5.

108. Desmond Keenan, *The Grail of Catholic Emancipation, 1793–1829* (Washington, DC, 2002), pp. 238–9.

109. Fraser, *The King and the Catholics*, pp. 93–4.

110. Ambrose Macauley, *The Catholic Church and the Campaign for Emancipation in Ireland and England* (Dublin, 2016).

111. Alessandro Roveri, *La Santa Sede tra Rivoluzione francese e restaurazione. Il cardinale Consalvi, 1813–1815* (Florence, 1974), pp. 127–8; and Lucio Bigi and Mario Mareddu, *L'orologio del Duomo di Firenze. L'unico al mondo che segna l'ora italica* (Florence, 2016).

112. Ibid.

113. Robert A. Maryks and Jonathan Wright (eds), *Jesuit Survival and Restoration: A Global History, 1773–1900* (Leiden, 2014); and Martín M. Morales, 'The restoration of the Society of Jesus and the vagaries of writing', in Ines G. Županov (ed.), *The Oxford Handbook of the Jesuits* (Oxford, 2019), pp. 953–73.

114. Van Kley, *Reform Catholicism*, pp. 235–45; and Jeffrey D. Burson and Jonathan Wright (eds), *The Jesuit Suppression in Global Context: Causes, Events and Consequences* (Cambridge, 2015).

115. Sabina Pavone, 'Anti-Jesuitism in a global perspective', in Županov (ed.), *The Oxford Handbook of the Jesuits*, pp. 833–54.

116. Jonathan Wright, 'The suppression and restoration', in Thomas Worcester (ed.), *The Cambridge Companion to the Jesuits* (Cambridge, 2008), pp. 263–77.

117. Boudon, *Napoléon et les cultes*, pp. 167–9; and Bindel, *Histoire religieuse de Napoléon*, II, pp. 78–9.

118. Burson and Wright (eds), *The Jesuit Suppression in Global Context*, chs 10 and 13; and Marek Inglot, *Compagnia di Gesù nell'impero Russo. 1772–1820 e la sua parte nella restaurazione generale della compagnia* (Rome, 1997).

119. Maryks and Wright (eds), *Jesuit Survival and Restoration*.

120. Geoffrey Cubitt, *The Jesuit Myth: Conspiracy Theory and Politics in Nineteenth-Century France* (Oxford, 1993); and Vincenzo Gioberti, *Il Gesuita moderno*, 5 vols (Lausanne, 1847).

121. Francisco Bethencourt, *The Inquisition: A Global History, 1478–1834* (Cambridge, 2009), pp. 416–39; and Emilio la Parra, *Fernando VII. Un rey deseado y detestado* (Barcelona, 2018), pp. 295–302.

122. Joseph Schmidlin, *Histoire des papes de l'époque contemporaine*, 2 vols (Paris, 1938), I, pp. 179–201; and Massimo Petrocchi, *La restaurazione. Il cardinale Consalvi e la riforma del 1816* (Florence, 1941), pp. 1–50.

123. Adolfo Omodeo, *Studi sull'età della restaurazione. La cultura francese nell'età della restaurazione. Aspetti del cattolicesimo della restaurazione* (Turin, 1974), pp. 438–47.

124. Consalvi, *Mémoires*, II, pp. 481–9.

125. For the best survey on neutrality, see Maartje Abbenhuis, *An Age of Neutrals: Great Power Politics, 1815–1914* (Cambridge, 2014), pp. 39–65.

126. Robinson, *Cardinal Consalvi*, p. 107.

127. Roveri, *La missione Consalvi*, I, p. 431.

128. Ibid., pp. 453–77.

129. Ibid., p. 454.

130. Ibid., p. 455.

131. Ibid., pp. 458–9.

132. Ibid., p. 460.

133. Ibid., pp. 461–2.

134. Pierre Branda, *Joséphine. Le paradoxe du cygne* (Paris, 2016), ch. 27.

135. Reinerman, *Austria and the Papacy in the Age of Metternich*, I, pp. 21–30.

136. Giuseppe Galasso, *Storia d'Italia*, vol. XV/4, *Il Regno di Napoli. Il Mezzogiorno borbonico e napoleonico, 1734–1815* (Turin, 2007), pp. 1,278–82.

137. Ibid., pp. 1,285–9.

138. Emmanuel de Waresquiel, *Talleyrand. Dernières nouvelles du diable* (Paris, 2011), p. 159.

139. Idem, *Talleyrand. Le prince immobile*, pp. 488–89.

140. Idem, *Talleyrand. Dernières nouvelles du diable*, pp. 165–7.

141. Omodeo, *Studi sull'età della restaurazione*, pp. 378–82 and 439; and Robinson, *Cardinal Consalvi*, pp. 111–12.

142. Omodeo, *Studi sull'età della restaurazione*, pp. 443–6.

143. Abbenhuis, *An Age of Neutrals*, chs 2–5.

144. Regoli, *Ercole Consalvi*, pp. 394–9.

145. Cencetti, *Le tre legazioni*, pp. 5–14.

146. Ibid.; and Pacca, *Mémoires*, II, pp. 316–19.

147. Braude, *The Invisible Emperor*, passim.

148. ASV, Segreteria di Stato, Epoca Napoleonica, Italia 16, fasc. 5, Diverse Diocesi, no. 5, letter to Bettini criticising Arrighi for his fidelity to Napoleon, 14 July 1814.

149. Lentz, *Nouvelle histoire du Premier Empire*, IV, pp. 179–210; and Mellini, *L'isola d'Elba*, pp. 275–83.

150. Roberto Adriani, 'Don Assunto Bartolini, figura chiave del clero Elbano durante il periodo napoleonico', *Rivista italiana di studi napoleonici*, anno XLIV, 1/2 (2011), pp. 133–51.

151. Braude, *The Invisible Emperor*, pp. 112–16 and 133–8; and Lentz, *Nouvelle histoire du Premier Empire*, IV, pp. 285–6.

152. Vincent Haegele, *Murat. La solitude du cavalier* (Paris, 2015), p. 686; and Jane Robins, *Rebel Queen: How the Trial of Caroline Brought England to the Brink of Revolution* (London, 2006), pp. 56–82.

153. Robinson, *Cardinal Consalvi*, p. 114.

154. Roveri, *La missione Consalvi*, III, pp. 101–21.

155. Ibid., p. 115.

156. Ibid., pp. 167–87.

157. Ibid.

158. Branda, *La guerre secrète de Napoléon*, pp. 346–60.

159. ASV, Segreteria di Stato, Epoca Napoleonica, Italia 12, fasc. 2, Fuga dal Elba, passim.

160. ASV, Segreteria di Stato, Epoca Napoleonica, Italia 12, fasc. 2, Fuga dal Elba, no. 17, Pacca to authorities in Frosinone, Rieti, Terracina and Subiaco, 3 March 1815.

161. ASV, Segreteria di Stato, Epoca Napoleonica, Italia 12, fasc. 2, Fuga dal Elba, no. 72, Garde-robe, Inventaire du lige et effets de SM l'empereur.

162. ASV, Segreteria di Stato, Epoca Napoleonica, Italia 12, fasc. 2, Fuga dal Elba, no. 83, Napoleon pursued by Miollis between Provence and Grenoble, 9–10 March 1815.

163. ASV, Segreteria di Stato, Epoca Napoleonica, Italia 12, fasc. 2, Fuga dal Elba, no. 93, Giovanni-Battista Nuti consigliere d'ambasciata Toscana to Pacca, 13 March 1815, Napoleon arrested by Masséna.

164. Emmanuel de Waresquiel, *Cent jours. La tentation de l'impossible, mars–juillet 1815* (Paris, 2008), pp. 306–12 and 353–62.

165. Haegele, *Murat*, pp. 691–2.

166. Lacour-Gayet, *Joachim et Caroline Murat*, pp. 282–3.

167. Pacca, *Mémoires*, II, pp. 258–60

168. Ibid., pp. 261–2.

169. Artaud de Montor, *Histoire du Pape Pie VII*, II, p. 400; and NAP NOUV CORRES, no. 39,241, Paris, 8 April 1815, XV, pp. 755–6.

170. Luigi Passerini, *Della origine della famiglia Bonaparte dimostrata con documenti* (Florence, 1856).

171. Pacca, *Mémoires*, II, pp. 274–8.

172. Angelo Remondini and Marcello Remondini, *Pio VII P.M. in Genova e nella Liguria l'anno 1815* (Genoa, 1872), pp. 19–24.

173. Roveri, *La missione Consalvi*, III, pp. 229–30.

174. Pacca, *Mémoires*, II, p. 286.

175. Farris, *Studi e documenti su Pio VII*, pp. 79–81 and 157–60.

176. Heimann, 'Catholic revivalism in worship and devotion'.

177. Pacca, *Mémoires*, II, pp. 294–5.

178. Lentz, *Nouvelle histoire du Premier Empire*, IV, p. 342; and Waresquiel, *Cent jours*, p. 101.

179. John Dunne, 'In search of the village and small-town elections of Napoleon's Hundred Days: A departmental study', *French History*, vol. 29, no. 3 (2015), pp. 304–27.

180. Guillaumin, *Les derniers républicains*, passim.

181. Henry Houssaye, *1815*, 3 vols (Paris, 1894), I, pp. 482–99.

182. ASV, Segreteria di Stato, Epoca Napoleonica, Francia 2, fasc. 3, prima parte Cardinale Fesch, nos 86–9, list of priests denounced in Lyon by neo-Jacobins, 1815.

183. AN, F19 5597, lettres du mois de juin 1815 relatives aux dénonciations contre les prêtres opposés au gouvernement imperial; and AF IV 1935, Council of State reports by Bigot on the clergy during the Hundred Days.

184. Ibid.

185. Tanguy Kenec'hdu, *Lamennais. Un prêtre en recherche* (Paris, 1982), pp. 77–81; and Bertier de Sauvigny, *Le comte Ferdinand de Bertier*, pp. 166–73.

186. Houssaye, *1815*, I, pp. 486–95.

187. NAP NOUV CORRES, no. 39,231, Paris, 8 April 1815, XV, p. 748; no. 39,547, Paris, 17 April 1815, XV, p. 796; no. 39,632, Paris, 15 May 1815, XV, pp. 1,914–15; and no. 39,776, Paris, 23 May 1815, XV, p. 977.

188. Lacour-Gayet, *Joachim et Caroline Murat*, p. 285.

189. Jean Tulard, *Murat* (Paris, 1999), pp. 363–66; Tulard's biography is excellent, but he is in error about the date of the Proclamation of Rimini, which he otherwise faithfully reproduces.

190. Richard Stites, *The Four Horsemen: Riding to Liberty in Post-Napoleonic Europe* (Oxford, 2014), ch. 3.

191. Haegele, *Murat*, pp. 696–706.

192. John A. Davis, *Naples and Napoleon: Southern Italy and the European Revolution, 1780–1860* (Oxford, 2006), pp. 270–4.

193. Roveri, *La missione Consalvi*, III, pp. 569–83.

194. Ibid., pp. 631–57.

195. Pacca, *Mémoires*, II, pp. 316–19.

196. Waresquiel, *Talleyrand. Dernières nouvelles du diable*, pp. 159–67.

197. Houssaye, *1815*, III, passim.

198. Lentz, *Nouvelle histoire du Premier Empire*, IV, pp. 515–19.

199. Lyonnet, *Le cardinal Fesch*, II, pp. 337–52.

200. ASV, Segreteria di Stato, Epoca Napoleonica, Italia 8, fasc. 41, patent conferring title of prince of Canino, 18 August 1814; and Simonetta and Arikha, *Napoleon and the Rebel*, pp. 241–65.

201. Christine Haynes, *Our Friends the Enemy: The Occupation of France after Napoleon* (Cambridge, MA, 2018), pp. 36–43.

202. Johns, *Antonio Canova*, pp. 171–94.

203. Charon-Bordas, *Inventaire des Archives de la légation en France*.

204. Chappin, 'Un mostro nell'Archivio segreto vaticano'.

205. Pacca, *Mémoires*, II, pp. 313–14.

## CONCLUSION: THE EMPEROR'S GHOST

1. Thomas H. Brooke, *History of the Island of St Helena, from Its Discovery by the Portuguese to the Year 1823* (London, 1824), pp. 46–60; and Jan Willem Drijvers, *Helena Augusta: The Mother of Constantine the Great and Her Finding of the True Cross* (Leiden, 1992), pp. 35–8 and 131–46.

2. Thousands of slaves were captured and 'freed' by the Royal Navy. During the second half of the nineteenth century, this campaign to stop the slave trade accelerated, and Saint Helena found itself interning thousands of debilitated slaves. Many died on the island, awaiting a repatriation that would never come. Indeed, recent archaeological excavations have found the graves of these slaves for whom their newly acquired freedom must have meant very little: Andrew Pearson, *Distant Freedom: Saint Helena and the Abolition of the Slave Trade, 1840–1872* (Liverpool, 2016).

3. For an accessible account, see Brian Unwin, *Terrible Exile: The Last Days of Napoleon on St Helena* (London, 2010).

4. Harold Bloom, 'Napoleon and Prometheus: The Romantic myth of organic energy', *Yale French Studies*, no. 26 (1960), pp. 79–82.

5. Philip Dwyer, *Napoleon: Passion, Death and Resurrection, 1815–1840* (London, 2018), pp. 27–129.

6. Ibid., pp. 21–2.

7. Aleksandr Antonovich Balmain, *Napoleon in Captivity: The Reports of Count Balmain, Russian Commissioner on the Island of Saint Helena, 1816–1820* (London, 1928).

8. Las Cases, *Mémorial de Sainte-Hélène*, pp. 368–9.

9. Thierry Lentz, *Bonaparte n'est plus! Le monde apprend la mort de Napoléon, juillet–septembre 1821* (Paris, 2019), pp. 51–2.

10. Robert Morrissey, *The Economy of Glory: From Ancien Régime France to the Fall of Napoleon* (Chicago, 2014), pp. 147–78.

11. Frédéric Bluche, *Le bonapartisme. Aux origines de la droite autoritaire (1800–1850)* (Paris, 1980), pp. 167–92; and Dwyer, *Napoleon: Passion, Death and Resurrection*, pp. 153–92.

12. Robert Gildea, *The Past in French History* (London, 1994), pp. 62–111; and Natalie Petiteau, *Napoléon, De la mythologie à l'histoire* (Paris, 2004), pp. 53–79.

13. Thierry Lentz (ed.), *Mémoires de Napoléon*, 3 vols (Paris, 2016); and Thierry Lentz, 'A brief history of an oft-forgotten secondary source for the Revolution and Empire period, the *Memoirs of Napoleon*', *Napoleonica. La revue*, no. 13 (2012), pp. 52–64.

14. The notable and excellent exception is Courtemanche, *Napoléon et le sacré*, pp. 221–61.

15. Ellis, 'Religion according to Napoleon'; and Casanova, 'Matérialismes, expériences historiques et traits originaux'.

16. Robert-Augustin Antoine de Beauterne, *Conversations religieuses de Napoléon. Avec des documents inédits de la plus haute importance ou il révèle lui-même sa pensée intime sur le christianisme et des lettres de MM. le cardinal Fesch, Montholon, Hudson Lowe, Marchant, et un fac-simile de l'écriture de l'empereur* (Paris, 1840).

17. Idem, *Sentiment de Napoléon sur le christianisme. Conversations religieuses recueillies à Sainte-Hélène par M. le général de Montholon* (Brussels, 1843).

18. Jay M. Smith, *Monsters of the Gévaudan: The Making of a Beast* (Cambridge, MA, 2011).

19. Luigi Mascilli Migliorini (ed.), *Napoleone. Conversazioni religiose sulla fede e sull'esistenza di Dio* (Rome, 2004), pp. 7–25.

20. Dwyer, *Napoleon: Passion, Death and Resurrection*, p. 115.

21. Courtemanche, *Napoléon et le sacré*, pp. 221–4.

22. Ibid., pp. 229–35.

23. Lentz, *Bonaparte n'est plus!*, p. 173.

24. Dwyer, *Napoleon: Passion, Death and Resurrection*, p. 112.

25. Ibid., p. 105.

26. Philip Mansel, *The Court of France, 1789–1830* (Cambridge, 1988), pp. 66–7.

27. Courtemanche, *Napoléon et le sacré*, pp. 270–2.

28. Ibid., p. 273.

29. Pierre Branda, *Le prix de la gloire: Napoléon et l'argent* (Paris, 2007), pp. 82–99; and Napoléon Bonaparte, *Testament de Napoléon* (Brussels, 1824), p. 5.

30. Michael Paul Driskel, *As Befits a Legend: Building a Tomb for Napoleon, 1840–61* (Kent, OH, 1993), esp. pp. 1–16.

31. Lentz, *Bonaparte n'est plus!*, pp. 105–24.

32. Dwyer, *Napoleon: Passion, Death and Resurrection*, p. 133.

33. Bluche, *Le bonapartisme*, pp. 193–203.

34. Lentz, *Bonaparte n'est plus!*, p. 204.

35. Artaud de Montor, *Histoire du Pape Pie VII*, II, pp. 476–7; and Pistolesi, *Vita del sommo pontefice Pio VII*, IV, pp. 175–6.

36. Giombi, 'Leone XII (Annibale della Genga Sermattei)', pp. 29–44.

37. Anderson, *Pope Pius VII*, pp. 196–201.

38. Monica Calzolari, 'Leone XII e la ricostruzione della basilica di San Paolo fuori le mura', in Piccinini (ed.), *Il pontificato di Leone XII*, pp. 87–106.

39. Artaud de Montor, *Histoire du Pape Pie VII*, II, pp. 560–75.

40. As a Protestant, Thorvaldsen was not allowed to sign his sculpture in Saint Peter's: Roberta J. M. Olson, 'Representations of Pope Pius VII: The First Risorgimento Hero', *The Art Bulletin*, vol. 68, no. 1 (1986), pp. 77–93, esp. p. 92.

41. David I. Kertzer, *The Pope who Would be King: The Exile of Pius IX and the Emergence of Modern Europe* (Oxford, 2018), pp. 113–22.

42. Roger Price, *The Church and the State in France, 1789–1870: 'Fear of God is the Basis of Social Order'* (Basingstoke, 2017), pp. 129–272.

43. Maurice Larkin, *Church and State after the Dreyfus Affair: The Separation Issue in France* (Basingstoke, 1974); Alain Boyer, *1905. La séparation églises-état. De la guerre au dialogue* (Paris, 2004); and Cesare Silva, *La separazione dello stato dalla chiesa in Francia del 1905* (Rome, 2019).

44. With the exception of Alsace-Lorraine due to the German occupation of 1870–1918: here, bizarrely, the Napoleonic Concordat remains in force to this day.

45. Philippe Reynaud, *La laïcité. Histoire d'une singularité française* (Paris, 2019); and Owen Chadwick, *The Secularisation of the European Mind* (Cambridge, 1978).

46. Edward Hales, *Pio Nono: A Study in European Politics and Religion in the Nineteenth Century* (New York, 1954); and Coppa, *The Modern Papacy since 1789*.

47. Antoine Roquette, *Monseigneur Frayssinous, grand maître de l'université sous la restauration (1765–1841). Évêque d'Hermopolis ou Le chant du cygne du trône et de l'autel* (Paris, 2007); and Gough, *Paris and Rome*.

48. Dan Kurzman, *A Special Mission: Hitler's Secret Plot to Seize the Vatican and Kidnap Pope Pius XII* (Cambridge, MA, 2007); and David I. Kertzer, *The Pope and Mussolini: The Secret History of Pius XI and the Rise of Fascism in Europe* (Oxford, 2014), pp. 59, 199 and 326–7.

## APPENDIX: THE FOUR GALLICAN ARTICLES OF 1682

1. Anon., *Déclaration du clergé de France faite dans l'assemblée de 1682 sur les libertés de l'Église gallicane et l'autorité ecclésiastique. Ouvrage contenant: I. Le texte du Décret de l'Assemblée du clergé de 1682, ou les quatre Articles du clergé de l'Église gallicane, avec l'Édit de Louis XIV, confirmé et renouvelé par S.M. l'empereur Napoléon. II. Le Rapport lu à cette Assemblée sur les quatre Articles, rapport composé par Bossuet dans le comité chargé de la discussion, et lu par M. de Choiseul-Praslin, évêque de Tournai. III. La Lettre des prélats de l'Assemblée de 1682, à leurs collègues, en leur envoyant les quatre Articles. IV. Le Discours de Fleury sur les libertés de l'Église gallicane. V. La Déclaration du chapitre métropolitain de Paris à S.M. l'empereur et roi, et les adresses d'adhésion des églises d'Italie* (Paris, 1811), pp. 1–8.

# FURTHER READING

Alas Napoleon's vexed relationship with Pius VII has not received much attention in Anglophone scholarship. The notable exception is Edward Elton Young Hales, *The Emperor and the Pope: The Story of Napoleon and Pius VII* (New York, 1961); now considered a classic, it is marred by a lack of citations and at under 150 pages in length it is also unhelpfully short. For Hales, a Catholic convert and civil servant working in the British ministry of education, the book was clearly a labour of love. Although he wrote with flair and brought the subject beautifully to life, Hales's undoubted scholarship remains hidden from view. He did spend some time in the Vatican Archives, but he left no clear record of his findings. Indeed, he missed the more salient and important papers relating to Pius's conflict with Napoleon and subsequent captivity. Admittedly, these sources are not easily accessible in a short space of time.

In Hales's defence the Napoleonic series in Rome consists largely of Cardinal di Pietro's papers, which were buried in the Vatican gardens when the French invaded in 1808. These manuscripts were only rediscovered during some landscaping work in 1889–90, thus bringing to light an invaluable archival find. There is a sense when perusing these papers that they were thrown together at random into fifty archival boxes: their contents are highly disordered. This is understandable given the fact that the Vatican Archives were transferred to Paris between 1809 to 1815 and were returned by the Bourbon authorities in a chaotic state of disorganisation not to mention with boxes missing which had fallen off carts during transit. In consequence, the combination of the papers from the curial archives that survived the journey back from Paris in 1815 with those discovered in the Vatican gardens in 1889 has created an archival series that is not only poorly organised but in a bad state of repair. Thankfully, the papers of the Epoca Napoleonica are at present being diligently recatalogued by the Rev. Father Marcel Chappin SJ, while some investment is being put into the restoration of the most badly damaged documents. One can only wish Father Chappin well in this Herculean task; the reordering of this series may well mean that my own citations will not map neatly onto the new catalogue once it is completed in future years. I spent the better part of 2018 and 2019 minutely analysing these papers, and they form the backbone of the research that underpins this book.

Those interested in further reading beyond Hales's slim volume will find it difficult to identify much relevant material in English. For Catholicism's struggle with the French Revolution one should immediately plunge into John McManners, *The French Revolution and the Church* (London, 1982); Owen Chadwick, *The Popes and European Revolution* (Oxford, 1980); and Nigel Aston, *Christianity and Revolutionary Europe, 1750–1830* (Cambridge, 2003): these all provide excellent syntheses of the scholarship on religion and revolution during the 1790s. John Martin Robinson has written an excellent – though sadly short – biography of Ercole Consalvi: *Cardinal Consalvi, 1757–1824* (London, 1987). There is a life of Pope Pius VII by Robin Anderson – *Pope Pius VII (1800–1823)* (Rockford, IL, 2001) – but regrettably the tone leans towards hagiography. The late Geoffrey Ellis published an insightful essay, 'Religion according to Napoleon: The limitations of pragmatism', in Nigel Aston (ed.), *Religious Changes in Europe, 1650–1914* (Oxford, 1997): this piece certainly paints Napoleon as an opportunistic and cynical agnostic. Michael Broers's *The Politics of Religion in Napoleonic Italy: The War Against God, 1801–1814* (London, 2002), is by far the most original contribution in English to the study of the Napoleonic Empire's persecution of the Roman Church. It focuses its attention, through minute archival research, on the conflict at a grassroots level in the Italian *départements réunis*.

In stark contrast to the paucity of work in English on Napoleon and the Papacy, the scholarship in Italian and French is vast. Polyglot readers can refer to my endnotes on the classic French and Italian works from 1850 to 1950 on this subject. I will use this opportunity to bring to the attention of the linguistically versatile some excellent recent work by French and Italian scholars. Of great note is Marie Courtemanche's *Napoléon et le sacré. Une vie spirituelle, une politique religieuse* (Paris, 2019), a game-changing and brilliant reinterpretation of Napoleon's complicated relationship with religion. Also to be highly recommended is Roberto Regoli's superb *Ercole Consalvi. Le scelte per la chiesa* (Rome, 2006): this doctoral student of Marcel Chappin certainly places Pius VII's secretary of state in his broadest diplomatic context with a shrewd and excellent analysis of his policies. Ivana Pederzani's *Un ministero per il culto. Giovanni Bovara e la riforma della chiesa in età Napoleonica* (Milan, 2002) is recommended, and so too is the older work by Filiberto Agostini, *La riforma napoleonica della chiesa nella Repubblica e nel Regno d'Italia 1802–1814* (Vicenza, 1990). Remarkably, Napoleon's French minister of religions, Félix Julien Jean Bigot de Préameneu, has never received a biography: this lacuna needs to be filled by an enterprising doctoral student. In terms of the history of law, one can read to great profit Daniele Arru's, *Il Concordato italiano del 1803* (Milan, 2003), a magisterial unpacking of the Italian counterpart to the French Concordat of 1801. There is still an echoing vacuum in the literature when it comes to Catholicism during the Hundred Days in 1815, and my book is the first attempt to reflect on how Napoleon's return from Elba impacted the church.

# ACKNOWLEDGEMENTS

My work and research have been enhanced immeasurably by the help and support received from so many friends and colleagues. Its flaws and limitations are inevitably my own. In the past twenty years it has been my privilege to study and work with outstanding scholars and specialists in the history of France and Italy during the age of revolutions. Their publications and monographs have made my life easier; what follows would have been impossible without their findings and insights. I am deeply in debt to my agent Robert Dudley, who believed in this project from the start: without him it would never have come to fruition. I look forward to future adventures with Rob. Equally, Lucy Buchan, Rachael Lonsdale, Marika Lysandrou and Heather McCallum of Yale University Press have been excellent editors: their enthusiasm for the project has been gratifying and I was delighted to follow their first-rate advice. The reports of Yale's two anonymous readers were extremely perceptive and brimming with brilliant suggestions for revision. My gratitude goes to these two unknown soldiers who, sadly, I will never be able to acknowledge in person: they richly deserve my thanks.

This book took over a decade to research and prepare. It began life in the office of Alan Forrest at the University of York, which for me has always been an incubator of good ideas. As ever, Alan, I am in your debt: for your kindness, and for instilling in me such a passion for the age of revolutions. One of the biggest and happiest changes in my life, since my first book, on Louis XVI, was published in 2012, has been to secure a permanent lectureship at the University of Kent. The past eight years have been a blissful and productive time; I have been truly blessed with outstanding colleagues and brilliant students. My special thanks go to Stephen Bann who, on my arrival in Canterbury, went above and beyond to make me feel at home. Since then he has been deeply generous with his time, ideas, good company and – dare I say it? – his cellar. I am exceedingly grateful to our professional services team (past and present) at the School of History in Kent, who have made my life so much easier through their efficiency and rigour. My deepest gratitude goes to Eloise Bates, Faye Beesley, Jon Beer, Rob Brown, Sian Draper, Jenny Humphrey, Tim Keward and the redoubtable Jackie Latham. Their hard work has freed up my research time immeasurably, and I cannot thank them enough. I acknowledge the School of History with immense appreciation for approving a year's research leave, in which the lion's share of my research at the Vatican Archives took place. My colleagues – Barbara Bombi, Philip Boobbyer, Tim Bowman, Leonie James, Gaynor Johnson, Mark Lawrence, Ben Marsh and Juliette Pattinson – have been magnificent and stalwart: my gratitude goes to them for making my working life such a pleasure.

My deepest debt at Kent goes to Andy Cohen, and his partner Helen Garnett, for their bonhomie, sense of mischief, northern groundedness and dark sense of humour. They have made even the darker moments of life bearable. My only regret at Kent has been the departure to the Sapienza Università di Roma of my aristocratic compatriot and dearest friend Giacomo Macola (his anarchic and seditious tendencies are deeply missed). My experiences in Lusaka and Monze diverge significantly from his own, but I have come to appreciate and in part share his Zambian and Congolese passions. His encouragement, iconoclasm and friendship in my early years at Canterbury were life-changing, and although he does not miss us, now that he is safely ensconced in the eternal city, we all deeply miss him.

My students over the past twelve years have deeply improved my writing abilities and helped me immeasurably to ask the right questions for this book. Some of course stick out more than others due to their industry and mighty intellect. Amongst these I include Joe Boucher, Matthew Boyd, Greg Cooper, Issy Cox-Jones, Kate Docking, Alex Echlin, Tom Eckett, Maria Edwards, Dom Gibson, Amy Harrison, Will Jarvis, Tom Like, Keith Minear, Stewart Murphy, Emily Parker, Barney Parr, Ralph Roberts, Joe Robertson, Gemma Steer, Jack Tracey, Lawrence White and Kesia Wills, all of whom made my life as a teacher not merely easier but incredibly rewarding. However, above and beyond the multitude stands George Evans-Hulme who now, for want of a better word, is gainfully employed at the British Parliament. His continued obsession with the history of the age of revolutions is reassuring. In his madness, he read an initial draft of my manuscript. His comments and suggestions as a very well-informed reader deeply enriched this text, and I am in his debt.

Archivists all over Europe have assisted me in finding new materials for this book. I am especially grateful to Gianfranco Armando and the Rev. Father

# ACKNOWLEDGEMENTS

Marcel Chappin SJ for being so generous with their time, and for taking me into the belly of the whale at the Vatican Archives. Without their support, archival insights and kindness this book would be much impoverished. In Lyon I was assisted in finding the private papers of Cardinal Fesch by Krystel Gilberton and Sophie Malavieille. This was quite a discovery and would have been impossible without their generous assistance and shared interest in the most pedantic of the Bonapartes. Others still have been prodigal with their time, advice and kindness. The Rev. Allan Doig, Lady Antonia Fraser and Munro Price read early drafts of this manuscript, enriching it immeasurably. It must be admitted that my research and writing has benefited enormously from discussions with many scholars. My deepest thanks go to Tim Blanning, William Doyle, Bettina Frederking, Rasmus Glenthøj, Mette Harder, John Hardman, Joanna Innes, Colin Jones, Luigi Mascilli Migliorini, Marco Meriggi, Marco Omes, the late Margery Ord, Morten Nordhagen Ottosen, David Parrott, and Geraint Thomas for allowing me to inflict Napoleon and the pope on them at unguarded moments. Naturally I cannot forget my dearest friends Edward and Kelcey Wilson-Lee, not to mention young Gabriel and Ambrose. Their continued support, encouragement and good humour are invaluable in impelling me onwards. It is always a thrill to see them in Cambridge.

Tragically, in January 2019, in the course of the writing of this book, I lost a great friend, Antti Matikkala. My thoughts go to his widow Mira, my godson Elias and his sister Laura: their bravery is an inspiration. It is heart-breaking that the world has lost a scholar of Antti's calibre so young. I shall miss his charm, conversation and monumental erudition; it is a source of the deepest regret that he will never know the contribution he made to my life and that of so many other academics. My sincere appreciation goes to Wilhelm Brummer for setting up a fund in Antti's memory so that a younger generation can continue his work and passion.

As ever my parents deserve the biggest thanks for their unconditional support for my research and career. For the past five years I have inflicted on them several holidays into *la France profonde*. They have inevitably had to swallow crumbling cathedrals, odd museums and provincial collections of obscure nineteenth-century art. Their love, patience and good cheer (apart from when it comes to selecting where to eat) remains a source of wonder, but I am supremely grateful. My father Paolo has always been my most committed reader and constructive critic. Despite his busy life, despite the fact that – how can I put this? – history is not a natural passion for him, he has now read every article, book and minor work I have produced. His support, and ability to respond to inopportune phone calls asking for advice at all hours of the day, remain treasured moments. He is the great inspiration of my life and I cannot express what our frequent conversations mean to me.

The most important acknowledgement must go to Michael Broers of Lady Margaret Hall, University of Oxford, who is the world's uncontested doyen of Napoleonic studies. My deep friendship with Mike started at the Antica Trattoria della Pesa in Milan. Several shots of grappa after the meal put me *hors de combat* for several days. Despite, or perhaps thanks to, this incident our friendship has grown steadily ever since. His enthusiasm for our subject and constant support has been awe-inspiring. The conference and edited collection we organised in 2016 was one of the most intellectually stimulating and challenging things I have ever done. Needless to say, without him it would have been impossible, let alone successful. His sage advice, formidable erudition, scintillating conversation, rich anecdotes and sheer good humour make him a treasured *maestro*. Without him the past ten years would have been impossible. That is why I dedicate this book to you, Mike. I hope it proves worthy of you. *Abbi cura di te!*

Canterbury, October 2020

# INDEX